The Quick-Reference Guide to
COUNSELING
WOMEN

The Quick-Reference Guide to

COUNSELING
WOMEN

TIM CLINTON
DIANE LANGBERG

BakerBooks

a division of Baker Publishing Group
Grand Rapids, Michigan

Published by Baker Books
a division of Baker Publishing Group
P.O. Box 6287, Grand Rapids, MI 49516-6287
www.bakerbooks.com

Printed in the United States of America

Library of Congress Cataloging-in-Publication Data
Clinton, Timothy E., 1960–
  The quick-reference guide to counseling women / Tim Clinton, Diane Langberg.
    p. cm.
  Includes bibliographical references.
  ISBN 978-0-8010-7234-5 (pbk.)
  1. Women—Pastoral counseling of. 2. Church work with women. I. Langberg, Diane. II. Title.
  BV4445.C56 2011
  259.082′03—dc22
                                              2011005547

To protect the privacy of those who have shared their stories with the authors, details and names have been changed.

11 12 13 14 15 16 17   7 6 5 4 3 2 1

Contents

Acknowledgments

We would like to say a special thank you to all involved in helping build a resource that we pray will be used to help counsel women all over the world, fostering lasting hope and true heart healing through the power and love of Jesus Christ.

A note of deep appreciation goes to Robert Hosack at Baker Books for believing in the project and to Mary Suggs and Mary Wenger for their excellence in editing.

Likewise, we extend sincere gratitude to the entire AACC team who helped in the writing, editing, and research of this project:

Joshua Straub, PhD

Pat Springle, MA

Laura Faidley

Paige Lloyd

Jena Manning

Brittany Dix

We would also like to thank our spouses, Julie and Ron, and our families for their love and support through the years. We could not enter into the work we do without you.

And to the entire AACC team and tens of thousands of pastors and Christian counselors who are literally entering into the darkness of the lives of hurting women. May this resource help you bring the light and hope of Jesus in every situation. We dedicate this series to you.

Introduction

On Being Female

Whatever else it means to be feminine, it is depth and mystery and complexity, with beauty as its very essence.

Stasi Eldredge

Every woman has a story, a story that is uniquely shaped by being female. For many women, that story is hidden, tightly locked inside a broken heart. But behind walls of fear, anger, and hurt, the wound festers. Behind the makeup and the pasted-on smile, women everywhere are hurting. They are confused, afraid, scared—and silent.

Consider the story of Melanie, a woman who was repeatedly raped as a child. Sitting across from me in the counseling office, she told me the story of how she had been stripped, placed in a circle of men, and gang raped. The impact on her life was profound; it was her greatest shame. She'd hidden her story from everyone, convinced that even God would have nothing to do with her.

"I cried all the time," Melanie told me (Diane). "I couldn't focus on work. I didn't want to go anywhere. I didn't want to remember anything anymore. I wanted to push it all away. I attempted to deny it all, as I had when I was a kid. But nothing was the same. Nothing and no one could be trusted. I wondered who I really was. I didn't know if I could go on. Life didn't seem worth living anymore."

Shame keeps women like Melanie silent. They are ashamed of the unspeakable evils that have been done to them or what they've done to themselves. Fearful of being known, of being judged and labeled, many women are bowed down under the weight of the shame they carry. Abuse, rape, incest, abandonment, divorce, pornography, abortions, chronic illness, infertility, or violence has defined them. And an untold number hide their stories and the shame and stigma that go with them.

Often the Christian community pretends that such things don't exist. In an effort to protect ourselves, we are silent and turn away from hurting women, distancing ourselves from their reality. It's hard to accept these facts:

1 in 3 women are sexually abused before age 18.

1 in 4 women are raped.

80 percent of women who work experience sexual harassment.

50 percent of marriages end in divorce.

1 in 4 marriages experience domestic violence.

21 million women have suffered emotional abuse.

1/3 of all females in relationships have experienced emotional abuse.

THE ROLE OF THE CHRISTIAN COMMUNITY

As the body of Christ, we are called to minister to the broken and hurting, not to ignore them, shut them up, and tell them to get over it and move on. Too often gossip and judgment within the church keep women from getting the help they so desperately need.

"Do you see the woman over there?" the church whispers. "She's the one who was raped . . . whose husband beats her . . . whose father had sex with her . . . whose husband left her. Poor thing!" This attitude does nothing to help and only adds to the pain and brokenness a woman has already experienced.

We label women by their circumstances not their heart. A for abuse, addiction, abortion, abandonment, adultery. D for depressed, domestic abuse, drugs. I for incest, immorality, infertility, insignificance. R for raped, ruined, rejected. S for stupid, silly, slut.

We condemn women. We push them away. We shame them. When a woman is defined by one word, reduced to that one shameful thing about her, it doesn't matter what she accomplishes or what other people might think about her. Beauty, brains, admiration, success, and respect do not touch that place of hurt. It is always there defining, shaming, frightening, and holding her in bondage to her past.

When the church adds to a woman's pain through an accusing, indifferent, or unloving attitude, we are in direct opposition to the gospel of Jesus Christ. In Isaiah 61 Jesus proclaims His mission on earth, and it should be our heartbeat if we are caregivers:

> . . . to preach good news to the poor . . . to bind up the brokenhearted, to proclaim freedom for the captives . . . to comfort all who mourn . . . to bestow on them a crown of beauty instead of ashes, the oil of gladness instead of mourning, and a garment of praise instead of a spirit of despair.
>
> verses 1–3

You and I cannot change women. As counselors, we cannot transform their minds and we cannot heal their brokenness. *But we know One who can.* And God gives us the privilege and responsibility of embracing women in their pain, weeping with them, listening to them, and ultimately, leading them to Jesus, who knows each of them intimately and longs to make them whole.

THE ART OF COUNSELING WOMEN

Everywhere we look, we find women who desperately need God's touch, women whose hearts are crying out for hope. Women in today's world live under the pressure of perfectionism. They are told that being a woman means being strong, confident, independent, put together—and not letting anything or anyone hurt you. This only reinforces the walls that women build to isolate themselves and perpetuate their silence. Yet a woman's heart remembers, and a broken, bleeding soul cannot be healed by any measure of material success or accomplishment.

Does any authentic remedy really exist?

We believe the answer is a resounding yes. And it starts with you. Since you are reading the introduction to this book, you have likely been called to the counseling ministry, to the work of authentic caregiving. You have been called and are likely trained to some degree to deliver care, consolation, and hope to the women in your church and community. As you work with women, remember that "the LORD is close to the brokenhearted; he rescues those whose spirits are crushed" (Ps. 34:18 NLT).

Many women feel tremendous pressure to hold it together, to be okay. In fact, they are afraid that if they face their past, their pain will overtake them and swallow them up. And so they run. They hide. They are silent. They exist and yet they desperately need hope. In His providence, God has chosen you as a vessel for the delivery of His special grace to hurting women; you have both the privilege and responsibility to deliver that care in the most excellent and ethical way possible.

Ministering to women must begin with looking at how Jesus ministered to women. As caregivers, we are called to follow in the footsteps of Jesus who went out of His way to stop and notice women, to listen to them, to love them, and to respond to their unique needs in a culture where women were belittled and devalued. They were viewed as second-class citizens, worthless and unclean.

In the Gospel of Luke alone, Jesus talks with a woman or speaks about a woman in His parables twenty-four times. Throughout His earthly ministry, Jesus loved and reached out to women—those who were hurting, desperate, and hopeless; those who were unclean; those who were broken and silent and hiding. No matter what their race, their social standing, or their disease, Jesus did not hesitate to reach out in love *every single time.*

Take, for example, the woman caught in the act of adultery (John 8:4–11), the woman with an issue of blood (Mark 5:25–34), the sinful woman who anointed his feet (Luke 7:36–50), the daughter of Jairus (Mark 5:35–43), the widow of Nain (Luke 7:11–17), the crippled woman (Luke 13:10–17), Mary Magdalene, who was possessed by seven demons (Luke 8:2), the Samaritan woman at the well (John 4:7–26) . . . and the list goes on.

Doug Clark writes:

He is the one man who dared to talk openly with the woman at the well. He breached every standard of his culture by doing that. And yet the woman, even while she was being exposed for everything that she was—a woman with multiple marriages and a sordid life—was never threatened. Jesus never humiliated her. He simply lifted her out of her filth and gently clothed her in the righteousness of her Heavenly Father. . . . Jesus lifted and affirmed every woman who came to Him.[1]

Jesus saw past the physical condition of women and ministered to them in the midst of their pain. He gave them freedom to be weak, broken, and needy. Many women are known by their past and they want to forget it, to move on and start over. As a caregiver, you have the privilege of helping women see that God wants to do something infinitely more beautiful than eradicating their past. He wants to transform it.

THE HEART OF THE MATTER

Every woman carries names, names that haunt and enslave her. And try as she might, she can't forget. God wants His daughters to remember so they will see that in this place—the worst, darkest, most evil place—is where He has come as healer, deliverer, the accepting one, the lover of souls, the opener of prisons, the comforter, the loving father, the bridegroom.

More than anything else, hurting women need to know this truth: *Jesus knows your deepest shame and humiliation and He wants to take what you most hate about yourself and use it to draw you to Himself. He is the restorer, the deliverer, the healer, the binder of broken hearts. God longs to use your greatest pain to reveal to you who He is and shape you to look like Him.*

Bring to Jesus your name and your greatest shame. He entered into your rejection so that you might be chosen, your humiliation that you might be honored, your ridicule that you might be precious. Abuse, rape, violence, depression, and fear can be caught up and used to transform us into His image. These things are evil, and God hates evil. But as evil as those things are, the depth of their evil doesn't incapacitate our God. His redemptive power isn't limited by what has been done to us or by the names we carry. He is able to enter redemptively into the greatest evil done to you or by you and set you free—free to follow Him.

This is what women need to know and believe. This is where they can live.

The woman who remembers who she was and where she has come from increases her capacity to love Jesus because remembering gives her a greater understanding of His wonderful, pursuing, rescuing love. The woman who thinks she's fine and has no great sense of need will love little and will see Him less clearly.

Remembering captivity points to the wonder of freedom. Remembering the darkness highlights the light. Encourage the women to whom you minister to remember and to meditate on the paradox of *I was . . . He is . . . so now I am*:

I was abused. He is the restorer of broken things. He is restoring me.

I was rejected. He is the lover of souls. In Him, I am chosen and loved.

I was proud and self-righteous. He is the bondservant who came down. I am humbled.

If we as Christian caregivers desire to be used by God, we must push past what's comfortable and be willing to go to the dark places and talk about the hard issues.

We must be willing to weep with women whose lives have been shattered. And it will make us uncomfortable. There are no easy answers, but Jesus is present in every conversation. And He who said, "It is not the healthy who need a doctor, but the sick" (Mark 2:17), is the only one who has the power to heal.

In this world there are hundreds of thousands of women named *forsaken* and *dying* because of AIDS. There are hundreds of thousands of women who are being stolen across borders of countries and sold into sex slavery. And there are countless women in your own community who are weighed down by addiction, divorce, eating disorders, unplanned pregnancy, abuse, and hopelessness.

Who will tell them the truth? Who will love them? Follow the example of Jesus. Love the rejected, the abused, the sick, the oppressed, the alienated. Bear His fragrance and share the hope of the gospel of Jesus as it applies to every single aspect of a woman's life.

THE THREE LEGS OF HELPING MINISTRY

Since the beginning of the American Association of Christian Counselors (AACC), we have been consistently asked to catalog and provide "quick reference" materials that pastors and counselors can easily access for the variety of issues we face. This *Quick-Reference Guide* on women's issues—and all the volumes in this series—is our response to that legitimate call. The topics for the quick-reference guides are:

Personal and emotional issues

Marriage and family issues

Sexuality and relationship issues

Teen issues

Women's issues

Singles' issues

Money issues

We are delighted to deliver to you this volume, *The Quick-Reference Guide to Counseling Women*, and trust that God will use it to bring hope, life, and freedom to millions of women all across the world.

This *Quick-Reference Guide* is designed for professional counselors, as well as pastors and lay counselors who desire to better understand and help women. We have written this book to apply to every leg of our three-legged stool metaphor. We advance the idea that the helping ministry in the church is made up of *pastors*, who serve in a central shepherding role, as the client nearly always returns to the role of parishioner; of *professional Christian counselors*, who often serve many churches in a given geographic area; and of *lay helpers*, who have been trained and serve in the church in individual or group leadership roles.

People serving at all three levels must develop both the character and the servant qualities that reflect the grace and truth of Christ Himself. God has also distributed His gifts liberally throughout the church to perform the various ministry tasks that are central to any healthy church, not the least of which is *caring for women*. No matter how skilled or intelligent we are, unless we rely directly on the Spirit of God to work in us to do the ministry of God, our service will not bear kingdom fruit.

God will bring us to the women He wants to love and heal through us, and we must learn to depend on Him to touch others in a supernatural way—so that people exclaim, "God showed up in that counseling session today!"

Pastor or Church Staff

If you are a pastor or church staff member, virtually every woman who walks through the doors of your church has been (or soon will be) touched by addiction, divorce, violence, depression, grief, confusion, loneliness, and a thousand other evidences of living as broken people in a fallen world. This guidebook will help you to:

- deliver effective counseling and short-term help to women who come to you
- teach others and construct sermons about the leading issues of the day with which women struggle
- provide essential resources and materials for staff and lay leaders in your church to advance their helping ministries

Professional Clinician

If you are a professional clinician, licensed or certified in one of the six major clinical disciplines, you are likely already familiar with most of the topics in this book. This quick-reference guide will assist you best to:

- review the definitions and assessment questions to use in your initial session with a new client
- understand and incorporate a biblical view of the client's problem as you develop a treatment plan
- deliver information to your clients that best helps them get unstuck and move forward more resolutely with the right thinking and focused action of this treatment process

Lay Counselor

If you are a lay counselor, this book will guide you in planning and delivering the best care you can from beginning to end. We recommend that you read through the entire book, highlighting the material most useful to you in either individual or group formats. This guide will help you:

- understand and accurately assess each woman's problem
- guide your discussions and delivery of helpful suggestions without assuming too much control or yielding too little influence
- remember key principles and guide you in the process of moving from problem to resolution more effectively

- remember the limits of lay ministry and assist you in making constructive referrals to others with more training

USING *THE QUICK-REFERENCE GUIDE TO COUNSELING WOMEN*

This guide includes chapters on forty of the most prevalent issues we see as professionals in the field of counseling women. You will see that we have divided each topic into an outline format that follows the logic of the counseling process. The goal and purpose of the eight parts are as follows:

1. **Portraits.** Each topic begins with a number of short vignettes that tell a common story about people struggling with the issue at hand. We have tried to include stories that you will most often encounter with the people you serve.
2. **Definitions and Key Thoughts.** This section begins with a clear definition of the issue in nontechnical language. Then we add a variety of ideas and data points to help you gain a fuller understanding of the issue and how it impacts lives and may harm the women who struggle with it.
3. **Assessment Interview.** Usually this section begins by suggesting a framework with which to approach assessment and is followed by a series of specific questions for gaining a more complete understanding of the woman's problem. There may be a section of "rule-out questions" that will help you determine whether referral to a physician or other professional is needed.
4. **Wise Counsel.** One or more key ideas are presented here that should serve as an overarching guide to your intervention—wise counsel that will help you frame your interventions in a better way. These key insights will give you an edge in understanding and working with the women you encounter.
5. **Action Steps.** This section—along with Wise Counsel—will guide you in what to do in your counseling interventions. It helps you construct a logical map and guide you and your client from problem identification to resolution in specific, measured steps—client action steps. Without a good action plan, it is too easy to leave women confused and drifting rather than moving in a determined way toward some concrete goals for change. Most Action Steps will be directed to the woman you are counseling. Any added notes for you, the counselor, will be in italics.
6. **Biblical Insights.** Here we provide relevant biblical passages and commentary to assist you in your counseling work from beginning to end. Embedding the entire process in a biblical framework and calling on the Lord's power to do the impossible are essential to authentic Christian counseling. You may choose to give your clients some of these verses as homework—ask them to meditate on them and/or memorize them—or you may want to use these passages as guides for the intervention process.
7. **Prayer Starter.** While not appropriate in every situation, many Christians want—and expect—prayer to be an integral part of your helping intervention. You should ask each client for her consent for prayer interventions. Even if she

does not join you, make it your habit to pray silently or in pre- or post-session reflection. You should pray for each client. Prayer is a critical aspect of spiritual intervention, and we prompt a few lines of prayer that can serve as effective introductions to taking counseling vertically, inviting God directly into the healing process.

8. **Recommended Resources.** We list here some of the best-known Christian and secular resources for further reading and study. Although by no means an exhaustive list, these resources will direct you to additional works, allowing you to go as deep as you want in further study of an issue.

As you learn more, know that your desire to break the silence as you help and care for women honors God. Christian counseling is a strong, effective case-based form of discipleship. In fact, it is often the door through which women walk to break through years of pain, misperceptions, and destructive habits that have kept them from being fully alive to God. We are honored to be partners with you in God's work and we trust that God will continue to use you in powerful ways to touch women's hearts and bring wholeness and healing to them.

ADDITIONAL RESOURCES

The American Association of Christian Counselors is a ministry and professional organization of nearly fifty thousand members in the United States and around the world. We are dedicated to providing and delivering the finest resources available to pastors, professional counselors, and lay helpers in whatever role or setting such services are delivered. With our award-winning magazine, *Christian Counseling Today*, and our training courses available through Light University, we also deliver a comprehensive range of education, training, and conference resources to equip you fully for the work of the helping ministry in whatever form you do it. While some of these resources are noted at the end of each chapter, several essential texts include:

The Bible for Hope: Caring for People God's Way by Tim Clinton and many leading contributors (Thomas Nelson, 2006).

Caring for People God's Way (and *Marriage and Family Counseling* and *Healthy Sexuality*—books in the same series) by Tim Clinton, Archibald Hart, and George Ohlschlager (Thomas Nelson, 2009).

Competent Christian Counseling: Foundations and Practices of Compassionate Soul Care by Tim Clinton, George Ohlschlager, and many other leading contributors (WaterBrook, 2002).

A Woman's Path to Emotional Freedom: God's Promise of Hope and Healing by Julie Clinton (Harvest House, 2010).

AACC's Light University also provides various biblical counselor training programs on video:

Caring for People God's Way

Caring for Kids God's Way

Caring for Teens God's Way

Breaking Free

Marriage Works

Sexual Addiction

Healthy Sexuality

Life Coaching

Extraordinary Women

Please visit www.aacc.net for other resources and services delivered by the AACC for the growth and betterment of the church.

Abortion

PORTRAITS 1

- Karen is in big trouble. She has a scholarship to her first-choice college, a nice boyfriend, and a leadership role in her church youth group, but the at-home pregnancy test she just took is positive. She cannot give up on all of her dreams for this one mistake, can she? *I don't have any other options*, Karen concludes. *My parents will kill me if they find out. I have a full-ride volleyball scholarship. Besides, it's a simple procedure, and no one else ever needs to know.*

- Growing up as a pastor's daughter, Julie knew that life was precious. But five years after the abortion her parents forced her to have, she is still angry, broken, and depressed. Shame and embarrassment kept her silent about her uncle's sexual abuse, but when she got pregnant, she couldn't hide it anymore. Julie was taken across state lines, her baby forcibly aborted, and she was forbidden to speak about it—until now. "I was a minor. I didn't have any say," Julie mumbles through tears. "All my parents cared about was keeping up their reputation."

- *I know I have been forgiven, but why can't I get over this?* Stacy wondered while at church with her two little children who squirmed beside her in the pew waiting to be released for children's church. She tried to concentrate on the pastor's words, but the Right to Life announcement in the bulletin claimed all of her attention. Her heart ached for the child who could have been sitting with her. *If only, if only . . . Oh God, I'm so sorry. I didn't realize what I was doing.*

DEFINITIONS AND KEY THOUGHTS 2

- The most common use of the term *abortion* is for *an artificially induced premature expulsion of a human fetus, as in a surgical or chemical abortion*; however, the term *abortion* actually refers to any premature expulsion of a human fetus, including those that are *naturally spontaneous, as in a miscarriage*. (If this is the case with your client, see the chapter "Miscarriage.")

- There are approximately *42 million abortions worldwide* per year and 1.37 million abortions in the United States per year.[1]

- The abortion ratio in 2006 was 236 legal abortions per 1,000 live births.[2]

- It is important that a woman with an unplanned pregnancy understand that *abortion is neither quick nor easy* and will carry repercussions for the rest of her life.

- Often a woman chooses to keep her abortion a secret, especially if she is part of a Christian community. Her own family members might not even know. *This secrecy may cause the grief and loss that surround an abortion to remain unprocessed for years.*
- In 2006, 62 percent of abortions were done *within the first 8 weeks of gestation*, well before family or friends were aware of the pregnancy.[3]
- Not only is abortion an issue in the community, it is *an issue in the church.* Protestant women (or those who attest to be Protestant) account for 37.4 percent of abortions, while 18 percent of abortions are performed on women who identify themselves as born again or evangelical.[4]
- In the United States, 52 percent of women who obtain abortions are *under the age of 25.*[5]
- Of all abortions, 1 percent occur because of *rape or incest*, 6 percent because of *potential health problems* regarding either the mother or child, and 93 percent for *social reasons* (usually because the child is unwanted or inconvenient).[6]
- *Some young women are forced to have an abortion by their parents.* In the past (prior to 1973), these young women were taken across state lines or out of the country and forbidden ever to speak about it. This only complicates the grieving process.
- An *abortion is experienced as not just a loss, but often as a trauma.* Women who have had an abortion may experience *emotional side effects*, such as reliving the procedure (in distressing dreams or flashbacks), attempting to live in denial, and avoiding any thoughts or feelings associated with the abortion.
- Other *possible side effects from the trauma of an abortion* include emotional numbing, sleep disorders, difficulty concentrating, hypervigilance, depression, guilt, and an inability to forgive oneself.
- *Trying to cope alone* with the reality of having had an abortion *is isolating and may reinforce the woman's sense of shame.* This shame may lead to self-destructive behaviors, such as substance or alcohol abuse, sexual promiscuity, eating disorders, or cutting. If a woman confides in you that she has had an abortion, realize that she has decided to trust you by sharing this experience. *Be cautious about your verbal and nonverbal behaviors.*

Myths about Abortion

Myth 1:   "It's a simple procedure; life will resume on Monday."

Myth 2:   "It's not a baby; it's a blob of tissue."

Myth 3:   "It's okay; abortion is legal."

Myth 4:   "My life will be ruined if I have this baby."

Myth 5:   "It's my choice, my responsibility, my decision."

Myth 6:   "It's okay to have an abortion if there's something wrong with the baby."

Myth 7:   "I am alone; no one cares about me."

Myth 8:   "I don't deserve forgiveness; I knew it was wrong."

Myth 9: "I got what I deserved; I did it more than once."

Myth 10: "This won't hurt; the pain will subside."

Myth 11: "It is my only option; he doesn't want the baby."

Myth 12: "It's okay in cases of rape or incest."[7]

ASSESSMENT INTERVIEW : 3

For the Woman Considering Abortion

1. How do you know that you are pregnant? Have you taken a pregnancy test or been examined by your doctor? (*These gentle questions about the pregnancy will help the counselee feel more at ease and take responsibility.*)
2. Do you know how far along you are in your pregnancy?
3. What are your present life circumstances?
4. How do you think your family will respond to your pregnancy?
5. Do you have sufficient social support? Who knows that you are pregnant?
6. Who is the father of the baby? What kind of relationship do you have with him?
7. What most scares you about your pregnancy?
8. Have you thought about any of the other options besides abortion? Have you considered carrying the baby to term? What are your thoughts about adoption?
9. How do you see your life if you have an abortion? How do you see your life if you make a different choice? (*Abortion is often chosen because the other options do not look like real options. The decision to have an abortion is sometimes made hastily to "solve the problem." Communicate to your counselee that she has some time to think about her pregnancy and make her decision. Help her see that her life will not be "ruined" if she makes the decision to carry her baby to term.*)
10. Do you have any questions about pregnancy or abortion? (*Do not assume that your counselee is fully informed about either.*)

For the Woman Who Has Already Had an Abortion

1. What is causing distress in your life at this time?
2. Take me back and share with me what happened. (*Listen carefully for any signs of post-traumatic stress; this may include disturbing dreams or triggers that bring back the event. When she decides to begin sharing her story with you, she is breaking her silence. Sharing her story is the beginning of the healing process, but this is also potentially upsetting because denial of the event is not possible anymore.*)
3. What were the main reasons that you made the choice that you did back then?
4. Do you feel depressed, down, or sad frequently?
5. Do you have difficulty eating or sleeping?
6. Do you ever have suicidal thoughts? (*If suicidal tendencies are apparent, get the counselee additional help immediately.*)
7. Are you using drugs or alcohol to deal with the pain?

8. How are things going in your life now? What triggers your pain?

9. Do you feel that God has forgiven you? Why or why not?

10. Do you believe that you can forgive yourself? Why or why not?

4 WISE COUNSEL

Be sure to provide practical support to the woman considering abortion to *encourage her to carry her baby to term*. Have information on hand about agencies that provide a home to stay in and medical care for pregnant women. Be sure to emphasize that she is making a decision for her life, as well as her baby's life. *Encourage her to look further into the future* than what is just ahead, such as starting college next semester or being able to play on her sports team.

Address immediately any behaviors that endanger her well-being, such as suicidal behavior or substance abuse.

Women who are faced with an unplanned pregnancy may be overwhelmed by fear and anxiety and feel isolated and alone. Most of them are not ready to be mothers and view abortion as an easy way out—with no consequences. As you speak with a client, take time to truly *listen and validate the emotions she is experiencing*. Educate her about the stages of pregnancy and the reality of the little life inside of her, but do not be too forceful or tell her that if she gets an abortion she is going to hell. Address the root issues of her anxiety and fear and work with her to develop a plan for handling her pregnancy.

Take the woman on a healing journey of forgiveness. If she has already had an abortion, *she is likely carrying a huge amount of guilt and shame*. Many women find it impossible to accept God's forgiveness and forgive themselves for taking the life of their innocent baby. *Grieve with the woman over her loss and allow her to express herself emotionally*. She may experience many symptoms that are normal to the grieving process, even though she never actually saw or felt her baby. Acknowledge the woman's sin and encourage her to ask God for forgiveness and to accept His unconditional love for her.

As the healing process progresses, *encourage the woman to volunteer* and serve in some way that helps pregnant young women.

5 ACTION STEPS

For the Woman Considering Abortion

1. Consider Options

- You may feel like your only option is abortion, but that simply isn't true. There are almost three thousand Crisis Pregnancy Centers (CPCs) in the United States where you can take a free pregnancy test, talk to a counselor, and learn about safe alternatives to abortion that respect your life and ensure your baby's future.

- You can find the nearest CPC in your community by looking in the Yellow Pages under the heading "Abortion Alternatives" or by calling 1-800-848-LOVE.
- Consider the best option for you and your baby's future. If you and your family are unable to provide a safe, loving home because of age, finances, or other life circumstances, adoption offers your baby the opportunity to grow up in a stable, loving, Christian environment. If you desire, many adoptions are "open," ensuring your continued relationship with your child.

2. Communicate

- It is very important that you communicate with your family members and the baby's father about the situation you are facing. While it may seem scary and overwhelming, as a woman bearing life inside of you, you have a right to rejoice and invite others to rejoice with you, no matter what the circumstances are surrounding the pregnancy.
- Assess the best way to talk with your family and the baby's father, while ensuring your safety and that of your baby (*depending on how much or what you know about her family members, you might need to be involved as a third party in such a conversation*). If your family is hostile, seek help and housing through a Crisis Pregnancy Center or your local church. Never put yourself in a situation that would endanger you or the baby.

3. Build a Support Network

- Even though you may regret your pregnancy, you can begin immediately to make some wise decisions regarding your baby's future. Don't try to navigate the journey of pregnancy by yourself.
- Evaluate your relationship with the baby's father. If he is not supporting you in your pregnancy or is acting in an abusive, manipulative manner, you may need to distance yourself from him to protect yourself and your baby.
- Make sure to follow up with your counselor with a future appointment and surround yourself with those who support you.
- Join a support group for pregnant women at your church or local Crisis Pregnancy Center.

For the Woman Who Has Already Had an Abortion

1. Tell Your Story

- Continue telling your story through future counseling sessions. It may also help to keep a journal. Don't hesitate to express the pain and anguish you feel. Bottling it up will only complicate the healing process.

2. Allow Yourself to Grieve

- Although you never met your baby, healing from abortion necessitates grieving the loss of your baby. Abortion can cause strange and unpredictable emotions.

- You may feel shame, anger, grief, frustration, and hopelessness at different stages in the grieving process. Allow yourself to work through each emotion and don't rush yourself to get over it.

3. Find Support

- There are several organizations and materials that exist to assist you in healing from abortion. Some organizations include A Time to Speak, Project Rachael, and Victims of Choice. (*Be aware of which ones exist in your area for a referral.*)
- If there is a confidential grief-support group in your area, plan to attend. (*Be ready to assist the woman in finding such a group.*)

4. Ask For and Accept God's Forgiveness

- Go to God in humility and brokenness, confessing your sin. Abortion is a sin, but no sin is beyond the redemption of Jesus Christ. He bore the punishment for every one of your sins, even this abortion.
- God will forgive you for having an abortion if you come to Him in humility and repentance. His love, acceptance, and delight over you are not based on what you do, but who you are as His child.
- Healing emotionally from an abortion is a process that cannot be accomplished in one session; however, healing is possible. Forgiveness, both forgiveness from God and forgiveness of yourself, is possible through God's grace.
- *Make sure you communicate, both verbally and nonverbally, your acceptance of the woman and God's willingness to forgive her.*

6 BIBLICAL INSIGHTS

If men fight, and hurt a woman with child, so that she gives birth prematurely, yet no harm follows, he shall surely be punished accordingly as the woman's husband imposes on him; and he shall pay as the judges determine.

Exodus 21:22 NKJV

Babies are precious to God. This verse shows how God protects the most defenseless people on the planet—unborn children in the womb. Causing a premature, though healthy, birth was a punishable offense under Old Testament law.

As the creator of everything, God is the champion of life. He has always protected women, children, and the weakest members of society and calls His followers to do the same.

For you created my inmost being; you knit me together in my mother's womb. I praise you because I am fearfully and wonderfully made; your works are wonderful, I know that full well. My frame was not hidden from you when I was made in the secret place. When I was woven together in the depths of the earth, your eyes saw my unformed body.

Psalm 139:13–16

Life begins at conception. In this passage the psalmist confirms that God knows and sees a baby's "unformed body" and is intimately involved in the process of development. From the moment of conception, God sustains and gives life to the baby.

Every life is a unique creation of God, and He alone has the power to give and take life. Life is precious and every life should be valued.

Behold, children are a heritage from the LORD, the fruit of the womb is a reward.

Psalm 127:3 NKJV

Children are truly a gift from God, and every new life is a miracle. No matter what the circumstances are surrounding a woman's pregnancy, the baby is innocent and should not be punished for the mistakes of his or her parents.

The birth of a child is always cause for celebration. Though there will be difficult adjustments in the process of pregnancy and motherhood, children bring great joy. They are a precious reward from God, the creator of life.

The LORD is compassionate and gracious, slow to anger, abounding in love. He will not always accuse, nor will he harbor his anger forever; he does not treat us as our sins deserve or repay us according to our iniquities. For as high as the heavens are above the earth, so great is his love for those who fear him; as far as the east is from the west, so far has he removed our transgressions from us.

Psalm 103:8–12

Just like any other sin, abortion breaks God's heart—not only because it takes the life of the unborn, but because it results in emotional pain and trauma for the woman. The psalmist speaks here of God's compassion, love, and willingness to forgive our sin.

Abortion is tragic but it is not beyond the redemption offered in Jesus Christ. He who took the punishment for all of our sins also promises to remove our transgressions, guilt, and shame—as far as the east is from the west.

PRAYER STARTER 7

God, we pray that Your grace and wisdom will pour out into _____'s life. She is worried and scared and needs some help from You. Surround her with Your peace, Jesus, and calm her anxious heart. We thank You for the assurance that You are close to us, God, in our brokenness and pain. Give _____ wisdom in the decisions she needs to make . . .

8 RECOMMENDED RESOURCES

Cochrane, Linda. *Forgiven and Set Free: A Post-Abortion Bible Study for Women.* Baker, 1999.

Florczak-Seeman, Yvonne. *A Time to Speak: A Healing Journal for Post-Abortive Women.* Love from Above, 2005. Books can be purchased at www.lovefrom aboveinc.com.

Focus on the Family. *Post-Abortion Kit: Resources for Those Suffering from the Aftermath of Abortion*, n.d.

Freed, Luci, and Penny Yvonne Salazar. *A Season to Heal: Help and Hope for Those Working through Post-Abortion Stress.* Cumberland House, 1996.

Klusendorf, Scott. *The Case for Life: Equipping Christians to Engage the Culture.* Crossway, 2009.

Reardon, David. *Aborted Women—Silent No More.* Acorn Books, 2002.

Smith, Gwen. *Broken into Beautiful: How God Restores the Wounded Heart.* Harvest House, 2008.

Aging

PORTRAITS : 1

- Wendy has been closely involved in her community for years ever since retiring from the school district. But her health has been failing recently and she's not sure how much longer she can live alone. She doesn't want to live at a retirement home or at an assisted living facility, but the last thing she wants to do is disrupt her children's lives. "I don't want to be a burden," Wendy insists, "so I just tell my kids I'm doing fine. But I'm not."

- Maggie is a devout member of her church and loves being a Sunday school teacher but lately she's been going through an emotional roller coaster. At times she feels great but at other times she cries for no reason at all. Frequently she experiences hot flashes, night sweats, and forgetfulness. Maggie lives with her daughter and son-in-law, who are pressuring her to give up teaching Sunday school, but Maggie refuses. The disagreement is leading to conflict and tension in the home.

- Carla has always been an independent woman, relying on herself to get things done. She prides herself in her work ethic and her accomplishments. Her forget-fulness, however, is really starting to worry her, but she doesn't want to accept the truth that she really does have a problem and may need help. Often she forgets where she is or what she's doing. *What is my life even about anymore?* Carla wonders. *I can barely even take care of myself.*

DEFINITIONS AND KEY THOUGHTS : 2

- *Aging is a natural process* that should not be presumed to lead inevitably to loss or to diminishing faculties. *The rate at which people age and progressively lose their abilities varies widely* according to many factors, such as family history, emotional attitude, chronic medical conditions, and lifestyle choices.

- In recent years, *the older population has increased significantly.* Currently 1 in 8 Americans are senior citizens. In 2008 there were 38.9 million people in the United States who were 65 years or older, but by 2030 it is estimated that there will be 72.1 million older persons.[1]

- Women entering their later years *experience many transitions*, such as retire-ment; moving from parenthood to grandparenthood; lessened physical abilities, strength, and energy; the deaths of friends and peers; lowered social status; economic stress; a tighter financial budget; and the loss of a spouse.

- Among women 65 and older, *the leading causes of death* are heart disease (28.7 percent), cancer (19.3 percent), and stroke (7.6 percent).[2]

- The *"sandwich years"* refers to the period when middle-aged people are *still raising children and are also caring for their parents*. They are "sandwiched" between these two generations, usually a stressful time that can feel like a vice grip or a well-coordinated dance.

- *Caring for aging parents can be gratifying but also stressful.* It depends on many complex issues, such as your own health, whether you are still raising children, financial resources, and emotional resilience. Even though being a caregiver is laudable, it is not necessarily the wisest decision if there are any other options.

- As women age, their *habits may become ingrained* and their idiosyncrasies tend to become more pronounced. Easygoing women may continue to be laid back, but those who were uptight at a younger age may become more anxious or paranoid as they get older.

- Although the risk of disability and illness increases with age, *poor health is not an inevitable consequence of aging*. Women with *healthy lifestyles* that include regular exercise, balanced diet, and no tobacco use have half the risk for disability of those with less healthy lifestyles.

- *Regular exercise slows aging.* Statistics show that of people sixty-five years old and older, women are less likely than men to have regular physical activities that maintain physical strength and endurance.[3]

- Women who live to age sixty-five can expect to live an average of nineteen years longer, but they often need assistance; *42 percent of aging women receive assistance in their overall daily living*. Eating assistance is twice as likely among females as it is among males. These statistics show that it is important to be realistic and plan ahead for an aging woman to get the help she needs.[4]

Health Issues in Aging Women

- *Depression is not a normal part of aging*, but more than 58 percent of older adults believe it is. Late-life depression affects some *six million adults, most of them women*, but only 10 percent of these women ever get treated. Twice as many women as men are diagnosed with clinical depression. This can be attributed to other chronic illnesses common in later life, such as diabetes, stroke, heart disease, cancer, chronic lung disease, Alzheimer's disease, Parkinson's disease, and arthritis.

- *Urinary incontinence is prevalent among elderly women.* Many times they are embarrassed or convinced that involuntary loss of urine is normal with aging, so they may be reluctant to seek medical assistance or talk about their problem.

- *Diabetes is a disease that has stricken 4.5 million women who are 60 years or older.* It is the sixth leading cause of death for elderly women, and one-quarter of them, 1.2 million, are unaware that they even have the disease.

- *Falls are to blame for 87 percent of all fractures for people sixty-five years and older.* Falls are also the *leading cause of injury deaths* and the second leading cause of spinal cord and brain injury in this age group.
- *Heart attacks occur more often in older women* because they tend to have higher rates of high blood pressure, high cholesterol, diabetes, obesity, and physical inactivity than younger women. Sixty-five percent of women *aged sixty-five to seventy-four and 79 percent of women aged seventy-five and older* have some form of cardiovascular disease.
- *Alzheimer's disease increases dramatically* with advancing age, and many more women than men live to the ages when Alzheimer's disease is most common.
- *Osteoporosis is seen in approximately eight million American women.* Women are *four times more likely* than men to develop osteoporosis because at menopause they lose estrogen, which blocks or slows down bone loss. *More than half of all women sixty-five and older have osteoporosis,* and it is usually not diagnosed until a fracture or break occurs.[5]

ASSESSMENT INTERVIEW 3

Remember that aging and caregiving take many forms. Try not to project your own values on the client, but instead protect the client's values. An older woman may value independence far more than you think is attainable or healthy, or a family member might be convinced that anyone older than sixty-five can't be independent. Listen first and then respond gently as necessary.

Rule Outs

1. Have you been ill? Is there a chance of depression, poor nutrition, dehydration, or other medical problems? (*Several medical conditions and depression can mimic the symptoms of dementia, so always be sure that medical problems and depression have been ruled out by medical and counseling professionals before making assumptions about a person's ability to live independently.*)
2. Have you experienced any feelings of loneliness or depression? On a scale of 1 to 10, with 1 being great and 10 being extremely depressed, where would you put yourself today? (*Loneliness can prompt a person to reach out for help, sometimes causing the person to act needier than she truly is. If depression is present, see also the chapter "Depression."*)

General Questions

1. Tell me about your life right now. What are your greatest challenges? What are the stressors in your life?
2. How has aging affected your [your loved one's] day-to-day life?
3. Who is taking care of you [your loved one]? If you must receive [give] help, how is this affecting you emotionally?

4. What level of care do you think you [your loved one] need? What specifically would you change to live better [assist your loved one to live better]? *Home-based care should be the option of first resort, and moving to a more structured environment the last resort.*

5. What are your [your loved one's] financial resources? Are you eligible for state or social security resources that haven't been tapped yet?

6. What medical issues are present? Are these issues terminal, chronic, permanent, debilitating, degenerative, or progressive? (*Clearly, if a medical condition is temporary, future plans will be very different than if it is terminal, progressive, or chronic.*)

7. Are you [your loved one] in danger? Dangerous conditions would include:

   — memory loss that could lead to accidental fires, wandering, or destructive behaviors
   — medical conditions that require constant supervision or that contribute to sudden loss of stability or consciousness
   — a residence that is deteriorated, unhealthy, or structurally too demanding (for example, too many stairs)
   — an emotional state that could lead to extreme despondency or psychosis (distorted thinking, such as dementia or paranoia)

8. Are you having a hard time accepting help? Do you feel the need to be strong and push through on your own?

9. When you think about the process of aging, what emotions do you feel? Do you feel anger, frustration, loneliness?

10. How do you feel about the possibility of having to get more care [give more care to a loved one]? What family members are available to help?

4 WISE COUNSEL

The later years in life can be a time of great joy, but the effects of aging and increasing health concerns can create added stress in the home. Talk about the issues from an informed position with the older person and her family, and *strive for mutually agreed-on decisions about any actions to be taken.*

When counseling a caregiver, impress on her *the complexity of issues related to aging* and the *wealth of resources for caregivers and for the elderly.* Encourage everyone involved to gather all the facts (from doctors, other family members, and neighbors) and approach the situation logically, rather than reacting under stress.

Listen to the elderly woman's side of the story. It is important to validate her because she may be feeling left out, misunderstood, and helpless. Remember, *it is always necessary to protect the elderly woman's confidences and seek her consent (based on mental capacity) before any decisions are made.*

The goal is to assess *how she is doing, what her needs are, and whether there are critical concerns.* Always strive to inform and involve the elderly woman in this process, even if all her wishes cannot be granted. Transitions through developmental challenges that accompany old age are smoother when *the woman is engaged in the primary decisions affecting her life.*

In the process of evaluation, it is essential to *assess whether there is any possibility of physical, sexual, or financial elder abuse or neglect.*

Financial abuse occurs when friends or family members take financial resources from the older woman for their own benefit. This is a particular risk when the woman is confused and no longer controlling her own finances. Don't expect the elderly victim to disclose what is happening. She may even deny it vehemently in the face of strong evidence, for fear of losing the contact and care of her family. It is critically important to emphasize and understand the entire situation from the elderly woman's point of view, even when your action may conflict with her desires.

Elder neglect occurs when a family member or caregiver neglects the needs of the older woman for food, clothing, shelter, a clean environment, and protection from extremes of temperature. Sometimes this occurs inadvertently when a previously healthy family member becomes confused or sick and is no longer able to provide a safe environment for the woman.

Elder abuse includes physical violence or emotional abuse directed at the elderly woman. This could be a form of domestic violence that has been going on for years or it could be abuse by an in-home caregiver. Such behavior must be reported to the appropriate authorities.

ACTION STEPS 5

For the Aging Woman

Poor health and the loss of independence are not inevitable consequences of growing older. Since limitations can and will occur at every stage of life, women of all ages and all levels of health must do what they can to prevent or limit disability and its costs. To preserve health and independence, consider the following strategies.

1. Maintain a Healthy Lifestyle and Seek Early Detection of Disease

- Screening to detect diseases early, when they are most treatable, saves many lives. Also, depending on your age and health, flu shots, pneumonia vaccines, and other important immunizations reduce a person's risk for hospitalization and death from illness. As much as possible, participate in assignments and interventions recommended by medical personnel.

- A healthy lifestyle is more influential than your genes in helping you avoid the decline traditionally associated with aging. Being active keeps you sharp mentally, physically, socially, and spiritually.

2. Prevent Injury and Have Injuries Properly Treated

- For older adults, falling is the most common injury. More than one-third of adults sixty-five and over fall each year, and of those, 20 to 30 percent suffer moderate to severe injuries that reduce mobility and independence.
- Remove tripping hazards in the home and have grab bars installed in key areas, like bathrooms. These simple measures will significantly reduce your chance of falling.

3. Learn Self-Management Techniques

- Consider getting involved in a community program that educates older women in self-management techniques. These programs will help you cope with and manage the transitions of your later years.
- To locate such programs, begin by asking your doctor if there are any groups or organizations in your area that meet regularly for support and/or social activities. In addition, services may be offered through your local community services agency within their older-adult care programs.

4. Maintain Relationships

- The number and quality of continuing relationships is critical to your physical and mental health. As you get older, you may feel that you live with perpetual loss because of dying friends and family members.
- Loneliness can often lead to feelings of depression and helplessness. Guard against this by maintaining and developing new relationships in your extended family, church, or community. (*For some elderly people, the risk of suicide or slow death from decided self-neglect increases substantially when he or she is left to live alone.*)
- Get involved in Sunday school, a small group, community bingo, the Red Hat Society, a reading group, or some other environment where you can build new relationships, laugh, and have fun, rather than isolating yourself.

For the Caregiver

Preparation for the future must include important conversations with family and/or friends who are acting as caregivers to discuss expectations.

1. Examine All the Options

- Many women have an idea of who they think will care for them but they don't discuss this with their potential caregiver. These discussions can be awkward and difficult, but they are critical to help minimize surprises.
- Discuss the changing levels of independence, financial planning (insurance, wills), and living arrangements, taking into account any physical or psychological issues.

2. Enlist Help

- As a spouse, child, or close family friend who cares deeply about the welfare of an older woman, you can easily grow overwhelmed by the day-to-day needs and stresses of caregiving. Get the help you need, as you see the demands increasing.
- To prevent burnout, it is essential to enlist the help of other people, rather than trying to handle everything on your own. Get advice from your extended family, friends, and your church community. Consider the possibility of using the help of a caregiver through an in-home care service. When possible, keeping the aging woman in a familiar environment will help maintain her quality of life.

3. Take Care of Yourself

- Take a step back from the undeniable fact of your love and concern for the elderly individual and assess realistically what you can and cannot commit to doing. As you ponder this decision, remember that it is not selfish to take care of yourself.
- Wearing yourself down will only make you stressed, frustrated, and angry. You may feel trapped, isolated, used, and unappreciated. To stay psychologically healthy, you must allow for personal time—time with God, time with friends, and time for rest.

4. Ask God for Strength and Wisdom

- The daily pressures and stresses of caregiving can be extremely taxing. Be honest with God about the emotions you are feeling and ask for His help each day as you serve the aging individual in your care.
- Compassion, empathy, and unselfishness are not attitudes you can drum up on your own. Ask God to develop these attitudes in your heart and give you wisdom as you serve your loved one.

BIBLICAL INSIGHTS 6

Moses was a hundred and twenty years old when he died, yet his eyes were not weak nor his strength gone.

Deuteronomy 34:7

Our generation tends to emphasize the importance of youth, but God uses servants of all ages. Age does not limit God's ability to work through people. As long as we have breath, we should be serving God, whether in big or small ways.

God says that His people "will still bear fruit in old age" (Ps. 92:14). Older believers have a lifetime of wisdom and experience that is valuable to the younger generation. Retirement is not an excuse to "check out" on life. Believers can and should grow spiritually and serve God, even in their later years.

Show me, O LORD, my life's end and the number of my days; let me know how fleeting is my life. You have made my days a mere handbreadth; the span of my years is as nothing before you. Each man's life is but a breath.

Psalm 39:4–5

Compared to the greatness and grandeur of God, our lives are like a vapor. Rather than ignoring the reality of death, David prayed that God would give him wisdom to use each day wisely.

One of the great challenges of aging is to understand that, while time is passing, God is working through us to make a difference in the world. No matter what our age, we must use our time wisely, fully, actively, and selflessly. We can give thanks for each new day and seek God's direction in how He wants us to serve Him.

Therefore we do not lose heart. Though outwardly we are wasting away, yet inwardly we are being renewed day by day. For our light and momentary troubles are achieving for us an eternal glory that far outweighs them all.

2 Corinthians 4:16–17

Often aging brings with it suffering, trouble, and pain, but to the Christian, this is no reason for despair. In this passage, Paul speaks of the inner vibrancy that sustains us, even in the midst of physical difficulties.

Health problems, suffering, and pain are *not* how God created the world to work. Sin has permeated and twisted our reality, but our hope is not in this life. Our hope as believers is grounded in the promise of eternal life with Jesus. In comparison with the glories and joys that await us in Jesus's presence, the difficulties of aging are "light and momentary."

7 PRAYER STARTER

Lord, we come to You today asking for Your wisdom and direction in _____'s life. Give her grace and peace in the midst of life's difficulties. God, we know You are faithful in every season of life, and You promise to walk with us and sustain us even in the uncertainties of aging. Reveal Yourself to _____ in a new way and reassure her of Your presence and Your love . . .

8 RECOMMENDED RESOURCES

Beach, Shelly. *Ambushed by Grace: Help and Hope on the Caregiving Journey*. Discovery House, 2008.

Bottke, Allison. *Setting Boundaries with Your Aging Parents: Finding Balance between Burnout and Respect*. Harvest House, 2010.

Buchanan, Missy. *Living with Purpose in a Worn-Out Body: Spiritual Encouragement for Older Adults*. Upper Room, 2008.

Focus on the Family. *Complete Guide to Caring for Aging Loved Ones.* Tyndale House, 2004.

Ieron, Julie-Allyson. *The Overwhelmed Woman's Guide to Caring for Aging Parents.* Moody, 2008.

Moll, Rob. *The Art of Dying: Living Fully into the Life to Come.* InterVarsity, 2010.

Morely, Patrick. *Second Wind for the Second Half: Twenty Ideas to Help You Reinvent Yourself for the Rest of the Journey.* Zondervan, 1999.

Tripp, Paul. *Lost in the Middle: Midlife and the Grace of God.* Shepherd Press, 2008.

Anger

1 PORTRAITS

- Sarah is the kind of woman you don't want to mess with. She can't keep a job for more than two weeks because of her anger. Being around Sarah is like walking on thin ice—any little thing can cause her to blow. People are afraid to approach her because they never know when she will snap. "This is just who I am," Sarah says. "My mom taught me to stick up for myself. I'm not the kind to hold my emotions inside. I say what I feel."

- At seventeen, Courtney and her mom, Julie, constantly battle about clothes, curfews, and choice of friends. Courtney gets so fed up that she begins to yell at her mother and throw things before retreating to her room, slamming her door, and blaring her music. Julie is at her wits' end and sometimes she just wants to knock some sense into Courtney. When Courtney mouthed off at her recently, Julie slapped her across the face before she even realized what she was doing.

- For most of her marriage, Marilee was abused by her ex-husband on a regular basis. Though she is free from this abusive lifestyle now, she feels intense hatred for all men. She can't even look at the opposite sex without resentment and rage fuming inside of her. "All my life, men have used me," she confesses. "My father, boyfriends, my ex—I can't trust them. I can't even talk to them. When I see a guy, all I want to do is smash his face in."

2 DEFINITIONS AND KEY THOUGHTS

- *Anger* is a *powerful, God-given emotion* (see Eph. 4:26) with intensity that ranges from being frustrated to severe fury. It can last from a few seconds to a lifetime. Anger itself is not a sin. What we *do* in our anger determines whether we sin.

- Anger is best understood as *a state of readiness*. It is a natural response to a real or perceived injustice or wrongdoing, and it inspires an alertness to defend good or attack evil. Even Jesus showed anger (see Mark 3:5).

- Anger is *mentioned more than five hundred times in Scripture*; the only emotion referred to more times in the Bible is love. Anger first appears in Genesis 4:5 and last appears in Revelation 19:15.

- Anger can lead to *healthy or unhealthy or sinful behavior. Careful assertiveness* is a healthy response to anger that involves problem solving and compassion.

Aggression is an unhealthy or sinful response to anger that involves hurting or controlling others, revenge, or hatred.

- Anger, when it is an automatic response to a situation, is considered a *primary emotion*. Anger can also be a *secondary emotion*, meaning it is felt in reaction to another feeling, such as hurt, sadness, or fear.

- In our culture in the past, women were expected to hold their anger inside and maintain a "ladylike" composure; however, in today's world, *an angry woman may feel free to express herself in raw, hurtful emotion*. Whether anger is verbally expressed or held inside, it *taxes the body physically.*[1]

- Statistics show that more than one in four people (28 percent) say that they *worry about how angry they sometimes feel*. More than one in ten people, or 12 percent, say they have *serious trouble controlling their anger*, but only 13 percent of those who admit having an anger problem have gotten help.[2]

Causes of Anger

- *External causes.* Anger can be a response to the harm someone has inflicted (a physical attack, insult, or abandonment) or to a circumstance in which there is no person at fault (100-degree days, physical illness, highway traffic).

- *Internal causes.* Anger is sometimes caused exclusively by an individual's mis-interpretations of reality or destructive thinking about normal life issues ("I should not have to pay taxes!"). Also, memories of traumatic past events as well as biologically rooted causes can be the internal impetus to anger.

Expressions of Anger

Anger always finds an *expression*.

- It may be *a response to a person, situation, or event*; to an *imaginary or anticipated* event; or to *memories* of traumatic or enraging situations.

- It may be *a response to a real or perceived injustice or hurt* in the form of frus-tration, betrayal, deprivation, exploitation, manipulation, criticism, violence, disapproval, humiliation, intimidation, and/or threats.

- It may be *a response when a boundary in a woman's life has been crossed*—when she feels violated, used, or devalued.

Levels of Anger

- *Irritation*—a feeling of discomfort
- *Indignation*—a feeling that something must be answered; something wrong must be corrected
- *Wrath*—a strong desire for revenge
- *Fury*—the partial loss of emotional control
- *Rage*—a loss of control involving aggression or an act of violence

- *Hostility*—a persistent form of anger; animosity toward others that becomes rooted in one's personality, which affects one's entire outlook on the world and life

Handling Anger

- *Internalization—repression.* Sometimes women repress anger. They stuff their emotion inside to maintain composure and peace. Some women actually *deny (or are unaware of) their anger.* This response is unhealthy. While a woman may not appear to be angry, the anger is still present—turned inward on herself. *Repressed anger can lead to various emotional and physical problems, including depression, anxiety, hypertension, and ulcers.*
- *Internalization—suppression.* Women may suppress their anger, meaning they acknowledge their anger and then bottle it up inside. With this approach to coping, they redirect anger-driven energy into unrelated activity. This can help manage their emotions; however, *it neglects addressing the root causes of anger.* One risk is that people who suppress anger may become cynical or passive-aggressive. Often they respond with indirect forms of revenge, such as sarcasm, lack of cooperation, gossip, and so on.
- *Rumination* is a common *unhealthy* response to a situation that has caused anger. *Women tend to go over and over in their head what happened, provoking increased anger.* This worsens any situation and leads to health issues like high blood pressure.
- *Physical symptoms* can develop *when anger is not handled properly.* These may include headaches, ulcers, stomach cramps, high blood pressure, colitis, and heart conditions.
- *Emotional symptoms of anger* include criticism, sarcasm, gossip, meanness, impatience, being demanding, withholding love, and refusing to forgive.
- *Healthy expressions of anger* are nonaggressive, assertive actions that maintain self-respect and show respect to others. A healthy response to anger *addresses problems in a constructive manner.*
- *Unhealthy or sinful expressions of anger* include acting in aggressive ways that hurt others. *Whether a woman yells, uses violence, or withdraws, the motivation involves revenge, manipulation, or "payback."* Women expressing anger in aggressive ways might say, "At least you know where I'm coming from!" However, they refuse to acknowledge the destructive force of their words and actions.

3 ASSESSMENT INTERVIEW

When women seek help for anger, *the problem is already out of control.* Such women may be experiencing shame and perhaps even fear because they do not yet understand how to identify and control their angry feelings. At the onset of counseling, *resist the urge to give advice.* Instead, *calmly hear the client's story.* It is important to ask the *rule-out questions* below to see if the problem is rooted in something other than anger. Then choose the appropriate questions from the remaining general questions.

Rule Outs

Depression has often been described as "anger turned inward." Women can express their anger as depression.

1. On a scale of 1 to 10, with 1 being "great" and 10 being "extremely depressed," where would you put yourself today? (*If depression is present, see also the chapter "Depression."*)
2. Do you have any thoughts of hurting yourself? (*If suicidal tendencies are evident, get professional help immediately.*)

Substance abuse is frequently an accompanying issue.

1. Are you ever under the influence of alcohol or drugs when you experience anger?
2. Do you use alcohol or drugs to avoid feelings of anger?

If you suspect that either depression or substance abuse is present, you should first deal with that underlying problem. Refer to the chapters on depression and addictions in this manual. Other underlying issues may include ADD/ADHD, brain trauma, personality disorders, attachment issues, and physical or sexual abuse.

General Questions

1. Who or what makes you angry?
2. How do you express your anger? When do you see your angry response crossing the line and becoming hurtful?
3. What is your first memory of feeling out of control when you got angry?
4. Do you ever take any action to redirect your anger by doing an unrelated activity?
5. Are you ever able to calm your anger? If so, how?
6. Has anger created any health issues?
7. How did you see anger expressed during childhood?
8. Could there be anger from your past that is affecting you now?
9. What is it like to be on the receiving end of someone else's anger?
10. How is the way that you express your anger harming your relationships?
11. Do you allow your anger to escalate? Do fights get physical?
12. When you get angry, how safe do you feel? How safe do those around you feel?
13. What would it be like to forgive the people with whom you are angry?
14. Do you pray to God about your anger? Do you deal with your anger "before the sun goes down"?

4 WISE COUNSEL

The emotion of anger, in and of itself, is not sin. Anger is a symptom of inner conflict, and the presence of this emotion shows that *a woman has hope that things can get better*. But left unresolved, anger can destroy relationships and cause deep heart wounds. As such, anger needs to be expressed and dealt with in constructive ways.

Rather than shaming a woman because of her anger, encourage her that *being willing to address the problem shows that she wants to change*. Investigate the emotions a woman feels in association with anger. Women tend to use anger to manipulate and control others. *When women repress their anger, it may lead to bitterness as well as physical health problems.*

Evaluate the history of anger expressed in the woman's life. It is possible that the anger the client feels today is not due to a "trigger" but is instead *rooted in anger from her past*. For example, a woman who is angry at her boss for being demanding might be thinking, *This man is heartless, just like my father was*. Such anger is misdirected at the boss, and the root issue of the woman's relationship with her father needs to be dealt with.

Anger leads to resentment (resentment is anger with a history), which then turns to bitterness or hostility.

5 ACTION STEPS

The goal is not to be anger free. Instead, it is to learn how to recognize anger and respond to it in a healthy manner.

1. Recognize Triggers and Warning Signs

- Focus on the source of the anger. List the triggers (during the counseling session and as homework). Until you can control your anger, you should avoid the triggers as much as possible.
- Learn to identify anger before it is out of control. How do you feel physically when experiencing anger? Do the following:

  — Identify angry feelings while they are still minor. State out loud, "I'm feeling angry right now."
  — Be aware of the first warning signs of anger, which may be physical changes. Anger promotes a sympathetic nervous system response (a physical state of readiness) and the following biological changes: rising heart rate and blood pressure, amplified alertness, tensed muscles, dilated pupils, GI tract disturbances, clenched fists, flared nostrils, and bulging veins.

2. Take a Step Back from the Situation

- Brainstorm ways to respond and not react in your anger.

  — Take a time-out; temporarily disengage from the situation if possible (twenty-minute minimum).
  — Perform light exercise until the intensity of anger is manageable.
  — Write don't fight; jot down troubling thoughts. This exercise is personal and writings should be kept private, possibly destroyed, not sent to anyone.

- Talk to a trusted friend who is unrelated to the anger-provoking situation. Don't just vent; ask for constructive advice.
- Pray about the anger, asking God to give you insight.
- Learn the value of calming. (*A person in a state of fury is not ready to manage an anger-provoking situation. Calming will let some of her angry feelings subside before expressing anger in a healthy way.* Note: *Ruminating is the opposite of calming, and makes anger worse by repeating destructive thoughts about an anger-producing event.*)

3. Learn to Express Feelings in a Healthy Way

- Brainstorm some ways to express your anger in a healthy way.

  — Respond (rational action); don't react (emotional retort).
  — Maintain a healthy distance until you can speak constructively (see James 1:19).
  — Confront to restore, not to destroy.
  — Empathize (get all the facts and try to understand the other person's perspective). Speak slowly and quietly (makes yelling difficult).
  — Surrender the right for revenge (see Rom. 12:19).

- If anger begins to escalate to wrath or fury, it is not the time to engage in interactions with others. Temporarily redirect your energy to solo activities. Get away from the cause of your anger until you can gain control and reestablish calm.

4. Ground Yourself in God

- Effectively managing anger is not something you can do in your own strength. The Bible says, "The fruit of the Spirit is love, joy, peace, patience, kindness, goodness, faithfulness, gentleness and self-control" (Gal. 5:22–23). The attitudes described in this passage are the direct result—the overflow—of a life directed by the Holy Spirit.
- You desperately need the help and grace of God to treat people as Jesus would. A life directed by the Holy Spirit doesn't just happen; rather, it is cultivated by concrete spiritual disciplines.

— Surrender to the Holy Spirit (Gal. 5:16).
— Reflect on the mercy and love God provides (Eph. 2:4).
— Pray and be honest with God about feelings and regrets (Matt. 5:43–45).
— Forgive and choose to let go of resentment and bitterness (Eph. 4:31–32).
— Avoid ruminating and revenge (1 Cor. 10:13; 1 Peter 1:13).
— Give respect to and receive it from those close to you (Eph. 5:22, 25).
— Love people, even those who anger you (1 Cor. 13).
— Remember what it is like to be on the receiving end of someone else's anger (1 Sam. 19:9–10).
— Resolve the root anger issues by talking about your frustrations and working toward resolution (Eph. 4:26).

- When we learn to control our anger and forgive those who offend us, we are following the example of Jesus, who forgave each of us. Ephesians 4:31–32 (NKJV) says, "Let all bitterness, wrath, anger, clamor, and evil speaking be put away from you, with all malice. And be kind to one another, tenderhearted, forgiving one another, even as God in Christ forgave you."

5. Seek Out Support and Counseling

- Underlying issues, such as abandonment, abuse, and betrayal, leave deep emotional wounds that do not heal overnight. In many cases, anger may be justified because of the wrong done to you, but the hurt and emotion still need to be worked through so that healing can take place. Otherwise, your bottled-up anger will spill over in other areas of your life.
- Make plans to work on such issues through additional counseling and support groups. A plan should be made for follow-up, perhaps:

— Find an accountability partner.
— Join an anger management group.
— Continue with individual counseling.

6 BIBLICAL INSIGHTS

If you do what is right, will you not be accepted? But if you do not do what is right, sin is crouching at your door; it desires to have you, but you must master it.

Genesis 4:7

Cain's problem with anger wasn't that he became angry. It was how he reacted in his anger. At first, Cain's anger was a positive response but it missed the mark. Instead of Cain making personal changes, his anger turned to deadly jealousy.

Anger must be ruled or it will rule. Uncontrolled anger quickly becomes destructive. When you invite God to help you identify your anger and take positive action, anger becomes a servant rather than a master.

"In your anger do not sin": Do not let the sun go down while you are still angry, and do not give the devil a foothold.

Ephesians 4:26–27

Note that these verses do not say, "Never be angry." Anger is a God-given emotion and, if handled well, will promote positive change. These verses challenge us to deal with the root causes of anger, rather than ignoring them.

Do not allow anger to cause you to act in ways that you will later regret.

Do not turn anger in on yourself or pretend you are never angry.

Deal with your anger as quickly (and responsibly) as possible—before the sun goes down—so that you do not "give the devil a foothold." Going to bed with unresolved conflict suppresses the immune system and leads to feelings of frustration, antagonism, and bitterness, which will destroy relationships.

Remember, Satan loves to use anger to divide the body of Christ. Seek to resolve differences with others respectfully, remembering that anger presents an opportunity for honesty, change, and growth.

And I became very angry when I heard their outcry and these words.

Nehemiah 5:6 NKJV

Nehemiah's anger was righteous indignation because many Jews were suffering at the hands of rich countrymen who had lent them money. Expressing his anger in a healthy way, Nehemiah called a meeting of the moneylenders who agreed to his firm requests.

When you feel anger burning beneath the surface, ask God to guide you toward a productive way of solving the conflict. Rather than reacting in rage and losing control, take a step back from the situation, pray, gain perspective, and try to work toward a healthy solution.

Do not make friends with a hot-tempered man, do not associate with one easily angered, or you may learn his ways and get yourself ensnared.

Proverbs 22:24–25

You may not be able to change the anger that others express but you can avoid close ties with furious people. Such people are ready to explode and anyone around will either catch the brunt of that fury or become similarly furious.

Choose carefully those who will be your closest friends, business partners, and spouse. You will eventually become like the people you hang out with. Anger leads to conflict, stress, and tension, and a perpetually angry person will only drag you into his or her drama.

PRAYER STARTER 7

Lord, we all get angry. Anger is a powerful emotion that You have given us. Your Word teaches us clearly about the constructive and destructive force that anger is.

Teach _____ to control and process her anger in a healthy way, even when she has been threatened or wronged. Give her wisdom to love and forgive other people and work toward positive change, rather than letting her anger paralyze her or cause her to withdraw. We need Your help, Jesus . . .

8 RECOMMENDED RESOURCES

Anderson, Neil, and Rich Miller. *Getting Anger under Control.* Harvest House, 2002.

Barnhill, Julie Ann. *She's Gonna Blow: Real Help for Moms Dealing with Anger.* Harvest House, 2005.

Carter, Les. *The Anger Trap: Free Yourself from the Frustrations That Sabotage Your Life.* Jossey-Bass, 2004.

Carter, Les, and Frank Minirth. *The Anger Workbook: A 13-Step Interactive Plan to Help You . . .* Thomas Nelson, 1992.

Chapman, Gary. *Anger: Handling a Powerful Emotion in a Healthy Way.* Northfield, 2007.

Clinton, Julie. *A Woman's Path to Emotional Freedom.* Harvest House, 2010.

Oliver, Gary, and Carrie Oliver. *Mad about Us: Moving from Anger to Intimacy with Your Spouse.* Bethany House, 2007.

Birth Control

PORTRAITS 1

- Bethany and her husband got married recently and are not ready for children just yet. After talking with her doctor about different contraceptives, Bethany left more confused than she was at the beginning of the appointment. She wants to be sure that the type of birth control she takes will not hurt her or lessen her chances of being able to have a baby in the future. "A friend told me that there is no safe birth control," Bethany says, "and the side effects the doctor mentioned are kind of scary."

- Jackie went to her friend's party ready for some fun, but after one too many drinks, she passed out. Waking up with a throbbing headache, Jackie was shocked to find that she was lying naked on a bed next to some guy she didn't even recognize. Grabbing her clothes, she dressed quickly and slipped out of the house. She has an idea of what probably took place and now she is trying to think of what to do. In a magazine, she sees an advertisement for a Plan B pill.

- Wendy and her husband have four kids and another one on the way. They feel that God is ultimately in control of the number of children they have, so they don't use contraception. Money is starting to get tight, though, and Wendy's health isn't very good. *After this baby . . . then what?* Wendy worries. *I'm not sure my body can handle another pregnancy.*

DEFINITIONS AND KEY THOUGHTS 2

- Birth control and family planning are *methods used to control pregnancy and birthing*, so that the process, timing, and the number of children born are a matter of a couple's choice rather than random occurrences. *The Bible does not address birth control specifically*, though many theologians and pastors suggest that there are biblical passages that provide some guidance for birth control–related decisions.

- Beliefs about contraception, even among Christians, vary greatly. *Some believe that any form of contraception, including abstinence from sex, is sinful.* These people tend to see the randomness of unplanned birthing as being in harmony with God's design and command to be "fruitful and multiply." On the other end of the spectrum are *people who feel that all forms of birth control, including abortion, are acceptable.* Most fall somewhere in between these two extremes, believing that certain forms of birth control are allowable.

- A core belief among conservative Christians is that life begins at conception (fertilization). Therefore, *birth control methods that prevent fertilization are generally accepted, because they do not destroy life.* However, any form of birth control that terminates a fertilized egg is considered unacceptable.

- *Every child is a blessing from God and has infinite worth.* While acknowledging that many Christians think a bit differently, we affirm that human life begins at fertilization (the union of sperm and egg), and as such, we do not believe that the prevention of fertilization is morally wrong. However, we would oppose any method that prevents implantation of the fertilized egg in the womb.

- In contrast to the position above, *some Christians do not see birth control that prevents implantation as a problem.* Research has shown that many fertilized eggs naturally do not make it from the point of conception to the point of implantation in a woman's uterus. Also some Christians contend that a fertilized egg is not a human in the same way that a chicken egg is not a chicken—it only holds the potential of being human. *This position, however, is nearly impossible to reconcile with biblical texts.*

- *Many families are made up of a combination of planned and unplanned children.* Many couples can point to one or more children that "just happened to come along" when they were wrestling with decisions about birth control and sterilization. Most families consider such children to be God's special gift, serving as a reminder that God alone is sovereign over the creation of a new life.

- Who uses what? *The most commonly used method of birth control is the Pill.* Nineteen percent of women ages fifteen to forty-four use the Pill, while 17 percent of women ages fifteen to forty-four use female sterilization. About 6 percent of women have used an emergency contraceptive.[1]

3 | ASSESSMENT INTERVIEW

Sometimes, women are prescribed birth control for reasons other than wanting to prevent pregnancy, such as PMDD (premenstrual dysphonic disorder), menstrual cycle regulation, pain regulation, and acne prevention.

For a woman who plans to use birth control to prevent pregnancy, start by educating her on the various kinds of birth control and the related issues and side effects that are possible with each. The following questions can help guide such a conversation. (Remember, however, since you are not a medical professional, to encourage the woman to talk to her medical doctor before making a decision, because medical and health issues may influence her choice of birth control.)

1. Why are you using or why do you need to use birth control? Is it to prevent pregnancy, regulate menstrual cycles, or for other health issues?
2. Are you currently using birth control? What side effects have you experienced? How has it been working for you?

3. Did you use a different birth control method in the past? Why did you switch to a different option?
4. When do you believe life begins—at fertilization, at implantation of the egg in the uterus, or sometime later?
5. What is your opinion about using birth control that probably prevents fertilization but will also prevent implantation if fertilization does take place?
6. Have you heard of the natural family planning method? How do you feel about abstaining from sex during certain times for the purpose of birth control?
7. How do you feel about using protection (male or female condoms)?
8. What does your husband think about birth control? Does he have a certain opinion or has he left it up to you?
9. How many (more) children do you want to have? When?
10. Have you and your husband talked about whether one of you would opt for sterilization or permanent birth control?
11. What are your concerns about using birth control?

WISE COUNSEL 4

Before marriage, the church admonishes a couple to *refrain from sexual contact*; however, after the wedding, the church admonishes the couple to *refrain from abstaining from sexual contact*.

A biblical basis for decisions regarding the timing of birth and methods used to control pregnancy should flow out of a couple's love for God and love for each other. *Together couples should determine the number and timing of children*, based in part on their financial position and the time they have to give to one another and to their children. All children need parents who love them dearly. These considerations could necessitate the use of birth control or the readjustment of a couple's lifestyle and commitments.

We believe that a husband or wife should not deliberately withhold sex from each other. *Abstinence is not a theologically suitable method of birth control for a husband and wife*. In 1 Corinthians 7, Paul writes, "Do not deprive each other [of sex] except by mutual consent and for a time, so that you may devote yourselves to prayer" (v. 5).

There are *many methods of birth control* that can be considered. Encourage the woman to use methods of birth control that value and preserve life—that do not terminate or interfere with life once fertilization has taken place.

As a counselor, if you will be dealing with this issue regularly, you will need to *keep up with medical trends and advances* as they appear (and in this field, changes and advances do happen regularly).

Advise the woman that *no contraceptive is 100 percent effective* (except abstinence or surgery). Usually contraceptive failures occur when birth control methods are used carelessly or improperly.

The following are some common contraceptive options for couples.

Timing Methods of Contraception: Natural Family Planning/ Fertility Awareness Method

The idea behind natural family planning (NFP) and the fertility awareness method (FAM) is this: *a woman is fertile during only a small window of time each month*. This small window is believed to be between 100 to 120 hours. Hence, if a couple abstains from intercourse during this time, pregnancy can be avoided. Conversely, NFP/ FAM could be used to help achieve pregnancy by couples wishing to have a child. To determine the window of fertility, a woman *charts factors*, such as menstrual cycle length, morning body temperature, and cervical mucus.

The question that most people ask concerning the various NFP/FAM methods is: how can I determine exactly the time of the window of fertility? If the time frame could be determined with 100 percent accuracy, then NFP/FAM would be a perfect method of birth control. However, *the window can only be estimated*, though with high probability if done correctly. There are numerous devices on the market to help determine when a woman is fertile. Couples using NFP/FAM methods correctly have *a much lower failure rate than condom users, and close to that of users of birth control pills*.

NFP is the only birth control method approved by the Roman Catholic Church. However, as discussed above, *some persons have theological problems with NFP* because it violates the biblical command to abstain from sex only for the purpose of fasting and prayer.

Barrier Methods of Contraception

Male Condoms

Male condoms are the most common type of barrier contraception. Condoms are made of latex or polyurethane (though "natural" pigskin and new synthetic materials are also used). *Latex condoms are the most popular, being the most affordable and very effective*. It should be noted that latex condoms can be used only with water-based lubricants, not oil-based lubricants, which harm the integrity of the latex. In addition, a small number of people have an allergic reaction to latex.

Polyurethane condoms are becoming widely available. These condoms are thinner and transmit heat more readily than do latex condoms, making intercourse feel more natural. It is not clear which are stronger—latex or polyurethane condoms—though some studies suggest neither is more likely to break. However, some say that since polyurethane condoms stretch less than latex condoms, there is an increased chance of breakage or slippage if the condom is too tight or too loose. Both oil- and water-based lubricants can be used with polyurethane condoms.

Condoms are probably the *least enjoyable method of contraception* for both women and men. Condom size (length and width) affects both comfort and effectiveness. To be most effective, condoms should be put on before there is any genital contact. After ejaculation, during intercourse, the penis must be withdrawn before any loss of erection, and the base of the condom needs to be held in place during withdrawal.

Female Condoms

The female condom has been available in Europe since 1992, and the United States Food and Drug Administration (FDA) approved it in 1993. The female condom is *a polyurethane sheath* about 6.5 inches in length that a woman wears during sex. It lines the vagina and helps prevent STDs.

At each end of the condom is a flexible ring. The closed end of the sheath, which has a slightly smaller ring, is inserted in the vagina to hold the prophylactic in place. At the other (open) end of the condom, the ring stays outside the entrance to the vagina to act as a guide during penetration and to prevent the sheath from bunching up inside the vagina. Since the condom does not move with the penis, *the sensation is more natural and enjoyable for the man* than with male condoms. However, some women find female condoms uncomfortable. *Note*: The female condom should not be used with the male condom because the friction between the two condoms could cause them to break.

Diaphragms, Cervical Caps, and Shields

Diaphragms, cervical caps, and shields are all similar in that they all are inserted into the vagina before sex and *cover a woman's cervix to prevent the union of sperm and egg.*

A *diaphragm* is a shallow, dome-shaped cup with a flexible rim.

A *cervical cap* is a silicone cup shaped like a sailor's hat. It is smaller in diameter than a diaphragm, though it still fits securely to cover the cervix.

A *shield (for example Lea's shield)* is a silicone cup similar to a cap, with an air valve and a tab to aid in removal.

Each method must be *used with spermicidal cream or jelly*. The spermicidal ingredient kills sperm, while the inserted device prevents sperm from entering the woman's cervix.

Diaphragms, caps, and shields are reusable items that must be fitted to a woman's body by a doctor. A new fitting is required if a woman gains or loses weight or has a vaginal birth. Caps are more difficult to fit in women who have given birth, and failure rates are higher. Accordingly, *sixteen out of one hundred women* who use a diaphragm will become pregnant during the first year of typical use. *Fourteen out of one hundred women* who have never been pregnant and use a cervical cap (FemCap brand) will become pregnant during the first year of typical use. *Twenty-nine out of one hundred women* who have given birth vaginally and use FemCap will become pregnant during the first year of typical use. *Fifteen out of one hundred women* who use the shield will become pregnant during the first year of typical use.[2]

Regarding user satisfaction, some people find using a diaphragm, cap, or shield to be a major interruption before sex, while others see it as a minor issue. Once in place, these methods are very comfortable for both the woman and the man, as neither should be aware of the product during intercourse.

Sponges

The contraceptive sponge is *a doughnut shaped piece of polyurethane foam containing spermicide* that is inserted into the vagina and placed over the cervix. Because of the spermicide, sponges work both to *block and kill sperm*. Similar to caps and dia-phragms, a sponge can be left in place for twenty-four hours and is considered good for multiple acts of intercourse (though more spermicide may need to be applied). Also similar to caps, the sponge must be left in the vagina for six hours after the last act of intercourse. On the negative side, some men claim they can feel the sponge or its removal tab during intercourse. Also the *failure rate with the sponge is high*: 9 percent for women who have not given birth, and up to 20 percent for women who have.[3]

Hormonal Methods of Contraception

Pills

Birth control pills, despite their widespread use, are quite *controversial*. This is because some birth control pills (as well as the other hormonal contraceptives listed below) *prevent fertilization of the egg*, while *others only prevent implantation*. To further complicate the topic, there is considerable debate about which hormonal methods prevent fertilization and which prevent implantation.

Basically, all hormonal methods of contraception contain a *progestin*, a synthetic form of progesterone (that prevents implantation), and some also contain a *synthetic estrogen* (that prevents ovulation and/or fertilization). These two chemicals are pre-sented in different amounts and strengths depending on the contraceptive being used.

There are two common types of birth control pill: *progestin-only pills* (POPs) and *combined oral contraceptives* (COCs) that contain both progestin and estrogen. POPs allow ovulation at least some of the time. This means that fertilization is possible, while implantation is inhibited. Therefore, if a woman believes that life begins at fertilization, POPs are the wrong choice for her. In contrast COCs are *so effective at preventing ovulation* that fertilization cannot occur.

Theoretically, the progestin in the pills could interfere with implantation, but if fertilization never occurs, this is irrelevant. Hence, COCs would be an acceptable form of contraception, even for couples who believe life begins at fertilization.

The Birth Control Shot

The birth control shot, also known as *combined injectable contraceptives* (CICs), is given every month or every three months, depending on dosages. This method is growing in popularity because of the *ease of use* (a woman does not need to re-member to take a daily pill), low side effects, and efficacy of the contraceptive. CICs contain *progesterone* and are quite effective in preventing ovulation. In one study, only *3 percent of sexually active women using the birth control shot became pregnant over the course of a year*.[4]

Implants

Implants consist of *small, match-sized tubes containing etonogestrel* that are sur-gically inserted by a physician in a woman's upper arm. The rods slowly release etonogestrel into the woman's bloodstream and can be *effective for up to three years*. This method works by thickening the cervical mucus, greatly reducing the changes of fertilization, as well as by thinning the uterine lining, making implantation impossible in the chance that fertilization does happen. After an implant is removed, women generally experience a fairly quick return of fertility.[5]

The Ring

The ring method, the most popular being the NuvaRing, is *a flexible circle of about two inches in diameter that is worn in the vagina for three weeks each month*, then removed for one week (during which menstruation usually takes place). Once the ring is inserted, the woman does not feel it because it molds to the body. During intercourse, most men report that they cannot feel the ring. The hormones contained within the ring, which are a combination of estrogen and progestin, are *absorbed directly in the bloodstream through the vaginal wall*. The method is very effective at preventing ovulation. In addition, with the use of the NuvaRing, the uterine wall becomes thinner than usual, which would inhibit implantation of a fertilized egg, if an egg were to become fertilized.

The Patch

Patches are becoming an increasingly popular delivery method for many types of medication, from smoking prevention to antidepressants. Their popularity is rooted in their providing a *convenient form* for receiving medication, with less chance of missing a dose. For birth control, a woman wears a small patch of approximately one inch for about *three weeks* a month. This patch works in the same way as the ring, implants, and intrauterine devices—it *prevents implantation* but not necessarily fertilization.

Plan B

Plan B (*levonorgestrel*) prevents pregnancy by 89 percent if taken *within three days of intercourse*, though efficacy increases the sooner the pill is taken after intercourse.[6] Though it is intended to be used after intercourse has occurred, Plan B is not the same as RU-486 (the abortion pill)—*it will not work if the woman is already pregnant*. Because the method often *destroys fertilized eggs*, it has been widely condemned by Christians. Plan B is considered an emergency contraceptive that can *prevent* a pregnancy after a contraceptive failure (such as forgetting to take a pill or having a condom break), unprotected sex, or sexual assault.

Intrauterine Device

An intrauterine device (IUD) is a small object that is placed in the uterus to prevent pregnancy. IUDs can last from *one to ten years*. The IUD is not noticeable during intercourse. While some claim that IUDs work by affecting the movements of the eggs and sperm to prevent fertilization, generally they function by *making the uterine lining unsuitable for implantation of a fertilized egg*.

Sterilization Methods of Contraception

Spermicides

Spermicides have been around for a long time, perhaps, according to some, since 1850 BC. Today there are a number of spermicides available as suppositories, gels, creams, foams, and even a plastic film. Many women and men like to use spermicides, either alone or in combination with some other form of birth control, because they are *relatively inexpensive, easy to use, and can be purchased without prescription*. Also spermicides have gained favor because they do not require a physical separation of the male and female genital organs, as do condoms.

However, spermicides do have disadvantages. The foremost is that they have *limited reliability when used alone*. Hence, many persons who use spermicides use them in conjunction with condoms or a cervical cap–type device. Other downsides include timing issues. That is, spermicides are *effective for only a limited amount of time—* typically an hour—and some need to be applied up to fifteen minutes before intercourse takes place. In addition, nonoxynol-9, a common active ingredient in spermicides available in the United States, is irritating to some women. The more frequently it is used, the higher the likelihood of irritation. When use is limited to no more than every other day, however, irritation is rare (3 percent more than with a placebo).

Vasectomy

The *vasectomy* has been described as the *most reliable form of birth control* available. On rare occasions a vasectomy can reverse itself; however, this occurs only 1 to 2 percent of the time.[7]

A vasectomy involves *cutting (or more recently, blocking) the vas deferens*, a tube that transports sperm from the testicles. *Procedural failure is very rare and complications are uncommon*. In addition, no change in sex drive is caused by vasectomy, although a few men seem to develop a psychosomatic response that interferes with normal sexual function. Also, since the testicles provide less than 5 percent of the seminal fluid that is ejaculated during orgasm, no difference in ejaculation is felt or noticed. Although vasectomies can sometimes be reversed, this is never assured and *the operation should be considered a permanent procedure*.

New methods for vasectomy include Vasclip, a method where a small plastic clip, about the size of a grain of rice, is clipped over the vas deferens, effectively closing it off.

Female Tubal Ligation

A female tubal ligation can be performed in the following ways:

Postpartum tubal ligation is usually done as a *mini-laparoscopy* after childbirth. *Laparoscopy* involves inserting a viewing instrument and surgical tools through small incisions made in the abdomen. Laparoscopy is frequently done with a general anesthetic. The fallopian tubes are higher in the abdomen right after pregnancy, so the incision is made below the navel. Often the procedure is done within twenty-four to thirty-six hours after the baby is delivered.

An *open tubal ligation* is done through a larger incision in the abdomen. It may be recommended if the woman needs abdominal surgery for other reasons (such as a cesarean section) or has had pelvic inflammatory disease (PID), endometriosis, or previous abdominal or pelvic surgery. These conditions may have caused scarring or sticking together (adhesion) of tissue and organs in the abdomen, making one of the other types of tubal ligation more difficult and risky.

Laparotomy (a surgical incision in the abdominal wall) or *mini-laparotomy* can be done using general anesthesia or a regional anesthetic, also known as an epidural.

Reversing a tubal ligation is possible but is not highly successful. Statistics report pregnancy rates of 31 to 73 percent, but successful pregnancy is sporadic at best. This is the reason tubal ligation is considered a *permanent method of birth control*.

One rare but serious complication of tubal ligation is *ectopic pregnancy*, in which the fertilized egg implants in a fallopian tube rather than in the uterus. This is an extremely dangerous situation that results in the death of the mother unless the pregnancy is identified early and terminated. The overall rate of ectopic pregnancy in traditional tubal ligation is estimated at 7.3 per 1,000 procedures.[8] The age of a woman has an impact on the chances of an ectopic pregnancy; women having a tubal ligation under the age of thirty have double the risk when compared to older females.

Abortion

The last, and for Christians most objectionable, form of birth control is abortion. Various procedures, at various stages of development of the fetus (including right up to the birth of the child), are used *to end the life of a fetus* and extract it from the womb.

In the United States abortion has been *legal since the US Supreme Court declared it so in the infamous Roe v. Wade and related cases in 1973*. For more than a decade now, the number of abortions in the United States has remained essentially stable—around 1.4 million each year.[9]

ACTION STEPS 5

1. Do Your Homework

- Research all of the options available for birth control to make an informed decision that is right for you. Talk to your doctor about the best options for birth control, considering your age, health concerns, personal beliefs, and past pregnancies.
- Look on the internet for information regarding birth control options. Websites that will provide helpful information are www.WebMD.com, www.cmda.org, www.healthywomen.org, and www.americanpregnancy.org.
- Search the Scriptures and get godly counsel from a trusted pastor at your church or another individual whom you see as a mature believer.

2. Pray Together

- Set a time to sit down with your husband and discuss the options and information you've found and then pray together about a decision.

- Schedule a day (after one or two weeks) on which the two of you will come back together for a decision. During the interval of one or two weeks, both of you should pray individually for God's guidance.
- After you decide on the best option for you as a couple, pray and thank God for His guidance. From this time on, trust that God knows what is best for your marriage and your family.
- *Be sure to emphasize the importance of both partners' seeking guidance from the Lord regarding this decision. You may want to suggest a time of fasting in addition to prayer.*

3. Seek to Honor God

- Love and respect each other. The greatest gift any mother can give her children is to love their dad. And the greatest gift any dad can give his children is to love their mother.
- God created sexual intimacy as an amazing gift to be shared in the context of the marriage relationship. And children are a precious blessing from the Lord.
- Using birth control to prevent pregnancy for selfish reasons does not honor God. He brought you and your husband together, and ultimately, God is sovereign in conception, no matter what birth control method you choose. Examine your priorities and underlying motives for using birth control.

6 BIBLICAL INSIGHTS

If any of you lacks wisdom, he should ask God, who gives generously to all without finding fault, and it will be given to him.

James 1:5

It is important to realize the need for God's wisdom and direction regarding birth control. There are many different viewpoints on the use of contraception, but more important is God's plan and desire for this couple.

God will bless the couple desiring wholeheartedly to do His will. By taking time to pray, and perhaps even fasting, concerning their birth control decision, discernment and understanding will come.

This is what the LORD says—your Redeemer, who formed you in the womb: I am the LORD, who has made all things, who alone stretched out the heavens, who spread out the earth by myself.

Isaiah 44:24

No form of birth control gives a 100 percent guarantee. But we can trust God, who is the Creator and Sustainer of life. For Him, no pregnancy is unplanned. If God decides to create a child within a mother's womb, He has a beautiful plan and will give the parents what they need to raise the baby, growing their faith in the process.

For you created my inmost being; you knit me together in my mother's womb. . . . My frame was not hidden from you when I was made in the secret place. When I was woven together in the depths of the earth, your eyes saw my unformed body.

Psalm 139:13, 15–16

Every conception is a miracle, a work of God. While birth control is often a responsible option, we must remember that God is sovereign and He is the author of life. Every child is a gift from His hand and should be treasured and loved as such.

PRAYER STARTER : 7

Father in heaven, who knows all things perfectly, give us wisdom as we consider the issue of family planning and birth control. There are many strong opinions, God, and many complicated issues to consider. Provide _____ and her husband with clarity and divine guidance as they seek to honor and obey You in the planning of their family . . .

RECOMMENDED RESOURCES : 8

Billings, John. *The Ovulation Method: Natural Family Planning.* Liturgical Press, 1984.

Grenz, Stanley J. *Sexual Ethics: An Evangelical Perspective.* Westminster John Knox Press, 1999.

Nelson, Tommy. *The Book of Romance: What Solomon Says about Love, Sex and Intimacy.* Thomas Nelson, 2007.

Paris, Jenell Williams. *Birth Control for Christians: Making Wise Choices.* Baker, 2003.

Weschler, Toni. *Taking Charge of Your Fertility.* Collins Living, 2006.

Cancer

1 PORTRAITS

- Sharon noticed a small, hard lump in her breast one day as she was showering but quickly dismissed it as hormonal. But when the abnormality hadn't gone away in several weeks, Sharon's concern turned to fear. *What if . . . what if . . .* she dared not say the words. With trembling hands, Sharon filled out the paperwork for her mammogram appointment. Part of her just wanted to ignore it, to pretend nothing was wrong. But she knew she couldn't.

- The doctor's words hit Amy like a ton of bricks: "I'm so sorry, but you have cervical cancer." It was just a routine checkup—Amy had planned to be in and out and back to her office. But now her mind was racing with anxiety, fear, anger, and shock. The feelings were overwhelming as Amy grabbed for her cell phone to call her husband, Tom. *How is this happening to me? I'm gonna die . . . I'm not ready to die! God, why? Why?*

- "I thought chemo was supposed to make me better," Katie moaned, "but I feel like it's killing me." Three weeks into her combined chemotherapy and radiation treatments, Katie was losing her hair by the handful. She hardly had enough energy to sit up, never mind take care of herself. As a marketing executive, Katie was used to calling the shots. Sitting in bed for hour upon hour wasn't just annoying, it was driving her mad. "I don't know who I am anymore," Katie muttered through tears.

2 DEFINITIONS AND KEY THOUGHTS

- *Cancer*, as defined by the National Cancer Institute, is *a term for diseases in which abnormal cells divide without control and can invade nearby tissues*. Cancer is not one disease, but the term is a general one that describes more than one hundred different diseases. Cancer can develop in any tissue of the body, described specifically by one of several categories:

  — *Carcinoma* is any cancerous growth that begins in the skin or in tissues that line or cover internal organs.
  — *Sarcoma* is any cancerous growth that begins in bone, cartilage, fat, muscle, blood vessels, or other connective or supportive tissue.

— *Leukemia* is any cancerous growth that starts in the bone marrow and is quickly spread through the bloodstream.

— *Lymphoma* and *multiple myeloma* are cancers that attack the cells of the immune system.

— *Central nervous system cancers* begin in the tissues of the brain and spinal cord.[1]

- Among women, *the most common forms of cancer* are:

  — skin cancer

  — breast cancer

  — lung cancer

  — colorectal cancer

  — reproductive cancer (cervical, ovarian, endometrial cancers)

- The word *cancer* can be one of the most terrifying words in the world. Every woman knows other women—a mom, sister, aunt, grandmother, friend, co-worker, roommate—who have battled or succumbed to some form of cancer. *Cancer is the second leading cause of death in women.*[2]

- *Breast cancer is the most common type of cancer* and the second most common type of cancer to result in death in women in the United States. (More women in the United States die from lung cancer than any other type of cancer.)[3]

- In 2010 more than 200,000 women in the United States were diagnosed with breast cancer, and there were nearly 40,000 breast cancer–related deaths in women. *It is estimated that 1 in 8 (12.5 percent) of women will develop breast cancer in their lifetime, and 1 in 4 women will develop some form of cancer.*[4]

- Hearing the news of one's cancer is frightening and overwhelming, and a woman may easily assume that death is inevitable. However, *cancer is not necessarily a death sentence*. As one example, in the United States, there are more than 2.5 million breast cancer survivors, and the American Cancer Society estimates that the five-year survival rate for breast cancer among women is 80–85 percent.[5]

- More than just a physical disease, *cancer affects a woman on every level—physically, emotionally, psychologically, socially, and spiritually*. The invasive nature of cancer treatments and the many negative side effects that result can make daily life very difficult; however, many women report that the hardest part of their battle with cancer was the emotional, psychological component.

- While a team of expert doctors may be overseeing a woman's cancer treatment plan and doing everything possible to ensure her *physical* well-being, very often women feel isolated and alone as they struggle to process the reality of their cancer. As such, *counseling is a vital part of the cancer treatment process.*

- A woman with cancer is facing the possibility of death, grieving the loss of her health and independence, and many times, struggling with feelings of depression and loss of purpose. *Breast and reproductive cancers can be especially damaging to a woman's sense of self-esteem and identity because disease or treatment may destroy the possibility of her having children in the future.*

- Physical changes, such as hair loss, weight loss, and surgeries to remove breasts or reproductive organs can lead a woman to feel robbed of her femininity and essence. She may be asking herself, *What makes a person a woman? Am I still beautiful? Do I matter to anyone?* These questions need to be addressed and answered in a safe, loving environment.

- Frequently friends and family members don't know how to interact with a woman who has cancer and they may view her disease as *a barrier to friendship and intimacy.* A woman with cancer needs genuine, *deep relationships with other women* who will choose to interact with her as a woman, not a blob with a disease. Additionally, if a woman is married, *it is essential that her husband be loving and understanding*, continuing to cherish, support, and care for her. No matter how cancer affects a woman's body, she is still a woman, a woman with hopes, dreams, fears, and aspirations.

3 ASSESSMENT INTERVIEW

1. Tell me about your experience with cancer. How did you find out? What was your initial response?
2. The news of cancer brings with it a whole torrent of emotion. What feelings have been most prominent and reoccurring for you?
3. What are you most afraid of?
4. Are you still able to do most of what you did before your cancer or has cancer limited your abilities and/or energy? Tell me about a typical day.
5. What are the biggest challenges for you right now and how are you handling these stressors?
6. What do you most love to do? How has cancer affected this?
7. What is your medical prognosis?
8. What treatment options have you chosen (chemotherapy, radiation, nutrition, and so on), and how are you handling the treatment physically and emotionally?
9. To whom are you talking? Who is supporting you emotionally and spiritually?
10. How are your relationships with your family and close friends? Are there any broken relationships you desire to be restored?
11. How is your relationship with God?
12. If you had one wish, what would it be?

4 WISE COUNSEL

Cancer is not just a physical disease. *Cancer adds a million complications to the daily stress of life*—evaluating treatment options, transportation to and from chemo or radiation treatments (sometimes long distances), side effects of treatment, the need for a caregiver, possible inability to continue in a job, the challenges of child care, fatigue, health complications, and the list goes on.

Be there for her. It is normal for a woman with cancer to feel angry, overwhelmed, sad, worried, distressed, fearful, isolated, and alone, and these feelings vary from day to day and moment to moment. While getting medical treatment is vital, *it is also essential that a woman with cancer have someone to talk to about what she's feeling, struggling with, and experiencing.*

Listen well. Every woman responds to the news of cancer differently. Give your client the freedom to talk, cry, or just sit and grapple with the reality of the diagnosis. Depending on where a woman is in the process—if she has just found out or has already been in treatment for a while—she will most likely be feeling different emotions. *Provide a therapeutic environment through active listening and unconditional positive regard.*

Assess and address key stressors. Try to ascertain how the woman is functioning in daily life and what her biggest stressors are. Then *work together to look for ways to manage the stress* and find ways for her to continue to enjoy her life. Identify coping skills and tools that will enable her to gain a healthy perspective and still find joy, beauty, and humor in the little things of life—a cup of coffee, a favorite television show, dinner with friends, a manicure, a new outfit, music, a good book, and so on.

Speak the truth. Cancer raises a host of questions in a woman's mind, many of which do not have easy answers. These questions may range from, Why would God allow this? and How could God love me? to Who will take care of my children? and What is death like? Rather than being completely preoccupied with the cancer, a woman needs to *gain perspective.* Help her do this by talking about *God's promises and faithfulness* to every single one of his children, even in the trial of cancer. Scripture says that nothing can separate us from the love of Christ, and that includes cancer or the possibility of death (see Rom. 8:38–39).

ACTION STEPS 5

1. Talk It Out

- You can't fight cancer alone, so don't isolate yourself or pretend you're okay. Talk to your family and friends about what you're feeling and experiencing and allow them to love, care for, and minister to you. For many of us it's hard to be weak and on the receiving end of ministry, but don't push away God's love and compassion as extended through His body.

- Join a support group so you can wrestle through the challenges of cancer with other people who have a similar battle. In this safe environment, talk honestly about your fears, anxiety, and frustrations. Bottling everything up may seem like a necessary and easy strategy, but it will eventually lead to an emotional breakdown. No one is meant to walk this road alone.

- Most important, talk to God about everything that's going through your head. He understands you completely, loves you unconditionally, and longs to give you peace and comfort.

2. Ask a Friend to Go Shopping

- If you are facing hair loss, ask a friend to go shopping with you and look for pretty scarves, hats, and wigs *before* you need them. Planning ahead will help ease the shock you feel at losing your hair and help you continue to feel fashionable.
- Shop for comfortable yet pretty clothes. Just because you have cancer doesn't mean you have to give up fashion. However, you may have to change your wardrobe slightly if you lose weight and to provide comfort.

3. Keep a Journal

- Buy a journal or start a blog where you can write out anything that you are feeling—your fears, questions, lessons you've learned, frustrations, goals, dreams. Many women find that writing helps them get things off their chest and helps them process everything they experience. Besides, you can read it later and see how you've grown and changed. You will be amazed as you are reminded of God's faithfulness along the way.

4. Be Intentional about Enjoying Life

- For many women, cancer is a wake-up call to the fact that life is short and there is no guarantee of tomorrow. Learn to live in the moment and look for the little blessings each day, rather than letting the weight of cancer overshadow every thought and every moment.
- Do what you love to do. While you may have to change and adjust your lifestyle, don't shut down, avoiding activities and interaction with people. If possible, exercise, eat out, enjoy time with friends, laugh, continue to pursue hobbies, read, spend time in God's creation, take a vacation. Do whatever fills you up and brings you joy. Grab life with both hands and *live*.
- Don't allow cancer to control or consume your life. Be intentional about building a life *outside of* your doctor's appointments and treatments. Take a bubble bath. Meditate on Scripture. Get lost in a good novel. Watch a comedy. Write a poem.

5. Rely on God's Promises

- Bask in the promises of God's Word and use the unchanging truth of who God is to fight the fear you feel. Make prayer a moment-by-moment reality as you talk to God about everything. Remember, He will never leave you or forsake you. He doesn't see you as ugly, worthless, or no good because of your cancer. In fact, He wants to use even this to make your heart more beautiful—to make you more like Jesus. God never wastes a wound!

BIBLICAL INSIGHTS : 6

I have told you these things, so that in me you may have peace. In this world you will have trouble. But take heart! I have overcome the world.

John 16:33

Many Christians believe wrongly that if they follow Christ, they will have an easy, comfortable life. However, this theology lies in direct contradiction to Scripture. Jesus tells His disciples ahead of time that trouble, pain, and suffering are all part of life in this fallen world. At the same time, however, this "trouble" promised by Jesus is not the ultimate reality, because Jesus also said, "I have overcome the world."

In every hardship we experience—even cancer—Jesus desires to shape and mold us into His image and to draw us into deeper intimacy with Him as He strips away earthly things that we rely on. So, rather than becoming frustrated and bitter about your cancer, your weakness, and the physical vulnerability you feel, embrace this opportunity to know Jesus more intimately. Run straight into His arms and find a safe place to rest. He is with you, even in the midst of cancer. And He loves you.

Therefore we do not lose heart. Though outwardly we are wasting away, yet inwardly we are being renewed day by day. For our light and momentary troubles are achieving for us an eternal glory that far outweighs them all. So we fix our eyes not on what is seen, but on what is unseen. For what is seen is temporary, but what is unseen is eternal.

2 Corinthians 4:16–18

Battling cancer is sure to shake a woman's faith and cause her to question God. However, Scripture encourages us to fix our eyes on Jesus, not the cancer. In the midst of trials and hardship, when Paul's life was at risk daily, he said confidently, "We do not lose heart." Paul's eternal perspective enabled him to see past his suffering to the "eternal glory that far outweighs" anything experienced in this life.

No matter how cancer affects a woman's body—even if it claims her life—she and her loved ones can take joy in the renewing grace of Jesus and the eternal hope of seeing Him face-to-face. For the believer, cancer is not a reason to despair.

This life is momentary, short, and fleeting, but Jesus Christ has taken away the sting of death, and we should not be consumed with fear. As followers of Jesus, we can look forward with anticipation to the day when we leave our failing earthly bodies behind and actually live *with Jesus*.

Yet I am always with you; you hold me by my right hand. You guide me with your counsel, and afterward you will take me into glory. Whom have I in heaven but you? And earth has nothing I desire besides you. My flesh and my heart may fail, but God is the strength of my heart and my portion forever.

Psalm 73:23–26

The hardship of cancer can easily overwhelm a woman and cause her to lose hope. David grounded his life in the reality of who God is. Compared to the glories of knowing and being with Jesus, "earth has nothing I desire," he wrote. Every joy and pleasure in this life is fleeting and temporary, but David knew that the source of life, joy, and pleasure is found in God.

That's why he—and we—have no reason to fear, even if our flesh fails. And it will. All of us will face death sooner or later, and along the way, we will all experience trials and suffering—if it's not cancer, it will be something else. Yet we can have confidence, like David, that God is always with us, holding our hands and guiding us. And when this short life is over, He *will* take us to glory.

7 PRAYER STARTER

Lord, even in the midst of our suffering, we come to You, because we know You are good and we can trust You. I pray for _____ as she struggles with the reality of cancer and all of the stresses and pressures it brings. Surround her with Your love and grace and draw her into deeper intimacy with You. Heal her body, Lord, if it is Your will, but more than anything, satisfy her soul with Your unfailing love and faithfulness. Give her doctors wisdom as they make decisions about her treatment and care. We thank You that nothing can separate us from Your love, not even cancer . . .

8 RECOMMENDED RESOURCES

Barry, Michael. *A Reason for Hope: Gaining Strength for Your Fight against Cancer.* David C. Cook, 2004.

Burkett, Larry. *Nothing to Fear: The Key to Cancer Survival.* Moody, 2004.

Delinsky, Barbara. *Uplift: Secrets from the Sisterhood of Breast Cancer Survivors.* Simon and Schuster, 2006.

Jeremiah, David. *When Your World Falls Apart.* Thomas Nelson, 2005.

Johnson, Nicole. *Stepping into the Ring: Fighting for Hope over Despair in the Battle against Breast Cancer.* Thomas Nelson, 2003.

Sorensen, Susan, and Laura Geist. *Praying through Cancer: Set Your Heart Free from Fear—A 90 Day Devotional for Women.* Thomas Nelson, 2007.

Turnage, Mac, and Anne Shaw Turnage. *Grace Keeps You Going: Spiritual Wisdom from Cancer Survivors.* Westminster John Knox Press, 2002.

DVDs

American Association of Christian Counselors. *Challenging Cancer* video series. Available at http://challengingcancer.aacc.net/.

Child Sexual Abuse

- Claire never told anybody what happened when she was growing up. She hoped that if she never talked about it, the memory would go away. But it didn't. Her uncle Steve worked from home, so he had always been around to play when she visited. He would ask her to play "a secret game" that involved watching naked people on television and letting Steve touch her. The "secret game" eventually led to being raped by her uncle. She tried to rationalize it away as "not a big deal," but now Claire is dating the guy of her dreams and finds herself unable to open up to him or trust him.
- When Amanda's two children—eight-year-old Olivia and five-year-old Michael—began visiting their grandparents, Amanda started having nightmares that would not stop. Her physician sent her to a therapist. During her treatment, Amanda realized that her nightmares were old memories she had long pushed away. When she was eight, the same age as her daughter, her father had sexually abused her.
- As a freshman in high school, Brittany was really excited to hang out with Chris, her new basketball coach and a recent college graduate. Chris seemed to single her out, complimenting her and making her feel special. When he asked her if she wanted to hang out on Friday night, Brittany was ecstatic. Chris said all sorts of wonderful things about her—that she was beautiful, sexy, and fun. Then he started touching her, reaching under her shirt, and putting his hands all over her body. Brittany tried to tell him no, but he insisted. Brittany feels violated, but she has no clue about what to do.

DEFINITIONS AND KEY THOUGHTS : 2

- *Abuse* is taking *unfair advantage of a position of power* to control someone else.
- The National Center on Child Abuse and Neglect defines *child sexual abuse* as "contacts or interactions between a child and an adult when *the child is being used for sexual stimulation* of the perpetrator or another person when the perpetrator or another person is in a position of power or control over the victim."[1]
- Child sexual abuse occurs when an adult exploits a person, *aged seventeen and younger*, to satisfy the abuser's needs. It consists of *any sexual activity—verbal, visual, or physical—engaged in with a minor.*

61

- Child sexual *abuse may include* oral-genital contact, masturbation, exhibitionism, fondling a child's genitals, having intercourse or oral sex with a child, having sex in front of a child, prostitution, rape, showing X-rated materials to a child, or using a child in any form of pornographic activity.

- Sexual abuse is most often perpetrated by an adult who has access to a minor by virtue of *real or imagined authority or kinship.* Around 10 percent of children are abused by strangers, 30–40 percent by a family member, and 40 percent by an older or larger child they know.[2]

- When a girl is abused by someone *she knows and even loves*, this may cause intense confusion about the meaning of love and intimacy and result in long-term emotional damage.

- The *statistics on child sexual abuse are startling*: two out of every ten girls are sexually abused by the end of their thirteenth year. And one in four girls is sexually abused by the age of eighteen.[3]

- It is estimated there are thirty-nine million survivors of childhood sexual abuse in America today, but more than 30 percent of victims never tell anyone about the abuse. *Shame and threats keep women quiet, or fear of not being believed.*[4]

- Child sexual abuse became a public issue in the 1970s and 1980s. *Prior to this time sexual abuse remained rather secretive, not spoken about in public.* Studies on child molestation were nonexistent until the 1920s, and the first national estimate of the number of child sexual abuse cases was published in 1948.

- *No child is psychologically prepared to cope with repeated sexual stimulation.* Even a two- or three-year-old, who cannot know that the sexual activity is wrong, can develop problems resulting from the inability to cope with the overstimulation.

- Often a young child who knows the abuser becomes *trapped between affection and loyalty* for the abuser and the sense that the sexual activities are terribly wrong. If the child tries to break away from the sexual relationship, *the abuser may threaten the child with violence or loss of love.* When sexual abuse occurs within the family, the child may fear the anger, jealousy, or shame of other family members, or she may be afraid the family will break up if the secret is told.

The Perpetrator Profile

- The *perpetrator* is the person who *coerces and initiates sexual abuse* with a child.

- There are *three types of perpetrators*: one type views the child whom he abuses as an adult, one type thinks of himself as a child, and the third type indiscriminately abuses a child without remorse or guilt.

- The first type of perpetrator struggles in maintaining healthy relationships with his peers. He doesn't fit in, feels inadequate, and behaves awkwardly. He desires to relate with adults but doesn't know how. As a result, the *child he abuses becomes the pseudo-adult.*

- The second type of perpetrator *believes that he is still a child* and will therefore engage sexually with someone he perceives to be at the same mental and emotional level.

- The third type of perpetrator could be labeled a sociopath. He is charming, manipulative, and callous. He feels little emotion and is not prone to experience remorse or guilt. He may even take pride in discussing his sexual exploits.

Physical Consequences

- *Long-lasting physical symptoms and illnesses have been associated with sexual victimization*, including chronic pelvic pain; premenstrual syndrome; gastrointestinal disorders; and a variety of chronic pain disorders, such as headaches, back pain, and facial pain.

Psychological Consequences

- Immediate reactions to sexual abuse include *shock, disbelief, denial, fear, confusion, anxiety, and withdrawal.*
- Statistics report that victims of child sexual abuse are more likely to struggle with *post-traumatic stress disorder, sadness and depression, school problems, eating disorders, and sexual activity at an early age.*[5]
- *Victims may experience emotional detachment, sleep disturbances, and flashbacks.* Approximately one-third of sexual abuse victims have symptoms that become chronic.
- Sexual abuse victims may experience *anxiety, guilt, nervousness, phobias, substance abuse, sleep disturbances, depression, alienation, suicidal behavior, and sexual dysfunction.* They may distrust others, replay the assault in their minds, and are at increased risk of revictimization.

Social Consequences

- Sexual abuse *adversely impacts relationships later in life* because of its negative effect on the victim's family, friends, and intimate partners. Victims of abuse find it difficult to trust other people and experience genuine relationships. Victims often cope with the pain and shame they feel by detaching from both their emotions and relationships with others.
- Victims of sexual violence are more likely than nonvictims to *engage in risky sexual behavior, including having unprotected sex, having sex at an early age, having multiple partners, and trading sex for food, money, or other items.*

Limits of Confidentiality

- As you counsel a person who has been sexually abused, *you must know the limits of confidentiality*.
- Sexual abuse of children is *illegal and must be reported*. Be sure to review state laws. You must *report it to the appropriate agencies*, such as local law enforcement, the Department of Social and Health Services, or Child Protective Services.

- You must report sexual abuse *within a period of time*, usually between twenty-four hours and seven days.
- Usually you can report by phone, in writing, or in person.
- Some states require counselors to report suspicions of abuse, even if it is not clearly stated by the client. *Take time to research the specific laws in your state for reporting child sexual abuse.*
- If a woman is over eighteen at the time of disclosure, reporting abuse may not be mandatory. However, *if the abuser still has access to children*, you may have an ethical obligation to report the abuse to protect the children.

3 ASSESSMENT INTERVIEW

Rule out any *suicidal risk, depression, or medical concerns* (especially if the abuse was recent).

Assess for the type of abuse perpetrated, including its degree and its history. Sometimes a woman will *seek help for other problems that actually stem from sexual abuse.* You need to get her to talk about the core issue. Be careful, however, not to retraumatize her with your questions. Trust and safety are of vital importance.

Use an intake form to explain and establish limits of confidentiality with the client. *Assume three things in the process of treatment:*

1. The problem is treatable and your client will be a survivor.
2. The client is not responsible for the abuse; she is responsible only for recovery.
3. To heal, your client needs to express, accept, and be prepared to deal with her issues.

General Questions

1. What has happened that has brought you here today?
2. Is this the first time you've sought help?
3. Tell me about your family. How are things going at home?
4. Tell me about your past. Have you had any painful or unusual things happen—even a long time ago?
5. How long did that go on?
6. Can you tell me who was doing this to you? (*If the person seems reticent, explain that you need to know to help her, others who might be abused, and the abuser. In addition, if she is a minor and still in contact with the abuser so that the abuse might recur, immediate action must be taken to keep her safe.*)
7. Do you know if others are being abused?
8. What problems are you currently having as a result of what happened? (*Listen to how the abuse affected her. No two people are alike in their experiences or the consequence of the abuse. Be aware that the victims tend to minimize the impact of the abuse.*)
9. How do you feel about what has happened to you? (*The client needs to have permission to feel her true emotions.*)

10. Do you feel responsible for the abuse? (*Reassure the client that she is not alone and that she is not responsible for the abuse.*)

11. What do you believe about yourself? (*Dig down for unhealthy beliefs that have developed as a result of abuse.*)

12. What do you believe about the person who is abusing you? (*Listen for rationalizations. "He couldn't help it; he was drunk." These defenses have helped the client cope but have also made her less capable of seeing herself as a true victim of abuse.*)

13. Have you ever tried to stop the abuse? What happened?

14. What would you like to have happen as a result of our meeting today?

15. What kinds of boundaries do you think need to be set up to protect you?

16. Who else have you told about this?

17. How did the person respond?

18. Who can help you maintain the boundaries that you set? Who will be your ally?

19. Where do you think God has been in all of this?

20. To heal from this, what do you need?

WISE COUNSEL 4

Women who have been abused have had their boundaries violated in a horrible way. Healing from abuse involves *restoration of healthy boundaries and trust*. The counseling process must be gentle and not contribute to an unintentional rewounding or shaming of the woman.

Follow the client's lead in the telling of her story. Allow her to *self-disclose in her way and at her own pace. Reassure her* that the abuse was not her fault. *Validate her pain* and *do not question the truth of her experience*. In the vast majority of cases, if a woman is brave enough to let the "secret" of her abuse out, she is desperate for help. Fabricated abuse reports constitute only 1–4 percent of all reported cases,[6] so unless you have specific reason to question her honesty, take her report as fact.

One of the questions frequently asked by someone who has been sexually abused is "Why me?" Feelings of worthlessness often result from sexual abuse. As a counselor, you need to keep your own emotions in check to provide a safe environment so the client is able to talk freely.

ACTION STEPS 5

1. Be Patient

- Healing from sexual abuse is a process, and women will vary in the amount of time required for their healing. It takes courage to seek help for healing, to talk about your experience, and to bring what was once in darkness into the light.

- *It is critical that there be an atmosphere of safety, unconditional positive regard, and reflective listening as the woman talks with you.*

- Talking is the first step to healing, but don't expect yourself to heal overnight. Sexual abuse is a complex and multifaceted issue. Far more than just a physical act, ramifications of the abuse can affect your self-esteem, identity, emotional health, and ability to have meaningful relationships.

2. Grieve Your Loss

- Much has been taken from you, and it is healthy to feel the pain and grieve the loss. Be honest with yourself. Allowing yourself to own the feelings will help you gain perspective and begin to heal.
- Attending a group for survivors of sexual abuse can be very helpful. Being believed and being able to say what happened in a safe context will free you from the dark secrets you carry.

3. Establish Boundaries

- Learn how to take care of yourself and reestablish healthy physical and emotional boundaries. You have a right to say no and to get out of any situation where you feel uncomfortable.
- Be sure trusted people are aware of these boundaries. That's the reason others will need to be let in on what's happening—no matter how painful. You may need their help in dealing with the abuse.
- Establishing boundaries may take the form of (1) speaking the truth to the abuser, (2) having the support of others in the Christian community, and/or (3) informed withdrawal from the abuser.
- If the abuser will not honor the boundaries, then other strategies may need to be put in place.

4. Trust God

- Know that God did not leave you and was not working against you as this abuse occurred. While it can be difficult to trust God in the midst of pain, He is the only one who knows you intimately and loves you unconditionally. Don't shut Him out of your pain and the impact of the abuse. Invite Him in.
- Plan on several more visits back to the counselor to discuss the spiritual concept of God's love even in the midst of such painful circumstances. In the wake of abuse, it can be extremely difficult to let God into the deep places of your heart, to truly feel and experience God's love. In this process of learning to trust again, be honest with God. He is faithful and He will heal you—one step at a time.

5. Get More Guidance

- *As much as you can help with the spiritual aspect, it's likely the woman will need some professional guidance to truly deal with the depth of the pain that sexual abuse causes.*
- *Refer her to a Christian counselor with expertise in this area.*

BIBLICAL INSIGHTS : 6

You intended to harm me, but God intended it for good to accomplish what is now being done, the saving of many lives.

Genesis 50:20

If anyone had a good reason for revenge, it was Joseph. His brothers' jealousy provoked them to horrible abuse—selling him as a common slave to be taken away forever (Gen. 37:11–28). Before being raised to power in Egypt, Joseph had lost thirteen years of personal freedom.

What Joseph's brothers did was evil, but Joseph did not live as a bitter, angry victim. Wisely Joseph understood that God had sovereignly overruled his brothers' abuse, making their evil turn out for good.

For a victim of sexual abuse, it may require some time and some healing before she can understand how this teaching applies to her. If a counselor refers to the example of Joseph and his attitude about his brothers' abuse too close to the woman's experience of abuse, it would likely be very difficult for her to accept.

Do not take revenge, my friends, but leave room for God's wrath, for it is written: "It is mine to avenge; I will repay," says the LORD. . . . Do not be overcome by evil, but overcome evil with good.

Romans 12:19, 21

God knows all that has occurred in our lives, even the abuse. He was present in the darkness and continues to walk with us. Because Jesus suffered abuse, He understands what we are going through. He weeps with us in our brokenness and is angered by the injustice of abuse.

And God promises to repay. In the journey of recovery, our focus should be on letting our guard down, being vulnerable in a safe environment, grieving what we have experienced, and finding healing in God's intimate, never-ending love.

We must not let evil overcome us; this only continues to give the abuser power in our life. We overcome the evil we have experienced by doing good to others and by letting God's love into this dark place of our past and trusting Him with our brokenness. Only He can heal us.

PRAYER STARTER : 7

We are facing an extremely difficult situation here today, Lord, a situation that You know about but is now just coming into the light for people whom we know and love. Give us wisdom to handle this situation correctly. Bring healing to _____, who has been used so wrongly . . .

8 RECOMMENDED RESOURCES

Allender, Dan. *The Wounded Heart: Hope for Adult Victims of Childhood Sexual Abuse*. NavPress, 2008.

Langberg, Diane. *Counseling Survivors of Sexual Abuse*. Xulon, 2003.

———. *On the Threshold of Hope*. Tyndale House, 1999.

Maltz, Wendy. *The Sexual Healing Journey: A Guide for Survivors of Sexual Abuse*. Collins Living, 2001.

Meyer, Rick. *Through the Fire: Spiritual Restoration for Adult Victims of Childhood Sexual Abuse*. Augsburg Fortress, 2005.

Morrison, Jan. *A Safe Place: Beyond Sexual Abuse*. Shaw Books, 2002.

Sands, Christa. *Learning to Trust Again: A Young Woman's Journey of Healing from Sexual Abuse*. Discovery House, 1999.

Sanford, Paula. *Healing Victims of Sexual Abuse: How to Counsel and Minister to Hearts Wounded by Abuse*. Charisma House, 2009.

Chronic Pain

- Charissa played volleyball all through college. During her junior year, she injured her back and had to drop off the team. Charissa is now thirty-four and struggling to carry out her responsibilities as a wife and mother of two toddlers. Pain is a constant in her life and sometimes she thinks she can't continue to endure it. *How do I go on? How do I function?* she wonders.
- Kathy has been to countless doctors and many psychologists in the hope of finding the reason she is in constant pain. She lives in agony with severe headaches daily. Time and time again she's been told it's a mental thing, but the appointments with the psychologists have not helped, and neither have the appointments with physicians. Kathy is running out of options.
- Marybeth's chronic pain from fibromyalgia has isolated her for years. Now she rarely socializes or goes out in public. Even simple tasks, like cooking dinner or leaning over to tie her shoes, are extremely painful. Her severe pain has forced her to spend most days alone in a dark room. Marybeth wonders if life is worth living anymore—*should she just end all the pain?*

DEFINITIONS AND KEY THOUGHTS 2

- *Chronic pain*, as defined by the American Chronic Pain Association (ACPA) is "*pain that continues a month or more beyond the usual recovery period for an injury or illness* or that goes on for months or years due to a chronic condition. The pain is usually not constant but *can interfere with daily life* at all levels."[1]
- Chronic pain may have *an unknown source or it may be caused by a diagnosed, chronic illness*, such as a degenerative or autoimmune disease.
- Chronic pain affects *one in ten Americans*; that's about twenty-five million people. Chronic pain is *more prevalent than heart disease or cancer*.[2]
- Often *chronic pain leads to* fatigue, depression, anxiety, frustration, lowered self-esteem, isolation, suicide or suicidal thoughts, confusion, skewed memory, and omission of regular daily activities.
- In the Voices of Pain Survey conducted in 2006, 60 percent of patients reported having *one or more instances of severe pain a day*, while 86 percent of patients reported *not being able to sleep well* due to pain. And 77 percent of people surveyed reported *feeling depressed*.[3]

- *Not only does chronic pain affect the individual suffering, but it affects those around her as well.* One-fourth of people with chronic conditions experience one or more daily limitations, many of them needing the help and assistance of a family member or caregiver.[4]
- Chronic pain can spring up sporadically or it can be a result of another disease or illness. *The most common types of chronic pain are backache, arthritis pain, and headaches*, but chronic pain is not limited to these.
- Chronic pain is a *medical, physical, and psychological* illness. It affects every aspect of a woman's experience—physical, psychological, social, and emotional.
- *Pain management* is a concept that suggests *accepting the pain* and coming up with a plan to *deal with the pain*. This may include medication, exercise, meditation, and dietary guidelines, among other things.[5]

3 ASSESSMENT INTERVIEW

1. When did your pain first begin? Where is your pain for the most part?
2. Is your pain a daily battle or does it come in sporadic bouts?
3. Do you suffer from any other illnesses (psychological or physical)?
4. Other than physical pain, what symptoms, feelings, or emotions are you experiencing?
5. Does your pain restrict your participation in daily activities or activities you used to do?
6. How have you coped with your pain to this point?
7. Do other people know that you have chronic pain or is this a private struggle?
8. What kind of thoughts has your chronic pain caused? What solutions have you considered? (*If the woman has suicidal thoughts, get professional help immediately.*)
9. What role have medications played in pain management for you? Have you ever become addicted to pain medications?
10. How has chronic pain affected your day-to-day functioning?

4 WISE COUNSEL

Often women suffering from chronic pain are accused of faking it to gain sympathy or attention. Be careful here. *The woman who is suffering may be going through significant pain, and if she feels she cannot talk about it, this will only worsen her emotional state.*

Research shows that it is possible for *emotional pain and unresolved conflict to manifest themselves as physical pain.* This is a rare but real condition called "somatization" and should not be confused with pain "being all in her head." In the case of somatization, *the emotional pain is so intense that it expresses itself physically*—it is not one or the other but both. Significant childhood trauma has been linked to somatization.

Frequently chronic pain funnels directly into *prescription drug addiction*. Be proactive in your assessment to determine this possibility, as well as the potential for overdose and/or hints of suicidal behavior.

Offer understanding and support. A woman in chronic pain may feel stuck—she wakes up with pain, lives through the day with pain, and falls asleep with pain. If a woman feels uncomfortable or grows weary of unrelenting pain, she is likely to withdraw, further isolating herself in her pain. As a counselor, take the initiative to persevere with her. *A woman needs to know she is being believed and heard.* Allow her to grieve, weep, and ask questions.

Depending on her diagnosis, she may be unable to do the tasks she loves or care for her family, her children, or even herself. She may view her illness and pain as *destroying her life, robbing her of a career or ministry, and imprisoning her.* She may be bedridden or suffer from side effects of pain medication. When suffering from chronic pain or illness, a woman may view her world as small and insignificant. Such a world can be made bigger only by *the entrance of others*, who are not turned off by her illness but who reach out in love.

When Jesus came to this world, He left glory and beauty and entered a reality of suffering and death. *Ask Him for strength to love and encourage in tangible ways women who are weary of pain.*

If issues arise later showing the pain is not legitimate or that the pain is a result of emotional pain, then that should be addressed once the client has a *better understanding and has built trust with you.*

Direct your client to the example of Joni Erickson Tada—a woman who was paralyzed in her youth and now lives with grave limitations and in constant pain. Her life and writings are *a testimony to God's work in and through suffering* (see www.joniandfriends.org).

ACTION STEPS 5

1. Seek Out Professional Help

- Consult a physician specializing in pain management and don't hesitate to get a second opinion. A qualified medical professional will help you pinpoint where the pain came from, such as somatization or chronic illness, and how the pain and pain medications you are on are affecting your life. Understanding what is going on in your body will help you participate in your own pain management.

- Talk to a professional counselor about the limitations your pain is causing. Your physical pain may be closely associated with emotional pain, as you grieve the loss of capacity and independence. Life becomes smaller—the size of a bed for some women—and you may have to let go of things you love to do or view as part of your identity (work, hobbies, the outdoors, and so on).

- Don't suppress the sadness, depression, frustration, anger, and isolation you feel. These emotions need to be validated, processed, and put in perspective within a therapeutic environment. Evaluate the stresses, relationships, and commitments in your life that may be exacerbating these emotions. Work with your therapist to find a new "normal."

2. Learn to Manage Your Pain

- Pain does not have to rule your life. As impossible as it seems, keeping occupied will help you manage your pain and continue to enjoy life. Engage in praise and worship. Read. Take a bubble bath. Watch a comedy. Incorporate laughter and humor into the day. Take time to do something for yourself. All of these activities will help relieve the stress of concentrating on the pain and the agonizing sensations and they will rebuild some positive emotions.

- Keeping a journal is another way of helping relieve the pain. By physically expressing the pain in writing, many women feel relief and are able to gain a healthier perspective on what they are experiencing. Write out what you're feeling—not only physically but emotionally—as well as how you are coping. Write out (and look for!) the blessings in your day, rather than letting your mind be overcome with negativity.

3. Lean on God

- The best place to find comfort during the pain is from God, our compassionate and loving Savior. Though the pain may be constant, God's promise to be faithful when we cry out to Him is constant as well.

- C. S. Lewis once said, "Pain is God's megaphone." Use this opportunity to get closer to Jesus. He is with you, even in the midst of pain, and He longs to draw you into deeper intimacy with Him. Relief may not come for whatever reason, but comfort, strength, and joy can and will, with focused dependence on God.

6 BIBLICAL INSIGHTS

But he said to me, "My grace is sufficient for you, for my power is made perfect in weakness." Therefore I will boast all the more gladly about my weaknesses, so that Christ's power may rest on me. That is why, for Christ's sake, I delight in weaknesses, in insults, in hardships, in persecutions, in difficulties. For when I am weak, then I am strong.

2 Corinthians 12:9–10

Don't let the first part of this verse frustrate you. If you are suffering from chronic pain, you may ask, "How is His grace sufficient? I'm in pain!" If you continue to read, you realize that it is more about the power of Christ getting you through the pain, and your relying on His power.

Our weaknesses show God's strength and grace because He carries and sustains us when we can't do it ourselves. If we rely on His power to get us through, our lives can be testimonies to God's goodness and faithfulness, even in the midst of suffering.

He was despised and rejected by men, a man of sorrows, and familiar with suffering. . . . Surely he took up our infirmities and carried our sorrows.

Isaiah 53:3–4

On this earth, Jesus suffered more than you or I can imagine. He became like us—even in the experience of pain—suffering for us and taking the punishment for our sins.

In the midst of your pain, don't run from God. Run to Him. He is "familiar with suffering" and He longs to carry your sorrow.

In my distress I called to the LORD; I called out to my God. From his temple he heard my voice; my cry came to his ears. . . . He reached down from on high and took hold of me; he drew me out of deep waters.

2 Samuel 22:7, 17

God listens and He cares. Verse 7 offers sound direction to women who are hurting, who are distressed. In your pain, *cry out to the Lord*. He will hear your cries and He will not abandon you.

Pain and suffering are a reality in this fallen world, but as believers, we have the assurance that we are not alone and that this life is not the ultimate reality. God weeps with you in your pain and longs for the day when you get to heaven and leap into His arms—forever free from the pain you feel now.

So then, those who suffer according to God's will should commit themselves to their faithful Creator and continue to do good.

1 Peter 4:19

Pain and suffering are not punishment from God. In fact, God can use such hardship to purify our faith and make us more like Jesus. All throughout Scripture, godly people experienced pain and were tempted to doubt God. Job, David, Isaiah, Jeremiah, Paul, Timothy—and Jesus Himself—are just a few examples.

Even in the midst of pain, you have a choice how you will respond. Chronic pain can easily embitter the soul and lead to resentment, if not viewed as a shaping tool in God's loving hand. In this passage, Peter encourages a godly response to suffering: commit yourself to God and keep doing good. Peter also doesn't hesitate to point out the promise we should cling to: God is faithful.

Our weaknesses showcase God's strength. As we cling tightly to Jesus and rely on His power to endure, He will enable us to live *with* our suffering and He will be honored in it.

PRAYER STARTER 7

Dear Lord, You have experienced pain on this earth and You fully understand our weaknesses. You know the pain and the agony _____ is experiencing. Father, we ask that You relieve her of this pain and give her wisdom as she learns how to manage it. Bring her comfort, peace, and strength as she fights this battle. Fill her life with Your joy, Lord, that is not based on circumstance but on the reality of who You are. Thank You that You are always with us . . .

8 RECOMMENDED RESOURCES

Boyd, Jeffrey. *Being Sick Well: Joyful Living Despite Chronic Illness*. Baker, 2005.

Morrone, Lisa. *Overcoming Headaches and Migraines: Clinically Proven Cure for Chronic Pain*. Harvest House, 2008.

Otis, John. *Managing Chronic Pain: A Cognitive-Behavioral Therapy Approach Workbook*. Oxford University Press, 2007.

Pratt, Maureen. *Peace in the Storm: Meditations on Chronic Pain and Illness*. Random House, 2005.

Schneider, Jennifer. *Living with Chronic Pain: The Complete Health Guide to the Causes and Treatment of Chronic Pain,* 2nd ed. Hatherleigh Press, 2004.

Wright, H. Norman, and Lynn Ellis. *Coping with Chronic Illness*. Harvest House, 2010.

Codependency and Relationship Addiction

PORTRAITS : 1

- "I feel so . . . stuck," Tracy moaned. Tracy had been dating Steve for over a year, and their relationship consisted of one thing: Tracy rescuing Steve. Steve had lost his job, and when he was evicted from his apartment, he showed up at Tracy's doorstep. Three months later Steve was still living with Tracy and now he'd just wrecked his car, which meant *she'd* be driving him everywhere, in addition to paying the bills. *What am I supposed to do?* Tracy wondered. *I love Steve, at least I think I do, but I can't live like this.*

- "Mom, you know I'm here for you. Just call me. Anytime." The words stuck in Beth's throat. Beth was over at her mom's house nearly every day, washing dishes, listening to her sob stories, giving her advice about guys. Ever since her mom had gotten a divorce three years ago, she'd relied on Beth for everything. "I don't know what I'd do without you," she would say. "It's like you've filled in where your father never could." And Beth hated it more every day. *I want to honor my mom,* she thought, *but I should be able to have my own life too.*

- Kiera stumbled sleepily into the bathroom, only to find her husband, Tom, collapsed on the floor. The pool of vomit and strong smell of alcohol confirmed what Kiera's heart feared. Tom had been drinking again. She was tired of it all—the fear she felt when she heard the door slam, the beatings when he was drunk, the shame of the bruises she tried to cover up. After hitting her, Tom would always tell her he was "so, so sorry," that he really loved her like crazy, that he promised to stop. *But it never stops.*

DEFINITIONS AND KEY THOUGHTS : 2

- *Codependency* is *a learned relational pattern that affects a woman's ability to develop emotionally healthy, satisfying relationships.* Often women who are codependent gravitate toward relationships that are emotionally destructive and abusive.

- *Forty million Americans, most of whom are women, are labeled as codependent.*[1] The original concept of codependency developed from responses and behaviors of those living with someone who battled alcoholism and/or substance abuse.

- In *Codependent No More,* Melody Beattie writes, "A codependent person is one who has let another person's behavior affect him or her, and who is obsessed with controlling that person's behavior."[2] *Codependent women are strongly influenced or controlled by another person's needs and feel obligated to rescue others and "fix" everything.* At the same time, codependent women feel the desperate need for another person to meet their need to feel "complete."

- Codependent behaviors are frequently developed in dysfunctional families, where conflict is not recognized or discussed. "The good of the family" is stressed to the point that family members *learn to repress their own feelings, desires, and needs to survive.* Family relationships easily become *enmeshed*, and addiction and abuse thrive unchecked in this environment, resulting in feelings of shame, fear, and anger that are either ignored or denied.

- *Enmeshment* is "when we use an individual for our identity, sense of value, worth, well-being, safety, purpose and security. Instead of two [healthy individuals], we become one identity . . . our sense of wholeness comes from the other person."[3]

- In short, *codependency is an addiction, and the drug is a relationship.* A woman who is codependent *struggles with who she is apart from the addictive relationship.* She defines herself by the other person, with no or few personal boundaries. She will do anything for anyone, staying in a physically, emotionally, or sexually abusive relationship *just to avoid being alone.*

- Phrases like "I need you"; "I can't imagine life without you"; "You're my everything" become the mantra and can *evidence signs of codependency.*

- *Many times a codependent woman feels frustrated, used, and stuck* but has no idea what the problem is, especially if she has grown up in a highly religious environment and been taught to love, serve, and sacrifice her needs and desires for others, especially the man in her life. While these are biblical principles, when taken to an extreme, a woman may feel that setting any boundaries in her life is sinful.

- The *characteristics of codependent people* are:

  — an exaggerated sense of responsibility for the actions of others
  — a tendency to confuse love and pity, "loving" people they can pity and rescue
  — a tendency to do more than their share, all of the time
  — a tendency to be hurt when people don't recognize their efforts
  — an unhealthy dependence on relationships; the codependent will do anything to hold on to a relationship to avoid the feeling of abandonment
  — an extreme need for approval and recognition
  — a sense of guilt when asserting themselves
  — a compelling need to control others
  — lack of trust in self and/or others
  — fear of being abandoned or alone
  — difficulty identifying feelings
  — rigidity and difficulty adjusting to change
  — problems with intimacy and boundaries
  — chronic anger

— lying and dishonesty

— poor communication

— difficulty making decisions[4]

ASSESSMENT INTERVIEW $\vert$ **3**

1. Tell me about your experiences in relationships. Have you ever lived with or been in a relationship with someone with a drug or alcohol problem?
2. What was your family environment like growing up?
3. Do you feel obligated to rescue, help, and serve other people? Do you find yourself trying to fix others' problems?
4. Do you have a hard time saying no and setting boundaries? Do you often find that you're overcommitted?
5. Do you have a hard time voicing your opinion or true feelings? Do you keep quiet to avoid arguments?
6. Do you have difficulty building friendships and just being yourself?
7. Are you overly concerned about what other people think?
8. Do you tend to feel selfish or guilty when you assert yourself?
9. Do you define yourself by the roles you fill in your relationships with other people, such as a wife, mother, daughter? Do you find your identity in meeting others' needs?
10. How much does the approval of other people matter to you? How do you feel when you make a mistake?
11. Do you feel stuck in any of the relationships in your life? If so, what feelings are most prominent in your interactions with that person? What would your life be like if that person were not a part of it?
12. Do you have a hard time identifying your true feelings and what *you* want? Do you have a hard time making decisions?
13. Who are you? What do you love to do and where are you going with your life? (*Look for signs of confusion or insecurity about personal identity.*)

WISE COUNSEL $\vert$ **4**

Codependency is not a disease. It's *an addictive behavior pattern* that is developed over time, often because of unmet needs. Learning how to live in freedom requires learning a whole new way of doing relationships. Codependency generally expresses itself in one of two ways:

A woman may be *needy, desperate, and clingy* in relationships, always needing to be rescued and unable to operate as an individual. The truth is, *she doesn't know who she is*, and above all, she's terrified of being abandoned and alone.

A woman may serve as the *enabler* in relationships. She takes on the serving, fixing, rescuing role in a relationship automatically, making everything "okay." Her family and friends grow to depend on her for everything. She defines her worth based on what she *does* to help other people, but aside from her actions, *she has no idea who she is.*

No woman wakes up one day and decides to become codependent. *These behavior patterns are developed and reinforced over months and years of watching and experiencing unhealthy, codependent relationships.* Frequently the roots of codependency are grounded in a woman's childhood years and past romantic relationships.

Breaking free begins with breaking down lies and letting God—not other people or your ability to help her—define who she is. The more a woman understands *who God is and His ability to meet her deep heart needs* and give her significance, the more she will be able to interact with other people in a healthy, genuine way. Rather than being timid or fearful, *she can confidently set boundaries and know that saying no does not make her a horrible person.*

5 ACTION STEPS

1. Ground Your Identity in Jesus

- Stop feeding on the approval of others. If you define yourself based on other people or by your ability to rescue them, your life will be a roller coaster of chaos and desperation. Study God's Word and find out who God says you are, rather than defining yourself by your friends or accomplishments.

- Rather than running to other people to meet your needs, go to God first. No human being can make you complete. And you definitely can't muster significance, identity, value, and worth from within yourself. You were created by God and for God—let Him define you. Live in freedom.

2. Refuse to Be an Enabler

- As a daughter of Jesus Christ, you have no business tolerating toxic relationships. Many women refuse to break up with an abusive boyfriend, and continue to enable him in his unhealthy behavior. Many husbands continue in drug or alcohol addiction without getting help because their wives feel a responsibility to keep the family together and cover for their husband's sin. This is abuse, not biblical submission.

- If you are in a toxic relationship and have been enabling or rescuing a boyfriend or husband, your codependent behavior is likely precipitating further abuse and dysfunction. Get wise counsel from church leaders and friends you trust about what steps you need to take to stop living this way.

- Tough love means saying no and refusing to continue to live in dysfunction. Continuing to excuse a husband's or boyfriend's abusive behavior is not love and will only hurt you and him. Don't continue to live as a victim.

3. Learn to Set Healthy Boundaries

- You are not God and you can't do everything. To develop healthy, balanced relationships, you must set boundaries—to define what is and is not your responsibility. If not, needy codependent people will be drawn to you like a magnet, reinforcing your unhealthy relational patterns.

- Realize that the way you have always done things is not necessarily right. No human being can meet the deepest needs that lie in your heart. If you have idolized people in the past, the idea of acting differently may feel strange and unnatural at first.

- Learn to be genuine and honest about who you are. As you begin to set healthy boundaries, you will likely feel lost and confused about your identity and purpose. That's okay. Over time you will begin to feel more comfortable with who you are in Christ.

BIBLICAL INSIGHTS 6

You shall have no other gods before me.

Exodus 20:3

They exchanged the truth of God for a lie, and worshiped and served created things rather than the Creator—who is forever praised.

Romans 1:25

God is jealous of our undivided worship of Him, because only He can satisfy the deep needs of our soul. Codependency sets up another person as an idol. Life revolves around pleasing that person and using him or her to feel better about ourselves.

But when we find our identity, value, worth, or purpose in another person—no matter how amazing that person is—we sin. We worship the creation rather than the Creator. And every time we worship something or someone other than God, we get hurt in the process. More than just an unhealthy behavior pattern, codependency is a sin because it robs God of worship that He rightfully deserves.

Just as the children of Israel disobeyed the commands of God by setting up and worshiping the golden calf, we exchange "the truth of God for a lie" when we lift up and value any person more than God.

You will know the truth, and the truth will set you free.

John 8:32

Codependency is a learned behavior, and as such, it can feel natural and comfortable. It becomes the norm. But relying on other people for our identity and worth will eventually spiral into chaos, hurt, and confusion. Many women feel stuck because they don't know who they are apart from another person, especially a man.

Breaking free from the patterns of codependency begins with *knowing the truth about God and about ourselves*. Over and over again, Scripture confirms that each of us is precious to God, made in His image, and valuable—not because of achievements or performance, but because *each woman is God's daughter*. Our true worth is grounded in God, not in how much we work or serve and not in other people's opinions of us. As we learn to live in the truths of who we are in Christ, the chains of codependency are broken and we are free.

So do not fear, for I am with you; do not be dismayed, for I am your God. I will strengthen you and help you; I will uphold you with my righteous right hand.

Isaiah 41:10

Many women struggling with codependency are desperately afraid of being alone, of being abandoned, of losing their identity because of losing a friend, boyfriend, spouse, or family member. Often, without saying the words, we act in a way that says, "You define me. I need you. I have to have you. I can't live without you." And in the moment, we fail to remember who God is and whose we are.

Scripture is replete with God's promises of love, provision, and concern. In this verse in Isaiah, God assures us that we have no reason to fear. The great I AM is not only with us, He is our God. He will strengthen us. He will help us. He will uphold us simply because He is God. In this one verse alone, God gives five specific promises, each of them grounded not in us but in Him.

Come to me, all you who are weary and burdened, and I will give you rest. Take my yoke upon you and learn from me, for I am gentle and humble in heart, and you will find rest for your souls.

Matthew 11:28–29

Codependency can cultivate a crazy, overcommitted, chaotic lifestyle, as a woman tries desperately to rescue, serve, and fix other people to affirm her own value and worth. Sadly, many teach that these behaviors are godly and biblical, but God never intended for us to live this way.

Beyond anything you or I can do, Jesus is concerned with our knowing Him and living in His abundance. Ultimately, codependency must be replaced with a genuine rest and trust in Jesus, which is a whole new lifestyle for the woman weary and burdened by codependent relationships.

7 PRAYER STARTER

Lord, thank You for creating relationships. We know, God, that You long for us to experience healthy intimacy and community, but some relationships can be really hurtful and scary. I pray for _____ as she struggles with codependency. I know,

Jesus, that it breaks Your heart to see Your daughter in this kind of bondage. Set her free, Lord, from this unhealthy desire to please and serve others. Open her eyes to who she is in You and teach her how to rest. Meet the deep needs of her soul, Lord, and help her create boundaries that will protect her heart . . .

RECOMMENDED RESOURCES : 8

Beattie, Melody. *Codependent No More: How to Stop Controlling Others and Start Caring for Yourself.* Hazelden, 1992.

Cloud, Henry, and John Townsend. *Boundaries.* Zondervan, 1992.

Engelmann, Kim. *Running in Circles: How False Spirituality Traps Us in Unhealthy Relationships.* InterVarsity, 2007.

Groom, Nancy. *From Bondage to Bonding: Escaping Codependency, Embracing Biblical Love.* NavPress, 1991.

Vernick, Leslie. *The Emotionally Destructive Relationship: Seeing It, Stopping It, Surviving It.* Harvest House, 2007.

Welch, Edward. *When People Are Big and God Is Small: Overcoming Peer Pressure, Codependency, and the Fear of Man.* P&R Publishing, 1997.

Depression

1 PORTRAITS

- Each morning Angela struggles to find the energy to get out of bed. She feels listless and down. Her kids need her, but she can't summon energy to even interact with them—much less prepare meals or clean the house. During the summer, Angela just thought her kids were wearing her out, but now, even after they've gone back to school, she still can't seem to pull it together. *What is wrong with me?* Angela wonders. *Why can't I just be normal?*

- Shannon witnessed her mom's murder when she was only eight years old. She never had a normal childhood because of the post-traumatic shock she experienced. Since her early teenage years, Shannon has been on strong antidepressants, but the drugs make her fatigued and don't really seem to help. Doctors have tried putting her on several different medications, but none of them take away the emotional pain that cripples Shannon.

- Grace is having a hard time thinking clearly. She lost her job and just can't seem to crawl out of the hole she feels she's fallen into. Because she's so down, she hasn't gone for job interviews; she just sits around at home, watches television, and plays on the computer. And she just keeps spiraling downward. *My life is so lame*, Grace tells herself over and over again. *I'm a loser. No one will ever hire me.*

2 DEFINITIONS AND KEY THOUGHTS

- *Depression* is "*a mental state characterized by a pessimistic sense of inadequacy and a despondent lack of activity.*"[1] Depression can evidence itself in different ways. The *most common symptoms* are decreased energy, fluctuating body weight, depleted concentration, irritability, bouts of crying, hopelessness or despair, a disinterest in pleasurable activities, social withdrawal, and thoughts of suicide.

- *Clinical depression* as a disorder is not the same as brief mood fluctuations or the feelings of sadness, disappointment, and frustration that everyone experiences from time to time and that last from minutes to a few days at most. Clinical depression is a *more serious condition that lasts weeks to months*, and sometimes even years.

- *Misdiagnosis of depression is common*. It is often labeled as anxiety, which is a common affect in many types of depression or other mood disorders. *Accurate assessment is the first step to proper treatment*.

- *Depression is on the rise*. People born after 1950 are *ten times more likely* to experience depression than their elders. Those between ages twenty-five and forty-five have the greatest percentage of depression, though teens have the fastest rate of depression growth.[2]

- Statistics show that *fifteen million adults suffer from clinical depression*. It is predicted that by 2020 depression will be the second leading common health problem in the world.[3]

- *Women are twice as likely to experience clinical depression as men*.[4] It is estimated that 12 percent of women will suffer clinical depression in their lifetime.[5]

- According to the National Institutes of Mental Health, depression causes *inestimable pain* for both those enduring the disorder and the persons closest to them. Depression destroys the lives of the victims and of their family members unnecessarily. Most sufferers *do not seek treatment* or believe their depression is treatable.[6]

- Recent research shows that around 80 percent of Americans who suffer from depression are not receiving any treatment. *Many women do not even believe depression is a real psychological illness* or refuse to acknowledge the reality of their consistently low moods.[7]

- *Depression differs from sadness*, which is a God-given reaction to loss that serves to slow people down so they can process grief. When one is sad, self-respect remains intact, intrinsic hope is maintained, and relief comes after crying and receiving support. Depression, however, results in *feelings of despondency and lack of hope and purpose for life*.

Types of Depression

- *Clinical/major depression* is distinct in that symptoms are so severe that they disrupt one's daily routine.

- *Dysthymic disorder* is a chronic, low-grade depression.

- *Bipolar disorder*, previously known as manic depression, is a type of mood disorder with severe changes in affect. A person may have periods of *euphoric elatedness* contrasted with periods of *severe major depression*.

- *Seasonal affective disorder* (SAD) is a severe onset of "winter blues" when one experiences depression, most often believed to be due to the lack of sunlight (or vitamin D).

- *Cyclothymia* is a *milder variation of bipolar disorder* where there is a recurring disturbance in mood from hypomania (irritable or elevated mood) and dysthymia (chronic, low-grade depression).

Causes of Depression

- Depression can be *caused by many life issues*, including anger; failure or rejection; family issues, such as divorce or abuse; fear; feelings of futility; lacking control over one's life; grief and loss; guilt or shame; loneliness or isolation; negative thinking; destructive misbeliefs; and stress. This is sometimes referred to as "*reactive depression*," and the symptoms may be least evident in the morning and increase throughout the day. *Note*: Persistent reactive depression will change one's chemical balances and may compound depression.

- *Medical and biological factors can also facilitate depression*, such as a genetic predisposition to depression, thyroid abnormalities, female hormone fluctuations, serotonin or norepinephrine irregularities, diabetes, B-12 or iron deficiencies, lack of sunlight or vitamin D, a recent stroke or heart attack, mitral valve prolapse, exposure to black mold, prescription drugs (antihypertensives, oral contraceptives), and recreational drugs (such as alcohol, marijuana, cocaine). When rooted in the biological, it is sometimes referred to as "*endogenous depression*," and sufferers may feel worse in the morning.

Symptoms of Depression

- According to the DSM-IV-TR, *major depression* is diagnosed when *five or more of the following symptoms are present*, with the presence of "(1) depressed mood or (2) loss of interest or pleasure":

  — depressed mood

  — lack of pleasure or interest in normal activities

  — significant weight loss or weight gain (change of more than 5 percent in a month)

  — inability to sleep or being overly tired

  — fatigue and lack of energy

  — crippling feelings of worthlessness or guilt

  — inability to concentrate or make decisions

  — thoughts of death or suicidal ideations[8]

- *There are many examples of depression in the Bible, with a variety of reasons and results*: David wrote of his feelings from unconfessed sin (Psalms 38; 51). God used depression to get Nehemiah's attention (Nehemiah 1–2). Job's losses led him to curse the day he was born (Job 3:1). Elijah was so depressed over the situation with Israel's leaders that he wished to die (1 Kings 19:3–4). Frequently depression comes with difficult circumstances, even in the life of a Christian.

ASSESSMENT INTERVIEW 3

Rule Outs

1. If 10 is extreme sadness, and 1 is feeling well, where are you today on a scale of 1 to 10? (*If the client is sad, find out the cause.*)
2. Are you using drugs or alcohol?
3. Are you currently taking any medications? Are you failing to take medications that you should be taking?
4. When was the last time you had a thorough physical examination? (*If the counselee hasn't seen her doctor recently, give a medical referral.*)
5. Do you have significant mood swings? (*Ask about the existence of mania or hypomania and, if they exist, give a psychiatric referral.*)
6. Have you had any thoughts about injuring yourself or of suicide? Have you ever attempted to kill yourself? Do you think of dying every day? Have you thought about how you might commit suicide? Does anyone else know that you are thinking about dying in this way? (*Sometimes the thoughts are vague, such as, it would be better if I were not here. Pay particular attention if the woman talks about a plan for carrying out these thoughts. Someone who is suicidal and imagines having an automobile accident has both a plan and a means to carry it out.*)

General Questions

1. How long have you felt depressed?
2. What was happening in your life when you first became depressed? (*Someone who is depressed needs acceptance and gentleness. The counselee may already be feeling as if she has failed in some way. Begin by listening to your counselee's story without judgment.*)
3. Have you been depressed before?
4. Do you have a family history of depression?
5. Do you have difficulty concentrating?
6. Have you lost interest in pleasurable activities?
7. Have you noticed changes in your eating or sleeping patterns?
8. Are you dealing with guilt or fear about anything? (*Fear is prevalent in many kinds of depression—anxiety and depression may coexist in women diagnosed with depression.*)
9. What do you see in your future?

WISE COUNSEL 4

Depression is a complex and multifaceted issue and is usually only a *symptom of a deeper issue.* As you talk to the woman, try to get to the heart of why she is feeling the way she is. Has she experienced any significant change in her life as of late? Has she lost relationships? Has her health condition changed? Listen to her story and *convey empathy and understanding, not judgment.*

Many women feel that a Christian should never be depressed, and this is simply not true. *Spiritual doubt and questioning may be a healthy part of spiritual formation,* and depressive feelings are a very real issue for many women.

The most dangerous symptom of depression is suicidal ideation. If you discover through your questions that the woman desires to hurt herself, do not hesitate to involve other family members or a mental health professional if necessary.

If you recommend that your client see a physician, make sure she understands that *it is okay to take medications,* if needed, to get depression under control. Communicate that using medication doesn't mean that the counselee is weak or lacks faith.

5 ACTION STEPS

1. Identify the Causes

- Overcoming depression starts with having the courage to admit that you are unsatisfied with your life and that you need help. Depression can be caused by many factors, but it's important to investigate the physical aspects first. Have a full-body physical to get the opinion of a medical professional and discuss the possibility of medication.

- Look at your schedule, commitments, and lifestyle. What changes have you experienced recently? What factors or stressors are affecting you most? Identify possible causes of the depression you feel. Is it situational (related to a current situation) or chronic (part of your behavior for a significant time period)? What would your life be like without depression?

2. Develop a Game Plan

- Thirty minutes of moderate daily exercise is very helpful in elevating mood. Build time into your schedule to exercise on a regular basis. Find a form of exercise that you enjoy—walk, jog, bike, swim, go to the gym. Invite a friend to work out with you or sign up to work with a personal trainer—it makes it harder to avoid the activity if someone is waiting for you.

- Work with a doctor or dietitian on a diet program. Better eating habits (for example, less sugar and more vitamins) can be a big help in boosting your mood. Try to avoid fried food, refined sugars, and too much caffeine, and eat more fruits, vegetables, and healthy proteins.

3. Refocus Your Thinking

- Self-defeating thoughts can cripple us. Take time to evaluate your thought patterns, perhaps even writing them down in a journal. Challenge each thought to see if it is really true. For example, if you find yourself thinking, *I'm totally worthless. I have nothing to give anymore*, change that statement to line up with the reality of Scripture: I am precious in God's sight. He made me in His image and loves me more than I can imagine.

- Refuse to let the stress and pressure of life steal your joy. Rather than focusing on the negative, look at each moment and each day as a gift from Jesus. Look for His blessings and providence—a caring friend, a day that goes well. Find joy in the little things—a beautiful spring day, a delicious meal, or a hot cup of coffee.

4. Get Social Support

- When you're feeling down, it's easy to isolate yourself. But sitting home alone will only further perpetuate your bad mood. Seek out social support and spend time with positive, uplifting, caring people.
- Get involved in your church and community. Put yourself out there; take the risk. Sure, new relationships can be scary, but the alternative is continuing to live the way you are now. Join a small group or Bible study. Hang out with friends. Be honest with others about how you're feeling.

BIBLICAL INSIGHTS 6

But [Elijah] went a day's journey into the wilderness, and came and sat down under a broom tree. And he prayed that he might die, and said, "It is enough! Now, LORD, take my life for I am no better than my fathers!"

1 Kings 19:4 NKJV

Often, like the highs and lows in a mountain range, low moods come right after the highs. Like Elijah, we may scale the heights of spiritual victory only to find ourselves quickly in the dark valley of depression.

While certain forms of clinical depression should be professionally treated, many depressed feelings are simply responses to life's ups and downs. Like Elijah, we should listen for God's "still small voice" (1 Kings 19:12) to comfort us and we should rest in the reality that He will never leave us or forsake us.

Then as [Elijah] lay and slept under a broom tree, suddenly an angel touched him, and said to him, "Arise and eat." Then he looked, and there by his head was a cake baked on coals, and a jar of water. So he ate and drank, and lay down again.

1 Kings 19:5–6 NKJV

Depression can drain energy, twist values, and assault one's faith. Depression can affect anyone, even a prophet of God like Elijah.

God provided care to Elijah on many levels. He provided food so that Elijah regained his physical and emotional strength. An angel touched Elijah, confirming to Elijah that he was not alone. Also, twice, God encouraged Elijah to rest.

God created us as physical beings—we need food and rest to be healthy. To admit these needs isn't being spiritually weak, it's being human. Healthy food, adequate physical rest, and personal time with God are all critical to overcoming depression. No one of these behaviors should be practiced at the exclusion of the others.

Why are you downcast, O my soul? Why so disturbed within me? Put your hope in God, for I will yet praise him, my Savior and my God.

Psalm 42:5–6

Feelings of depression cause some women to turn away from God in bitterness and anger. Other people, like David, allow those disquieted, anxious feelings to make them "hope in God," remembering His goodness, even when everything else in life seems to be falling apart.

During such times, living by faith takes on a whole new meaning. No matter what you are feeling, you are not alone. God is with you—and He knows every intimate detail of your mind and heart. He is constantly present in the midst of your despair, even when you can't feel or sense Him.

Trust means continuing to believe, even when you cannot feel or see. So run to God. Pour out your heart to Him. Be honest with Him, as David was, because the only source of true joy is communion with God, not anything on the earth.

To comfort all who mourn, and provide for those who grieve in Zion—to bestow on them a crown of beauty instead of ashes, the oil of gladness instead of mourning, and a garment of praise instead of a spirit of despair. They will be called oaks of righteousness, a planting of the LORD for the display of his splendor.

Isaiah 61:2–3

The Bible recognizes the heaviness and reality of depression. Loss, heartache, pain, and change may all result in feelings of depression—and this is a normal part of life in this fallen world. The good news is that we're not stuck there.

God's unending love is far more powerful than the depression or discouragement we feel. God promises to give consolation, beauty in place of ashes, oil of joy in place of mourning, and a garment of praise instead of a spirit of heaviness.

We don't have to battle depression alone. We can invite God into our struggle and be honest with our family and friends. The goal isn't to hold it together. The goal is that God may be glorified, and He is glorified most when we rely on Him in our weakness.

7 PRAYER STARTER

Lord, at times we all feel downhearted. Today _____ feels as though she is walking in darkness with no way out. I pray, Lord, that You will provide healing. Please help us discern what is going on deep in her heart. If there is deep pain or loss, guilt or shame, give us discernment to bring it into the light and confess it to You . . .

RECOMMENDED RESOURCES 8

Anderson, Neil, and Joanne Anderson. *Overcoming Depression*. Regal, 2004.

Burns, David. *The Feeling Good Handbook*. Plume, 1999.

Hart, Archibald D., and Catherine Hart Weber. *A Woman's Guide to Overcoming Depression*. Revell, 2007.

Minirth, Frank, and Paul Meier. *Happiness Is a Choice: The Symptoms, Causes, and Cures of Depression*. Baker, 2007.

Rogers, Timothy. *Trouble of Mind and Disease of Melancholy*. Soli Deo Gloria Ministries, 2002.

Tan, Siang-Yang, and John Ortberg. *Coping with Depression*. Baker, 2004.

Diet and Nutrition

1 · PORTRAITS

- Kathy has been overweight all her life. Growing up in a dysfunctional home, Kathy would use junk food to comfort herself—Doritos, M&Ms, Twinkies, ice cream—you name it. Kathy has tried many new diets but she gives up on them because of her cravings for sugar. As soon as Kathy strays from one of her fad diets, she regains the weight she lost and she gets really frustrated. "I hate being overweight," Kathy mumbles through tears, "but I can't seem to stop eating."

- Erin is a full-time ER nurse and single mother of three. Her job and children leave little time for healthy, home-cooked meals. Usually dinner consists of a pizza, McDonald's hamburgers, or prepackaged frozen dinners. Erin's busy lifestyle is contributing to a poor diet and lifestyle for her kids, but she doesn't know what to do differently. *I'm not a supermom*, she muses, *but I want to raise healthy kids.*

- Carol is a workout-aholic. Before going to the office in the morning, after getting off at night, whenever she has free time, she's at the gym. Although she's been athletic all her life, Carol is extremely worried about gaining extra weight as she sees her metabolism change with age. In fact, SlimFast shakes and Healthy Choice meals are about the only things Carol eats. But recently she's been having severe muscle cramps whenever she exercises, and the doctor says she might be nutrient deficient.

2 · DEFINITIONS AND KEY THOUGHTS

- *Nutrition* is defined as "the processes by which an organism assimilates food and uses it for growth and maintenance."[1] Good nutrition leads to *health, prevention of disease, and proper development both physically and mentally* and is attained by *eating healthy, nutrient-rich foods* that are necessary for the effective functioning of the mind and body. *Nutrient-rich foods* are foods containing high levels of vitamins, minerals, and other nutrients.

- A person's *diet* refers to her *pattern of eating or types of foods she eats. Diet* can also refer to a plan of eating and/or refraining from eating certain foods. Research shows that *45 percent of American women are on a diet on any given day.*[2] There are many diets, including South Beach Diet, Atkins Diet, and Weight Watchers. Popular diets or diets that are new on the market are often called *fad diets.*

- *Dietitians* and *nutritionists are experts* in the field of proper diet and nutrition. They can help individuals develop and maintain a healthy eating lifestyle. As of 2010, according to the Centers for Disease Control and Prevention, 75 percent of women age twenty and over have visited a physician's office for *diet and nutrition counseling and related medical complications.*[3]

- As of 2008 only 28.6 percent of women were consuming five or more servings of fruit and vegetables a day. That leaves *72.4 percent of women not getting enough healthful nutrients in their daily diet.*[4]

- Improper dieting and/or poor nutrition can tax a woman's health and well-being. *More than one in ten women (14 percent) in the United States who are eighteen years or older are in poor or fair health.*[5]

- *Many women resort to unhealthy dieting plans because of skewed ideas of "health" presented by the media.* Studies show that the average American woman is 5'4" tall and weighs 140 pounds. The average American model is 5'11" tall and weighs 117 pounds. That makes most fashion models thinner than 98 percent of American women.[6]

- Aside from the physical and psychological stress extreme dieting puts on the body, *most diets are ineffective long-term.* Ninety-one percent of women recently surveyed on a college campus had attempted to control their weight through dieting, and 22 percent dieted "often" or "always." However, 95 percent of all dieters will regain their lost weight in one to five years.[7]

- Many women don't eat a healthy diet because they don't think they can afford it. Others fall prey to "magic" diet plans that are often expensive and ineffective. *Studies show that Americans spend more than forty billion dollars on dieting and diet-related products each year.*[8]

- *Poor diet and nutrition can be a result of*

  — cultural eating habits
  — poverty
  — mental health disorders
  — lack of time
  — eating disorders
  — lack of education in proper diet and nutrition

ASSESSMENT INTERVIEW 3

Begin with a synopsis of the client's diet. Also take into consideration the body mass index (BMI), a formula that measures body fat. BMI = (weight in pounds) / (height in inches) x (height in inches) x 703. You can use an online BMI calculator at http://www.bmi-calculator.net/.

Some significant details to talk about with your client include the following:

1. Tell me about your eating habits. What do you eat? When do you eat?

2. What health issues do you presently have? What health risks do you have based on genetics?
3. Have you talked to your doctor about the role of diet and nutrition in your health? Have you seen a dietitian?
4. How does your lifestyle (job, family, kids) influence your eating choices?
5. What is keeping you from getting proper nutrition and developing healthy eating habits?
6. What steps (diets, exercise, indulging in eating disorders, medication) have you taken in the past to manage your weight? What was the result?
7. Describe how you feel when eating. Do you tend to use food to comfort yourself?
8. Is exercise a part of your life? If not, why not?
9. Do you feel that you can control your eating, or does eating control you?
10. What steps could you take right now to build a healthier lifestyle?

4 : WISE COUNSEL

For many women, diet and nutrition are more about *their outside appearance and what others think of them* than *their own personal health*. This is the reason many women are driven into unhealthy diets and eating disorders, which deprive their bodies of critical nutrition and nutrients. Many women assume that the key to losing weight and being healthy is eating less. While food portions are important, *what you eat is just as important* (if not more!) *than how much you eat.*

Change the focus to better health and lifestyle. A focus on proper diet and nutrition demands discipline and simple changes in thought patterns that the client may not realize.

Consider underlying issues, such as poor self-esteem, childhood abuse or neglect, or depression. Women tend to indulge in *comfort or emotional eating and social eating* to handle stress, conflict, loss, or grief. If this is the problem, the focus needs to be on *changing behavioral patterns.*

When poor diet and nutrition are the result of *poor behavior or lifestyle choices*, behavior changes are still going to be the main focus. Lack of time, lack of self-control, and lack of knowledge on proper diet and nutrition are not *short-term challenges.* Dealing with them properly requires *a lifestyle change.* Sometimes those "lack of" issues also result from underlying control issues.

Many women assume that they don't have the time, money, or energy to eat healthy because to them "eating healthy" means buying fancy organic foods that are cost-prohibitive. However, this is simply not true. While getting proper nutrition requires some time in food preparation, eating at home is nearly always cheaper than eating out. Eating a balanced diet of fruits, vegetables, proteins, and carbohydrates is quite possible on a budget, but many women don't know where to begin. Encourage your client to speak with a nutritionist or dietitian, if possible, and *develop a healthy eating plan*, without resorting to an extreme diet.

Discuss with your client the possibility of enrolling in a healthy weight-loss program (such as Weight Watchers) and working with a personal trainer to develop an appropriate exercise program. Steps like these will help a woman avoid emotional eating or compulsive exercise.

ACTION STEPS 5

1. Assess Your Lifestyle Choices

- Track your diet for two weeks, including calorie, fat, and carbohydrate intake, as well as related nutritional data. Examine these habits to see if they are nutritionally sound. Also take time to track your exercise regimen for two weeks.

- Do some research on the physical risks and long-term effects of poor nutrition. Often facing the facts and getting a grip on reality is the best way to jumpstart better health. Acknowledging the risks and consequences of poor diet and nutrition is the first step to change.

- It's easy in the moment to rationalize your eating choices as "just this once," promising to start dieting tomorrow. However, it is critical to understand that the choices you make today will affect your health tomorrow. What you eat today will determine how you feel tomorrow.

- Building a healthy lifestyle is about far more than dieting. In reality, many fad diets rob your body of critical nutrients needed for good health. Starving yourself is never a healthy option—it will only put your body in "survival mode" and shut down your metabolism. Evaluate any dieting plan you are currently following.

2. Evaluate the Emotional Aspects

- Whether you're overeating, dieting obsessively, or just eating junk food, emotions are frequently involved. Pinpoint the emotional or mental aspect of your poor diet and nutrition choices by asking, *Why am I dieting (or eating junk food)? What are my comfort foods? What thought processes are guiding my eating behaviors?*

- This may be a painful process if it involves unresolved issues from the past about body image, self-esteem, or abusive relationships. Consider your family and your history. Though painful, this part of the process is critical to healing and starting on a new diet and nutrition plan. Until you get to the root issue of your eating habits, it's likely you won't change.

3. Watch for Triggers

- Believe it or not, you are not a victim of your body's cravings. Everything your body craves isn't necessarily good for you, either. Hunger is a complex physical and psychological process, influenced by many factors. Begin to look for triggers that lead you to eat unhealthily. Is it stress, conflict, lack of time, habits, convenience, depression, loneliness?

- Once you identify the triggers, you can begin to adjust your schedule and lifestyle to make healthy eating more feasible. If you're "too busy" to eat healthy, slow down. Say no to some things. Research healthy options for eating on the go. If you find yourself turning to food when you're sad and lonely, start putting yourself in more social situations and change what you snack on when you do eat. In your decisions, focus on balance. Don't set unreasonable standards for yourself.

4. Make a Plan

- Breaking the cycle of poor diet and nutrition may take time, but the long-term benefits are critical. Behaviors form lifestyles. You can begin making choices today that will cultivate a healthier you. Make sure you are realistic—there's nothing worse than setting unachievable goals. Here are a few ideas to get you started:

  — Stay away from minimalistic, starvation-style diets.
  — Write a master grocery list that eliminates junk food.
  — Snack on vegetables, fruits, and nuts.
  — Stay away from sweet, rich desserts.
  — Build time into your schedule to exercise (and do something you actually enjoy).
  — Drink plenty of water and avoid sodas.
  — Choose healthy options for eating out.
  — Develop new, more active hobbies (hiking, running, walking, swimming, and so on).
  — Take a multivitamin and dietary supplements.

6 BIBLICAL INSIGHTS

Do you not know that your body is a temple of the Holy Spirit, who is in you, whom you have received from God? You are not your own; you were bought at a price. Therefore honor God with your body.

1 Corinthians 6:19–20

Our earthly bodies are temporary but they are temporary vessels for the use of our Savior. Our bodies are to be cared for and kept pure because we are not our own—we are God's. It is our responsibility to take care of our body as the temple of God.

Both excess food and voluntary deprivation of food can be damaging to the body. As God's servants on this earth, we should do everything in our power to be healthy and have the strength and energy to serve Him well. Poor diet and nutrition habits are most often due to laziness, habit, and convenience, and this displeases God, who created our bodies "fearfully and wonderfully" (Ps. 139:14).

"Everything is permissible for me"—but not everything is beneficial. "Everything is permissible for me"—but I will not be mastered by anything. "Food for the stomach and the stomach for food"—but God will destroy them both.

1 Corinthians 6:12–13

God created human beings with free will—to make choices and live with the choices we make. As a follower of Christ, Paul points out in this passage that we are not to "be mastered by anything"—even food. While the New Testament gives no direct commands about diet and nutrition (aside from removing the Old Testament dietary laws), junk food and fad diets are not "beneficial."

Food can be a powerful force in destroying a woman's health, yet it is, of course, a requirement for life. As a provision of God, food offers us sustenance and nutrients necessary for the energy and daily function of our bodies, but when food (or the lack of food) becomes an obsession, it is sin. When we choose to eat poorly, we choose to endanger our bodies, which really aren't ours at all, but God's. We should not allow anything, even food, to have power or control over us.

Put a knife to your throat if you are given to gluttony.

Proverbs 23:2

You, my brothers, were called to be free. But do not use your freedom to indulge the sinful nature.

Galatians 5:13

Scripture is full of admonitions about not being controlled by our cravings. These passages speak to the seriousness of being under the control of our appetite. We may argue that the terms are not literal in Proverbs 23 ("put a knife to your throat"), but the premise is clear—if you give way to your appetite and are controlled by your desire for food, your life is no longer your own. In essence, you become lifeless. You live in bondage to what you crave.

Do not allow your eating habits to control your life. Do whatever is necessary to get your eating under control. In the New Testament we are commanded to glorify God in everything—"whether you eat or drink or whatever you do," Paul says (1 Cor. 10:31). God wants to set you free from being ruled by your cravings for food. As you look at your diet and lifestyle, ask yourself, *Am I glorifying God by what I eat, by what I refrain from eating, and by how I take care of my body?*

PRAYER STARTER 7

Lord, You are our power and our stronghold. Father, give _____ the strength to resist the behaviors and the temptation to let food be her power and her stronghold.

God, give her wisdom to make the correct choices that will benefit and better the body that You gave her to use for Your glory . . .

8 : RECOMMENDED RESOURCES

Arterburn, Stephen, and Dr. Linda Mintle. *Lose It for Life: The Total Solution—Spiritual, Emotional, Physical—for Permanent Weight Loss.* Thomas Nelson, 2007.

Hadden, Julie, and Ashley Wiersma. *Fat Chance: Losing the Weight, Gaining My Worth.* Guidepost Books, 2009.

Hobbs, Chantel. *Never Say Diet: Make Five Decisions and Break the Fat Habit for Good.* WaterBrook, 2008.

Morrone, Lisa. *Overcoming Overeating: It's Not What You Eat, It's What's Eating You!* Harvest House, 2009.

Shepherd, Sheri Rose. *Fit for My King: His Princess 30-Day Diet Plan and Devotional.* Revell, 2009.

Swenson, Richard, and Robert Tamasy. *In Search of Balance.* NavPress, 2010.

Divorce

PORTRAITS : 1

- Jennifer was served divorce papers after her husband, Tom, had an affair with a co-worker. She was devastated and begged him to attend counseling—to at least try for the kids' sake. "It's time to move on," Tom said. "I don't love you anymore." Relocating to another state with his new girlfriend, Tom hasn't contacted Jennifer or the kids in four years. Jennifer is broken, hurt, and confused. She picked up a second job and tried to move on but she's still really angry at Tom.

- Katie's husband has beaten and abused her since they were married six years ago. His fits of rage are unpredictable. Little things like cold coffee or a puddle in the bathroom make him lose it, so Katie spends her days walking on thin ice, trying to keep him happy. After an incident, when she's often black-and-blue, he apologizes and promises he'll "do better," but then it happens again. "As a Christian, I feel I have to stay with him," Katie explains, "but I'm tired of being a punching bag."

- "You have to fight for your marriage. Respect your husband. Support him." Everywhere she turns, Jackie hears this advice from well-meaning Christians. But Jackie's marriage is falling apart. Respect and support aren't cutting it. Jackie's husband, Chris, is addicted to pornography, and she recently walked in on him and another woman. When she confronted Chris about it, he was belligerent. "So what?" he said. "I can be with whoever I want." Jackie doesn't think she can live one more day like this but is clueless about what to do.

DEFINITIONS AND KEY THOUGHTS : 2

- *Divorce* is "the *legal termination* of a marriage by a court in a legal proceeding, requiring a petition or complaint by one party."[1]

- *A divorce may be filed as a "fault" or "no-fault" dissolution.* A fault divorce is "a judicial termination of a marriage based on marital misconduct." An individual must present tangible evidence of extramarital sexual activity or significant abuse to file a fault divorce proceeding.[2]

- In a no-fault divorce, however, "neither party is required to prove fault." The decision may be justified based on *personal testimony of "irretrievable breakdown" and "irreconcilable differences."*[3]

- Research by The Barna Group shows that among Americans who have vowed "'til death do us part," one in three (33 percent) have been divorced at least once. *In Christian circles, the divorce rate is nearly identical* (32 percent).[4]

- Far more than just the breaking of vows, divorce has been shown to have *significant negative effects on women*. Divorced women have a greater risk of low self-esteem, depression, heart problems, and cancer, due to drastic increases in psychological distress.[5]

- *While divorce may seem like an easy solution to marital conflict, statistics suggest otherwise.* Associated Content reports that women who "were unhappy but stayed married were more likely to be happy five years later than those who divorce."[6]

- According to the National Center for Health Statistics, divorced women have a 50 percent chance of remarrying. However, *second marriages are not immune to divorce.* Statistics show that 23 percent of second marriages end in divorce within five years, and that figure jumps to 39 percent after ten years.[7]

Scriptural View of Divorce

- Divorce was never intended as part of God's perfect plan. Malachi 2:16 says that *the Lord hates divorce.* However, the rest of the verse reveals that Malachi was speaking to men who were disloyal to their wives. *God's compassion toward the injured party is clear.*

- In a fallen, broken, and messed-up world, divorce will happen. Jesus spoke of divorce happening because of "the hardness of your hearts" (Matt. 19:8 NKJV). *The destruction of a marriage relationship always stems from sin and selfishness of some kind.* But divorce, just like any other failure in life, is not beyond the reach of God's grace.

- Many women who seek help wrestle with a divorce that was not their decision. Scripture commands us to "weep with those who weep" (Rom. 12:15 NKJV). *Rather than judging women who are experiencing the trauma of broken marriage, the body of Christ is called to:*

  — share in their sorrow
  — offer compassion
  — give reassurance that their church family will not reject them
  — impart hope that God is working and will not forsake them
  — offer them opportunities to serve in the church

Biblical Reasons for Divorce

- *Sexual activity outside of the marital covenant* breaks the marriage vow. In Matthew 19:9, Jesus said that if a spouse had committed this type of sin, divorce was permitted. This does not mean divorce is required or commanded in instances where sexual sin has been committed, but it is permitted. *Even when there are biblical grounds, divorce is never easy.*

- Some theologians maintain that *the abandonment* of a believer by a nonbelieving spouse leaves the believing spouse free to divorce the deserter (see 1 Cor. 7:15).

Reasons for Separation

- *Physical abuse* is not addressed in the Bible as a reason for divorce, but nowhere does Scripture command a woman to stay in a home where she or her children are being physically abused. *In these situations, separation is necessary for physical safety.*

- *Sexual abuse* of one's spouse or children betrays trust on a deep, intimate level. In cases when a man becomes a predator rather than a protector of his family, separation becomes a basic necessity.

- *Mental or verbal abuse* is devastating to a woman's heart and involves severe belittling or demeaning behavior.

- *Chemical addictions* involve addictive patterns in the use of drugs or alcohol that result in harmful behavior to the spouse or children.

- *Physical neglect*, such as not providing appropriate food, clothing, shelter, or supervision of the children, can result in troubling, life-threatening situations. *The spouse has a duty to remove the children or the addict from the home, to provide a safe environment for the children.*

- *Many times, separation and mediation can prevent divorce.* As a result, we recommend that any separation be done judiciously, with the intent of healing and restoration of the marriage.

Biblical View of Reconciliation

- *Restoration after abuse* should be predicated on *true repentance* and a *significant change in the abuser's behavior* that lasts for an extended period of time. Abuse of any kind destroys the fundamental trust on which relationships are built. While the Bible does call us to forgive, forgiveness does not mean continuing to put oneself in dangerous and hurtful situations, hoping desperately for a corrupt man to change. Sometimes, change, recovery, and healing cannot happen unless a husband and wife separate for a time and seek help for their own personal issues.

- In this confusing process, *the church plays an essential role*—to create a safe haven for the victim and hold the abuser accountable to change his behavior. *The church can serve as a protector of the abused* by helping her find a safe place to stay, offering counseling, providing financial assistance, and using church discipline to hold the abusive spouse accountable.

Consequences of Divorce

- Divorce *destroys the beauty of the marriage relationship*. Marriage is more than a contract between a man and a woman—it is a covenant bond created by God and serves as *a picture of God's relationship with us, His bride.*

- Divorce *tears apart relationships*. When harsh words fly and emotions get out of control, divorce may seem like a "quick fix," the easy way out. However, divorce is not just the ending of a marriage relationship. *It tears apart two families, destroys close relationships, and leads to pain and brokenness.*
- Divorce *devastates children*. Research shows that, for most children, the pain they feel from the breakup of their home is just as painful ten years after the divorce as it was at the time of the divorce. The pain often follows them into adulthood, and can *drastically influence their personality and life choices.*

3 : ASSESSMENT INTERVIEW

For a Woman Contemplating Divorce

When a woman comes to counseling with divorce in mind, you are usually the last stop before a lawyer.

Rule Outs

1. Do you have reason to believe that you are in danger?
2. Has there been any type of abuse (physical, verbal, or sexual) to either you or your children? (*If there has been physical or sexual abuse, the first step is to get the abused woman and her children away from the abuser and to a safe place. Counseling cannot begin until this takes place. Individual counseling is recommended so that the woman can heal and the man can deal with his abusive behaviors and work toward reestablishing trust. This is an essential step before marital counseling is safe to do, or makes sense.*)

General Questions

1. What has prompted you to come to counseling?
2. What do you hope the outcome of counseling will be?
3. Tell me about your marriage. How long have you been married?
4. Do you have any children?
5. How did you meet? What first attracted you to each other?
6. How did you know that this was the man you wanted to marry?
7. What was your first fight about?
8. When did the problems that bring you here today first arise?
9. How have you tried already to solve these problems?
10. Do you feel there is any hope of reconciliation? What would it take for you to want to reconcile?
11. Do you both want a divorce? Do you have biblical grounds for divorce?
12. Are both you and your husband believers? How is your walk with the Lord?
13. Tell me about your background, your parents, your siblings. What was your parents' relationship like?
14. What do you think divorce will accomplish for you?
15. How do you think the divorce will affect your children?

For a Victim of Divorce

When a woman suffering the pain of divorce comes to counseling, it is a positive sign that she feels worthy of help. Many times, a woman's *self-worth is demolished by the divorce.*

In your initial meeting, reinforce the woman's proactivity in seeking out help as a sign that she wants to work through her pain and find healing.

Rule Outs

1. On a scale of 1 to 10, with 10 being joy and 1 being hopelessness, where would you put yourself? (*You will want to rule out the presence of clinical depression.*)
2. Have you had any thoughts of hurting yourself or others? (*If you feel the woman is a danger to herself or others, refer her to a professional counselor.*)

General Questions

1. What brought you here today? What do you hope to gain from counseling?
2. Tell me about your marriage. How did you meet your husband?
3. What attracted you to him? Did you notice any character qualities that gave you concern?
4. Did your feelings change during the marriage? How?
5. How did your parents feel about your husband?
6. When did you first realize that there were problems?
7. How did your husband tell you he wanted to end the marriage?
8. What were your feelings? What did you say or do?
9. To whom did you go for help? Was the person helpful?
10. What was the reaction of your family, your husband's family, and your close friends?
11. Do you have any children? How old are they?
12. How did they react to the news? How are they doing now?
13. What feelings have you gone through? Be honest. Have you been able to talk to anyone about these feelings?
14. What support do you have around you? Are your friends and family supportive? Do you belong to a support group?
15. How are you and your children doing financially?
16. Do you feel the Lord has rejected you or forgotten about you?

WISE COUNSEL 4

For a Woman Contemplating Divorce

Share what God says about divorce. Explain that *God hates divorce because of the hurt and devastation it brings to people.* Still, He loves the people involved.

Talk through the *biblical reasons for divorce*, as described earlier in the chapter: sexual activity outside of the marriage covenant (Matt. 19:9) and abandonment (1 Cor. 7:15).

Discuss the *implications of divorce*. Make it clear that people are not commanded to divorce in these situations but are allowed to. *Forgiveness and restoration* are also options when the guilty party is truly repentant and willing to change.

Empathize with the pain and hurt both spouses are going through, but be straightforward about the new problems divorce will likely bring:

- financial difficulty of two separate households
- conflicts involved in splitting joint possessions and resources
- probability of custody battles
- stress of single parenthood
- guilt from seeing the children's world torn apart
- dealing with sending the children back and forth between parents
- feelings of anger, loneliness, and grief

For a Victim of Divorce

Assure the woman that *God sees her troubles and cries with her in her pain*. It grieves and angers Him to see His daughter hurt and suffering (see Isa. 40:27–28). Drawing Scripture from the Biblical Insights section, help the woman realize that God loves her and totally accepts her, even as a divorced woman. *Jesus understands her feelings of betrayal and rejection completely* because He too was betrayed and rejected.

Explain *the importance of grieving* and the time it takes to come to terms with the death of a marriage and a new phase of life. Usually healing takes *two to five years and consists of five stages*: denial, anger, bargaining, depression, and acceptance. Many times, a woman goes through these stages multiple times (and in no particular order) before she finds a new "normal."

Do not rob the woman of her grief. *Validate the hurt done to her.* Empathize with her pain but assure her that she can *live as a survivor* rather than a victim. God is still sovereign and present, and His arms are strong enough for her to rest in as she works through the process of grief.

Investigate her *emotional state* since the divorce. Has she felt shame, guilt, condemnation, or anger at her ex-husband? Encourage her *to process these feelings* but explain that her feelings *may not accurately represent reality all of the time.* Caution her on acting out of emotion, as such decisions may be rash and harmful. Reinforce the importance of building a *support team* around her during this time of transition and healing.

Encourage her to release the hurt and find healing as she *forgives her husband and herself.* If she continues to carry around anger and resentment, she will live controlled by these feelings. (For more, see the chapter "Forgiveness.")

ACTION STEPS : 5

For a Woman Contemplating Divorce

1. Put the Divorce on Hold and Get Counseling

- Take a step back from the divorce paperwork and attend marriage counseling. Talk with a mediator and do everything in your power to reconcile with your husband.

- Begin to meet with a trained marriage mentoring couple or coach who can come alongside to encourage and instruct you.

- Count the cost. Take some time to consider the impact of divorce on you and your family. Study the Word with a spirit of openness, praying that God will lead and direct you.

2. Be Proactive about Confronting the Root Issues

- Work with a counselor to dig into the root issues causing your conflict. Be willing to look for and admit underlying problems. Your marriage is at stake here! Honestly express to your husband what you feel, what you are frustrated about, and the hope you see for change.

- You are not alone. Most likely another couple has experienced a similar conflict or struggle as you and your husband. Often it is extremely helpful to read what has helped others.

3. Seek Out God's Wisdom

- Many women who had given up hope now have healthy and fulfilling marriages, so don't throw in the towel too soon. Ask God to give you wisdom as you consider the possibility of reconciliation.

- Only God can change your and your husband's hearts and re-create genuine love for each other. Ask God to develop unselfish love in your heart for your husband, while at the same time setting healthy boundaries. You are precious to God, and being submissive does not mean letting your husband walk all over you.

For a Victim of Divorce

1. Build a Support Network around You

- Frequently divorce splinters friendships and extended family relationships. Even well-meaning people can take sides, defend one party, and act in a harsh and judgmental manner. To heal, you need to step back from the drama and seek out loving, supportive friendships within the body of Christ—even if it means building some new friendships or going to a new church.

- Start attending a divorce recovery group. A support group offers the opportunity to connect with other people suffering the pain of divorce, share stories, and find hope and healing. Many churches offer these groups. (For more information, visit www.divorcecare.com.)

- Set up weekly counseling appointments with a professional counselor. Healing fully from the pain of divorce requires working through the root issues and emotions. This can be a confusing and overwhelming process, and it's important to enlist professional help.

2. Try to Avoid Making Major Decisions

- Healing from the pain and betrayal of divorce takes time and will probably put you in an emotionally vulnerable state. During this time, it's unwise to make major life changes that may add to emotional stress.
- Realize that you don't have to figure it all out on your own. There will be difficult decisions to make, whether or not you feel prepared to make them. Decisions, such as custody of children, relocation, career change, and romantic relationships, should be made only with the advice and support of your counselor and pastor.

3. Guard against Rebound Relationships

- Divorce may leave a woman feeling empty, alone, and incredibly lonely. While it may seem natural to pursue a new romantic relationship, extreme caution is needed. Dating too soon can set a woman up for yet another dysfunctional relationship.
- Rebound relationships are often motivated by a woman's desperate desire to feel loved and validated. However, if you do not first work through the root issues of pain, betrayal, and low self-esteem, you will likely carry around significant emotional baggage for the rest of your life.
- Seek out friendships with other women whom you can talk honestly with and spend time with on a regular basis. Learn to enjoy the simple things of life and focus on letting God fill the emptiness inside you. As you look to relationships in the future, you can be a whole, healed woman, not a desperate, hurting victim.

6 BIBLICAL INSIGHTS

"Why then," they asked, "did Moses command that a man give his wife a certificate of divorce and send her away?" Jesus replied, "Moses permitted you to divorce your wives because your hearts were hard. But it was not this way from the beginning."

Matthew 19:7–8

In God's perfect plan, divorce was never intended. God created marriage as a covenant between one man and one woman—for life (see Gen. 2:24). In the Old Testament law, God did allow divorce, but only because of the people's hard, self-absorbed hearts. Divorce is permitted under certain circumstances, but marriage vows should not be taken lightly.

Marriage is not just a contract. It is a picture of Jesus's relationship with His bride, the church. As such, God would have couples do their best—with His help—to seek reconciliation and work through their problems, rather than viewing divorce as an easy out. In situations where divorce does occur, God's compassionate and unconditional love can heal even the deepest wounds, but significant consequences still exist.

But I tell you that anyone who divorces his wife, except for marital unfaithfulness, causes her to become an adulteress, and anyone who marries the divorced woman commits adultery.

Matthew 5:32

But if the unbeliever leaves, let him do so. A believing man or woman is not bound in such circumstances; God has called us to live in peace.

1 Corinthians 7:15

In today's individualistic culture, many women view divorce as a quick fix to marital problems—ditch the guy and start over again. However, Jesus's teachings make it clear that the grounds for justifiable divorce are only marital unfaithfulness (clear sexual sin) or abandonment.

God takes marriage seriously. He desires marriages to last. Because sin has infected all relationships, however, some marriages do not survive. The Bible does not give people an easy way out of their commitments, but when there is no hope of reconciliation, God offers hope and healing. As a woman, your identity is defined by Jesus Christ, not your marital status.

"But I will restore you to health and heal your wounds," declares the LORD, "because you are called an outcast."

Jeremiah 30:17

A bruised reed he will not break, and a smoldering wick he will not snuff out. In faithfulness he will bring forth justice.

Isaiah 42:3

No pain is too great for Jesus Christ to heal, including the pain of a broken marriage. The Bible is replete with promises of unconditional love and faithfulness. Tragically, many times divorced women feel like outcasts in the Christian community, which is the direct opposite of God's heart.

God does not see divorced women as "less than." The Christian gospel is a message of *grace*, and that grace is always extended *in spite of* our weaknesses and failures—not because of our good works. God weeps over the pain, betrayal, and injustice that divorced women experience, and He longs for every single one of His daughters to experience healing and grace in the body of Christ.

7 PRAYER STARTER

Lord, we know that You hate divorce because it can destroy the picture of Your relationship with us. You hate how it tears apart families, how it hurts women, how it destroys the intimacy and love You created. And yet, God, we live in a messed-up, sinful world. We want Your will, Lord. _____ desperately needs Your wisdom. She is hurting, Lord, and her trust in You doesn't make the pain magically go away. Guide her in Your truth. Give her clarity to make God-honoring decisions and get the help she needs. Protect her, Lord, and bring her through this struggle by Your power . . .

8 RECOMMENDED RESOURCES

Carder, Dave. *Torn Asunder: Recovering from an Extramarital Affair*, 3rd ed. Moody, 2008.

Carter, Les. *Grace and Divorce: God's Healing Gift to Those Whose Marriages Fall Short*. Jossey-Bass, 2004.

Clarke, David, and William Clarke. *I Don't Want a Divorce: A 90-Day Guide to Saving Your Marriage*. Revell, 2009.

Clayton, Brenda. *Desperate Wives: Help and Hope for Women Considering Separation or Divorce*. Beacon Hill, 2005.

Clinton, Tim. *Before a Bad Good-bye*. Thomas Nelson, 1999.

Hawkins, David. *Living beyond a Broken Marriage*. Revell, 2008.

Kniskern, Joseph. *When the Vow Breaks: A Survival and Recovery Guide for Christians Facing Divorce*. B&H, 2008.

Leonard, Kathy. *Divorce Care: Hope, Help and Healing during and after Your Divorce*. Thomas Nelson, 2005.

Smoke, Jim. *Growing through Divorce*. Harvest House, 2007.

West, Karrie, and Noelle Quinn. *When He Leaves: Help and Hope for Hurting Wives*. Harvest House, 2005.

Drug and Alcohol Addiction

- For fourteen years Peggy was a heavy drinker and a regular illegal drug user. She never thought of herself this way, though. She was a successful businesswoman with a large, expensive house, a classy car, and three young children. But not a day went by when Peggy didn't inject herself with heroin and drink at least a few beers. *It's just a little bit*, Peggy rationalized. *I need it to relax.* Looking back now, she sees things differently: "I had a nice car; my kids were in private school; I looked all right. Problem was, I was dying."

- Brittany struggled with severe pain as a daily reality. The doctors couldn't find a cause for her migraines, so they prescribed her several strong medications to manage the pain. While the medications worked for the pain, they also were very addictive, so addictive that Brittany would often go to the ER just to get more meds. Frequently she took three to four times the suggested dosage. Prescription drugs helped her cope, forget the pain—and everything else in her life. Brittany's friends knew something was wrong but they weren't sure what.

- Sarah's husband kept telling her that she had to quit smoking for the sake of their family and her health. She knew he was right and promised she would stop—and she really did try. But each time she tried, she felt as though she were going to die. So she gave up trying. Now she keeps the cigarettes in her car and sprays her clothes down with a deodorizer before arriving home each day. *As long as no one knows, I'm okay*, Sarah thought. *At least I'm not drinking all the time, like some of my co-workers.*

- An *addiction* is a *dependence on a substance* (alcohol, cigarettes, prescription medicine, marijuana, or street drugs) *or activity* (gambling, shopping).

- An *addiction* is *a physical* (as in alcohol or most other drugs) or *psychological* (as in gambling or shopping) *compulsion to use a substance or activity to cope with everyday life*. For example, without alcohol, the alcoholic does not feel "normal" and cannot function well.

- An *addiction* is a *behavior that is habitual and difficult or seemingly impossible to control*. It leads to activity that is designed solely to obtain the substance or cover up its use—the housewife hiding bottles all over the house, the drug addict shoplifting to support the habit, the gambler embezzling to pay off debts.

- *Drug addiction is the biochemical dependence on a substance.* Over time the body needs the substance in ever-increasing amounts to stave off the symptoms of withdrawal.

- *Alcohol addiction*, better known as *alcoholism*, involves *regular, heavy use of alcohol as a part of everyday life.* Alcoholism is the number one drug problem in America. Statistics show that fifteen million Americans are dependent on alcohol.[1]

- Alcohol can be described as the "*gateway drug*," because many women who start out with alcohol *eventually progress to illegal drug use.* Ninety percent of cocaine users smoked, drank, or used marijuana before trying cocaine.[2]

- Characterized by the *defense mechanisms of denial, minimization, and blame-shifting*, the addict blames her problems on someone else or some difficult situation—the boss is too demanding, the job is too stressful, the spouse isn't affectionate enough, the kids are disobedient, or the friends are too persuasive. *The addict usually refuses to take responsibility or admit to the seriousness of the problem.*

- Many counselors assume that drug and alcohol addiction is *primarily a male problem, but this is simply not the case.* Research shows that 16 percent of women in America have used illegal drugs.[3] Nine million women in the United States consume illegal drugs every year.[4] An estimated four million women in the United States drink so that it threatens their health and safety.[5]

Key Characteristics

There are several *key characteristics of addictions*:

- patterns of out-of-control substance usage or behavior for a year or more
- mood swings
- increasing usage or pattern of behavior over time
- increasing feelings of shame or worthlessness
- obsessing over a certain substance or behavior
- increasing unmanageability of the addiction
- increasing guilt, shame, fear, and anger
- failed efforts to control the addiction
- negative consequences of the addiction suffered by self and others

Causes of Drug and Alcohol Addiction

- Some *common triggers* for drug and alcohol abuse are the *death of a loved one, divorce, or physical pain.*
- Many people turn to substance abuse to "medicate the pain" when struggling with *challenging emotional issues like depression or anxiety.*

- Drug and/or alcohol addiction is not just an addiction. The American Medical Association classifies these addictions as a *disease* that *alters the chemical makeup of the brain and the flow of chemicals, such as dopamine.*
- *Genetics* can influence addictive behavior.
- An individual's *personality* may affect her likelihood of drinking. Women who are under *high levels of stress* may drink to help drown out their problems. A woman who is *shy, depressed, or anxious* may turn to alcohol for what may seem like a confidence boost.

Effects of Drug and Alcohol Addiction

- *Physical effects*: brain damage, severe liver damage, changes in blood cells, blood clotting, weight gain, fetal alcohol syndrome when pregnant, alcohol poisoning, and depressed immune system
- *Emotional effects*: psychiatric disorders (for example, depression or anxiety), problems in relationships, and guilt

ASSESSMENT INTERVIEW 3

Remember that a key characteristic of addiction is denial. According to the client, the substance use is usually "not an issue." Understanding the extent of denial is part of your job in assessment (if it already seems clear that dependency exists).

When interviewing the user, focus on asking concrete questions about her circumstances, events, and symptoms. If asked in a nonthreatening and nonjudgmental way, she should respond fairly honestly. When speaking with a family member, reframe the following questions and ask them about the user.

Rule Outs

1. Has your substance use increased or decreased over the years? Has there ever been a time when you did not use substances? (*Tolerance, or the need for increased amounts of the substance, is a key distinguishing factor between a substance abuse and dependency. You also want to assess strengths, including support system, treatments that have helped, and family dynamics.*)
2. (*If alcohol is the substance*) Have you ever experienced a time when you did not remember what you did while you were drinking (you had a blackout)? Have you ever experienced anxiety, panic attacks, shakes, or hallucinations after not drinking for a while?
3. Have you ever been treated for an addiction or been in counseling for any other reason? (*This is to assess severity and the success or failure of prior treatment, as well as to assess for any prior mental disorder.*)
4. Has anyone in your family ever been hurt by your using or said anything to you about your using? Is your husband threatening to leave you? Are you in

any legal trouble as a result of your using? (*This is to assess the need for family help, crisis intervention, or legal referral.*)

General Questions

1. Has anyone ever suggested that your use of drugs or alcohol is a problem?
2. Have you been concerned about your use of drugs or alcohol?
3. How often do you consume this substance and how much at each use?
4. Do you ever try to hide your use from family and friends, or are they aware?
5. At what age did you start using the substance?
6. Have you ever done anything while under the influence of this substance that you later regretted?
7. Did anyone in your family of origin use a substance in excess while you were growing up?
8. Has your use of this substance ever affected your job or your family? What happened?
9. Have you ever tried to quit before? What happened when you did? How did you feel?
10. How do you think your life will be different if you stop using this substance?

4 : WISE COUNSEL

Safety is always a key issue when counseling for substance abuse. Try to find out if the woman has been driving under the influence or has small children at home who might be endangered. If so, *take immediate steps to protect all individuals involved.*

If possible, *speak with other family members* who are old enough to understand how to handle the user's behaviors, in particular, driving under the influence. Family members must learn to say no to rides with the woman when she is under the influence and to get help if children are being abused or neglected.

If there is *any fear of harm or abuse*, encourage family members to go to a relative's home or a shelter and report the behavior to appropriate authorities. If *verbal abuse* is an issue when the user is under the influence, encourage family members to seek counseling, especially counseling or group sessions for family members of addicts.

5 : ACTION STEPS

1. Sign a Contract and Seek Out Accountability

- If you truly desire change, you must be willing to take definite actions to remove yourself from situations where drugs or alcohol are present. Talk to your counselor about how this would work in your life. For example, it might mean letting go of certain friendships, getting all of the drugs and alcohol out of your house, or enrolling yourself in rehab.

- Sign a contract with your counselor stating what you agree to do—stop using alcohol and drugs and get immediate help for the addiction, or at least agree not to use substances until your next counseling meeting.
- Seek out and attend some type of Christian recovery program or a local AA gathering. Get a sponsor—an accountability partner. Don't try to fight this addiction on your own.

2. Take Responsibility for Your Behavior

- You are not a victim of your behavior. Left untreated, an addiction can destroy your life, but you have the choice to get help. Drug and alcohol use have definite consequences—even the possibility of your own or others' injury or death.
- Talk to your counselor about putting accountability measures in place to protect yourself against operating a vehicle under the influence of drugs or alcohol. (*This means a responsible adult in the counselee's life will take the keys to the vehicle if she drinks or uses drugs. It would be a good idea for the plan to be signed by both the counselor and the client to enhance accountability and participation.*) This sets a clear boundary regarding substance abuse and imitates what will happen if a DUI citation is imposed or you are caught with illegal drugs in your possession.

3. Get Professional Help

- Make an appointment with a counselor specializing in chemical dependency to assess whether the substance use is an addiction. Such assessments are available at community mental health agencies, some hospitals, and community substance abuse centers (*common in urban and suburban areas and through county governments in many rural areas*).
- A medical exam will determine any medical problems caused by use of the substance. An addiction such as alcoholism in its late stages progresses to a diseased state, so treatment from a doctor is certainly recommended.
- A physician can also prescribe any medicine that may be helpful in maintaining sobriety, especially when a dual disorder is involved.
- A professional counselor can also be very helpful in assessing and treating an addiction. Depending on the severity of your addiction, consider enrolling in rehab, so you can get the help you need to recover fully.

BIBLICAL INSIGHTS 6

Woe to those who rise early in the morning to run after their drinks, who stay up late at night till they are inflamed with wine.

Isaiah 5:11

Many alcoholics are so dependent on alcohol that they begin early in the morning and continue drinking until late at night. The tragedy of addiction is that it influences and dominates the desires and choices of the addicted. The even greater tragedy is that addicted people reject the Lord's work in their lives.

Alcohol and drug use is a bondage and it never satisfies. The feelings of euphoria and pleasure are short-lived and fading, and the body always craves more. God alone can provide the lasting comfort, joy, and relief that people mistakenly seek in alcohol. No mind-altering substance, regardless of how powerful, can ultimately satisfy the needs of a woman's soul.

Be self-controlled and alert. Your enemy the devil prowls around like a roaring lion looking for someone to devour.

1 Peter 5:8

Addictions are powerful enemies that Satan uses to enslave us and damage our relationship with God. Whether the addiction is to alcohol, drugs, sex, pornography, gambling, web-surfing, shopping, or busyness, addicted women can attest to their apparent inability to control their desires.

Usually addictions begin subtly—an experience or a substance that brings pleasure begins to take over and become an obsessive drive. Eventually, the obsession takes control, and in the process of trying to gain pleasure, a woman may damage herself, as well as her relationships with family and friends.

Addictions destroy individuals, families, friendships, reputations, and careers. Rarely can a woman escape addiction without some form of intervention.

No temptation has seized you except what is common to man. And God is faithful; he will not let you be tempted beyond what you can bear. But when you are tempted, he will also provide a way out so that you can stand up under it.

1 Corinthians 10:13

As Christians, we have the Holy Spirit living inside of us. No sin—even the power of addiction—is stronger than the power of God, the same power that raised Jesus from the dead. Addiction is a sin, and just like any other sin, it is covered in the blood of Jesus Christ. However, addictions are so powerful because they make us dependent on another substance rather than God for our feelings of happiness, security, and enjoyment.

Breaking free from addiction doesn't happen overnight, but God's Word promises that God is faithful and that He will strengthen us to resist temptation if we call out to Him for help and grace. God desires for us to live free—slaves to no one and nothing—except Himself. He will walk with us every step of the way in our recovery from addiction. With Him, all things are possible.

7 PRAYER STARTER

Dear Lord, thank You that _____ has come here today to seek help for an addiction. Please help her be open to considering that this might be a true addiction for which she needs to get practical day-to-day help. Lead us by Your Holy Spirit to the resources that will be most helpful, and thank You for Your willingness to forgive and heal even addiction . . .

RECOMMENDED RESOURCES 8

Anderson, Neil T. *Freedom from Addictions: Breaking the Bondage of Addictions and Finding Freedom in Christ.* Gospel Light, 1996.

Clinton, Tim. *Turn Your Life Around.* Faith Words, 2006.

Clinton, Tim, Archibald Hart, and George Ohlschlager. *Caring for People God's Way.* Thomas Nelson, 2006; see the chapter on addictions.

Hart, Archibald D. *Healing Life's Hidden Addictions: Overcoming the Closet Compulsions That Waste Time and Control Your Life.* Crossway, 1991.

May, Gerald. *Addiction and Grace: Love and Spirituality in the Healing of Addiction.* Harper One, 2006.

Moore, Beth. *Breaking Free: Discover the Victory of Total Surrender.* B&H, 2007.

VanVonderen, Jeff. *Good News for the Chemically Dependent and Those Who Love Them.* Bethany House, 2004.

Welch, Edward. *Crossroads: A Step by Step Guide Away from Addiction.* New Growth, 2009.

Eating Disorders

1 PORTRAITS

- Sara hated exercising, but she really wanted to lose weight. Her friend suggested she start taking laxatives after her meals. When she started to shed unwanted pounds, she began to feel more confident about herself, but issues that developed with her bowel system started to worry her, so she resorted to throwing up whenever she felt full. Now it has become a daily routine, and Sara can hardly hold a meal down.

- Emma wanted to lose a couple of pounds so she started to count her calorie intake and to exercise every day. As she began to see results, she became increasingly obsessed with her routine, going to the gym two or three times a day. Daily she decreased her calorie count and increased her workout time, seeing how long she could go without eating anything but salads. Emma is addicted to exercise and she gains huge satisfaction from depriving herself of food. "It's all gonna be worth it, the aching muscles, the hunger pangs . . ." she says, but what Emma doesn't realize is that she's already underweight.

- Nancy hated looking in the mirror, because all she saw was a fat, ugly pig. It didn't help that she lived at the beach and constantly saw bikini-clad women. Nancy loved food and couldn't help but indulge—not only at meals but also in between. Sometimes Nancy eats several cartons of ice cream at a time. After she eats, she is overcome by guilt and the desire to be in control. As a result, she forces herself to vomit.

2 DEFINITIONS AND KEY THOUGHTS

- Women with *eating disorders* are characterized by a primary *obsession with food* (either eating a lot or not eating enough) *and compulsive behaviors related to eating.* These behaviors may be a *misdirected attempt to gain control and deal with anxiety and stress.*

- Compulsive overeating and milder forms of obsession with food or weight can also be considered eating disorders if the practices produce *unhealthy and obsessive behaviors* and/or altered thought processes or body image.

- In the United States it is estimated that *as many as ten million females struggle with anorexia or bulimia,* while many women also struggle with unhealthy binge-

114

ing.[1] Statistics show that one in five women is currently struggling with an eating disorder.[2]

- Often eating disorders result from *an unhealthy self-image*, which is perpetuated by the media. Research shows that more than 80 percent of American women are dissatisfied with their body.[3] *In fact, two out of five women would trade three to five years of their life to obtain their goal body weight.*[4]

- Estimates indicate that *one out of every three women will have an eating disorder–related problem at some time in her life.* Between 1988 and 1993, the incidence of bulimia in ten- to thirty-nine-year-old females tripled.[5]

- Eating disorders are especially *prevalent among young women.* Ninety percent of females with eating disorders are between ages twelve and twenty-five.[6] One study reports that "one out of every four college-aged women uses unhealthy methods of weight control—including fasting, skipping meals, excessive exercise, laxative abuse, and self-induced vomiting."[7]

- Of all mental disorders, *eating disorders have the highest mortality rate.* In women ages fifteen to twenty-four years old, the annual death rate for anorexia alone is twelve times higher than any other cause of death.[8]

- Because of the shame and secretiveness associated with eating disorders, *the vast majority of women do not get the help they need.* Statistics show that only 6 percent of people with bulimia receive mental health care. And only one-third of people with anorexia receive mental health care.[9]

Anorexia Nervosa

- *Anorexia nervosa* is a psychological disorder "characterized especially by a pathological fear of weight gain leading to faulty eating patterns, malnutrition, and usually excessive weight loss."[10] Women suffering from anorexia nervosa *starve themselves to feel thin.*

- Even when weighing twenty to thirty pounds below the lowest recommended weight for their age and height, women suffering from anorexia *still believe they are fat. Their body image is extremely distorted.*

- Anorexics consider hunger pangs to be good—evidence of their success at weight loss. They *obsess over what they eat and how much they exercise.*

- Research indicates that as many as 20 percent of anorexics *die of starvation.* According to one estimate, "5–10 percent of anorexics die within ten years of onset, 18–20 percent die within twenty years of onset, and only 50 percent report ever being cured."[11]

- Most anorexics are *girls between the ages of fourteen and eighteen.* A symptom of the disorder is that *they stop menstruating* or never start.

- Many anorexics come from homes where their parents held them to *high or perfectionist standards*, which they were successful in meeting early in life. They may resort to anorexia where standards become unclear.

- *The attempt at perfectionism is fueled by several fears:*

115

— fear of fat

— fear of failure

— fear of being less than perfect

— fear of rejection

— fear of losing control

- Eventually, *the only thing a woman feels she can control* is her eating—to the point that what she is controlling begins to control her.

Bulimia Nervosa

- *Bulimics* (those with *bulimia nervosa*) *binge on high-calorie, fatty, and/or sweet foods*, secretively eating hundreds or thousands of calories in one sitting. Afterward, to counteract the effect of eating, they *self-induce vomiting, overdose on laxatives, or exercise excessively.*
- Bulimia tends to occur most often in girls in *late adolescence*, such as the last years of high school and early college.
- Bulimia can lead to complications related to *electrolyte imbalances and destruction of tooth enamel.*
- Bulimics may be of *normal weight.* Though they are worried about fat, *they do not suffer from severe distortion of body image that plagues those with anorexia.*
- They are not usually particularly thin, yet, like anorexics, they are *obsessed with food and fat.*
- While anorexics feel they are right about their extreme diets, bulimics *know that bingeing and purging are not normal.*

Common Barriers to Treatment

In most cases there are *multiple barriers that keep women from receiving the proper treatment* for an eating disorder.

- *Access.* Sometimes finding treatment from someone who specializes in eating disorders is difficult.
- *Considering it an act of will.* There are emotional, spiritual, and interpersonal complexities involved in the healing of eating disorders. *Women with an eating disorder cannot simply "will themselves" out of it.*
- *Denial.* Frequently women with an eating disorder have *distorted body images* and may deny the level of harm they inflict on themselves.
- *Fear of treatment.* Treatment involves discomfort and facing pain and hurt and it can be a difficult and frightening process. This prevents some women with eating disorders from seeking treatment.
- *Financial barriers.* Unfortunately many treatment options for eating disorders are expensive.

- *Idols.* With eating disorders, food is not about sustenance; it is *preoccupation* and *obsession* similar to idolization. A disordered woman's world and priorities revolve around food.

- *Lack of faith.* Women with eating disorders may have lost hope that any counselor or treatment can overcome their addiction.

- *Minimizing the problem.* Many women deny treatment because they minimize the grasp the problem has on their lives, and they believe it might go away on its own.

- *Pride.* It's not easy to admit to self, others, and God that something is out of control.

- *Shame and guilt.* Secrecy and shame may shroud eating disorders for long periods of time. It is *very hard* to admit that there is a problem. *It is embarrassing to admit to not eating or bingeing and vomiting.*

Warning Signs

- secretive behavior coupled with trips to the bathroom after eating
- laxative or diuretic abuse
- heart palpitations
- depression
- social withdrawal
- restrictive dieting
- frequent and obvious weight fluctuations
- preoccupation with body weight and appearance

ASSESSMENT INTERVIEW 3

First, *rule out immediate medical problems.* Then ask the following questions. Your questions need to be probing but nonjudgmental, keeping in mind that a woman with an eating disorder is probably in denial about the severity of her behavior.

1. Tell me a little bit about your eating habits. Are you more prone to overeat or eat too little?
2. What do you weigh? (*If her weight is 10 percent below the lowest recommended weight for her age and height, she should be taken to a doctor for a thorough medical exam. Medical condition is always a significant concern for those with eating disorders.*)
3. If you greatly restrict your calorie intake or binge and purge by vomiting, how long has this been going on? What led to this behavior pattern? (*If she has done this frequently, she should have medical and dental exams to check for health complications.*)
4. What advantage does weight loss (through starvation or purging) afford you? How does it make you feel about yourself?

5. What disadvantages have you seen from these actions? Have you seen any changes in your health as a result?
6. How do stress and anxiety influence your eating habits?
7. When you look in the mirror, how do you see yourself? Have your eating habits changed this?
8. Has anyone ever told you that you are beautiful or ugly or fat? Who and when?
9. How do feelings of helplessness and control influence your attitude toward food?
10. What were meals like when you were growing up? Did your family ever eat together? Was it a pleasant or tense environment? Did your parents force you to clean your plate? Did you snack often?
11. What change would you like to see in your eating habits and lifestyle? Have you tried to stop bingeing and purging or starving yourself before? What happened as a result?

4 : WISE COUNSEL

Eating disorders can be *very complicated and even life-threatening*. If a woman's eating habits are damaging her health, *do not attempt to treat her on your own*. When an eating disorder is controlling and endangering a woman's life or well-being, she needs to be *under the direct care of a physician, in the hospital, or in some type of intensive treatment program*. The most effective programs use a collaborative treatment approach using medical, nutritional, and counseling professionals. If a woman is dangerously malnourished, suffering from medical complications, or showing signs of severe depression or suicide, she needs *to be hospitalized*.

Watch for evidence *of suicidal feelings* and get help immediately if you see signs. If the behavior has gone on for some time, *seek the assistance of a professional* who is a specialist in eating disorders. Women with anorexia seem to respond well to family therapy, while those with bulimia tend to do well in group counseling. The woman's health will *continue to be compromised* until she gets help.

Most eating disorders are *not ultimately about food*. Women binge, purge, starve themselves, or exercise excessively as a way of self-medicating their emotional pain and insecurity. At the root of the issue, *eating disorders are about control*. While setting up a plan for healthy eating and regular accountability can be helpful, merely changing eating habits is rarely successful in overcoming an eating disorder. *Issues of low self-esteem, insecurity, past abuse, and a woman's relationship with her father* need to be addressed for her to truly heal. Eating disorders are challenging but *not impossible* to overcome.

ACTION STEPS : 5

1. Enlist the Help of a Doctor and Dietitian

- Recovering from an eating disorder does not happen overnight. It requires openness, accountability, and the willingness to get professional help. Your will power is not strong enough to fight your body's urges and cravings on your own.
- Have a thorough medical examination to assess for any health complications as a result of your eating behaviors. Get a referral to a dietitian or nutritional consultant to assess your current diet and to develop a balanced plan of eating.

2. Identify a Target Weight

- Women with an eating disorder are usually obsessed with losing weight, but extreme weight loss can jeopardize your health. It is important to identify an ideal weight and a target weight. Ideal weight refers to the best weight for a woman when her height and body type are taken into account. The body mass index (BMI) is the most accurate measure to determine healthy weight guidelines.
- A target weight is described as your lowest safe weight. Target weight is calculated as 90 percent of the midpoint of the ideal weight. Talk to your doctor or dietitian, make an agreement about weight-loss goals, and stick to it.

3. Develop Strategies for Fighting Your Urges

- Overcoming an eating disorder isn't just about changing what you eat. It requires changing how you view food. Many women use food (or food deprivation) as a way to cope with stress, anxiety, and uncertainty and to gain some type of control in their lives.
- Evaluate the role of food in your life and identify what triggers your starving or bingeing behavior. Identify the situations that aggravate unhealthy eating behaviors. Chances are, some kind of anxiety or stress influences your decisions and behavior toward food.
- Take your focus off food and eating. *Unless the woman is in immediate danger of starvation or electrolyte problems, examine what weight loss means to her, what eating stands for, and what she fears most about eating.*
- Consider other ways of dealing with stress and anxiety, rather than turning to food. Many women must physically remove themselves from the presence of food and go for a drive, a run, or pick up the phone and call a friend when the urge to binge comes. Women who starve themselves must intentionally sit down for three meals a day and actually eat, rather than using the excuses of "I'm too busy" or "I'm not hungry."

4. Accept Yourself the Way You Are

- A common theme, especially among anorexic women, is the tendency toward perfectionism. Examine your view of beauty, fitness, and health. Chances are, you have a perfectionist mind-set, and can't accept your body as it is. While there is nothing wrong with watching your diet and wanting to look good, an eating disorder takes these desires to an extreme, leading women to destroy their health, trying to look like a movie star.

- Do some research on the media and beauty in today's culture. As you do, you will see a vast disproportion between healthy weight and the weight of today's models. For example, the average American woman is 5'4" and weighs 140 pounds, whereas the average American model is 5'11" and weighs 117 pounds. That makes most fashion models thinner than 98 percent of Americans.[12]

- Read Psalm 139 and meditate on what it says about how God views you. God knit you together in your mother's womb and He made you beautiful. Accept yourself the way God made you—the way you are. You don't have to look like a model to be beautiful. In fact, if you try to copy the way models look, you will most likely destroy your health.

- Journaling can be a very effective way to express a lot of what is happening on the inside and the patterns in your everyday life. It can also be a valuable tool to gauge changes in thoughts and behavior.

6 BIBLICAL INSIGHTS

The rabble with them began to crave other food, and again the Israelites started wailing and said, "If only we had meat to eat! We remember the fish we ate in Egypt at no cost—also the cucumbers, melons, leeks, onions and garlic. But now we have lost our appetite; we never see anything but this manna!"

Numbers 11:4–6

Preoccupation with food (or fear of food) can indicate an eating disorder. When women become overly focused on food, their dependence on God suffers. Food, which God graciously provides for health and sustenance, can become an idol and a bondage.

The Israelites, while not suffering from an eating disorder, did experience a "perspective disorder" because of their focus on food. Their preoccupation on foods they did not have caused them to lose sight of God's miraculous and loving provision of manna.

When women become preoccupied with anything other than God, they can lose their perspective of God's care for them. Women with eating disorders need to refocus on their worth in God's eyes and be thankful for God's provision, rather than letting food control them.

So I say, live by the Spirit, and you will not gratify the desires of the sinful nature.

Galatians 5:16

A woman who lives with the daily reality of an eating disorder—whether it is an addiction to food or an obsession to go without it—understands the power of that addiction. Many women find themselves trapped in emotional eating, leading to such problems as obesity and bulimia.

There must be a balance between enjoying what God has provided and using food to meet emotional needs and thus allowing it to control one's life. Self-control, a fruit of the Spirit, applies to many areas of life, including eating. God alone can fill the emptiness of a woman's heart, while no amount of food (or feelings of control from starving oneself) can.

Only the power of the Holy Spirit can help a woman overcome unhealthy eating patterns.

Whether you eat or drink or whatever you do, do it all for the glory of God.

1 Corinthians 10:31

Food isn't the problem. Food is a blessing and gift from God; without it, we could not exist. God provided food to sustain the animals and people He created. A food obsession takes the focus off God and puts it on one's food or stomach—both of which will eventually no longer be needed.

The purpose of our lives as God's children is to glorify Him. This passage points out that, even in eating, we can glorify God by taking care of our bodies, which are the temple of His Spirit. As you make choices about what you will and will not eat, ask God to give you wisdom. You may feel helpless to change your eating habits, but remember, God delights in showing His strength through your weakness. Your healing can bring glory to Him.

PRAYER STARTER 7

Dear Lord, I thank You that _____ is seeking help. Please help her be honest with herself and know that she is loved. Set her free, God, from this unhealthy, destructive obsession with food. Give her wisdom and a spirit of humility as she seeks out professional help. Thank You, Lord, that there is nothing too hard for You. Be with her every step of the way to healing. Change her heart and mind and let her be controlled by Your Spirit, not by the urges of her body . . .

RECOMMENDED RESOURCES 8

Alcorn, Nancy. *Starved: Mercy for Eating Disorders*. WinePress, 2007.
Costin, Carolyn. *The Eating Disorder Sourcebook*. 3rd ed. McGraw-Hill, 2006.

Davidson, Kimberly. *I'm Beautiful? Why Can't I See It? Daily Encouragement to Promote Healthy Eating and Positive Self-Esteem.* Tate Publishing, 2006.

Dillinger, Jesse. *Reasonably Thin.* Thomas Nelson, 1998.

Jantz, Gregory L. *Hope, Help, and Healing for Eating Disorders: A New Approach to Treating Anorexia, Bulimia, and Overeating.* Shaw Books, 2002.

Organizations

Gürze Books specializes in eating disorder publications (800-756-7533 or www. bulimia.com).

Remuda Ranch provides inpatient and residential programs for women, girls, and boys suffering from anorexia, bulimia, other eating disorders, and related issues. Their Christian programs offer hope and healing to patients of all beliefs (800-445-1900 or www.remudaranch.com).

Emotional Abuse

- "Don't you get cocky with me, you lazy, good for nothin' witch." Mary Beth cowered as these hateful words flew out of her boyfriend Matt's mouth. She and Matt fought a lot, and Matt was convinced he was always right. Sometimes Mary Beth thought about breaking up with Matt but she was terribly afraid of being alone. And Matt told her she couldn't last a day without him there. *Maybe what he says is actually true*, she thinks.

- Growing up, Debbie was taught that a woman's role is to submit to a man—no matter what. Debbie works as an assistant to Steve, a company executive. Steve is very driven and overbearing by nature, and he requires Debbie to come in on weekends, babysit his kids, and do the work of several employees. Despite Debbie's best efforts, however, Steve is always cutting her down. "C'mon, Debbie, get with the program here. I'm counting on you." Debbie hates her job and her life but doesn't see a way out.

- Susan's husband, Tim, is very controlling—checking the mileage on her car, giving her money for only three gallons of gas at a time, forbidding her to spend time with friends, and forcing her to stay home and serve him 24-7. He made her quit the job she loved two years ago to help him with his remodeling business. He constantly belittles her in front of the kids and recently he made her work through the night to get a job done. Susan is burning out physically and she wonders where to draw the line of personal respect.

DEFINITIONS AND KEY THOUGHTS 2

- *Emotional abuse*, also known as *psychological maltreatment*, is the *debasement of a person's feelings that causes him or her to perceive self as inept, not cared for, and worthless.*

- Emotional abuse is the systematic tearing down of another human being by *rejecting, ignoring, terrorizing, isolating, or corrupting* him or her. It is the use of emotional power to *control, manipulate, or intimidate another.*

- Emotional abuse is more subtle than other forms of abuse but no less damaging. *Though there may be no physical bruises, such abuse results in heart wounds that do not easily heal.*

- Often emotional abuse *accompanies physical and/or verbal abuse*. Persistent patterns of treating a child or spouse as if he or she were *nonexistent or invisible, while blocking the victim from outside contact with other human beings, has a debilitating effect* on a person—crushing identity, destroying self-esteem, and making the person into little more than a slave.

- Statistics are hard to find on emotional abuse, because many instances of abuse go unreported. Especially in Christian circles, *some women are taught that being controlled, manipulated, and intimidated is what biblical submission means*. In reality, nothing could be further from the truth.

- Research shows that *more women experience emotional abuse than physical abuse*. It is estimated that more than one in three women (35 percent) who have been in a long-term relationship or marriage have been emotionally abused.[1]

- In one study of a thousand women fifteen years of age or older, 36 percent had experienced *emotional abuse while growing up*, 43 percent had experienced *some form of abuse as children or adolescents*, and 39 percent reported experiencing *emotional abuse in a relationship* in the past five years.[2]

- *Emotional abuse is prevalent in dating/cohabitation relationships*. The United States Department of Justice reports that three in ten college women have been injured emotionally or psychologically while being stalked.[3]

- *Emotionally abusive relationships are very hard to get out of*, because it's not uncommon for the abuser to apologize after an episode of abuse and promise to "do better," with very little real follow-through. Usually an emotionally abused woman leaves her partner an average of five times before ending the relationship.[4]

Physical Consequences

- Contrary to the old adage, "Sticks and stones may break my bones, but words will never hurt me," words *really do* hurt. Emotional abuse takes a toll on any woman who has been abused. Although emotional abuse has more psychological consequences than physical, there are still *possible physical consequences* that may be experienced.

- Women who have experienced emotional abuse tend to *lack self-confidence, a personal identity, and the ability to function on their own*, especially later on down the road, if they were abused as children.

- These women may be *overly obliging and kind*. They will do anything for anyone and tend to let themselves be treated like a doormat, which greatly heightens the likelihood of physical or sexual abuse in the future.

Psychological Consequences

- Those who have suffered from the emotional and verbal abuse of another person can develop *depression, suicidal thoughts, post-traumatic stress disorder, cutting, and alcoholism or drug abuse*.

- Persistent emotional abuse often leads a woman to develop unhealthy coping mechanisms that involve withdrawal from other people to survive and be safe. *A woman builds up walls to protect herself, and as a result, has a hard time trusting or being vulnerable with anyone.*

- The closer the individual is to the abuser, the harsher the consequences tend to wear on the abused individual. Emotional abuse causes inner damage that *demolishes self-esteem and self-confidence, leading a woman to live in insecurity and fear.*

- Emotional abuse is damaging because it tears down a person. As Proverbs 18:21 puts it, "The tongue has the power of life and death." *In God's perfect plan, close, intimate relationships are a critical means of encouragement, support, and identity building.* When a parent, spouse, sibling, teacher, employer, or close friend engages in emotional abuse, he or she robs a woman of the safe, intimate, loving relationships God intended.

ASSESSMENT INTERVIEW 3

Assess for the *type of perpetrated abuse*—its degree and its history. Sometimes a woman is *seeking help for other problems* that actually stem from emotional abuse. You need to get her to talk about the core issue: what's being said and done in her closest relationships. Be careful, however, not to retraumatize the woman with your questions. Trust and safety are of vital importance.

Rule out any *suicidal risk, depression, or medical concerns* (especially if the abuse was recent).

Assume three things in the process of treatment:

- The problem is treatable and your client will be a survivor.
- The client is not responsible for the abuse; she is responsible only for recovery.
- To heal, your client needs to express, accept, and be prepared to deal with her feelings.

1. What specifically happened that has brought you here today?
2. Is this the first time you've sought help?
3. Tell me about your family. How are things at home?
4. Describe the severity and frequency of what you're experiencing. What do you hate most about the abuse?
5. What problems are you currently having as a result of how you have been treated?
6. How do you feel about the way you have been treated? Do you feel responsible?
7. What do you believe about yourself? (*Dig down for unhealthy beliefs that have developed as a result of abuse. For example, what does the person think about herself since she has allowed the abuse to continue?*)
8. What do you believe about the person who continues to emotionally abuse you?
9. Have you ever attempted to stand up for yourself to stop the abuse? What happened?
10. Who else have you told about the abuse you've been experiencing? How did that person respond?

11. Who can help you maintain the boundaries that you set? Who will be your ally?
12. Where do you think God has been in all of this?
13. To heal from this abuse and mistreatment, what do you need?

4 WISE COUNSEL

It has been said that it takes twenty positive statements to counter one negative interaction. Women who have been abused have had their boundaries violated in a horrible way. Emotional abuse is like mutilation of the heart and soul, and tragically, many times a woman eventually comes to view this treatment as normal.

Especially in a romantic relationship or marriage, many women think that fighting is just part of life. The question is not ultimately if conflict happens (because it inevitably will), but *how* a couple handles that conflict. Angry, cruel, and belittling words are not part of a healthy relationship.

Healing from abuse involves *restoration of healthy boundaries and of trust*. The counseling process must be gentle and not contribute to an unintentional rewounding or shaming of the woman. *Follow the woman's lead* in how she tells her story.

Sometimes *feelings of worthlessness* result from the emotional abuse. Many people who have been emotionally abused ask, "What did I do to deserve this?" Reassure her that *the abuse is not her fault*, nor does she deserve it.

5 ACTION STEPS

1. Be Honest with Yourself

- Many victims of emotional abuse live in a state of denial. "He's not that bad." "He was having a rough day." "He was just upset; he didn't really mean it." Stop making excuses for your abuser or yourself and face the reality of the situation.
- Being able to admit how hurt and abused you are is tough. This alone is a huge step in the healing process. For many, it's easier to deny or rationalize the abuse away. Ask the Holy Spirit to show you any abuse present and how it has affected you.
- You may feel that much has been taken from you. Now is the time to tell yourself that you are on the way to healing just by coming to the realization that you have been abused.

2. Tell Your Story

- Silence perpetuates abuse. Find a trusted friend, mentor, pastor, or counselor to talk to. Being believed and being able to express your feelings about how you have been treated in words is vitally important to healing.

- Through God's Spirit and the support of people you trust, you have the power to stand up for yourself when someone is trying to control you or degrade the value of your true worth. You don't have to keep living this way.
- Acknowledging and speaking about abuse requires courage and may bring with it a variety of emotions. You may feel anger, fear, loss, and grief over what has been done to you, as well as a certain freedom because the abuse is no longer a secret.
- Attending a group for survivors of emotional abuse can be an excellent next step.

3. Establish Healthy Boundaries

- Emotional abuse can destroy all personal boundaries and skew your thought patterns so that you begin to view degradation and control as normal. Establishing boundaries may include (1) speaking the truth to the abuser, (2) having the support of others in the Christian community, and/or (3) informed withdrawal from the abuser (informing the abuser and physically removing yourself from interactions with him or her).
- Get godly counsel from a pastor or counselor to begin setting boundaries and standing up for yourself. Be sure that your trusted friends are aware of the boundaries you have established so they can keep you accountable. The last thing you want is to be sucked back into the emotional abuse because it is all that you have ever known.
- Seek professional help and guidance as you deal with emotional baggage and begin changing the way you interact with the abuser. Counseling can help you assess the severity of the situation and ensure your safety as you work for change.
- If the abuser does not honor the boundaries, then other strategies may need to be put in place.

4. Ground Your Life in Jesus

- You may have lost some self-confidence and struggle with feelings of worthlessness but you are not ruined for the future. God can heal you and make you the confident woman He designed you to be. You belong to God. You're His child, His precious possession, and He has not given up on you.
- God invites you to let Him transform your heart and mind (Rom. 12:2). This is a process that takes time and intentionality and it starts with listening to God, not the abuser, and living your life based on the truths of Scripture, not on how you have been treated in the past.

6 | BIBLICAL INSIGHTS

Come to me, all you who are weary and burdened, and I will give you rest. Take my yoke upon you and learn from me, for I am gentle and humble in heart, and you will find rest for your souls.

Matthew 11:28–29

Even in the midst of the pain of emotional abuse, God is present and He longs for His daughters to find hope and healing. God invites you to stop striving, stop working, and just rest in His strong arms.

Many times, an emotionally abused woman reacts against those in positions of authority, even viewing God as a tyrant. But God is not harsh, cruel, and heartless. This passage describes Jesus as "gentle and humble in heart," a safe place to rest. Jesus's love for His daughters is unconditional and He desires to replace the fear, hurt, and pain of emotional abuse with hope, peace, and security. As God's children, we belong to Him, and He will never leave us or forsake us.

He heals the brokenhearted and binds up their wounds.

Psalm 147:3

When God sees His children hurting, He does not just sit back and let us handle things on our own. In the Old Testament, God tells Moses, "I have indeed seen the misery of my people. . . . I have heard them crying out . . . and I am concerned about their suffering" (Exod. 3:7). In the midst of your heartache and emotional pain as a result of the abuse you have experienced, Jesus hears you. He understands you. He knows the deepest aches of your soul.

Jesus longs to bring healing to your heart and remind you of the truth of who you are as His daughter. So don't pretend you're okay. Cry out to Jesus and ask Him to heal you, to bind up your wounds and set you free from the lies you've been told about who you really are.

Be strong and courageous. Do not be afraid or terrified because of them, for the Lord your God goes with you; he will never leave you nor forsake you.

Deuteronomy 31:6

God does not take lightly any abuse or hurt committed against His daughters. If you struggle with the pain of abuse, never forget that God is with you at all times. He is powerful beyond belief and beyond any other person who may try to hurt you. He is just and He will avenge your wrong.

Get help and support so you can take action and set boundaries against those who are hurting you emotionally. Remind yourself often that just because you are labeled something—dumb, ugly, no good—does not make it true. God, not people, defines who you are.

As you get godly counsel and begin to set personal boundaries, do not be afraid. God loves you deeply and He is actively present in your life and situation. His love for you is far stronger than your abuser's desire to degrade you and cut you down.

PRAYER STARTER : 7

We are facing an extremely difficult situation here today, Lord. It is a situation You know about but is now just coming into the light for people whom we know and love. Give us wisdom to handle this situation correctly. Bring healing to this child of Yours who has been used so wrongly . . .

RECOMMENDED RESOURCES : 8

Clinton, Julie. *A Woman's Path to Emotional Freedom*. Harvest House, 2010.

Hegstrom, Paul. *Angry Men and the Women Who Love Them: Breaking the Cycle of Physical and Emotional Abuse*. Beacon Hill, 2004.

Jantz, Gregory, and Ann McMurray. *Healing the Scars of Emotional Abuse*. Revell, 2009.

Meyer, Joyce. *Beauty for Ashes: Receiving Emotional Healing*. FaithWords, 2003.

Omartian, Stormie. *Finding Peace for Your Heart: A Woman's Guide to Emotional Health*. Thomas Nelson, 1999.

Osborn, Susan, Karen Kosman, and Jeenie Gordon. *Wounded by Words: Healing the Invisible Scars of Emotional Abuse*. New Hope, 2008.

Vernick, Leslie. *The Emotionally Destructive Relationship: Seeing It, Stopping It, Surviving It*. Harvest House, 2005.

Envy and Jealousy

1 PORTRAITS

- Jaclyn is a shop-until-you-drop kind of woman. Money doesn't matter to Jaclyn, but looking good does. She spends most of her free time shopping for all the latest styles. Jaclyn can't stand the thought of not being the most fashionable woman in the room. Her husband, Steve, complains that they are never able to get ahead because of Jaclyn's constant spending. Jaclyn doesn't seem to care, however. She feels too important not to be on top of the latest styles and not to look as gorgeous as possible.

- Brittany has advanced education and a successful career. She's smart, talented, and ahead of the game financially but she can't shake the resentment she feels for her best friend, Lindsey, who seems to turn guys' heads without even trying. Lindsey is a natural when it comes to relationships with guys, but Brittany tends to be more shy and introverted. *Why can't I be more like Lindsey?* she wonders.

- Because her father had an affair, Karrie is overcome with fear that her husband, Tim, will leave her for another woman. Karrie is suspicious of any woman who interacts with Tim, whether it's his secretary, a neighbor, or her girlfriend. She feels especially threatened by the women she feels are more attractive than she. Controlling and possessive, Karrie is constantly accusing Tim of being unfaithful. "You're my husband," Karrie threatens. "You shouldn't even be talking to other women."

2 DEFINITIONS AND KEY THOUGHTS

- *Jealousy* and *envy* are two *closely related cousins* that develop from a *toxic mix* of anger, anxiety-based insecurity, and an obsessive habit of comparing oneself with others.

- *Envy* is *desiring what someone else has*, whether relationships, possessions, money, or popularity. This addictive drive is often referred to as "keeping up with the Joneses."

- Left unchecked, *envy can develop into hatred, malice, contempt*, and ultimately, the destruction of precious relationships. When a woman is envious, she resents others' prosperity and success and frequently cuts other people down.

- Envy is always evident in one's *dislike of another person.* Many times the woman who is envious may not consciously be aware that the dislike is prompted by envy.

- Envy is *fueled by the expectation of deserving* more success or recognition than another person. As such, envy is closely linked to pride and greed.

- *Jealousy* stems from the fear that something valuable will be taken away. It may be evidenced in *feelings of insecurity, anxiety, and undue suspicion.* Jealousy is usually rooted in fear—the fear of losing the love or praise of other people.

- Jealousy involves *a triangular relationship.* The jealous person becomes fixated on an (often misperceived) rival, who is viewed as competing for the attention of a third person.

- Scripture says that love is "as strong as death" and will produce jealousy that is "as cruel as the grave" (Song of Sol. 8:6 NKJV). Even in the Christian woman's life, *envy and jealousy are powerful emotions* that have the potential to destroy her relationships.

- Envy and jealousy *stand in direct contrast with love and humility.* It is impossible for a woman to be humble and jealous at the same time. *Unselfish love rejoices over the good of others. Envy seeks to destroy others* with the motive of personal gain.

- Envy and jealousy are ultimately the human heart's *rebellion* against one's own finiteness and God's provision. When women struggle with envy, they reject God's provision for their life. *They stop believing that God is enough* and they refuse to accept the unique woman God created them to be.

Causes of Envy and Jealousy

- *Dissatisfaction with God's provision.* The woman may be focusing on what God *hasn't* provided rather than what God *has* provided.

- *Comparison with others.* From childhood, many women fall prey to the monster of comparison. They define their worth by being smarter, more attractive, and more popular than other women, leading to *insecurity, dissatisfaction, and the need to cut other women down.*

- *Self-absorption.* Envy is driven by the false notion that a woman "deserves" the good life, a life of comfort, happiness, and personal success. When a woman lives this way, *life becomes all about her.*

- *Low self-esteem and seeking significance.* When a woman believes that she is worthless and no-good, she will *constantly try to find significance in her achievements, possessions, and relationships,* rather than finding her deepest needs met in an *intimate relationship with Jesus Christ.*

- *Value of worldly gain.* A woman may be *obsessed* with money, status, appearance, talents, or achievements as evidence of *her value or place in the world.*

Expressions of Envy and Jealousy

- *Resentment toward others.* A woman may be highly critical or judgmental of other people, *belittling and cutting them down.*
- *Competition in relationships.* The *desire to be number one*—the *best* at everything—is often an indicator of envy or jealousy. A woman may exhibit a *drive toward overachievement* and have an *attitude of superiority.*
- *Depression.* A woman may be highly self-critical because she has fallen short of the *unachievable standards she has set for herself.* Often this mind-set leads women into a rut of hopelessness, when life loses its purpose and meaning.
- *Lack of contentment.* American culture bombards women with the lie that material gain will lead to greater personal happiness. Most likely an envious or jealous woman is *not content with what God has provided.*
- *Gossip about others.* A woman concerned with "keeping up with the Joneses" will criticize the object of her envy. Talking negatively about other people *makes her feel better about herself.*

Stages of Envy and Jealousy

The following list summarizes how envy and jealousy develop over time, progressing from an internal desire to a destructive and consuming pattern of behavior.

- *Comparison.* Frequently envy and jealousy develop when a woman compares herself or her possessions, successes, or relationships with other people. The result is *a desire for what someone else has or is.*
- *Scorn or disdain.* When a woman continues to think about and nurture her feelings of envy and jealousy, she begins to *scorn, disdain, and even hate another person*, simply because this man or woman is a constant reminder of what she is lacking. This is expressed in contempt.
- *Malice.* As a root of envy or jealousy grows, feelings of disdain bloom into malice. A woman begins to *desire to destroy the good she sees in another's life.* She believes that if she cannot have what another person has, she will destroy any pleasure the individual has from it.
- *Domination in relationships.* A jealous or envious woman is usually desperate to be in control, so she seeks to dominate every relationship in her life. Some women who have faced abuse or abandonment in their past bring this pathology into their marriage, becoming *domineering, nagging, and suspicious* toward their husband, rather than loving and respecting him.
- *Consuming cycle.* Unresolved issues from a woman's past may serve as the impetus for developing a vicious cycle of hurtful emotion. Far more than a passing thought, jealousy and envy become *a mind-set* and *a lifestyle.* A woman will use self-pity, lies, threats, and other forms of manipulation to control her relationships and get what she wants. When a friend or spouse resists, the jealous woman reacts by becoming more conniving. As time goes by, this cycle destroys meaningful relationships in her life.

ASSESSMENT INTERVIEW : 3

Other issues may mask the presence of envy or jealousy in a woman's life. A woman may speak of the unfairness of life or express resentment toward someone else. She may talk about the need always to be the best at anything she does.

Envy and jealousy may also stem from resentment and a lack of forgiveness because the woman has been hurt by someone else and desires revenge.

Listen to the core issue not just the symptoms. Is the woman resentful toward what another person has done to her? Is she jealous because someone else has achieved something that she has not?

Do not use the label "envious" or "jealous." Instead, listen and acknowledge the person's struggle and experience.

1. What is the situation that has prompted these emotions for you?
2. Do you get upset when others advance in their career or social standing?
3. Do you find that it is difficult for you to celebrate the blessings of those around you?
4. Do you sometimes feel that God has disappointed you or not come through for you?
5. Do you find yourself often thinking, *If only I* _____ (fill in the blank with what you wish were different in your life)?
6. Where do you find that most of your money goes? What are your shopping habits like?
7. Do you feel secretly pleased when someone you admire experiences a setback or failure?
8. Are you critical or judgmental of other people?
9. Do you find that you are not content unless you are the "best at something"? Do you often feel inadequate?
10. Do you tend to put others on a pedestal?
11. Do you find yourself cutting other people down to validate yourself?
12. How do you feel about your husband's friendships and activities? Has your husband ever given you reason to doubt his faithfulness to you?

WISE COUNSEL : 4

Overcoming envy and jealousy is a process—there is no magic prayer, test-proven pill, or easy answer. Ultimately these destructive emotions stem from *a heart driven by selfishness*. Envy and jealousy are futile attempts to fill the deepest longings of a woman's heart for significance, love, and security. Envy and jealousy drive a woman to seek what someone else has or to control what someone else does.

The *process for overcoming* envy and jealousy is threefold:

1. understanding God's unconditional love
2. finding contentment in God's provision
3. learning to love other people with God's love

Envy and jealousy in a woman's life have the *potential to destroy her relationships and distance her from the people she loves* the most. In the heat of the moment when emotion flares, it is easy to forget that other people have emotions too. When a woman acts out of selfishness, she fails to remember or care about the impact of her behavior on others.

Counseling women through these damaging emotions requires compassion and understanding. *Harsh reproof for sin is unlikely to get to the root issues in a woman's heart.* Envy and jealousy are likely only *symptoms* of insecurity, pride, or low self-esteem. A woman who is struggling should be gently and consistently pointed to the *love and sufficiency of Jesus.*

Rather than finding their identity and significance in possessions, money, or success, women need to be encouraged to look honestly at their heart's desires. *True recovery involves readjusting one's focus.* Rather than comparing herself with others, a truly free woman learns to rejoice in her unique identity as a precious, loved daughter of Jesus Christ.

5 ACTION STEPS

1. Be Honest

- It is easy to deceive ourselves in a multitude of ways. While we may not feel we are struggling with envy or jealousy, these feelings may be disguised in many different forms, including criticism, contempt, gossip, self-pity, and manipulation.

- Refusing to confront the destructive emotions in your life will only lead to further hurt and brokenness—both for you and for those you love. Ask God to reveal the true motivations of your heart.

- In your interactions with other people, consider whether you are primarily concerned about what you can *get* or what you can *give.* Confess to Jesus the areas where envy and jealousy are controlling your relationships.

- Take some time to write down in a private journal what God has shown you. Repent of your sin and accept God's forgiveness and grace.

2. Focus on Jesus Christ

- God sees you as His own beloved child. He is not expecting you to get your act together or perform to a certain standard without His help. Begin each day by committing yourself to God and absorbing the truths of Scripture, asking Him to give you the strength to obey.

- When you feel insecure and start comparing yourself with other people, consciously take a step back and remind yourself of what you *know* is true: God loves you *now,* just the way you are, and He is in the process of transforming your heart if you belong to Him.

3. Develop a Lifestyle of Gratitude and Worship

- Rather than focusing on what you *don't* have, count your blessings. Even when you don't feel like it, discipline your mind to recount what you *know* to be true about God. He is a God of love, goodness, faithfulness, and provision, even when you can't see it.
- Read the Psalms as personal prayers, praising God for who He is and what He has done in your life. Write out key passages and post them in places where you will see them around your home or office.
- Fill the dead time in your day with Christ-centered music that will help you develop an attitude of thankfulness, rather than wallowing in your circumstances.
- As you wind down at the end of your day, reflect on the provision and blessings you received from God during the day. Thank God for His constant love and care.

4. Confront the Habits of Comparison and Manipulation

- Spend time in malls only when there is a specific item you need to purchase. Avoid window or impulse shopping.
- Become more aware of your controlling, manipulative tendencies. When you notice envious, jealous thoughts or words popping up in your mind, intentionally stop your thoughts and insert healthy, God-honoring thoughts. Instead of allowing these emotions to take over, ask God to cleanse your heart and mind.
- Ask Him to help you truly love—"love does not envy . . . thinks no evil" (1 Cor. 13:4–5). When you feel jealousy or envy rising up in you and you want to lash out and hurt someone with your words, stop and pray: *Lord, help me to love _____ and treat her[him] as Your child, not my enemy.*
- Ask yourself what it is about the person that causes you to envy him or her. Does this person have strong social skills? Is he or she deeply compassionate? Thank God for the redeeming qualities you see in this person and ask God to form those qualities in your own heart.

BIBLICAL INSIGHTS 6

This . . . is the law of jealousy.

> Numbers 5:29

The ancient Israelites had a complex ritual for dealing with jealousy. Their detailed process (Num. 5:11–31) recognized the destructive potential of a jealous husband or wife. The most important part was that they dealt with this issue before the Lord (v. 30). Jealousy can drive a wedge of distrust into a friendship, partnership, or marriage and ultimately destroy it.

Every relationship, no matter how close or intimate, is prone to jealousy. Protection from the wedge of this divisive emotion begins with honesty—

before God and the other person. Stuffing feelings of jealousy and pretending everything is okay will only lead to relational breakdown. Scripture teaches that jealousy and envy must be dealt with candidly and straightforwardly.

The question, What makes me jealous? serves as a great starting point for facing jealousy honestly and fighting it. Admitting jealous feelings takes a lot of courage but it is a proactive step to fight for healthy relationships. Complete honesty and trust will help obliterate jealousy.

A heart at peace gives life to the body, but envy rots the bones.

Proverbs 14:30

For where you have envy and selfish ambition, there you find disorder and every evil practice.

James 3:16

Envy causes hurt, dissension, and division. As women who desire to please God, we should desire to be holy in every aspect of our conduct (1 Peter 1:15). When we compare ourselves with other people, we are refusing to be content with the way God has created us and the blessings He has given us. The rat race of envy will always leave us as women feeling less-than and not-good-enough, "rotting" our God-given identity and purpose.

Envy is a deadly emotion. It has motivated people to steal, cheat, lie, and even kill. Whenever we women choose to dwell in envy, we are in essence telling God, "You're not good enough," just as Eve did. Envy is not a sin to play around with. It may come naturally, and we may see it all around us, but the Bible clearly tells us that envy leads to "disorder and every evil practice."

Do nothing out of selfish ambition or vain conceit, but in humility consider others better than yourselves. Each of you should look not only to your own interests, but also to the interests of others. Your attitude should be the same as that of Christ Jesus.

Philippians 2:3–5

Many times jealousy stems from prideful self-absorption; we look out for our own interests and feel that we are *better, smarter, more beautiful, more accomplished* than other people. We care about being right, being number one, and being in control. Jealousy is natural. Caring for others runs against the grain of our selfish ambition.

As Christians, however, we are called to live for more than ourselves. Being a Christian means following Jesus, and we are never more like Jesus than when we set aside our own plans, desires, and wishes and begin truly to love and care about the people around us. Jesus set aside the riches and glories of heaven to live and walk among us and die for us—His enemies.

Love that is truly unselfish comes from God. It's not something we can drum up or try harder to have on our own. We must take our jealousy to God, asking

Him to help us appreciate others' talents, while showing us how best to use our own. And we must ask Him to help us love as He does.

Do not worship any other god, for the LORD, whose name is Jealous, is a jealous God.

Exodus 34:14

I am jealous for you with a godly jealousy. I promised you to one husband, to Christ, so that I might present you as a pure virgin to him.

2 Corinthians 11:2

The word *jealous* can be used positively or negatively. God's jealousy stems from His holy desire for us to worship and delight in Him only. As the One who created us as women, God knows that idolatry steals the joy and intimacy He created us to experience with Him.

Writing to the Corinthian church, Paul speaks of a "godly jealousy" he feels. Here, Paul's jealousy was not a desire for his own advancement, but for the growth and spiritual maturity of the Corinthian church. While this type of jealousy is motivated by the desire for the good and welfare of others, ungodly jealousy always has a primary focus on self, whether the focus is looks, wealth, popularity, or power.

PRAYER STARTER 7

Lord, we thank You for all of Your blessings in the life of Your precious daughter. Your Word says that You know what we need before we even ask You. We praise You, Jesus, that You know us intimately, even the deepest desires of our hearts. Today, Lord, _____ struggles with the pain of desiring more, of being enticed by the monster of comparison. Open her eyes to see the unique, beautiful, and gifted woman she is, the person You created. Teach her contentment, Lord, and ground her heart in intimacy with You. Reveal Yourself to her and show her the emptiness of possessions and success compared to the delights of knowing You . . .

RECOMMENDED RESOURCES 8

Clinton, Julie. *A Woman's Path to Emotional Freedom: God's Promise of Hope and Healing.* Harvest House, 2010.

DeMoss, Nancy Leigh. *Lies Women Believe and the Truth That Sets Them Free.* Moody, 2002.

Dillow, Linda. *Calm My Anxious Heart: A Woman's Guide to Finding Contentment.* NavPress, 2007.

Kendall, R. T. *The Sin No One Talks About: Jealousy.* Charisma House, 2010.

Myers, Ruth, with Warren Myers. *31 Days of Praise.* Multnomah, 2005.

Samson, Will, and Lisa Samson. *Enough: Contentment in an Age of Excess*. David C. Cook, 2009.

Sandford, Paula. *Healing for a Woman's Emotions: Released from Damaging Thoughts and Feelings*. Charisma House, 2007.

Sorge, Bob. *Envy: the Enemy Within*. Regal, 2003.

Stanley, Charles. *Landmines in the Path of the Believer: Avoiding the Hidden Dangers*. Thomas Nelson, 2007.

Fear and Anxiety

PORTRAITS : 1

- Jessica's timid voice, shy manner, and furtive glances seem to indicate insecurity, but Jessica is more than just insecure. She lives in fear every day. Jessica's mom was abused as a child, and her life mission became to protect her daughter from a world "full of hurt and danger." So she controlled everything in Jessica's life and worried about everything. As Jessica grew up in this atmosphere, a deep-seated, unhealthy sense of fear was nurtured in her and she can't seem to break free of it.

- Nadia's persona of an independent, modern woman was a mask to hide her overwhelming fear of being in groups. Nadia would often have a panic attack when she was in a restaurant eating with friends or in a group meeting at work. Even though it seemed irrational, she would become overwhelmed with anxiety, sure that she would say something foolish, spill food on her shirt, or begin to stutter. "Sometimes, I have to excuse myself because the knot in my stomach spreads to my chest and I feel like I'm having a heart attack," Nadia says. "I can't catch my breath. I can't make it go away."

- When Rebecca was asked to lead a women's Bible study at her local church, she was initially excited. However, as she prepared, she got more nervous and fearful. The morning of the Bible study she felt sick to her stomach. Then when Rebecca began the study, reading the opening verse, she began to hyperventilate and shake uncontrollably. She couldn't stop the panic attack and had to be taken to the emergency room.

DEFINITIONS AND KEY THOUGHTS : 2

Fear

- Fear is *a physical and emotional response to a perceived threat or danger.* Whether the threat or danger is justified or not, fear is automatic, based on internal beliefs about self, others, and one's environment.

- While most women experience fear as a negative emotion, *fear also has a positive component.* If you find that you have turned down a one-way street and see a car heading directly at you, fear triggers an autonomic response that sends a signal to your brain to flee the potentially dangerous situation.

- Fear becomes a problem when a woman is *afraid of things that are not real* or when the feeling of fear is *out of proportion* to the real danger present.

- Fear is an emotion in response to real or perceived danger that draws a woman into a *self-protective mode*. This can be called "fight or flight" syndrome—a state of readiness to respond to the threat—either by lashing out or withdrawing.

- More often than not, fears are related to *what a woman perceives as a threat* to her safety and security. She may fear losing her job, having her home burglarized, or having conflict in a relationship.

- Many women are plagued with *fears of what could happen*. A recent survey reports that women's *top fears* include:

  — fear of unplanned pregnancy
  — fear of getting an incurable disease
  — fear of losing a man
  — fear of losing one's beauty and attraction
  — fear of being overweight
  — fear of something happening to one's children[1]

- There are *four major relational fears* that can significantly alter a woman's quality of life:

  — fear of failure
  — fear of rejection
  — fear of abandonment
  — fear of death or dying

Anxiety

- *Anxiety is a constant fearful state*, accompanied by a feeling of *unrest or dread*. A woman who is anxious has "a relatively permanent feeling of worry and nervousness . . . usually accompanied by compulsive behavior or attacks of panic."[2] The woman may not be aware of what is creating the anxiety.

- In contrast, *worry* is not an emotion as much as a problem with negative thinking that is closely linked to the emotion of anxiety.

- Anxiety is aroused by a *number of factors*:

  — external situations (viewing the nightly news, a fast-paced lifestyle)
  — physical well-being (lack of sleep, blood sugar imbalance)
  — genetics (brain chemistry, personality)
  — modeling (parents who are highly anxious)
  — trauma (difficult life events, situations that may be similar to experiences of the past that caused great pain)

- *Anxiety's symptoms* can include inability to relax, tense feelings, rapid heartbeat, dry mouth, increased blood pressure, jumpiness or feeling faint, excessive perspiring, feeling clammy, constant anticipation of trouble, and constant feeling of uneasiness.

- In the United States, about *forty million people ages eighteen and older struggle with consistent, overwhelming fears evidenced as an anxiety disorder*. And *women are almost 6 percent more likely* to be diagnosed with anxiety than men.[3]

- Anxiety disorders are the *most common mental health disorders* in the United States, but only about one-third of those suffering from anxiety disorders seek treatment.[4]

Phobias

- A *phobia* is "an anxiety disorder characterized by extreme and irrational fear of simple things or social situations."[5] Phobias are *fears of specific things*.

- Phobias are fears that are *out of proportion* to the object, situation, or activity feared. A woman may have a phobia of social situations, spiders, snakes, heights, dark rooms, being alone, flying, or speaking in public. For example, a woman who exhibits a phobia of spiders may refuse to ever enter a room again because once she saw a small spider on the ceiling there.

- It is estimated that *one in twenty-three people (4.5 percent) has a phobia*. Research has found that "females are more prone to irrational fears than males. Roughly twice as many women as men suffer from panic disorder, post-traumatic stress disorder, generalized anxiety disorder, and specific phobia."[6]

- One of the most prevalent phobias is social phobia, *an overwhelming fear of being in group situations, being in the spotlight, or having to speak in public*. Statistics estimate that 5.2 million Americans suffer from social phobia.[7]

Panic Attacks

- Panic attacks are sudden, overwhelming, fearful reactions that affect the body and the mind with feelings of impending doom.

- In a panic attack, the woman feels *out of control and often may believe she is dying*. Symptoms include being out of breath, sweating, dizziness, nausea, diarrhea, ringing ears, choking, vertigo, and an overwhelming fear of leaving home for fear of another attack.

- The woman generally has *no clear idea* of what prompted the reaction and then becomes *afraid of another episode occurring*.

- The woman *may feel as if she is going crazy* or having a heart attack. *Note*: More than three attacks in a month or the onset of refusing to go out of the house indicate the *need for professional assistance*. In some situations, medication may be necessary.

- Research estimates that about *2.4 million American adults have panic disorder*. Frequently panic disorder comes to the surface in late adolescence or early adulthood.[8]

- Approximately one in three individuals with panic disorder also develop *agoraphobia*, a condition in which the person is overcome with fear of being in any environment where escape might be difficult if a panic attack happens.

3 ASSESSMENT INTERVIEW

As you speak with the woman, it is important to assess whether her fears are based on reality. Try to detect if she is struggling with ungrounded fears or if she has legitimate reason to be concerned.

1. What are you afraid or anxious about?
2. What would happen to you if your fears came true?
3. How long and to what extent has this fear or anxiety been occurring for you?
4. What situation or object or person causes you the most distress?
5. Do you find there are times when you are more anxious than others? If so, when?
6. Of the things that cause you fear, which seem reasonable and which seem more unreasonable?
7. When do the feelings of anxiety go away?
8. How have you tried to cope with the anxiety?
9. Do you have any health problems and/or medications that may contribute to the anxiety?
10. What would your life be like if you were free of this anxiety?

4 WISE COUNSEL

Fear and anxiety are *defused by knowledge*. (For example, fear of snakes is often defused by learning about all of the different types, their habitats, and how to avoid encounters with a snake.) The more a woman can defuse the perceived threat, the less anxiety she will experience. For instance, if a woman is deathly afraid of someone breaking into her house and raping her, talk with her about the measures she has taken to ensure her safety. If she locks her doors, has a security system, and has some method of self-protection (pepper spray or stun gun), confront her with the irrationality of her fear. If her concerns are grounded, work with her to develop a plan so she can feel more safe, rather than living in constant fear.

Generally, the fearful woman has established a whole system of irrational beliefs that is creating anxiety in her mind. *Try to gain an understanding* of what lies or deceptions are contributing to the anxiety. What past experiences have made her anxious? Are her fears grounded? How does she cope with the panic and fear she feels? How is it affecting her daily life?

Most anxiety reactions are *learned behavior*. Be intentional in your efforts to encourage the person to develop hope that she will be able to overcome the anxiety or fears by *learning new behaviors rooted in truth*. Work with the woman to develop behaviors that reduce anxiety and fear.

Anxiety can be *contagious.* Those who experience strong anxiety tend to elicit anxiety reactions in those who are around them. You need to be aware of your own anxiety level and how you cope personally with anxiety when it occurs.

Be patient with the woman as she sorts through her feelings and root causes of her fear. Changing patterns and learning new behaviors take time, and during this time, your support, insight, and reassurance are essential.

ACTION STEPS : 5

1. Change Your Thought Patterns

- Take time to clarify what thoughts and experience have led to the fear response. Work to defuse the intensity of these feelings with reality testing and truth.
- As Rick Warren put it, "God is real, no matter how you feel." Rather than focusing on your anxiety or fear, begin to discipline your thoughts to focus on what you *know* is true about God.
- It is important to dispute negative thoughts and lies with the truth of Scripture (Phil. 4:8). You may not be able to extinguish the *feelings* right away, but by filling your mind with the truths of God's Word every time you are anxious or afraid, you are building healthy thought patterns from which healthy emotions will spring.

2. Focus on God

- As a loving Father, God delights in comforting and protecting His children, so don't try to fight your fears on your own. Run to Him whenever you are anxious, worried, or afraid, rather than trying to figure it out yourself.
- Holding on to your anxieties and fears is actually denying God His right to be God—to have control over every aspect of your life and to take care of you. God already knows what you need before you ask Him. He longs for you to trust and relinquish all fears to Him, especially through prayer (Phil. 4:4–6). To have peace, keep your thoughts on God's love (Isa. 26:3).
- Remember, you're not a victim of your emotions. Often anxiety springs from a lack of trust. God is fully capable of taking care of you, so don't believe the lie that you have to hold yourself all together. God's perfect love is the only thing strong enough to conquer your fears, so don't push Him away.

3. Watch for Triggers

- Become proactive in identifying and minimizing activities that cause anxiety, if possible. For some women, driving during rush hour, shopping in a crowded mall, or being alone in the dark induces feelings of anxiety. Whatever your trigger is, look for ways to change your lifestyle so you're not continually putting yourself in anxiety-causing situations.

- Stop yourself when you begin to focus on negative, fearful thoughts. In each situation, stop and pray. Then work to replace these thoughts with reality and truth.

4. Move Forward

- Rather than ignoring or minimizing your fears, face them. Name them. And look for the root cause of your anxiety. Fears and anxieties don't have to keep you in bondage, but you must be proactive in continuing to face down your fears.
- Seek out supportive, encouraging relationships with other women with whom you can be yourself and honestly express your fears and anxieties. Every woman struggles with anxiety on some level, so don't feel that you're alone and don't hide your struggles.

6 BIBLICAL INSIGHTS

Trust in the LORD. . . . Delight yourself in the LORD. . . . Commit your way to the LORD. . . . Be still before the LORD and wait patiently for him; do not fret when men succeed in their ways, when they carry out their wicked schemes.

Psalm 37:3–5, 7

David encouraged God's people to focus on the Lord—to trust, to delight, to commit, to be still. Many things in this life are beyond our control. When we stress and worry and try to figure everything out on our own, we fail to experience the joy of relying on God.

Trusting focuses our faith and deepens our commitment. Delighting in God means that we experience pleasure in His presence. Committing our way to God means entrusting everything in our lives to His guidance and control. Waiting patiently is sometimes difficult but often it is the ultimate test of our trust in God.

In this passage, we are challenged to exchange our worry and fear for the joy found in simply trusting Jesus. He is sovereign over everything and He is always working for our good and His glory.

The LORD is my light and my salvation—whom shall I fear? The LORD is the stronghold of my life—of whom shall I be afraid? . . . Though an army besiege me, my heart will not fear; though war break out against me, even then will I be confident.

Psalm 27:1, 3

When I am afraid, I will trust in you. In God, whose word I praise, in God I trust; I will not be afraid. What can mortal man do to me?

Psalm 56:3–4

Fear is an automatic human response to feelings of danger, but here, David rejoices in the fact that, because he knows God personally, he has nothing to fear. God is a stronghold, a refuge, a safe place to whom we can run.

No place could be safer than with God! Even when we are afraid, we can make the choice to put our trust in God, rather than letting fear hinder and control us. Our loving Father promises to protect us and never to leave us. This does not imply that we will never suffer or face difficulty, but it does assure us that we don't need to fear because "perfect love drives out fear" (1 John 4:18), and Jesus is our perfect love.

Trust in the LORD with all your heart, and lean not on your own understanding; in all your ways acknowledge Him, and He shall direct your paths.

Proverbs 3:5–6 NKJV

Do not be anxious about anything, but in everything, by prayer and petition, with thanksgiving, present your requests to God. And the peace of God, which transcends all understanding, will guard your hearts and your minds in Christ Jesus.

Philippians 4:6–7

It's one thing to trust God with our eternal destiny, but often it's harder to trust God with the challenges and difficulties of daily life. Naturally, we want to take control and figure everything out on our own, but trusting God means surrendering each day to Him and being led by His Spirit.

God promises to direct us and give us wisdom. We need to trust God to help us handle the difficult situations we face, even in cases where we can't begin to see how He could do it. Remember, He is the God of the impossible. Nothing is too hard for Him!

The best antidote for fear and anxiety is daily dependence on God. Trust isn't just a theological idea; it's a matter of submitting ourselves to Him each moment and letting His Spirit, not our fears, control us. The Bible commands us to bring our fears, anxieties, and requests to God in exchange for peace, even when we don't exactly understand how it will work. Our confidence is in God—the Creator of the universe—not ourselves. If we know and follow Him, He promises to watch over and protect us. We have no reason to fear.

PRAYER STARTER 7

Lord, we all experience fear and anxiety sometimes. _____ feels overwhelmed right now. Calm her, Lord. Help her know that You are in the midst of everything that is happening and that You are in control. Surround her with Your peace and help her to feel safe, Lord. Give her wisdom in dealing with fearful situations. Let her not be crippled, Lord, by her feelings. You hold us in Your hands, God, and that is the safest place to be. We pray expectantly as we look to the days ahead, knowing that You are with us and are for us . . .

8 RECOMMENDED RESOURCES

Anderson, Neil, and Rich Miller. *Freedom from Fear: Overcoming Worry and Anxiety.* Harvest House, 1999.

Fitzpatrick, Elyse. *Overcoming Fear, Worry, and Anxiety: Becoming a Woman of Faith and Confidence.* Harvest House, 2001.

Hart, Archibald D. *The Anxiety Cure.* Thomas Nelson, 2001.

Stanley, Charles. *Finding Peace: God's Promise of a Life Free from Regret, Anxiety, and Fear.* Thomas Nelson, 2007.

Welch, Edward. *Running Scared: Fear, Worry, and the God of Rest.* New Growth, 2007.

———. *When I Am Afraid: A Step by Step Guide away from Fear and Anxiety.* New Growth, 2009.

Young, Ed. *Know Fear: Facing Life's Six Most Common Phobias.* LifeWay Christian Resources, 2003.

Forgiveness

PORTRAITS | **1**

- Becky hasn't spoken with her father in five years. He walked out on her family when she was a teenager. His last words still ring in her ears, "You're nothing but a bother. I need to live my life, and you aren't part of it. You're just like your mother." Becky has tried to move on but she still has a deep-seated hatred for her father. She keeps having nightmares about his abuse and she is having a hard time trusting the guy she's dating. "I don't know how to forgive my father," Becky says. "I don't know if I ever could."

- Linda was shocked to find out that her friend and co-worker, Amy, has been criticizing and making negative comments to their boss about Linda's work. Then her friend was promoted, while Linda was demoted. Linda feels hurt, betrayed, and angry. She can't stop thinking about ways to get even with Amy. "That conniving little b—," Linda fumes. "I am going to get revenge. She can't get away with this."

- Kelly and her twin sister, Kendra, have been at each other's throats since they were little girls. The tension really got bad in high school—each trying to outdo the other. Kendra finally trumped Kelly when she started dating and is now engaged to Kelly's ex-boyfriend. Kelly absolutely loathes her for it. She feels betrayed and doesn't think she can ever forgive Kendra.

DEFINITIONS AND KEY THOUGHTS | 2

- *Unforgiveness* involves *refusal to let go of an offense.* It is a state of anger, resentment, bitterness, hatred, hostility, fear, and stress toward an individual who has transgressed in some way. *Unforgiveness is a cancer that eats away at the very soul of a person.*

- Researchers have discovered that *holding on to a grudge* in one's mind puts a woman's body through the same strains as a major stressful event: *muscles tense, blood pressure rises, and sweating increases. Bitterness suppresses the immune system,* leading to compromised health.[1]

- *Forgiveness* means "canceling a debt"—a wrongdoing or injustice done against you. Forgiveness occurs when a woman *chooses to let go of resentment, indignation, and anger held toward the offender,* rather than holding a grudge or seeking revenge. When a woman forgives, she *chooses not to hold past offenses or hurts against the other person.*

- *Forgiveness is never fair*—it always means extending grace to the offender *when he or she does not deserve it.* Forgiveness wells up out of a heart that is full of love and gratitude to God for His infinite forgiveness through Christ's work on the cross. In Luke 7:40–47 Jesus tells us the truth that *those who have been forgiven much love much.*
- More than fifty-five studies have been conducted on the *effects of forgiveness,* with results confirming that *forgiving others leads to* "reduced stress, better heart health, stronger relationships, reduced pain, and greater happiness."[2]
- Forgiveness is *essential to physical and emotional health.* ABC News reported on research on forgiveness that revealed: "Studies show that letting go of anger and resentment can reduce the severity of heart disease and, in some cases, even prolong the lives of cancer patients."[3]
- *Forgiveness is critical to building healthy relationships.* A recent study found that women who *forgave their spouse* and felt benevolent toward him solved their conflicts more effectively and found greater joy in their relationship.[4]
- *Letting go of past hurt and anger has been shown to increase quality and enjoyment of life.* Research at Stanford University found that people who forgave others evidenced a 24 percent increase in productivity and a 23 percent decrease in symptoms of stress. They reported being *happier, focusing better, and getting a better night's sleep.*[5]
- The ways women respond to heartache and pain have significant impact on their daily life. *Research shows that bitterness is detrimental to spiritual, psychological, and physical health.*[6]

3 ASSESSMENT INTERVIEW

1. Can you tell me about your background?
2. What do you think is the source of your concern?
3. What led you to come to counseling?
4. What do you hope to accomplish?
5. What incident or incidents are you having trouble forgiving?
6. How did the incident make you feel?
7. What can you tell me about the person who hurt you?
8. Have you tried to forgive? Why do you think it's so difficult?
9. How have you protected yourself from being hurt again by this person?
10. How can you tell that you haven't forgiven this person?
11. Did you ever see any examples of forgiveness in your home while you were growing up?
12. When is the first time you can remember someone offending you? How did you handle it?
13. Can you see a pattern in how you respond when people offend you?
14. Do those responses help or hurt you?

15. God says in His Word that we should forgive others as God has forgiven us. Do you think this applies to your situation? Why or why not?
16. What do you think forgiveness is?

WISE COUNSEL : 4

When a woman seeks help to forgive, it is often because the irritability of unforgiveness has started to *disrupt her personal, emotional, or spiritual life.* A lack of forgiveness (due to the stress it creates) may be the source of *physical problems*, such as sleeplessness, lack of energy, headaches, joint pain, or back pain. It also may be the root cause of *depression or anxiety* or an *inability to build healthy relationships.*

Sometimes a woman *does not realize* that the origin of her problem is a *lack of forgiveness*, and you may need to gently lead her to this knowledge.

Share the truth about forgiveness and how, biblically, it is always our responsibility. Frequently a woman has not forgiven because she doesn't understand what forgiveness is. It is best understood as *an act and a process.* When a woman forgives, her heart will begin to heal. We can forgive when we realize that we have been forgiven by God (Eph. 4:31–32), whether or not the offender is willing to restore communication or work toward reconciliation.

What Forgiveness Is and Is Not

Many women misunderstand what forgiveness is, confusing it with letting the perpetrator get away with the offense or being okay with future hurt and abuse. If the woman is reluctant to forgive, thinking it's just letting the offender off the hook, explain that forgiveness lets *her* off the hook and *protects her* from the *destructive power of unforgiveness.* Discuss with the woman the following characteristics of true, biblical forgiveness.

Forgiveness *does not mean that any wrongs done to you were acceptable.*

Forgiveness does not diminish the evil done against you, *nor is it a denial of what has happened.*

Forgiveness *does not require reconciliation.* Reconciliation involves rebuilding trust and restoring the relationship, and in some cases, especially when abuse is involved, is not always possible or recommended. *It takes two to reconcile but only one to forgive.*

Forgiveness is a key part of *not letting past wrongs hurt you any longer.*

Forgiveness *does not take away the consequences* the other person will face because of his or her sin.

Forgiveness is letting go of your desire to hurt the other person. Simply put, forgiveness means *you cancel a debt.*

Forgiveness is a *difficult and uncomfortable* process. When you make the decision to forgive, *God provides the grace and strength to forgive and to maintain a heart of forgiveness.*

Forgiveness is *not weakness*. It is the most powerful thing you can do. Refusing to forgive allows Satan to continue to hurt you; forgiveness *stops that destructive power of Satan*.

Forgiveness *does not depend on the other person's actions* and it is not probationary (for example, saying, "I will forgive you as long as you quit drinking").

Forgiveness *does not require you to become a "doormat"* nor does it require you to allow the offender to hurt you again.

Forgiveness is *a gift you give to the offender. Trust*, on the other hand, *must be earned*. You must set boundaries.

Forgiveness *does not mean that you necessarily forget*. Forgiveness is a choice as well as a constant process—one that you may have to remind yourself that you granted.

Forgiveness shows how much *you trust God to take care of you*.

Forgiveness is experiencing *empathy* for the offender, *humility* about your own sinfulness, and *gratitude* for being forgiven by God and others.

Seek to *identify the woman's emotions*. Empathize with her and acknowledge the evil that has occurred. Encourage the woman to *grieve the offense* and the losses that have resulted from any wrong committed against her.

Explain that *hurt and anger are not sinful*; they are normal responses to an offense. It is important that she *identify and express her feelings* about the offense committed—both how she felt when it was happening and how she feels now.

Work with the woman to decipher what must be done *to keep the offender from perpetrating the same hurt again*. This involves the way in which the person maintains an ongoing relationship with the offender. For instance, she can be polite (safe boundary) without being a best friend (unsafe boundary). Likewise, she can listen without taking advice.

Unsafe people are those who hurt without regard to the damage it creates in another's life. Help the woman *learn not to look for approval from another person who will likely cause pain*. Work with her to recognize that she does not need another's approval to live a free and fulfilling life. *The only approval she needs is God's.*

Know that *God can use offense* to promote spiritual growth and dependence on Him for His plan and His glory. Ask for the intervention of the Holy Spirit to heal her emotional wounds.

Ask God to help the client love the offender. Since those who transgress are often lost, broken, or hurting themselves, the woman who was wronged may feel pity and compassion for the offender as she experiences forgiveness in her life. *Praying for the offender* will help a woman's feelings move from wanting revenge, to not wanting harm, and finally to wanting the best for the transgressor. When the woman reaches the latter stage, she will know true freedom.

Reasons to Forgive

Help the woman understand the following benefits of forgiveness.

Forgiveness *sets you free* to move on with your life.

It refuses to let the person who hurt you have any *power over your life*.

It *opens up your relationship with God* (see Matt. 5:43–48).

Forgiveness *keeps you from becoming bitter* and thus protects those around you.

It keeps you from becoming like the person who hurt you.

Unforgiveness hurts *you.*

Scripture commands us to be forgiving (Matt. 18:21–35).

ACTION STEPS 5

Psychologist Everett Worthington Jr., who has conducted extensive research on forgiveness, has developed a useful acrostic for navigating the process of forgiveness. It is known as R-E-A-C-H:[7]

1. Recall the Hurt

- It is difficult but necessary to recall the hurt. Recalling your hurt is not for the purpose of finger-pointing, but a means to review objectively what has occurred.
- Journaling is a great way to work through anger and hurt. It organizes your thoughts and helps you acknowledge the truth in clear black and white.
- Sometimes writing a letter to the offender is helpful, but don't mail the letter.
- *Don't minimize or deny the woman's pain and don't make excuses for the offender.*

2. Empathize with the Offender

- Write a letter as if you were the offender. You should write about your thoughts, feelings, insights, and pressures. Make this a letter of apology. Think about how difficult it would be for the offender to do this.
- By placing yourself in the shoes of the person who hurt you, it may help you understand the reasons the person did it.
- This does not remove blame from the individual but does serve to show that the individual who hurt you is likely hurting deeply too.

3. Altruistic Gift of Forgiveness

- Think about the "giving" of forgiveness. Think of a time when you did something wrong and were forgiven. Reflect on the wrongdoing and the guilt you felt. How did it feel to be forgiven? Would you like to give the gift of forgiveness to the person who hurt you?
- Write a blank check of forgiveness. Write in your journal that this day you released the offender from the debt that he or she owes you. Forgiveness is a choice, not a feeling, so don't wait until you feel ready to forgive.
- You may want to write down the offenses the person has done and then write "Canceled" or "Paid in Full" over them.
- Through this step, also recall the great mercy and grace of God toward you.

4. Commit Publicly to Forgive

- Write a certificate or letter of forgiveness stating that you will not ruminate on the wrongs done to you anymore, but don't send it.
- By participating in some outward expression of forgiveness, such as writing a letter, you will be more apt to remember that you have forgiven and are thus freed from the bondage of unforgiveness.
- Share with those you trust (family, close friends, small group, pastor) about your decision to forgive. By disclosing your forgiveness to others, you will be held accountable to your decision to forgive the transgressor.

5. Hold On to Forgiveness

- Hold on to forgiveness when doubts arise. There is a difference between remembering a transgression with an unwillingness to forgive and remembering it but knowing you have forgiven the person. Forgiveness doesn't mean that you will necessarily forget; it means not seeking revenge anymore.
- Make "Stones of Remembrance." After God parted the Jordan River so the Israelites could go through on dry land, God told Joshua to have each tribe choose a stone so they could all be piled up as a memorial to the great things God had done that day. The stones served as a reminder to the people and their children in times to come (Joshua 4). It is good to have something concrete to help you remember the day you set your offender (and yourself) free. Your "Stones of Remembrance" may be notes, pictures, or some other physical object that jogs your memory about the choice you made to forgive.
- Let it go. Holding on to anger and bitterness hurts only yourself. When Corrie ten Boom (a Nazi concentration camp survivor) was reminded of an offense someone had done to her, she responded, "I distinctly remember forgetting that." Though you will never completely forget, you can remember your choice to forgive.

6 BIBLICAL INSIGHTS

Then the king summoned Absalom, and he came in and bowed down with his face to the ground before the king. And the king kissed Absalom.

2 Samuel 14:33

Absalom had betrayed his family and his father, David, but despite all that Absalom had done, David allowed for the possibility of reconciliation by forgiving his son. Absalom, however, had no tears, no repentance, and no change of heart. Indeed, Absalom would eventually try to take his father's throne (see 2 Sam. 15:10–12).

One person can forgive, but it takes two to reconcile. Forgiveness does not guarantee reconciliation. But forgiveness does set us free, enabling us to let go of the hurts and wrongs done by others.

I, even I, am he who blots out your transgressions for my own sake, and remembers your sins no more.

Isaiah 43:25

When the guilt of past sins weighs us down, we must remember that when we seek forgiveness, God "blots out" our transgressions and forgets our sins. The idea of blotting out sins is a picture of wiping the slate clean. Whatever sins we have committed, God promises to erase them—to "cancel" our debt by taking the punishment for every one of our sins. He knows the deepest secrets of our heart, yet chooses to forgive us and offer us His righteousness.

Because God has forgiven us our sins, we must forgive ourselves.

Then Peter came to Him and said, "Lord, how often shall my brother sin against me, and I forgive him? Up to seven times?" Jesus said to him, "I do not say to you, up to seven times, but up to seventy times seven."

Matthew 18:21–22 NKJV

In this passage, Jesus was saying, Don't even keep count; just keep on forgiving. Then He told a parable about a man who, after receiving forgiveness for a large debt he owed to someone, refused to forgive a person who owed him a small debt. Jesus was illustrating the fact that God has graciously forgiven us and continues to forgive us daily, over and over again. We should be just as gracious in forgiving others, by the power of the Holy Spirit.

Bear with each other and forgive whatever grievances you may have against one another. Forgive as the Lord forgave you.

Colossians 3:13

For if you forgive men when they sin against you, your heavenly Father will also forgive you. But if you do not forgive men their sins, your Father will not forgive your sins.

Matthew 6:14–15

Conflicts, misunderstandings, and pain are part of life in this broken world, but how we respond to hurt is our decision. Part of living as the body of Christ is bearing with each other in our weaknesses and sins, rather than becoming bitter or trying to get even.

Jesus stated that God's forgiveness of us is somehow related to how we forgive others. When we accept God's forgiveness of all the wrongs we have done Him, we should be so grateful that we offer forgiveness to those who have wronged us.

To refuse to forgive shows that we do not understand or appreciate how much God has forgiven us and have not allowed God's grace to transform us.

7 PRAYER STARTER

Lord, _____ has been deeply hurt. She wants to let go, to be free of the pain, but she is finding it very difficult. Her emotions go all over the place, and she doesn't want this pain affecting one more waking moment. Please help her let it go. Please help her forgive the offender as You have forgiven her. Please give her life once again . . .

8 RECOMMENDED RESOURCES

Hunt, June. *How to Forgive . . . When You Don't Feel Like It*. Harvest House, 2007.

Kendall, R. T. *Total Forgiveness*. Charisma House, 2007.

Lutzer, Erwin. *When You've Been Wronged: Moving from Bitterness to Forgiveness*. Moody, 2007.

Sande, Ken. *The Peacemaker: A Biblical Guide to Resolving Personal Conflict*. Baker, 2003.

Stanley, Charles. *The Gift of Forgiveness*. Thomas Nelson, 2002.

Stoop, David. *Forgiving the Unforgivable*. Regal, 2005.

Worthington Jr., Everett L. *Handbook of Forgiveness*. Brunner-Routledge, 2005.

DVDs

Stoop, David. *Forgiveness: Getting beyond Your Past and Pain*. American Association of Christian Counselors Courageous Living Video Series. See www.aacc.net for more information.

Gossip

- Sarah couldn't believe what she heard about her small group leader. She knew it was a personal, private matter but she couldn't control the urge to share the surprising and controversial news. "You'll never believe what I just found out," Sarah texted a friend, and before she knew it, she had spilled the whole story. Sarah didn't think much more about it, but at their next small group, her leader shared how hurt she had been by the rumors circulating about her.

- When Jena got in an argument with her supervisor, Mark, she didn't hesitate to let the whole office know what a "lazy, insensitive jerk" Mark really was. Sure, she'd never say it to his face, but Jena gained a certain evil pleasure in demonizing her boss. Almost overnight, he went from being everybody's favorite co-worker to being given the cold shoulder. When the news got back to Mark and he called her out for her backstabbing, nonprofessional behavior, she rationalized, "It's just who I am. I can't hold things inside."

- Megan and Katie have been best friends for years. Recently Megan has been struggling with her boyfriend about sex. Her active role in the youth group keeps Megan from going "all the way," but the temptation is so strong that she often confides in Katie, asking for prayer and accountability. In conversations with youth group members, Katie shares Megan's situation and asks for prayer. The "prayer request" spreads, and Megan's whole reputation is compromised. Megan feels hurt and betrayed and isn't sure that she can ever trust Katie again.

DEFINITIONS AND KEY THOUGHTS 2

- *Gossip exploits the personal issues* or matters of another person. Someone who gossips "habitually reveals personal or sensational facts about others."[1] Such conversations typically involve "rumors, opinions, or inside information. . . . [Gossip] is not an innocent pastime. It is sin."[2]

- *Slander* is a direct partner of gossip. Slander includes *malicious and hurtful talk* about another person. It is "the utterance of false charges or misrepresentations which defame or damage another's reputation."[3]

- The Social Issues Research Centre found that *55 percent of men's conversation* and *67 percent of women's conversation* involve gossip. Research shows that women are more likely to participate in gossip than men.[4]

- Whether women call it "networking," "catching up," or "staying current," such conversations may begin something like, "Can you believe what I heard . . . ?" and *revolve around relationships, popularity, social standing, and character* (or lack thereof). Usually the information spread is *more rumor than fact*, and even when the details are accurate, it is in most cases personal, private information.
- Gossip is rampant, not only among friendships, but also in the professional world. In a study that videotaped thirteen teacher meetings that lasted around forty minutes, twenty-five instances of gossip were observed in the actual business portions of the meetings.[5]

3 : ASSESSMENT INTERVIEW

1. Has anyone ever betrayed your trust, shared a secret, or gossiped about you? How did it make you feel?
2. Are you the victim or perpetrator of gossip?
3. Do you feel sometimes as if you don't fit in with the crowd which you are in?
4. Do you often compare yourself to others and feel inferior?
5. Do you find yourself focusing on the negative or the controversial?
6. Do you seek affirmation and approval from others?
7. Why do you gossip? What benefits does it provide? How does it make you feel?
8. What do you see as the positive and negative effects of gossip?
9. How have you seen gossip change friendships and relationships?
10. What do you think is a healthy response to gossip?
11. What are some strategies you can put in place to safeguard your heart and your friendships?

4 : WISE COUNSEL

For many who participate in it, *gossip* is about *attention and a means of covering insecurity*. A woman who gossips may feel the *need to turn the attention to herself* or feels that she is *gaining approval, status, or acceptance* by sharing information. Many times the old adage is true: information is power.

Gossip can be a window into understanding the self-esteem of the gossiper. Many women mistakenly think that by cutting others down, they are building up their own public image and identity, when, in reality, gossip destroys trust and openness in relationships.

Sometimes gossip is hard to discern because it's hidden in *prayer requests or other expressions of concern* that, in reality, are *ways to reveal intimate or personal details or rumors about others' lives*. Concern may become a *justification for gossip*. Discernment is vital for detecting gossip and choosing not to participate in it.

For some women, gossip stems from the desire to be in control and "in the know." While there is nothing wrong with keeping up with local news, gossip involves sharing details about someone who isn't present with people who are neither part of the problem nor the solution. *Confidentiality is essential to developing trusting relationships.* Though many women think sharing gossip is fun, many others have discovered that being gossiped about *destroys friendships and can easily mar one's character.*

ACTION STEPS : 5

1. Ask for Help

- Gossip is hurtful and destructive and it's a sin. Confess this behavior to God and repent, and then ask for His help in resisting the temptation to participate in gossip.
- When trying to escape the hold gossip has on you, rely on others to help you change your patterns of thinking, acting, and talking. Being up-front and honest about your tendency to gossip is the first step in releasing yourself from gossip's grip. Ask a friend to hold you accountable and call you out when you slip into gossiping.

2. Consider the Reasons People Gossip

- As noted previously, gossip can be cloaked as a "concern" or a "prayer request." It is vital that you become aware and use great discernment in these situations as to whether the information is truly a prayer request or gossip. Awareness of your tendency to gossip is a large part of "taming the tongue."
- *Help the client learn to dig deeper into her motives and reasons for gossiping. Is it to gain approval? Is she lacking self-worth? Does she feel jealous or envious of the person she is gossiping about? Has being "in the know" become an idol for her? Does she feel affirmed by cutting others down?*

3. See People as God's Children

- Often gossip comes from boredom and selfishness. A life with meaning, purpose, and activity results in meaningful conversation versus gossip-centered conversation. As you speak and interact with others, consider their interests and needs, not just your own.
- The Golden Rule challenges us: "Do to others as you would have them do to you" (Luke 6:31). Spreading rumors or personal information about other people to build up your own security and identity is selfish and damaging.
- Rather than using other people to feel better about yourself, practice listening. Invest your time in helping and serving someone else—building up relationships and encouraging, rather than tearing down and destroying. See people as God's sons and daughters in Christ.

4. Think on These Things

- Philippians 4:8 gives perfect advice for the woman struggling with gossip. Think on things that are true, noble, right, pure, lovely, admirable, excellent, and praiseworthy.
- The heart and mind are connected. Your words show your heart attitudes. Jesus said, "What you say flows from what is in your heart" (Luke 6:45 NLT). By disciplining your mind to think on the good, you will influence what comes out of your mouth.

6 BIBLICAL INSIGHTS

If anyone considers himself religious and yet does not keep a tight rein on his tongue, he deceives himself and his religion is worthless.

James 1:26

Spiritual maturity and control of the tongue go hand in hand. Being a true Christ-follower and keeping control of our tongue are closely related. Gossiping is a habit that is hard to break. After all, in our own strength it is impossible to truly love and care for others. Left to ourselves, we will continue in a life of selfishness. But God, by the power of the Holy Spirit, desires to transform us, including the way we think, act, and speak.

Fundamental to Christianity is the command to "love one another." Gossip and loving one another cannot coexist. Those entrapped in the snares of gossip must realize and acknowledge their inability to escape the strong hold of the Evil One on their tongue without the power and grace of the Holy Spirit. Healing begins when we grasp God's call to encourage and love others, rather than tearing others down with our words.

They get into the habit of being idle and going about from house to house. And not only do they become idlers, but also gossips and busybodies, saying things they ought not to.

1 Timothy 5:13

Do not let any unwholesome talk come out of your mouths, but only what is helpful for building others up according to their needs, that it may benefit those who listen.

Ephesians 4:29

The individuals described in 1 Timothy 5 are idlers, gossips, and busybodies. Women like them do not care about the needs of others. Instead, they are known as busybodies. They may be nosy, conniving, and manipulative in their attempts to gain information, because knowledge gives them control over others.

Gossip, by its very nature, is not wholesome or beneficial for building others up. In fact, it does quite the opposite. To apply Ephesians 4:29 is to cultivate wholesome conversations that are helpful and beneficial to others who are listening. Build one another up. Encourage and pray for one another. This is how we are called to live as the body of Christ. This makes us different from the world.

A gossip betrays a confidence, but a trustworthy man keeps a secret.

Proverbs 11:13

A perverse man stirs up dissension, and a gossip separates close friends.

Proverbs 16:28

Proverbs is full of admonitions about the danger of the tongue and the destructiveness of gossip. A woman who gossips will continually find it difficult to develop honest, open relationships, because her friends will learn not to trust her with their secrets and struggles.

In this way, a gossip misses out on life; she fails to enjoy the blessing and treasure of helping others carry their burdens (see Gal. 6:2).

PRAYER STARTER : 7

Father, Your Word speaks of edification and uplifting speech, not speech that is malicious or slandering. Lord, You know that _____ is struggling with this. Please honor her honesty and admission of this stronghold in her heart. Lord, we ask that You release her from this bondage of gossip. Give her love and heartfelt concern for others, rather than insensitivity and the tendency to tear them down with her words . . .

RECOMMENDED RESOURCES : 8

Barthel, Tara, and Judy Dabler. *Peacemaking Women: Biblical Hope for Resolving Conflict*. Baker, 2005.

Bridges, Jerry. *Respectable Sins: Confronting the Sins We Tolerate*. NavPress, 2007.

DiMarco, Hayley. *Mean Girls: Facing Your Beauty Turned Beast*. Baker, 2004.

Kuhatschek, Jack. *Self-Control: Mastering Our Passions*. Zondervan, 2001.

Mayhall, Carole. *Words That Hurt, Words That Heal*. NavPress, 2007.

Peace, Martha. *Damsels in Distress: Biblical Solutions for Problems Women Face*. P&R Publishing, 2006.

Pegues, Deborah. *30 Days to Taming Your Tongue: What You Say (and Don't Say) Can Improve Your Friendships*. Harvest House, 2005.

Rose, Shirley. *The Eve Factor: Resisting and Overcoming Temptation*. NavPress, 2006.

Grief and Loss

1 PORTRAITS

- "What? How?" Katie collapsed in shock and horror, the phone falling out of her hand. Her best friend and former roommate, Brittany, had been hit by a drunk driver and died on the scene. At the funeral, Katie was numb. *How could God . . . ? It doesn't make any sense. It just hurts. A lot.* Katie was angry at God, at the drunk driver, at the world. *Where do I go from here? How do I move on? I can't pull myself together. I need help.*

- Tina couldn't seem to stop crying. She was angry at herself for agreeing to move and angry at her husband, Bill, for taking a job a thousand miles from her hometown. She missed everyone—her church, the friends she had grown up with, and most of all, her family. She didn't want to be here, and she *certainly* didn't want to make new friends. Tina didn't have a job yet, so she spent most of her days at home, watching television or talking to her family back home. She rarely ventured out, except to buy groceries. When her husband confronted her, Tina exploded. "I'm hurt. I'm grieving. I've lost everything I've ever known. It's like starting all over again, and I'm not sure I want to."

- Amy couldn't drive past the hospital without feeling that sick, clenching feeling in her gut. She had spent two years watching her mom struggle with breast cancer. Her days, and her nights for that matter, had revolved around taking care of Mom. And now she was gone. Amy felt empty inside, as though there were a big hole in her heart. She cried until there were no more tears to cry and still, every time she thought about her mom, she broke down. *Maybe I just need to forget it and move on,* Amy thinks. *But I can't. She was my mom.*

2 DEFINITIONS AND KEY THOUGHTS

- *Grief* is the *intense emotional suffering* and *deep mental anguish* experienced as a result of loss. More than mere sadness, grief affects a woman on every level—physically, emotionally, psychologically, socially, and spiritually.

- Psalm 23 describes grief as "the valley of the shadow of death." Grief is *painful*. It is a *lingering process*. But it is also the beginning of a *healing journey* that can last anywhere from three months to more than two years, and can affect a woman for a lifetime.

- Grief is an *appropriate and healthy response* not only to death but also to any significant change or loss in life—*relationship breakup, divorce, broken friendship, unemployment, disaster, or misfortune.*

- It's estimated that, each year, 13 million Americans grieve the death of a friend or loved one, 2.5 million Americans experience the grief of divorce, and 15.6 million Americans suffer the grief of a romantic breakup.[1]

- *Grieving the loss of a child* can be one of the most difficult circumstances of life. The United States government's statistics show that 228,000 children and young adults die every year.[2]

- Despite the fact that many people experience grief, the National Institute for Mental Health reports that *only about 10 percent of people who experience a significant loss ever seek professional help.*[3]

- More than just a feeling, grief is actually *a complex set of emotions*, which manifest differently in women, depending on personality, coping mechanisms, and past experiences. Women who are grieving may experience loss *psychologically* through feelings, thoughts, or attitudes; *socially* as they interact with others; and *physically* as it negatively affects their health.

- A woman who is grieving the loss of a loved one may experience *intense feelings of guilt* for an aspect of her relationship with the deceased person. Especially when death is unexpected, a woman may *wish she had done something more* and may struggle with *regret and unfinished business.*

- A *sudden death* (for example, car accident, heart attack, suicide) can be more difficult to grieve because of the *shock factor.* There is no warning, no chance to say good-bye, and no opportunity to prepare for the loss.

- Sometimes feelings of anger and sadness are *projected onto God.* When a loss doesn't seem to make sense, a woman may *blame God* as the cause of her pain. She may view God as distant, cruel, or uncaring.

- Often *well-meaning friends are at a loss to help* a woman who is grieving. They may think they need to cheer her up or help her move on, but this can actually add to a woman's stress, *causing her to either avoid friends or fake feeling okay*, rather than expressing her true feelings.

- The process of grieving *cannot be rushed.* Every woman is different, and there is *no right way to work through the emotions* of loss. Attempting to hold oneself together or be strong will only *slow down the journey of healing* and may lead to further pain in the future.

- Sometimes loss is cumulative and a new experience of loss *awakens memories of early losses* that were never fully grieved. Often grieving can *intensify during certain times of the year*, such as the month a person died, family holidays, and birthdays and an anniversary.

Stages of Grief

Grief can be *felt in many different ways.* It has *several stages* that were originally identified by Elisabeth Kübler-Ross.[4]

1. *Denial and shock.* Intellectually, a woman may comprehend the loss of her loved one, but her emotions may not experience the pain yet. In this state of numbness, she may feel as if the death or loss isn't real.

2. *Anger and blame.* Once the reality of the loss begins to sink in, a woman may experience intense feelings of anger. Often this anger is directed toward God for not intervening. A grieving woman may become preoccupied with memories of what has been lost and withdraw for a time.

3. *Bargaining.* In case of impending death or loss (of a job, a marriage, and so on), a woman may bargain with God for herself or a loved one. During this phase, a woman may call on God and attempt to negotiate her circumstances.

4. *Depression.* Pain and loss are finally *felt* during this phase. A woman may cry uncontrollably and experience heartache and deep emotional pain. It's a time of emotional instability, and many women feel disorganized and wonder if life can ever be normal again.

5. *Acceptance.* Eventually a woman begins to come to terms with the death or loss she has experienced. She is able to express her pain in words and talk openly about the subject of her loss. She takes steps to reorganize her life, fill new roles, and reconnect with family and friends. Verbalization serves as a key sign of acceptance.

- Although these stages serve as a helpful outline, *every woman's experience of grief is unique.* A person will probably not experience the stages sequentially; rather, they are a cycle, and *grieving women may experience these emotions in different orders and for varying lengths of time.*

- Many people describe grief as a roller coaster of pain. It is important to give a grieving woman the freedom to *feel* the pain, rather than trying to cheer her up. Thankfully, "weeping may endure for a night, but joy comes in the morning" (Ps. 30:5 NKJV).

- The goal of grieving is *not to get things back to normal.* After a loss, a woman's entire life may change. The goal is to *find and accept a new normal.*

3 ASSESSMENT INTERVIEW

In the healthy process of grieving, it is important to assess for the presence of *complicated grief*—when a woman gets *stuck* in grief and falls into debilitating depression.

Rule Outs

1. On a scale of 1 to 10, with 1 being great and 10 being extremely depressed, where would you put yourself today? (*If depression is present, see also the chapter "Depression."*)

2. Do you have any thoughts of hurting yourself? (*If suicidal tendencies are evident, get professional help immediately.*)

General Questions

Note: These questions are directed toward a woman who is grieving over a death but could be easily rephrased for a woman who is grieving some other form of loss.

1. Who has died? How did it happen?
2. Was the death unexpected or traumatic? (*For example, was it a suicide, a sudden accident, or a death at home?*)
3. How did you find out? Where were you when the death occurred? (*Listen for ways that the woman may be blaming herself or feeling guilty for what happened. For example, was she driving the car that had the accident? Was she out of town? Was she present?*)
4. How did you feel after the death? What hit you the hardest?
5. What emotions have you had since the death? What feelings are most prominent or reoccurring?
6. How are you handling or processing the pain? Who have you been talking to about it?
7. Tell me about your relationship with _____. How close were you? When was the last time you talked?
8. Does this loss remind you of any other loss that you have experienced?
9. What does the loss mean for you personally?
10. At what level are you functioning right now? Are you able to carry on most of your regular activities? Do you spend most of the day in bed? Do you cry a lot? Tell me about a typical day.
11. When are your best times and your worst times?
12. Who else knows what you are going through? Who is supporting you emotionally and spiritually?

WISE COUNSEL 4

Any feelings a grieving woman may experience of *wanting to die* or *not having a reason to live* must be taken very seriously. Give a referral for immediate professional care and/or medication, if necessary.

Assess how the woman is *functioning in daily life* and what help she might need. Reassure the woman that the process of grief *takes time* and that the range and intensity of emotions she is experiencing are *the body's normal way of processing loss.* Those who love deeply also grieve deeply.

Give the woman the freedom to talk honestly about what she is feeling and *practice reflective listening.* Do not rob her of her pain or cheapen the anguish she feels with cliché Christian statements, such as, "God loves you" or "All things work together for good" or "Trust God." While these statements are theologically true, when a woman is experiencing the anger, grief, and disbelief of tragic loss, *she will probably not be capable of processing such truth right away.* Give her the freedom to experience and work through the pain and loss. Telling her to paste on a smile, trust God, and move on will only *complicate her healing process*. Instead, *provide a therapeutic environment*, but be careful not to tell her what to feel.

Remind the woman that no two people process grief in exactly the same way, while at the same time *normalizing the process* by identifying her feelings as common with other people suffering an important loss.

5 : ACTION STEPS

1. Allow Yourself to Feel the Pain

- You have experienced a significant loss. Pain and grief are normal. It would be more of a concern if you seemed to be feeling totally fine than if you seem to be falling apart. Allow yourself to take the time to actually work through the grieving process and heal emotionally.
- Trying to just push through and hold yourself together might seem easier, but it will only hurt you more in the long run. If your grief is not felt and resolved, it will keep you tied down to the past.
- Take a step back from some of your commitments, if possible, and try not to attempt too much. Direct your energies toward healing and make sure you take care of your body. As you work through the healing process, eat regularly and get a good night's sleep every night.

2. Maintain Friendships

- While some alone time is healthy, allowing you to think and process what has happened, too much isolation can lead to feelings of depression and hopelessness and cause you to lose a healthy perspective.
- Spend time with people you trust and let yourself be weak around them. Talk about what you are feeling and thinking. Talk about the memories you have of your loved one, and don't be afraid to discuss your fears and anxieties as well. Let others comfort you and share in your journey toward healing.
- Attend a grief support group at a local church or counseling center. In this safe environment, you will have the opportunity to process what you are feeling with other people who are experiencing similar losses.

3. Realize That Grief Is Normal and Healthy

- Grieving is a normal, expected, and healthy reaction in the wake of loss and it cannot be rushed. Grief serves as confirmation that you are actually processing your pain rather than bottling it up inside.
- Trying to hide your feelings of loss will only cause problems in other areas—emotionally, spiritually, or physically. However, the grieving process can be a major avenue of growth and life-transforming change if you allow yourself to work through it.

- The intensity of your pain is normal and eventually it will begin to subside as you heal and gain perspective. The pain will probably never disappear completely but it will become bearable.

4. Rest in God's Strong Arms

- As you begin to process your loss, a million questions will likely flood your mind. Some of them can be answered, but many times there simply are no satisfactory answers to the pain you feel. Don't feel pressured to figure it out.
- Be honest with God as you grieve. He weeps with you in your pain and, more than anything, He longs for you to be honest with Him. Whatever you're feeling—anger, frustration, pain—talk to God about it. He may not answer all your questions, but He does offer peace and rest.

BIBLICAL INSIGHTS 6

When Jesus saw her weeping, and the Jews who had come along with her also weeping, he was deeply moved in spirit and troubled. . . . Jesus wept.

John 11:33, 35

Expressing sorrow is a healthy response to grief. Even with the full knowledge that He would bring Lazarus to life only moments later, Jesus wept. He was angered to see the ravaging effects of sin on His precious child.

Being a Christian does not mean being happy all the time. Jesus Himself was "deeply moved in spirit and troubled" at death. Jesus knows the pain of loss and deep sorrow. He knows the incredible power of death, and understands our pain.

Jesus said to her, "I am the resurrection and the life. He who believes in me will live, even though he dies; and whoever lives and believes in me will never die. Do you believe this?"

John 11:25–26

Because of sin, death comes to all of us (Rom. 5:12–14). Though we may try to ignore it, we cannot escape it. Feared or embraced, expected or not, death still occurs. When we are faced with the reality of loss, we begin to grasp that death is not normal.

Even in the midst of sorrow, Jesus *is* life. As believers, we do not grieve as those who have no hope, because death is not eternal for Christians. "The sting of death is sin" (1 Cor. 15:56), but death is no more than a passing shadow between this earth and God's presence.

Even though I walk through the valley of the shadow of death, I will fear no evil, for you are with me; your rod and your staff, they comfort me.

Psalm 23:4

Cast your cares on the Lord and he will sustain you; he will never let the righteous fall.

Psalm 55:22

In our deepest moments of grief and loss, we need only look to Jesus. Rather than trying to be strong, we can rest in His arms, confident that He is strong enough to carry us when we are too weak and broken to walk.

God is faithful, and even when it seems as though our world is falling apart, He promises never to leave us or forsake us. On the cross, Jesus was stricken, smitten by God, and afflicted (see Isa. 53:3–4). He is no stranger to pain and suffering.

Even in the dark place of pain, anguish, and grief, we can be confident that Jesus is right there with us. He weeps with us in our sorrow and longs to heal our broken hearts.

He will wipe every tear from their eyes. There will be no more death or mourning or crying or pain, for the old order of things has passed away.

Revelation 21:4

As Christians, this is our future. While death is a reality in this sinful, fallen world, it is not the final reality. By rising again from the dead, Jesus conquered death and now holds "the keys of death and Hades" (Rev. 1:18).

Believers have the ultimate assurance. We believe that Jesus died, rose again, ascended, and is coming back; and we also believe that He will bring with Him all believers who have died. One day, all believers will be reunited with Him forever.

7 PRAYER STARTER

Lord, today our hearts are heavy, and the hurt goes deep. There are a lot of questions, God, and very few answers. We choose to trust You, because we know that You are good. Give _____ comfort and peace. Wrap her up in Your strong arms and make Your presence real to her as she grieves. God, I thank You that not only do You cry with us, but You also promise to heal our broken hearts, to bind up our wounds . . .

8 RECOMMENDED RESOURCES

Cox, David, and Candy Arrington. *Aftershock: Help, Hope, and Healing in the Wake of Suicide*. B&H, 2003.

Dunn, Bill, and Kathy Leonard. *Through a Season of Grief: Devotions for Your Journey from Mourning to Joy*. Thomas Nelson, 2004.

Kübler-Ross, Elisabeth. *On Death and Dying*. MacMillan, 1969.

Lewis, C. S. *A Grief Observed*. HarperOne, 2001.

MacArthur, John. *Safe in the Arms of God: Words from Heaven about the Death of a Child*. Thomas Nelson, 2003.

Neff, Miriam. *From One Widow to Another: Conversations about the New You*. Moody, 2009.

Sittser, Jerry. *A Grace Disguised: How the Soul Grows through Loss*. Zondervan, 2004.

Wangerin, Walter, Jr. *Mourning into Dancing*. Zondervan, 1996.

Wright, H. Norman. *Experiencing Grief*. B&H, 2004.

Yancey, Philip. *Where Is God When It Hurts?* Zondervan, 1997.

CDs

Clinton, Tim. *An Invitation to Comfort*. Maranatha Music, 2008.

Website

GriefShare is a grief recovery support group network where you can find help and healing after the loss of a loved one. For more information, or to find a group near you, visit www.griefshare.org.

Infertility

1 PORTRAITS

- Sarah and Ron are hurt and discouraged. They have been trying to have a baby for three years. Their doctor told them the only way they will likely be able to conceive is through in vitro fertilization, but they are hesitant to choose this option because of their religious beliefs. *Will we ever be able to have the family we've always dreamed of having?* Sarah wonders. *I want a baby so badly.* Sarah is beginning to think that God is punishing her and Ron for their past sexual failures.

- Anna has had four miscarriages and has never been able to carry a baby to term. Each time, the excitement of a child, followed by the pain of loss, plunges Anna into depression. In the past she's started feeling better after a few months, but this time there's just no reason to hope anymore. Anna is fixated on her failure to have the son that her husband has always wanted. Lately her feelings of hopelessness and anger have led to thoughts of suicide. *If I can't give my husband any children*, Anna questions, *what's the point of even living? All I am is a failure.*

- Several years after losing her husband and only child in a horrible automobile accident, Brenna began to contemplate what she had done as a young college sophomore—she had given her eggs, that were then frozen, for an experimental reproduction study being done at the college's medical school. Recently she has been wondering if she could be a parent to a test-tube baby that is still waiting to be unfrozen . . . or if it's even ethical. "I want another child," Brenna says, "but I don't see myself getting married again. And I'm not just going to go out and have sex with somebody to get pregnant."

2 DEFINITIONS AND KEY THOUGHTS

- *Infertility* is *the inability to conceive or carry a child to delivery.* A couple is usually considered *infertile after they have not conceived after having intercourse regularly for one year without using birth control. Sterility* is when there is a *lack of sperm production* in the male or the *inability to ovulate* in the female.

- Infertility may be caused by unknown problems or by problems in the male, female, or in both the male and female. About 30 percent of reported cases of infertility are due to *problems in the male*; another 30 percent are due to *problems in the female*; and the remaining 40 percent are due to *unknown problems or problems in both the male and female.*[1]

- Infertility may be caused by *any interruption in the natural process* of fertilization, pregnancy, and birth. This natural process includes ejaculation of normal amounts of healthy sperm, passage of the sperm through the cervix and into the fallopian tube of the female, passage of an ovum (egg) down the fallopian tube from an ovary, fertilization in the fallopian tube, implantation of the fertilized egg in a receptive uterus, and the ability to carry the fetus to term. The most common problems in women are the *failure to ovulate and a blockage of the fallopian tubes.* The most common problem in men is *low sperm count.*

- There could also be underlying problems with infertility. This includes *diseases*, such as diabetes or mumps (in adult men), hormonal imbalances, endometriosis, pelvic inflammatory disease (which is often caused by sexually transmitted diseases); *alcohol or drug abuse*; and exposure to *workplace hazards* or *environmental toxins.* Uterine *irritation* or *infection* that sometimes accompanies the use of an IUD could also negatively affect fertility. Sometimes there may be a chemical, hormonal, or immunological *incompatibility* between the male and female. Psychological factors are difficult to evaluate due to the stressful nature of infertility itself.

- The Centers for Disease Control report that 7.3 million (11.8 percent) women between the ages of 15 and 44 have "an impaired ability to have children." While pregnancy is not impossible in this case, the *chances of conceiving without medical intervention* are quite unlikely.[2]

- Infertility is a *widespread concern among women*, with 2.1 million (7.4 percent) married women between the ages of 15 and 44 considered infertile (unable to get pregnant for at least 12 months).[3]

- Statistics show that 7.3 million women between the ages of 15 and 44 have *used infertility services.*[4] Often medical procedures are successful in treating infertility, but some couples may struggle with the intrusiveness and ethicality of certain options. Some women are simply *unable to conceive or carry a child.* Acquiring this knowledge will likely lead to a period of grief for a woman and her husband.

ASSESSMENT INTERVIEW 3

1. How long have you been struggling with infertility?
2. Have you seen your doctor for this problem? What did your doctor tell you? Did he or she recommend any treatment options? Are you currently receiving any type of treatment for infertility?
3. Do you have any other children? If so, were there any complications during the pregnancy or labor?
4. Have you fully discussed the subject of infertility with your husband? How do you feel about the way the conversation went? Did you believe that he heard and understood you?

5. Have the two of you discussed other alternatives for having a child, such as adoption? What was the conclusion of these discussions?

6. In what ways has infertility impacted your relationship? Do you still feel connected to your husband? Do you ever feel distant from him?

7. How do you think you will feel if you are unable to conceive a child?

8. Do you feel any pressure from family or friends to conceive? Do you feel supported by family and friends? What has been the overall response you have received from others?

9. What do you feel is the biggest issue that you are struggling with right now related to infertility? Is it your marriage, your relationship with God, or something else?

10. Would you be willing to commit to the counseling process to discuss these issues?

4 : WISE COUNSEL

Testing for Infertility

When a couple is faced with infertility, it is *important that their doctor examine both the woman and the man.* The doctor may want to begin by *testing the husband's semen.* The doctor will look at the number, shape, and movement of the sperm. Sometimes doctors may suggest *testing the level of a man's hormones.*

The first step in testing a woman for infertility is to *find out if she is ovulating* each month. There are several ways to test this. A woman can track her ovulation at home by

recording the changes in her morning body temperature (basal body temperature) for several months

recording the texture of her cervical mucus for several months

using a home ovulation test kit (these are available at drug or grocery stores)

The woman's doctor can also check if she is ovulating by doing blood tests and an ultrasound of her ovaries. *If the woman is ovulating normally, more tests will be needed.* Some common tests of fertility in women include:

Hysterosalpingography. In this test doctors use X-rays to check for *physical problems of the uterus and fallopian tubes.* They start by injecting a special dye through the vagina into the uterus. This dye shows up on the X-ray, allowing the doctor to see if the dye moves normally through the uterus into the fallopian tubes. With these X-rays doctors can find blockages that may be causing infertility. *Blockages can prevent the egg from moving from the fallopian tube to the uterus and can also keep the sperm from reaching the egg.*

Laparoscopy. During this surgery the doctor makes a small cut in the lower abdomen and inserts a laparoscope to see inside the abdomen. With this instrument, the doctor can *check the ovaries, fallopian tubes, and uterus* for *disease and physical problems.* Doctors can usually find *scarring and endometriosis* with laparoscopy.

As more couples are making *the decision to postpone childbearing to a later age,* there is a greater need for treatment for infertility. In women, *fertility begins to decline in the mid-twenties* and continues, more and more rapidly, until menopause. Male fertility declines gradually until *age forty* and then declines more quickly.

Treatment for infertility is geared toward the specific problem. The first step may be the *treatment of underlying disease* and having men avoid substances that might negatively affect sperm count. *Fertility drugs,* some of which increase the possibility of multiple births, are often prescribed. A *surgical correction of blocked tubes* may be attempted if necessary.

Assisted Reproductive Technology

Assisted Reproductive Technology (ART) is a modern treatment term that describes several methods used to help infertile couples. ART involves *removing eggs from a woman's body, combining them with sperm in the laboratory, and putting the embryos back into a woman's body. Success rates vary* and depend on many factors. Some things that affect the success rate of ART include:

age of the partners

reasons for infertility

policies of the clinic

type of ART

if the egg is fresh or frozen

if the embryo is fresh or frozen

The United States Centers for Disease Control and Prevention (CDC) collect success rates on ART for some fertility clinics. According to the 2003 CDC report on ART, the average percentage of ART methods that led to a healthy baby were as follows:

37.3 percent in women under the age of 35

30.2 percent in women ages 35–37

20.2 percent in women ages 38–40

11.0 percent in women ages 41–42[5]

ART can be expensive and time-consuming but it has allowed many couples to have children, who otherwise would not have been conceived. Common *methods of ART* include the following.

In vitro fertilization (IVF) means fertilization outside of the body. IVF is the most effective ART. Often it is used when a woman's fallopian tubes are blocked or when the man produces too few sperm. Doctors treat the woman with *a drug that causes the ovaries to produce multiple eggs.* Once mature, the eggs are removed from the woman. They are put in a dish in the lab along with the man's sperm for fertilization. After three to five days, *healthy embryos are implanted in the woman's uterus.*

171

Zygote intrafallopian transfer (ZIFT) or tubal embryo transfer is similar to IVF. Fertilization occurs in the laboratory. Then the very young embryo is *transferred to the fallopian tube* instead of the uterus.

Gamete intrafallopian transfer (GIFT) involves transferring eggs and sperm into the woman's fallopian tube, so *fertilization occurs in the woman's body.* Few medical practices offer GIFT as an option.

Intracytoplasmic sperm injection (ICSI) is used for couples in which there are *serious problems with the sperm.* Sometimes it is also used for older couples or for those with failed IVF attempts. In ICSI *a single sperm is injected into a mature egg.* Then the embryo is transferred to the uterus or fallopian tube.

Sometimes ART procedures involve the use of *donor eggs* (eggs from another woman), *donor sperm, or previously frozen embryos.* Donor eggs are sometimes used for women who cannot produce eggs. Also donor eggs or donor sperm may be used when the woman or man has a genetic disease that can be passed on to the baby. *This procedure raises a number of ethical issues that are important to consider from a Christian perspective.*

If the woman is seeking counsel because she wants to find out what is causing the infertility in her marriage or know whether or not she and her husband will ever have children, you should *provide a referral* to a primary care physician. Be sure to *continue counseling with follow-up sessions* as she and her husband progress through this process.

Doctors will search for the cause of infertility by doing a complete fertility evaluation on both the woman and her husband. Usually this process begins with physical exams and by taking health and sexual histories. If there are no obvious problems, such as poorly timed intercourse or absence of ovulation, tests will be needed. *Finding the cause of infertility can be a long, complex, and emotional process.* It may take months for the doctor to complete all the necessary tests. The woman and her husband may need *ongoing encouragement and guidance* from a counselor to get through this difficult time.

5 : ACTION STEPS

1. Get a Thorough Checkup from an Infertility Specialist

- You and your husband should begin by getting a medical evaluation. It is also important that you address any emotional experiences or relationship problems that may be occurring at this difficult time.
- *Provide your client with a referral list of reputable doctors in your area who specialize in fertility.*

2. Talk to Your Husband and Consider the Options

- Become informed about all of the options that your doctor may suggest. You and your husband need to become students of infertility, knowing its causes and treatment options rather than just taking the word of your doctor.
- Whatever is the cause of the problem, good communication and genuine expressions of empathy and support will help strengthen the relationship between you and your husband during this time.

3. Pray with Your Husband

- When a medical cause is ruled out or discovered, spend time with your husband in prayer, and pray individually as well. Ask for God's peace and wisdom.
- You and your husband may also want to consider a time of fasting before making a decision regarding how you will deal with the issues that have been discovered.

4. Face Any Emotional Roadblocks

- Numerous emotions may surface during this time. Anger, confusion, stress, frustration, sadness, grief, and loss are just a few common and normal responses. It is important to express these emotions, or they will begin to form a root of bitterness in your heart that is capable of destroying your relationship with your husband.
- Be honest about the emotional damage and destructive reactions that may be present in your response to infertility.
- *Help the woman and her husband express their inmost feelings and learn how to communicate them to each other in a positive manner.*

5. Consider Attending a Support Group with Your Husband

- Attending a group for couples with infertility issues could be a healing next step. Getting to know other couples who have also struggled with infertility will allow you and your husband to learn from their experience, feel less alone in your pain, and give you a chance to encourage those in the group.
- *Provide the woman and her husband with a list of groups that meet in your area.*

6. Consider Adoption

- Adoption is an extremely viable option for an infertile couple. Spend time in prayer about the possibility of adopting and begin looking into and meeting with adoption agencies in your local area.
- *Help the couple compile a list of adoption options and the issues involved, for example, the financial requirement and the challenges adoption can pose.*

7. Get Involved with Children

- Getting involved with serving children can help fill your need to nurture and care for little ones, especially if adoption is not a viable option. You could serve in a Sunday school class, nursery, or mentoring program. In this way you will be passing a legacy of faith and strength on to the next generation, investing in "spiritual children" if not biological children.

6 BIBLICAL INSIGHTS

Is anything too hard for the LORD? I will return to you at the appointed time next year and Sarah will have a son.

Genesis 18:14

Every conception is a miracle. Sarah and Abraham were old, and she was past the childbearing age when God showed his grace and blessed them with a son, Isaac. This story shows that there is nothing impossible with God. If God desires for you to have a child, He will work out every single aspect.

But the angel said to him: "Do not be afraid, Zechariah; your prayer has been heard. Your wife Elizabeth will bear you a son, and you are to give him the name John. He will be a joy and delight to you, and many will rejoice because of his birth."

Luke 1:13–14

God sent an angel specifically to tell Zechariah that God had heard his prayers and that Elizabeth would have a son. God is intentional and intimately involved in the process of childbearing. He is sovereign and He listens carefully to every single heartache, worry, and fear.

I will bring health and healing; . . . I will heal my people and will let them enjoy abundant peace and security.

Jeremiah 33:6

Through whatever happens, God wants to give you healing and peace. Whether or not God chooses to bless you with a child, His love for you is unchanging. God is not punishing you with infertility but He does use trials to grow our faith and increase our intimacy with Him.

7 PRAYER STARTER

God, thank You for Your goodness and Your love for _____ and her husband. We pray to You today because they want to begin a family and they are having trouble conceiving a child. We ask that Your will be done in this situation and for You to bring comfort during this time. We thank You for the love this woman and her husband have for one another and ask that You bring children into their lives for them to love and raise up in the days ahead . . .

RECOMMENDED RESOURCES : 8

Glahn, Sandra. *The Infertility Companion: Hope and Help for Couples Facing Infertility*. Zondervan, 2004.

Saake, Jennifer. *Hannah's Hope: Seeking God's Heart in the Midst of Infertility, Miscarriage, and Adoption Loss*. NavPress, 2005.

Schalesky, Marlo. *Empty Womb, Aching Heart: Hope and Help for Those Struggling with Infertility*. Baker, 2001.

Vredevelt, Pam. *Empty Arms: For Those Who Suffered a Miscarriage, Stillbirth, or Tubal Pregnancy*. Multnomah, 2001.

Weschler, Toni. *Taking Charge of Your Fertility*. HarperCollins, 2006.

Woodward, Shannon. *Inconceivable: Finding Peace in the Midst of Infertility*. David C. Cook, 2006.

Lesbianism and Same-Sex Attraction

1 PORTRAITS

- Kay dated casually when she was in high school but she always seemed to feel more comfortable around her girlfriends. One day Nancy, a new girl in school, asked her to run an errand with her. On the way Nancy drove to a secluded park, stopped the car, and gently leaned into Kay. "I want to kiss you so much it hurts," she whispered. She kissed Kay, first tenderly, and then passionately. Kay's emotions exploded. She enjoyed the attention and sexual attraction but she felt terribly ashamed and confused. After a week of emotional torture, she confided to her school counselor, "I don't know who I am anymore. Am I a lesbian?"

- Heather was always a "loner." Her mother worked late hours and her father was always traveling for business. Growing up, Heather rarely felt as if she belonged in any group of people. When she went off to college, her "loner" reputation followed. Amber, who was in Heather's philosophy class, seemed to mirror Heather's image. Quickly Amber and Heather became friends and they roomed together their second year of college. As Heather and Amber grew closer, they met each other's need for affection. Then Heather realized she was attracted to Amber. She began to wonder, *Am I in love with Amber?* One night, after a long conversation, Heather and Amber decided to test out their feelings of attraction.

2 DEFINITIONS AND KEY THOUGHTS

- *Same-sex attraction* is a sexual predisposition toward members of the same sex. *Same-sex behavior* is the engagement of any sexual activity between two people of the same sex.

- Probably no other topic elicits *such powerful emotions from people having entrenched and conflicting perspectives* as does homosexuality, especially in the Christian community. Many hold to the biblical view that homosexuality is a perversion of God's design for sex and a distortion of human identity. Others argue that homosexuals don't have a choice about their sexual preference and they lobby for acceptance of the people and their behavior.

- *Identifying the causes of homosexuality* has proven to be a difficult and explosive issue. *Some argue that people choose homosexuality based on the influences of their social environment; others say that homosexuality is genetically predetermined.*

At this point, no definitive study has conclusively established the etiology of homosexuality, but several factors seem to contribute.

— A person's *family background*, and especially one's relationship with the same-sex parent, can shape emerging sexuality in adolescence.
— *Social interactions*, especially during the formative years, teach and reinforce sexual norms.
— *Early sexual experiences* and particularly seductive, abusive, and homosexual experiences can shape a child's self-concept and perception of sexuality.
— *Biological causes* have received the most attention in recent years. However, only ambivalent research results exist. These have often been presented as "proving a biological or genetic cause" for homosexuality. Such a conclusion is compelling to those who espouse a gay lifestyle because it no longer would be considered a choice but a *biological imperative* and, therefore, *not a sinful orientation* requiring a spiritual solution.

• Research reports that 86 percent of women said they are *attracted to males only*. Ten percent of women said they were attracted *mostly to males*. And 3.4 percent of women said they were attracted *only or mostly to females*, or *equally attracted to both* sexes.[1]
• Research shows that 4 percent of women have had a *sexual experience with another woman* in the past year. Another 3 percent of women have *had sex with both males and females* in the past year.[2]
• *Sexual attraction is not a clear-cut issue*. Research shows that even among women who have had sexual relations with another woman, 65 percent say they are heterosexual.[3]
• According to the *Duke Journal of Gender Law and Policy*, more than 68 percent of lesbians report having had a range of *mental health problems* in the past, including long-term depression and sadness, constant anxiety and fear, and other mental health concerns.[4]
• The *passionate and risky nature* of homosexual encounters may make individuals more vulnerable to various *sexually transmitted diseases*, including HIV/AIDS.

ASSESSMENT INTERVIEW 3

1. Tell me a little bit about the closest relationships in your life. Who are your best friends? Whom do you talk to when you're upset or stressed?
2. How have you related to members of the opposite sex? Are you attracted to them? Have you had dating relationships with the opposite sex?
3. Do you fantasize about members of the same sex? How many of these fantasies have come true (or close to true)?
4. When did your same-sex attraction begin? How did you become aware of these feelings?

5. Have you acted out your urges? If so, tell me about your experiences.

6. Are you currently engaging in sexual relationships?

7. Have you told anyone about your same-sex urges (and behaviors)? How have they responded?

8. What are your hopes and fears about your sexuality?

9. What are your goals for counseling?

10. Talk about your relationship with your family of origin. How is your relationship with your mother and father? Were they present in your home when you were a child? Were Mom and Dad actively involved in your life? How did (do) they express affection toward each other? How do they express affection toward you?

11. When was your first sexual experience? What happened? How did it affect you at the time?

12. Have you ever been sexually abused? If so, was it by a same-sex or opposite-sex perpetrator?

4 : WISE COUNSEL

Don't compromise your professionalism by demonstrations of shock, judgment, or disapproval. Accept the woman as a wonderful creation of God who is wrestling with her sexuality. Most lesbians are *hypersensitive* and *hypervigilant* regarding this dynamic. Stay engaged and express any opinions in a matter-of-fact manner.

The client has come to you for help (or perhaps has been brought to you by someone else) and is in a very *vulnerable emotional state.* Her progress may depend on your ability to make her feel safe and to help her be honest about hurts, fears, and hopes for the future. So while you may be opposed to homosexual behavior, *empathy and understanding are essential* tools at the outset of counseling. *As a professional counselor, if you have a conflict of values, you need to refer the client judiciously to someone else.* At this time it is extremely important to *let your client know you accept her as fully deserving of God's love.*

Explore her feelings and attitudes about her homosexual urges and behaviors. In many cases, *clients come because they feel confused and ashamed.* (Those who feel satisfied and justified in their homosexuality will rarely, if ever, come for help.) She may experience *significant anxiety* over her sexual orientation and behaviors, and her fears may cloud her thinking processes.

One of the first tasks is to *help her resolve her identity confusion* and *decide who she is.* Put to her the challenge of answering the following crucial questions first. They will help clarify the identity puzzle.

Am I in fact gay? Answering yes would mean she is embracing a sexual identity.

Am I instead a woman who is struggling with homosexual attractions and desires? It is key to note that same-sex experimentation is not grounds for homosexual labeling. Often in adolescence, or in preadolescence, experimentation with homosexuality occurs. Usually this phase passes and the individual becomes exclusively heterosexual.

Avoid "Bible thumping" at all stages of counseling. Many clients already know that the Bible says homosexuality is sin and they have avoided coming to a pastor or Christian counselor because they don't want anyone to preach condemnation to them. It is important, however, to draw out what they understand the Bible to say about homosexuality and then discuss what that means and where the *dissonance* is. For instance, how does the woman deal with the Bible's statements? What does she want to accomplish to please God and to know His strength and purpose in her life?

Clients with same-sex attraction may be engaged in *addictive sexual activity.* This is most commonly found in men, but it does occur in women. Stopping addictive activity will *help a woman clarify her sexual orientation.* Many Christian counselors use an *addictions treatment model* in helping clients with same-sex attraction—and often in the context of group therapy for sexual addictions. This model is based on *several assumptions*, including the possibility of predispositions, the client's desire for change, turning to God for hope and strength, taking a fearless and searching moral inventory of urges and behaviors, genuine repentance, mutual support, and a long-term perspective about change.

Like alcoholics or drug addicts, individuals with same-sex attraction may never consider themselves "cured," but by acknowledging their powerlessness over the condition, they begin a process and learn day by day to walk in a way that can lead to a *new freedom in Christ.*

If you are not specifically trained in addictions counseling, you may want to *refer the client to a therapist* specializing in this type of treatment.

ACTION STEPS 5

Every Christian counselor should be prepared to help the client define her goals and move in a constructive direction toward resolving the confusing ambivalence around identity and behavior.

1. Identify Your Personal Goals

- Think about what you would like to achieve in counseling. What would you like your life to be like at the end of the counseling process? Share these thoughts with your counselor.

- *Determine if your goals and the client's goals are compatible with your faith and practice. As a professional counselor, if the client feels affirmed in her gay identity and lifestyle and wants help to have better relationships with same-sex partners, you should seek a referral for your client, since you do not believe that same-sex behavior is right before God. Remember, however, that clients may assume that a Christian counselor is rigid and condemning and they may be defensive until you demonstrate empathy and understanding. Help the client clarify her life goals by offering the stark choice of choosing a lesbian-affirming posture versus change therapy.*

- *If a woman admits her confusion and conflicting emotions about homosexual urges and behaviors and wants to change, offer her a realistic pathway on which she can experience peace, freedom, and joy in Christ, as well as engaging in meaningful nonsexual relationships with people of both genders.*

2. Explore Your Beliefs about Sexuality

- Discuss with your counselor what you have been taught in the past about sexuality and your past sexual experiences. What do you believe about same-sex attraction? How has this contributed to your current behavior system? What do you consider normal and abnormal?
- *Many who experience same-sex urges and behaviors come to counseling with a wealth of misinformation about causes, diseases, the definition of "normal" sexuality, and a host of other topics related to the problem. Some have been taught that they've committed a sin God won't forgive and they feel not only ashamed but also hopeless. Help the client understand God's design for sexuality, as well as His willingness to forgive and pardon all sin (see 1 John 1:9).*

3. Be Honest about Your Fears and Hopes

- If you are seeking counseling for same-sex attraction, you must be willing to be honest in exploring your emotions. This is an important step in feeling understood, building trust with your counselor, and moving forward.
- Many people hope that a counselor will give them a quick and easy solution and make them feel better right away. This, of course, won't happen. Same-sex attraction requires rugged realism about the process and goals for change. Change is possible but will require hard work and time, and even then, the urges may continue.

4. Realize the Importance of Mental Self-Control

- Be open to learning how thoughts and feelings dictate actions. Through the counseling process, practice new ways of interpreting and analyzing unwanted thoughts and feelings prior to acting on them.
- *The combination of sexual passion and shame causes many homosexuals to be preoccupied, even obsessed, with their sex life and identity. For some, their sexuality is primarily a fantasy world, but this world consumes their life. Sex becomes an obsession, and they can't stop thinking about it. Teach the client to identify thoughts, songs, passages of Scripture, and inspiring messages to focus on and confess aloud when unwanted or intrusive fantasies come into her mind.*

5. Be Encouraged by Each Step Forward

- Changing identity and a lifestyle is a monumental task. Other people with challenging issues, such as alcoholics, drug addicts, compulsive gamblers, and those with eating disorders, have successfully taken steps out of their darkness toward hope and health, and those suffering with homosexuality and lesbianism can do the same.

- Don't be ashamed of your past; instead, celebrate each step forward. Even if you slip, all is not lost. God loves you and He is in the process of helping you change. You can begin to move forward again by repenting, receiving the Lord's forgiveness, and focusing on biblical goals.

- *Provide strong encouragement that the benefits of progress are worth the struggle of moving forward.*

6. Consider Participating in a Support Group

- The encouragement that you will receive in a Christ-centered support group can be invaluable as you go through the process of change. In an environment of mutual support and accountability, you will hear from others who struggle with similar problems as you make courageous decisions and experience the joys of real change.

- *Provide a referral to a support group in the area for your client or start one yourself.*

BIBLICAL INSIGHTS 6

Therefore God gave them over in the sinful desires of their hearts to sexual impurity for the degrading of their bodies with one another. They exchanged the truth of God for a lie, and worshiped and served created things rather than the Creator—who is forever praised. Amen.

Because of this, God gave them over to shameful lusts. Even their women exchanged natural relations for unnatural ones. In the same way the men also abandoned natural relations with women and were inflamed with lust for one another. Men committed indecent acts with other men, and received in themselves the due penalty for their perversion.

Romans 1:24–27

Scripture is clear that sexual intimacy between a man and a woman within the marriage relationship is a beautiful gift and creation of God. However, this passage in Romans speaks about the misuse of that gift—"exchang[ing] natural relations for unnatural ones" and being "inflamed with lust for one another." If God created sex for a man and a woman, as Genesis states, any same-gender sexual activity lies outside the bounds of God's purpose and intent for sexual intimacy and as such cannot be blessed.

The belief that God ordained sex only for a man and a woman is not popular in today's relativistic society, where the truth of God has been exchanged for lies. Many in our society worship sexual pleasure, but the biblical teaching is that we must be in submission to God, and this includes the desire for sexual intimacy and all our desires. As Christians, our lives should not be about satisfying our desires, but obeying God and letting Him satisfy us.

Therefore, my dear friends, as you have always obeyed—not only in my presence, but now much more in my absence—continue to work out your salvation with fear and trembling, for it is God who works in you to will and to act according to his good purpose.

Philippians 2:12–13

Our obedience to God is a response to His goodness and greatness. We don't just obey if we feel like it. All of us have hard choices as we follow Christ, but God promises to work powerfully in us by His Spirit to equip us, change us, and inspire us to keep moving forward. God's desire for women and men is that we have a full life, not a life of destruction, which the Evil One desires for us (John 10:10).

You were taught, with regard to your former way of life, to put off your old self, which is being corrupted by its deceitful desires; to be made new in the attitude of your minds; and to put on the new self, created to be like God in true righteousness and holiness.

Ephesians 4:22–24

The process of change requires objectivity and tenacity. It does not just happen automatically. In this Ephesians passage, Paul says it's like changing clothes. We take off our old behaviors and thoughts; then our minds are renewed by the Scriptures, and we put on new, healthy, positive behaviors that honor God. To change clothes we have to be intentional about what we take off and put on. It's the same way with changing our lifestyle.

Therefore, prepare your minds for action; be self-controlled; set your hope fully on the grace to be given you when Jesus Christ is revealed. As obedient children, do not conform to the evil desires you had when you lived in ignorance. But just as he who called you is holy, so be holy in all you do; for it is written: "Be holy, because I am holy."

1 Peter 1:13–16

The measurement of our lives isn't what our society permits (or what it thinks is amusing or acceptable). Ultimately we answer to God alone, and one day we will give an account to Him for our behavior and lifestyle. This realization reframes our choices and helps us clarify our direction in life and the way we live.

PRAYER STARTER : 7

Father, You are wise and strong. _____ is struggling with her desires and she wants to change. Lord, You offer hope that change is possible. Give wisdom about the steps that can be taken to replace old fantasies with new, healthy thoughts. Provide courage for her to take the steps she needs to take and to keep moving forward when she feels discouraged . . .

RECOMMENDED RESOURCES : 8

Comiskey, Andrew. *Naked Surrender: Coming Home to Our True Sexuality.* InterVarsity, 2010.

Dallas, Joe, and Nancy Heche. *The Complete Christian Guide to Understanding Homosexuality: A Handbook for Helping Those Who Struggle with Same-Sex Attraction.* Harvest House, 2009.

Haley, Mike. *101 Frequently Asked Questions about Homosexuality.* Harvest House, 2004.

Hallman, Janelle. *The Heart of Female Same-Sex Attraction.* InterVarsity, 2008.

Heche, Nancy. *The Truth Comes Out: The Story of My Heart's Transformation.* Gospel Light, 2006.

Howard, Jeanette. *Into the Promised Land: Beyond the Lesbian Struggle.* Monarch, 2005.

Klein, Walter. *God's Word Speaks to Homosexuality.* Wine Press, 2007.

Paulk, Anne. *Restoring Sexual Identity: Hope for Women Who Struggle with Same-Sex Attraction.* Harvest House, 2003.

Stott, John. *Same Sex Partnership? A Christian Perspective.* Baker, 1998.

Yarhouse, Mark, and Stanton Jones. *Ex-Gays? A Longitudinal Study of Religiously Mediated Change in Sexual Orientation.* InterVarsity, 2007.

Masturbation

1 PORTRAITS

- Masturbation is a love-hate relationship for Laurel. Whenever she's stressed, anxious, or overwhelmed, she finds herself retreating once again to the practice, even using objects to increase the sensation. Yet every time she masturbates, Laurel is overwhelmed with feelings of guilt and shame. *Why am I doing this to myself? I am so sick. Will I even be able to enjoy sex with my husband one day?*

- As a little girl, Katie was molested by her cousin, Billy, who told her that he was just teaching her how to feel good. This incident confused Katie—she didn't like the idea of Billy touching her private parts but she did like the warm, ecstatic feeling it produced. Now, as a teenager, Katie masturbates compulsively. Every time she gets in a fight with her boyfriend or has an argument with her mom, she retreats to her room to "make it all go away."

- Carla enjoys sex with her husband, Ray, but she really enjoys using a vibrator too. Sometimes she feels guilty for getting so much pleasure out of a sex toy but she can't wait to use it again.

- A single woman in her mid-thirties, Beth has all but given up on getting married. "You might as well try the whole porn thing out," her friend Sharon mentions one day. "It helps ease the pain of not having someone, and, hey, it's not as bad as actually having sex with a guy." *Is masturbation a safe way to enjoy orgasms?* Beth wonders.

2 DEFINITIONS AND KEY THOUGHTS

- *Masturbation or self-sex* is *self-stimulation of the genitals* to achieve *sexual arousal and pleasure, usually to the point of orgasm* (sexual climax). It is commonly done by touching, stroking, or massaging the clitoris until an orgasm is achieved. Some women also use stimulation in the vagina to masturbate or use sex toys, such as a vibrator.

- Women masturbate for *a variety of reasons.*

  — It feels good.
  — One's partner isn't available for intercourse.
  — It relieves sexual tension and stress in general.
  — It avoids the risk of pregnancy and sexually transmitted diseases.

- In a study among college-aged women, 44 percent had masturbated before. Women who masturbated did so at *an average rate of 4.7 times a month.*[1]
- Often there is teaching that masturbation is a form of sexual perversion, and in the past, some believed that it led to blindness or paralysis or other terrible outcomes. Today most people view it as *a developmental behavior* that in and of itself *isn't wrong.* Researchers estimate that 25 percent of women masturbated for the first time when they were *eleven to thirteen years old.*[2]
- The challenge of masturbation, however, comes down to two primary issues: *fantasy* and *self-control.*
- In *The Act of Marriage after 40*, Tim and Beverly LaHaye observe:

  > All forms of masturbation have to be evaluated, not in the light of the physical experience, but in the mental attitude at the time. . . . Masturbation can also become self-addicting. . . . I think masturbation is a matter between the individual and God. If you can do it without feeling the need to confess it as sin, the physical function of bringing oneself to orgasm is not in itself a sinful act.[3]

- We agree that the act of self-sex in and of itself is not wrong. But when women masturbate *in conjunction with pornography or illicit sexual fantasies,* which is often the case, the act is sinful. Moreover, *masturbation is addictive.* What began as a way of relieving sexual stress can quickly become a chronic behavior, and Paul challenged each of us to let nothing master or control us except Christ (1 Cor. 6:12; 1 Thess. 4:3–5).
- Many single women assume that masturbation can help them deal with being single until they get married. They fail to realize, however, that *when the practice becomes habitual, it may threaten the beauty and intimacy of marital sex in the future.*
- Self-sex provides a sexual experience that misses the essential *purpose of sex: the joining of two to become one flesh, physically and emotionally.* Hence, we believe that masturbation *should not be used as a substitute for healthy, normal sexual activity in marriage.* When it becomes a distraction or a substitute for sexual and emotional interaction in marriage, it is a problem that needs to be addressed and *may signal that the relationship isn't healthy.*
- Some women use *sex toys,* such as vibrators, to *enhance sexual stimulation with their spouse or during self-sex.* For couples struggling sexually, sex therapists may recommend them. However, some partners feel threatened because they can't compete with the sensation provided by the toy. It is possible to get *addicted to the use of sex toys* so that sex becomes primarily or exclusively a self-absorbed means of orgasmic pleasure.
- Should we have pleasure and enjoyment in our sexuality? Absolutely, but not to the exclusion of building relational intimacy. Besides, *no woman is going to die because she didn't have sex.*

3 ASSESSMENT INTERVIEW

1. Talk with me about your self-sex behavior. Are you concerned about your own behavior or the behavior of your partner?
2. When did you first masturbate?
3. Is pornography or fantasizing part of your masturbation practices?
4. What is your attitude toward the use of vibrators and other sex toys?
5. Has the frequency of your self-sex changed since you first masturbated?
6. How often do you masturbate?
7. Do any specific stresses or pressures bring on the urge? Can you stop giving in to the urge?
8. Is masturbation (or your preoccupation with it) interfering with your relationships and healthy communication? If so, explain how.
9. What would you describe as a healthy and appropriate use of masturbation for you personally?
10. Is there any history of sexual abuse in your past? Have you had past sexual experiences (wanted or unwanted) involving another partner?

4 WISE COUNSEL

Many women *experiment with masturbation in their developmental years*, but the concern comes when masturbation becomes an obsessive, habitual practice. A lot of women experience intense feelings of guilt and shame but can't seem to stop because of their body's cravings for sexual pleasure.

Obsessive masturbation is a clear symptom of a deeper issue. If a woman has been molested, raped, or abused in the past, especially in her developmental years, she may turn to masturbation as a safe way to release sexual tension and unresolved heart wounds from the past abuse. If a woman has been deprived of healthy, intimate, trusting relationships within her family (and specifically, with her father), she may develop a habit of masturbation as a way of calming or soothing herself. (If this is the case, see the chapter "Child Sexual Abuse.")

A wise counselor needs to assess the woman's view of the subject of masturbation. Does she see it as normal? Does she feel guilty about the practice? Does she desire to stop? Does the behavior stem from a deeper, unmet need for trust and intimacy in relationships? Is past abuse a factor? Clearly, *when masturbation is coupled with lustful fantasies or serves as a substitute for healthy intimacy within marriage, it is wrong and needs to be addressed.*

The Bible has *very little, if anything to say about masturbation*, but it has a lot to say about God's amazing gift of sex in marriage and the sinful abuse of God-designed pleasure outside of that context. Scripture teaches that sex is more about giving than receiving: "The wife's body does not belong to her alone but also to her husband. In the same way, the husband's body does not belong to him alone but also to his wife" (1 Cor. 7:4).

ACTION STEPS : 5

1. Talk about Your Perceptions of Self-Sex

- What were you taught in your past about masturbation? Many women have never talked about this behavior because of associated feelings of shame, but the first step to changing is openness and honesty.
- Get to the heart of your motivation for engaging in this behavior. By exploring your perceptions and belief system about masturbation, you will be able to identify any underlying issues that may be present and causing distress or confusion.

2. Address the Root Issue

- Obsessive masturbation is often a sign of unhealthy past or present relationships. Many women who can't trust other people around them or who don't feel free to discuss their fears, anxieties, and insecurities will turn inward to calm or self-soothe—away from God and away from the joy and healing of openness within the body of Christ. Masturbation may seem like a "quick fix" to tension and heartache, but only within the context of healthy, trusting relationships can we truly be healed of past wounds. Be willing to talk with your counselor about sexual experiences in your past, as well as your use of self-sex now, and your feelings about this practice.
- *When a woman brings up the topic of masturbation, she may be seeking an answer to the question, Is it wrong? rather than asking Why am I doing it? Ask questions to get to the root issue of the woman's behavior. Explore her background, her understanding of the practice, her own experiences with self-sex, and her feelings about them.*

3. Explore God's Design for Sex

- In today's sex-saturated culture, it's easy to forget God's intended design for sex. Spend some time reading Scripture and the recommended resources your counselor will give you to explore God's design for sexual pleasure.
- *Gently correct any misinformation the woman may have about masturbation. Explain the nature, beauty, joy, and purpose of sex in marriage, and encourage her not to shortchange love, sex, and romance.*

4. Recognize and Deal with Shame and Guilt

- Some women carry around the shame and guilt of masturbation their whole lives and never tell anyone about it, for fear of being viewed as a sick, perverted person. The truth is that many women masturbate and many women feel stuck because they can't stop. But an addiction to masturbation, like any other sin, is not outside the realm of God's grace and mercy. Talk to God about how you feel about your self-sex.

- If you have developed the habit of turning to masturbation for comfort and security, rather than to Christ, confess your sin and lack of trust that He really can provide all you need. Accept God's forgiveness and rest in His unconditional love for you as His daughter.

5. Develop Healthy, Trusting Relationships

- For some women, the struggle with masturbation is only overcome when they learn to trust other people and build healthy, trusting relationships. Discuss and explore with your counselor any fears or mistrust that may be driving your self-sex practices.
- Seek out genuine, honest friendships in the body of Christ. Rather than turning inward to handle your stress and anxiety so that others won't know about it, learn to be open and honest about your weaknesses, struggles, and stresses.

6 BIBLICAL INSIGHTS

For you have been called to live in freedom, my brothers and sisters. But don't use your freedom to satisfy your sinful nature. Instead, use your freedom to serve one another in love. . . . So I say, let the Holy Spirit guide your lives. Then you won't be doing what your sinful nature craves.

Galatians 5:13, 16 NLT

Sexual desire was created by God, and as God's idea, it is not wrong, evil, or dirty. On the contrary, it is amazing and precious. However, perversions of God's design for sex threaten to mar the beauty and wonder of two becoming one. Every woman's sexual drive is different, but for some women, especially women who have habitually masturbated, sexual pleasure can be like a drug and self-sex an unhealthy addiction.

"Everything is permissible"—but not everything is beneficial. "Everything is permissible"—but not everything is constructive. Nobody should seek his own good, but the good of others.

1 Corinthians 10:23–24

By its nature, self-sex is self-focused. Though it is used by teens who are beginning to learn about their sexuality and by lonely adults who feel the need for the intimacy of a sexual relationship, it is not part of God's plan for a husband and wife. If it becomes an obsessive behavior or interferes with the sexual intimacies of a marriage, then it is a problem that must be addressed.

While in some cases, masturbation may be permissible, it may not be beneficial or constructive—and it is never God's best. To a certain extent, such behavior before marriage robs a husband and wife of the beauty and delight of sexual exploration and pleasure in the marriage bed.

But the fruit of the Spirit is love, joy, peace, patience, kindness, goodness, faithfulness, gentleness and self-control. Against such things there is no law.

Galatians 5:22–23

A primary concern in masturbation is self-control. Many times, the behavior becomes all-consuming and often includes pornographic lusts and fantasies that do not please God. Even when pornography is not associated with the behavior, if the desire for the sexual pleasure of masturbation controls a woman's life, she is dishonoring God. We are God's children, and Scripture commands us to be controlled by the love of Christ, not our earthly passions.

PRAYER STARTER 7

Father, thank You for _____'s concern about her sexuality. You have given sex as a wonderful gift to be enjoyed, but it is also a powerful desire that can easily control us. We ask for Your wisdom, God, as this woman strives to honor You with her sexuality. Help _____ submit even the desire for sexual pleasure to Your control. By Your Spirit, set her free from any addictive patterns and help her develop trusting, genuine relationships with other people, and most important, Lord, with You . . .

RECOMMENDED RESOURCES 8

Ethridge, Shannon. *Every Woman's Battle: Discovering God's Plan for Sexual and Emotional Fulfillment*. Random House, 2003.

Penner, Clifford, and Joyce Penner. *The Gift of Sex: A Guide to Sexual Fulfillment*. Thomas Nelson, 2003.

Rinehart, Paula. *Sex and the Soul of a Woman: The Reality of Love and Romance in an Age of Casual Sex*. Zondervan, 2004.

Roberts, Ted. *Pure Desire: Helping People Break Free from Sexual Struggles*. Gospel Light, 1999.

Rosenau, Douglas. *A Celebration of Sex: A Guide to Enjoying God's Gift of Sexual Intimacy*. Thomas Nelson, 2002.

Smith, Winston. *It's All About Me: The Problem with Masturbation*. New Growth Press, 2010.

Menopause

1 PORTRAITS

- Kay jerked upright in bed. It was 2 a.m. on a chilly November night, and she was covered in sweat. *What is wrong with me?* she wondered as she tossed and turned, unable to fall back asleep. Recently she'd had mood swings like crazy, almost like PMS that never went away. And she felt as though she'd lost all passion for intimacy with her husband, Tom. *I'm not sure if I can handle getting old! Will I ever be normal again?*

- "We'll need to schedule the hysterectomy as soon as possible," Tracy's gynecologist told her. *I can't believe this is happening to me*, Tracy thought. *I've always been the active, athletic type and now I'm about to lose my ability to give life.* "Make sure you read this," the doctor said as he handed her an information sheet. Tracy glanced down and read, "After a hysterectomy you may experience any of the following side effects: hot flashes, fatigue, insomnia, depression, urinary problems, weight gain, heart palpitations, vaginal dryness . . ."

- Looking at herself in the mirror, Maura was shocked. *Oh my! What is happening to me?* Her mom had always told her she couldn't keep her sexy figure forever, and Maura was starting to believe her. Since Maura's monthly cycles stopped last year, she'd been fighting an uphill battle with her waistline. And it didn't help that, most of the time, she simply had no energy to exercise. Every day Maura woke up feeling sore and bloated for no reason. Her body just didn't work the way it used to.

2 DEFINITIONS AND KEY THOUGHTS

- *Menopause* is defined as *a natural biological process in which a woman's ovaries produce less estrogen and no progesterone, resulting in a permanent cessation of menstruation.* A woman is considered to have reached menopause when she has not had a menstrual cycle *for at least twelve months.*

- *Perimenopause* is defined as *the time when a woman begins experiencing menopausal symptoms, even if she is still menstruating.* During this time, ovulation is less predictable, fertility declines, and a woman may notice changes in her menstrual periods. While it is still possible to get pregnant during this time, it is quite unlikely.

- According to the North American Menopause Society, the *average age for the onset of perimenopause* is 47.5 years and the *average age for menopause* is 51.4 years. More than 90 percent of women have reached menopause by age 55. The menopause transition lasts an average of 4 years, but may last only 2 years.[1]

- Menopause may be *brought on prematurely* by chemotherapy, radiation treatments, or the surgical removal of a woman's ovaries in a procedure called bilateral oophorectomy. This surgery is often accompanied by a hysterectomy (removal of the uterus). While *natural menopause is marked by a gradual decrease in sex hormones, surgery-induced menopause ends abruptly the production of estrogen and progesterone*, which frequently results in sudden and severe menopausal symptoms.

- In some rare cases, a woman experiences premature ovarian failure, which is the *loss of normal function of the ovaries before the age of forty*. The ovaries don't produce eggs or normal amounts of estrogen and the woman's periods may be sporadic or nonexistent.

- Every woman's *experience of menopause is different*, as the body adjusts to decreased levels of hormones and the absence of a monthly cycle. *Common symptoms* include

  — irregular periods (shorter, lighter cycles; heavier cycles; missed cycles)
  — hot and/or cold flashes, night sweats, clammy feeling
  — trouble sleeping through the night
  — loss of sexual desire, vaginal dryness
  — mood swings, irritability, unpredictable tears
  — fatigue, anxiety, difficulty concentrating
  — breast tenderness, loss of breast fullness
  — hair loss or thinning
  — tingling in the extremities, electric shock sensation under the skin

- *Decreased hormonal levels* result in the increased possibility of *health problems*, such as

  — weight gain (especially around the waist)
  — osteoporosis
  — urinary incontinence
  — cardiovascular disease

- *Postmenopause* refers to *the years following menopause*, in which a woman no longer has a monthly cycle nor is capable of bearing children. While menopause is a significant biological transition, the cessation of a woman's cycle *does not mean the end of her femininity and sexuality*. On the contrary, many women enjoy not having to worry about periods or pregnancy, and statistically speaking, most women spend one-third to one-half of their life in postmenopause.[2]

3 ASSESSMENT INTERVIEW

1. Tell me about your experience with menopause. What symptoms are you experiencing? Were your symptoms brought on by radiation or surgery?
2. What changes have you seen in your body? (*Try to ascertain where the woman is in the menopausal process—perimenopause, menopause, postmenopause.*)
3. Have you seen a doctor recently? Have you experienced any other significant changes in your health?
4. How have you reacted to the changes of menopause? What thoughts or emotions have you experienced?
5. How have your moods been affected by the hormonal changes in your body? What words best describe how you feel?
6. How has menopause changed your daily life and relationships? How has your experience changed the way you interact with your family, friends, spouse, and co-workers?
7. Have you discussed these issues with anyone? Do you know any other women who are going through menopause?
8. How do you cope with change and stress? Are there other issues complicating the menopausal process for you (divorce, empty nest, job change, marital conflict)?
9. Do you feel as if you have lost your sense of identity, femininity, and sexuality as a woman?
10. What do you hope to gain from counseling? What do you desire your life to be like in postmenopause?

4 WISE COUNSEL

Menopause is far more than just the physical event of a woman no longer having her period. *It is a time of physical, mental, and emotional transition as a woman is faced with the reality of her aging, grieves the loss of her ability to bear any more children, and restructures her life to adjust to the changes in her body, health, and lifestyle.*

The menopausal years are often a time of *midlife crisis* for women who have invested a significant portion of their life in bearing and raising children. At the same time a woman is *adjusting to the physical and hormonal changes* that come with menopause, she may also be struggling to let her children go and coping with *the loneliness of empty-nest syndrome.*

Thus menopause is not just a medical issue; it is a *multifaceted transition* that needs to be addressed as such. Like a second adolescence, menopause presents a woman with biological changes in her body that make her uncomfortable with herself and cause her to *question her identity, femininity, sexuality, and purpose in life.* Many women view the loss of their fertility as the loss of their womanhood and need to be reassured that menopause is *a normal part of aging* and not a death sentence.

A menopausal woman needs *confidence and the right perspective* to be able to evaluate her lifestyle, adjust to the changes she is experiencing, and still find meaning, purpose, and joy in her life. Encourage the woman to get connected with other women who are or have experienced menopause and look for ways to enjoy these relationships. While health restraints may force a woman to slow down her pace of life, help her see that her life is not over. *Brainstorm together about ways for the woman to exercise regularly, develop a healthy lifestyle, and get involved in friendships and community.*

ACTION STEPS 5

1. Recognize and Accept the Changes of Menopause

- Menopause is a transition, not a disease. There is no getting around the reality of aging, yet some women are hesitant to talk about menopause for fear that dwelling on it will make it worse. During this time of transition in your life, it is vitally important that you be honest about how you're doing and don't try to just hold it together while trying to continue life as normal.

- Although your body is transitioning out of the childbearing years, that does *not* mean your life is over. God is intimately involved in every aspect of your life—even menopause. After all, He is the one who created your body and best knows your heart. So don't hesitate to talk to Him about the emotions, fears, and anxieties you are experiencing with this change.

2. Build a Healthy Lifestyle

- Look for ways to stay active. Though you may not have the energy you did as a teenager, you can still have a healthy and fulfilling life, and exercise is critical. Walk, bike, swim, whatever activity you enjoy. Build it into your schedule and don't hesitate to invite some of your friends along.

- Develop healthy eating habits, including adequate amounts of fruits, vegetables, proteins, and whole grain foods. With menopause, your metabolism and cravings will likely change. Resist the urge to feed your sweet tooth. What you eat has a direct effect on your energy levels, mood, and overall health.

- Talk to your doctor and consider supplementing your food intake with vitamins and minerals (especially calcium and B vitamins) to ensure that your body is getting the nutrition it needs.

3. Embrace This New Season as a Gift from God

- Often women feel isolated and misunderstood during menopause. Changes in mood and energy can make it difficult to keep up friendships, but be proactive in spending time with your girlfriends and focus on enjoying life.

- Remember, menopause isn't a death sentence. It's the beginning of a whole new chapter of your life! So embrace this new season as a gift from God. It probably means the kids are out of the house, so you have more free time to do the things you love to do.

4. Ground Your Identity in Jesus

- God—not your health, your ability to have children, or your accomplishments—defines who you are as a woman. God created you as a woman, and you will always be a woman, despite the changes in your body caused by menopause.

- Rather than focusing on what you *can't* do, choose to embrace each day as a gift from Jesus and ground your identity in who you are as His daughter. Rejoice in the things that you *can* do and choose to age with grace. This will only add to your inner, lasting beauty, which does not diminish but only grows over time.

6 BIBLICAL INSIGHTS

Come to me, all you who are weary and burdened, and I will give you rest. . . . I am gentle and humble in heart, and you will find rest for your souls.

Matthew 11:28–29

In the midst of hot flashes, mood swings, and all that menopause brings, Jesus longs for His daughters to find rest in His presence. Don't try to push through on your own. Seek out times with Jesus to vent your frustrations, soak up His love, and be reminded of where your true identity lies.

Rather than obsessing about the changes and circumstances in your life, obsess about Jesus. Let this time of transition push you deeper into His arms. Don't keep stumbling along, weary and burdened. He offers rest for your soul. Take it.

Even to your old age and gray hairs I am he, I am he who will sustain you. I have made you and I will carry you; I will sustain you and I will rescue you.

Isaiah 46:4

Menopause can cause women to lose confidence in themselves and see themselves as ugly and no good. However, this passage affirms that "old age and gray hairs" do not change our relationship with God.

God's promises never change. In the midst of health problems, confusion, and pain, God promises to sustain, carry, and provide for His children. He loves us not because of what we look like or what we do, but simply because we are His daughters.

But our citizenship is in heaven. And we eagerly await a Savior from there, the Lord Jesus Christ, who, by the power that enables him to bring everything under his control, will transform our lowly bodies so that they will be like his glorious body.

Philippians 3:20–21

As believers, every year that goes by and every transition in our lives only make the gospel sweeter and more real as we cling to and treasure the promises of

Scripture. Paul's glorious reminder of our future with Jesus is a sure antidote for feeling down in the dumps, used up, and worthless.

Our citizenship really is in heaven—with Jesus—and that is something we can look forward to with excitement, no matter what challenges come along the way. Like Paul, we can "eagerly await" the transformation of our earthly bodies when we see Jesus face-to-face.

PRAYER STARTER 7

Lord, we thank You for Your faithfulness in every season of our lives. Be with _____ as she struggles to adjust to the changes that menopause and midlife bring. Make Your presence and Your promises real to her and sustain her with Your grace as she charts these new waters. Allay her fears, Lord, with reassurances of Your love and care. We thank You that You promise to care for us and sustain us, even through menopause . . .

RECOMMENDED RESOURCES 8

Bolton, Martha. *Cooking with Hot Flashes: Discovering New Talents in Middle Age.* Bethany House, 2004.

Boston Women's Health Book Collective. *Our Bodies, Ourselves: Menopause.* Simon and Schuster, 2006.

Demetre, Danna. *The Menopause Guide.* Revell, 2009.

Fitzpatrick, Elyse. *The Afternoon of Life: Finding Purpose and Joy in Midlife.* P&R Publishing, 2004.

Kalb, Kate Bracy. *The Everything Health Guide to Menopause*, 2nd ed. Adams Media, 2010.

Smith, Pamela. *When Your Hormones Go Haywire: Solutions for Women over 40.* Zondervan, 2005.

Walker, Laura. *Mentalpause.* Revell, 2007.

Miscarriage

1 PORTRAITS

- Marilyn hadn't eaten in three days and she was exhausted from crying. Her baby, her precious little girl, was gone. She and her husband, Luke, were crushed. When her cycle was late, Marilyn had wondered if she was pregnant and she was ecstatic to announce the news to Luke. Every day they had prayed for their little one together. Marilyn and Luke had even begun decorating the baby's room. But now . . . now what? *How could God allow this to happen to my baby?* Marilyn sobbed.

- A sharp pang stabbed Amy in the heart as she realized that today would have been his birthday—*would have been* because little Benjamin never lived to take his first breath. Ben was stillborn one year ago, and Amy still couldn't forget that haunting, peaceful little face. Her heart wouldn't let her forget. *Will my life ever be normal again? Could I ever love another child?* Amy wonders.

- When Matt brought up the subject of trying again, Sharon couldn't shake the gut feeling of fear that enveloped her. "God, I don't understand. I'm scared," Sharon blurted out one afternoon as she sat in rush hour traffic. "I just want to have a baby but I don't know if I dare go through it all again." Sharon and her husband, Matt, have been trying to have kids for almost four years, and Sharon has had three miscarriages. *Will I ever get to hold a baby in my arms? What is wrong with me?*

2 DEFINITIONS AND KEY THOUGHTS

- *Miscarriage* is defined as *a natural, unexpected termination of pregnancy when the baby is incapable of sustaining life outside the womb in the first twenty weeks of gestation.*

- Miscarriage can occur for *a number of unexplainable reasons.* Many times doctors cannot pinpoint exactly what caused the miscarriage, but the following can be factors:

  — ectopic pregnancy or improper implantation in the uterine wall
  — chromosome abnormalities of the fetus
  — hormonal imbalances or other maternal health complications

— lifestyle risks (smoking, drinking, drug use, exposure to toxic substances or radiation, poor nutrition, excessive caffeine)

— maternal age or trauma

• Most miscarriages take place *during the first trimester* (three months) of pregnancy. Research shows that 10–25 percent of all pregnancies end in miscarriage, but *risk of miscarriage changes based on childbearing age.*

— Women under thirty-five have a 15 percent chance of miscarriage.

— Women thirty-five to forty-five have a 20–35 percent chance of miscarriage.

— Women over forty-five can have up to a 50 percent chance of miscarriage.

— A woman who has had a previous miscarriage has a 25 percent chance of having another (only a slightly elevated risk compared to nonmiscarrying women).[1]

• *The process of miscarriage can drag out* for several days and can be physically exhausting and painful. As the uterus expels the fetus, a woman may experience heavy bleeding accompanied by blood clots or tissue, severe cramping, and sometimes crippling back pain. But *long after the physical trauma, the pain of unexplainable loss lingers.*

• Miscarriage is a *complex biological process* involving many factors. Several specific terms to be aware of are:

— *Incomplete or inevitable miscarriage.* Symptoms are abdominal or back pain and bleeding through an open cervix. Loss of the baby is inevitable when the cervix is dilated and membranes have been ruptured.

— *Missed miscarriage.* This occurs when a woman experiences a miscarriage without knowing it. Fetal life ceases, but there is no expulsion of the embryo.

— *Blighted ovum/anembryonic pregnancy.* This occurs when a fertilized egg is implanted in the uterine wall, but no fetal development takes place.

— *Ectopic pregnancy.* This is when a fertilized egg implants itself in abnormal places of a woman's reproductive system, rather than the uterus. Immediate medical intervention is necessary to avoid serious complications.

— *Molar pregnancy.* This is a result of genetic error during the development of the placenta, leading to abnormal tissue growth within the uterus. This tissue growth prevents the development of an embryo, but common symptoms of pregnancy (including positive pregnancy test, missed period, nausea, and so on) are present. An ultrasound is often required to detect a molar pregnancy.

3 ASSESSMENT INTERVIEW

1. Tell me about your experience of miscarriage. When did it happen and what were the details surrounding it?
2. How did you feel? What hit you the hardest?
3. How did you respond to the news and cope with the pain of your loss?
4. What emotions have you had since the miscarriage? What feelings are most prominent or reoccurring?
5. How are you handling and processing the pain? Have you been talking with anyone about it?
6. Have you allowed yourself the freedom to grieve?
7. Is this your first miscarriage? How do you feel about the possibility of trying to conceive again in the future?
8. How has this miscarriage affected you and your husband's relationship? How do you think he is handling it?
9. Tell me about your interactions with God. Are you angry at Him? Are you hurt, upset, or bitter that He let this happen?
10. How has this miscarriage changed your life? What hurts the most right now?

4 WISE COUNSEL

Frequently the experience of a miscarriage *raises many questions* about who to blame, what went wrong, how God could allow such a thing, and other difficult questions. As you talk with a woman about her loss, *don't be pressured to give answers* to all of these questions, and *don't resort to cliché Christian answers*, like "God loves you" or "All things work together for good" or "Trust God." While these statements are theologically true, when a woman is experiencing the anger, grief, and disbelief of a miscarriage, she may not be capable of processing such truth right away. *Give her the freedom to experience and work through the pain and actually come to grips with the fact that she has lost her baby.* Telling her to paste on a smile, trust God, and move on will only complicate her healing process.

Instead, *provide a therapeutic environment* and *practice reflective listening*, giving the woman freedom to grieve and being careful not to tell her how to feel. Offer a listening ear and sympathize with her pain. Sometimes a grieving woman finds simply *having someone with her* most meaningful.

Losing a baby is a very traumatic experience. Grieving the loss in the case of miscarriage is especially difficult because a woman is *grappling with the death of a child she never met or knew, yet a child that she carried and nurtured in her own body.*

A mother's love runs deep and does not die easily. Many women describe the emotional anguish of a miscarriage as *one of the most intense pains they ever experience in their lives*, and healing takes time and a willingness to deal with the pain.

Encourage the woman to *let herself grieve. Let her talk openly* about her loss, about the baby, and about how she is doing emotionally and spiritually, not just physically. Often a woman is surrounded with love and support for the first week following the miscarriage, and then everything returns to normal for others, and *the woman is left to wonder if things will ever be normal for her again.*

Many women blame themselves for the loss of their baby, wondering what they did wrong. While in some cases, such as through improper nutrition or drug use, personal decisions may have been a factor, *many times, there is no medical explanation for a miscarriage.*

Encourage the woman not to blame herself for this loss and not to isolate herself from other people. While the grief process is different for every woman, healing comes from grieving together and finding hope together in the promise of eternal life.

ACTION STEPS : 5

1. Have a Thorough Physical Examination

- Normally, following a miscarriage, the body recovers on its own, but in some cases complications or infection can occur. Make sure you follow up with your doctor and have a physical examination.
- Give your body time to heal. Aside from simply losing a lot of blood, your body is undergoing significant hormonal changes. Don't rush getting back to your regular routine and make sure you consult your doctor before engaging in sexual activity with your husband.

2. Give Yourself Time to Grieve

- Losing a baby that you never met is a strange and heart-wrenching experience. Because there is no body physically present, many people assume that the grieving process is easier, but it isn't. If anything, it's harder.
- Realize that grief is a normal and healthy response to loss. So don't bottle it up, stuff it inside, or hold back the tears. Don't pretend to be okay and don't put on a mask. Face the reality of your loss head-on, and allow yourself to feel the pain.
- Surrounded by the strength and comfort of Jesus, you can be confident that grief is not only a healthy closure but also an opportunity to get closer to Jesus, grow in faith, and experience greater depths of His intimate love and care for you in the midst of heartache.

3. Talk about It

- It's essential in the healing process that you talk about how you're doing, how you're feeling, and the questions and doubts that are spinning through your head. Talk openly with your husband and a few trusted friends about these issues, and allow the body of Christ to minister to you in your weakness.
- Attend a grief support group at a local church or counseling center. In this safe environment, you will have the opportunity to process what you are feeling with other people who are experiencing similar losses.

4. Find Your Hope in God

- As a daughter of God, even in the midst of heartache and unimaginable loss, you don't have to despair. God cares intimately about you—your aching heart, your questioning mind, and even your anger and frustration.

- Be honest with God about what you feel. Rest in His loving embrace and let Him heal your broken heart. Rather than waiting for life to get back to normal, ask God to give you grace to find a new normal. Life will never be exactly the same again, and you will always miss your baby, but God still longs to reveal His love to you and use you to share that love with others who are experiencing similar loss and pain.

5. Trust God for the Future

- The process of healing from a miscarriage takes time, patience, and support from family and friends. If you and your husband desire to get pregnant again in the future, you may experience anxiety and fear about the possibility of having another miscarriage. This is normal. Many times the thought of trying to have another baby—even months or years after a miscarriage—can be terrifying for a woman. While physical healing generally takes a few months, emotional healing is a much longer process. As you discuss family planning, be honest with your husband about these fears and doubts and seek medical counsel if you suspect physical problems that may impede pregnancy.

- If your doctor gives you the okay to try to conceive again, and you and your husband decide to move ahead, realize that God is sovereign over every single part of your life, including your womb. Embrace this step as an opportunity to trust God with your future children or a future without children. Rather than dwelling on what-ifs, meditate on the faithfulness and promises of your loving heavenly Father.

6 BIBLICAL INSIGHTS

Before I formed you in the womb I knew you.

Jeremiah 1:5

For you created my inmost being; you knit me together in my mother's womb.

Psalm 139:13

From the moment of conception, a developing baby is alive. Your baby was not just a piece of tissue, but a real, live, tiny little person that God created. Though you never met your baby, he or she was very much real—and very precious to God. As you work through the process of grieving both the loss of a child and being barren at the present time, you can rest in the knowledge that God knew your baby in the womb and still knows him or her.

In Scripture there are many examples of barren women—Sarah (Gen. 16; 18:1–15; 21:1–7), Rebekah (25:19–23), Rachel (30:1–24), Samson's mother (Judg. 13), Hannah (1 Sam. 1), and Elizabeth (Luke 1) to name a few. These women wrestled through the pain of desperately wanting a child and not being able to conceive for a time. Take time to read the stories of these women and identify with their pain, loss, and honest prayers. Be careful, however, not to assume that God always answers this prayer eventually with a child. Sometimes, in God's plan, this is not the case. Be honest with God, just as these women were, and rest in His sovereignty and love for you.

There is a time for everything, and a season for every activity under heaven . . . a time to weep and a time to laugh, a time to mourn and a time to dance.

Ecclesiastes 3:1, 4

Sometimes life hurts, and there are no easy answers. The loss of a child is a jarring reminder that the consequences of living in a fallen world permeate every aspect of our lives. Every woman goes through the stages of grief differently, but Scripture affirms that grief is a normal and healthy response to the loss of a child. Weeping, mourning, and feeling the pain of a child's loss are not selfish, and in the moments of our greatest weakness and pain—when we realize we have nothing else to cling to but Jesus—He eagerly desires to minister to us, wrap us in His loving, strong arms, and weep with us as we weep.

God is our refuge and strength, an ever-present help in trouble. Therefore we will not fear. . . . The LORD Almighty is with us; the God of Jacob is our fortress.

Psalm 46:1–2, 11

Our God is not a distant, uninvolved deity. David described God as his refuge, his strength, his help, his fortress, his reason for not being afraid. Even when it seems that the world is spinning out of control and God is silent, Scripture reminds us that He is a safe place to take refuge in the storms of life, when we can't go on alone.

Even in the terrible tragedy of a miscarriage, we can cling to the truth that "the LORD Almighty is with us"—right here, right now, in the midst of anguish, questions, and doubt. And nothing can take us out of His loving care.

He heals the brokenhearted and binds up their wounds.

Psalm 147:3

Cast your cares on the LORD and he will sustain you; he will never let the righteous fall.

Psalm 55:22

Not only does God weep with us, but He also promises to heal us, to bind up our wounds. Nowhere in Scripture does God promise to give us all the answers to our questions—to tell us *why* He allowed the loss of a child—but we can rest assured that He will carry us and sustain us along the way. Jesus will never forsake His children and He longs to use every trial and heartache to draw us closer to Him.

7 PRAYER STARTER

Lord, Your daughter is hurting. We don't understand why You've allowed these circumstances, but because we know You are good and sovereign, Lord, we choose to trust You. Just as You were with Sarah, Rebekah, Rachel, and others in the Bible, so too you are here with _____, in this time of sorrow. Make Your presence very real to her as she works through the pain of this loss. Be very near and present in her life and surround her with love and support from family and friends. You are the only one, Jesus, who can heal our brokenness and give us new life. We need You . . .

8 RECOMMENDED RESOURCES

Barrett, Elise. *What Was Lost: A Christian Journey through Miscarriage*. Westminster John Knox Press, 2010.

Gamino, Louis, and Anne Taylor Cooney. *When Your Baby Dies through Miscarriage or Stillbirth*. Augsburg Fortress, 2002.

Hinton, Clara. *Silent Grief: Miscarriage, Child Loss, Finding Your Way through the Darkness*. New Leaf, 1998.

Lafser, Christine. *An Empty Cradle, a Full Heart: Reflections for Mothers and Fathers after Miscarriage, Stillbirth, or Infant Death*. Loyola, 1998.

Schroedel, Jenny. *Naming the Child: Hope-Filled Reflections on Miscarriage, Stillbirth, and Infant Death*. Paraclete Press, 2009.

Vredevelt, Pam. *Empty Arms: For Those Who Suffered a Miscarriage, Stillbirth, or Tubal Pregnancy*. Multnomah, 2001.

Wunnenberg, Kathe. *Grieving the Child I Never Knew: A Devotional Companion for Comfort in the Loss of Your Unborn or Newly Born*. Zondervan, 2001.

Obesity

PORTRAITS : 1

- Rachel has a tight schedule at her job, working in a cubicle in a busy office. She has very little time for physical activity and seldom takes time for a healthy, nutrient-rich breakfast and lunch. Her meals are usually quick and on the go—fast food. Rachel knows she is overweight—technically, she is obese—but she's not sure what to do differently. "I can't quit my job," Rachel rationalizes, "and when I get home, I'm too tired to exercise."
- Since Karla was twelve years old, she has been considered obese. Although she tries to eat a healthy diet, Karla cannot seem to lose weight. Her doctor has told her that her weight issues are a result of her genes and her "slow" metabolism. Karla is frustrated and confused about why God would make her this way. She wants to lose weight but doesn't know where to start or what to do differently.
- Christy decided to join a local gym to combat her obesity. Her fear of what other women would think of her has kept her from going in the past but she determined she was not going to let that be the case any longer. But then she saw the pointing, heard the comments, and noticed that the other women in the gym were staring at her. After a half hour of feeling humiliated during her workout, she stormed out of the gym in tears, determined that she would never go to a gym ever again.

DEFINITIONS AND KEY THOUGHTS : 2

- *High caloric intake and low physical activity* are the primary reasons for *obesity*. According to the Centers for Disease Control and Prevention (CDC), "A *calorie* is defined as a unit of energy supplied by food. A calorie is a calorie regardless of its source. Whether you're eating *carbohydrates, fats, sugars, or proteins*, all of them contain calories."[1]
- To maintain a *healthy weight*, a balance is needed between the calories consumed and the calories used (by physical activity, exercise, and normal bodily functions).[2]
- *Diseases and drugs* are common factors in obesity. The most common drug to cause weight gain is *steroids*. Other medications, such as *antidepressants and birth control pills*, may also cause weight gain. *Genes* may play a role as well. Although it cannot always be determined that weight gain is caused by our

genes, heredity and the predisposition for a slower metabolism may increase the chances of being obese.

- *Behavior and environment* are also major links to obesity. Late night meals and the *convenience of unhealthy food* contribute to obesity. The United States alone has 12,804 McDonald's restaurants as of 2007.[3] This type of convenience, as well as the *appeal of the low cost*, has had a large impact on the obesity rates in the United States.
- *Lack of exercise* is a major factor in obesity. Research shows that only 30 percent of women eighteen years and older participate in *regular, leisure time physical activity*.[4]
- According to the CDC, *an adult must have a BMI (body mass index) of 30 or higher to be considered obese*. For example, someone at 5 feet 9 inches, weighing 203 pounds or more would be considered obese. In some rare cases, body mass index may not hold true, especially among athletes, due to height and muscle mass. However, overall, it is a good guideline for determining healthy weight.[5]
- *Obesity is a significant issue for women in America*. Statistics reveal that 57 percent of women over 20 years old are overweight, while 35 percent of these women are obese.[6]

3 ASSESSMENT INTERVIEW

1. How long have you been obese?
2. When did the weight gain begin?
3. Can you pinpoint the cause of your obesity; for example, overeating, low activity, genes? (*Not all clients will be able to pinpoint one specific reason for their obesity.*)
4. Are your parents or grandparents overweight or obese?
5. Do medications play a role? If so, what medications are you on?
6. If eating is a cause, do you feel that your emotions drive your eating or do you eat out of boredom?
7. What is your home environment like? Is there a lot of tension and/or arguing? Are you often home alone?
8. What are the emotional, physical, and medical consequences of your obesity?
9. Do you have a support system to aid in your weight loss?
10. Do you have a diet and exercise program? If so, describe it.

4 WISE COUNSEL

For the obese client, *lifestyle changes have to be made*, and often these lifestyle *changes take time*, depending on how deep the roots are. If the obesity has been a lifelong issue, the process will obviously take longer than for someone who has become obese in the past few years. Obesity may take longer to overcome if it is a result of a trauma that caused the client to turn to food for comfort. *The deep-rooted issues of the trauma must be addressed as new behaviors are introduced to cope with and control the emotional issues.*

A new way of living to control weight is a difficult thing for many women to accomplish. Many setbacks may occur. Stress to your client the importance of having *a strong support system*. This may be found in family, friends, co-workers, and an organized support or workout group, offered at community centers, gyms, or churches. Such groups can be extremely helpful to a woman who is trying to change her lifestyle and diet and exercise habits. The encouragement of others and positive peer pressure are *extremely powerful in helping women develop new habits*. In fact, it may have been lack of a support system that played a role in the obesity.

To eat a proper diet and control weight, *an understanding of nutrition* and of *how to read food nutrition labels* is important. Encouraging the client to see a nutrition counselor may be a beneficial step. A *food journal* may also be a helpful tool. Until the client sees on paper her daily intake of food, she may not realize how much she is really eating. And finally, *an exercise plan* is an important part of the journey toward weight loss and lifestyle change. It is wise to seek out the *counsel of a medical professional* who can evaluate the client's ability to exercise.

ACTION STEPS : 5

1. Get a Medical Evaluation

- To control obesity, you must know where it begins. Is it diet, activity, illness, medication, genes, or some combination of these? Is it the result of a trauma, an emotional issue, or a habit? A medical professional will be able to help you answer these questions and suggest specific changes in your life to help you address the root issue of obesity.

2. Get Active

- Whether the obesity is a result of overeating or underactivity, more physical activity is likely necessary. After seeking the advice of a medical professional to ensure that exercise is an appropriate step, join a gym or get a group of women together to walk, run, or do a workout class. Set achievable goals for yourself and ask a friend to set goals with you so you can hold each other accountable to exercise. Make the activity fun so that you will be more apt to do it consistently.

- Consistency is a key to losing weight. You must do the activity regularly—at least four to five times a week for at least thirty minutes. Mix up the routine if it gets boring or too ritualistic. Pick a few of your favorite activities (perhaps Pilates, tennis, running, or swimming) and put them in a rotation.

- Sign up with a fitness trainer or nutrition coach if you can afford it. The reality is that, in many cases, you can't afford not to, so cut out other things you don't need. As you lose weight, you will be able to live a happier, healthier, and longer life.

3. Control the Intake

- You *must* learn to stick to proper portions of food—healthy food. You don't have to deprive yourself of the occasional treat, but most of the food you consume should be healthy and nutrient rich. We eat to live, not live to eat.

- A food journal is a great way of keeping track of how much you consume. Also kitchen scales are a great tool to measure the amount of food for meals. Equip yourself with the proper tools to control the amount of food you eat so that you will successfully lose weight.

- Seek out the advice of a nutrition counselor or dietitian to develop a personalized, healthy diet plan. Your food intake should provide your body with the nutrition it needs, while avoiding junk food and excess calorie intake. For instance, it is generally better to eat six small meals or snacks a day than to eat three large meals. This schedule reinforces portion control and keeps your metabolism stable.

4. Think Natural

- Processed food and fast food will wreck a healthy diet and slow the process of weight loss. The best way to get the most out of your food is to eat it as close to how God made it as possible. You want the most nutrient-rich options, which are the most natural options. When you feed your body wholesome food, it will be able to use more of the food for fuel and energy, leaving fewer calories in your body stored as fat.

6 BIBLICAL INSIGHTS

Do not be wise in your own eyes; fear the LORD and shun evil. This will bring health to your body and nourishment to your bones.

Proverbs 3:7–8

We are holistic people—created with physical, emotional, and spiritual components that are all interconnected and interrelated. When we focus on our spiritual journey, we are more likely to want to take care of our physical bodies. When we neglect our physical health, the consequences are fatigue, obesity, increased likelihood of diseases, among other problems—all things that can impede our ability to enjoy life, as well as to connect with and glorify God.

Beloved, I pray that you may prosper in all things and be in health, just as your soul prospers.

3 John 2 NKJV

Just as Christ desires a soul that is spiritually healthy, He desires a body that is healthy. There needs to be a balance of all things—we should neither neglect nor indulge ourselves in food or in physical activity. The better our physical health, the more able we are to serve God to the fullest—in every way. Our bodies are a gift of God. To neglect them or overindulge them is careless and ungrateful for the gift we were given.

"Everything is permissible for me"—but not everything is beneficial. "Everything is permissible for me"—but I will not be mastered by anything. "Food for the stomach and the stomach for food"—but God will destroy them both. . . . Do you not know that your body is a temple of the Holy Spirit, who is in you, whom you have received from God? You are not your own; you were bought at a price. Therefore honor God with your body.

1 Corinthians 6:12–13, 19–20

Our bodies belong to God, not to us. Food was created to sustain us, not to control us. We have the free will to choose to eat and live as we wish, but after a time, when we choose to live in excess with the things God intended to be used moderately (such as food), God's mercy in sustaining us will subside. We must not take our focus off Him and put it on food. Where our mind abides, our motives thrive. If our mind is focused on food, our motives will be to acquire it. If our mind is focused on Christ, our motives will be to know Him better.

PRAYER STARTER : 7

Our hearts, our minds, and our bodies are Yours, Father. Please help our sister, _____, submit herself and her body to you. God, please let her choices be honoring and her focus be on You. Give her wisdom and discipline in losing weight and aid her in presenting her body a living sacrifice to You . . .

RECOMMENDED RESOURCES : 8

Ayres, Desiree. *God Hunger: Breaking Addictions of Anorexia, Bulimia, and Compulsive Eating.* Creation House, 2006.

Hadden, Julie, and Ashley Wiersma. *Fat Chance: Losing the Weight, Gaining My Worth.* Guidepost Books, 2009.

Hampton, Diane. *The Diet Alternative.* Whitaker House, 2001.

Linamen, Karen. *A Waist Is a Terrible Thing to Mind: Loving Your Body, Accepting Yourself, and Living without Regret.* WaterBrook, 2010.

Sears, Barry. *Toxic Fat: When Good Fat Turns Bad.* Thomas Nelson, 2008.

Physical Abuse

1 PORTRAITS

- Marge stared in the mirror at the new bruise on her face. She had never imagined that this would be happening to her. She knew her husband, Paul, was sorry; he had told her so again last night after he had seen marks on her face where he had hit her. This morning before he left for work, he had promised that it wouldn't happen again if she would just give him another chance.

- Janet didn't know what to do. The wedding was only weeks away, and she had always thought that she and Randy made such a good couple. But lately he was becoming more controlling of her time and demanded to know where she was going when he wasn't with her. He was also getting jealous when some of her other friends spent time with her. But last night had been the worst. When she disagreed with him, he actually grabbed her arms and shook her. Janet was scared. *But surely he'll calm down once we're married, won't he?*

- Sarah didn't see it coming. She and her husband went out one night for a few drinks with some of his friends when his ex-girlfriend arrived. Sarah became very upset when her husband sat his ex on his knee and gently kissed her on the cheek. Sarah raced immediately to the car, locking herself in. When her husband came stumbling out of the bar after her, he realized the car was locked. After arguing with her and yelling at her to open the door, he put his fist through the glass and punched her in the head, while screaming at her for wandering off.

2 DEFINITIONS AND KEY THOUGHTS

- *Abuse* is anything that is harmful or offensive. There are several types of abuse, one of which is *physical*.

- *Physical abuse* involves *physical contact intended to cause feelings of intimidation, pain, injury, or other physical suffering or bodily harm*. Physical abuse includes things like hitting, burning, pushing, biting, shaking, restraining, scratching, blocking the victim's way, and beating with an object. *It is, in essence, physical power that is used to control, manipulate, or intimidate another person.*

- Physical abuse can also be when the perpetrator *uses his body to threaten a woman's safety* by punching holes in the wall, breaking things, and so on.

- Physical abuse or *intimate partner violence* (IPV) may follow a three-step circular pattern:

— *Tension builds* until the abuser loses control.

— *Battering occurs.* The batterer lashes out in anger, feeling that the victim deserves it or that he needs to teach her a lesson. Often the abuser and/or the victim rationalize the battering and minimize the seriousness of the abuse.

— *Remorse.* The batterer is sorry and asks for forgiveness. The tension is gone, and he wants reconciliation. At this point the batterer may make promises that "it will never happen again" and behave in very loving and contrite ways.

- The third stage of the cycle looks a great deal like true repentance. However it is due only to an absence of tension and the feeling on the part of the abuser that the victim has "learned her lesson." *When this situation changes and the tension again increases, the battering can recur.*

- Physical abuse is *rarely a one-time occurrence and many times goes unreported.* The National Institute of Justice reports that "women who were physically assaulted by an intimate partner averaged 6.9 physical assaults. . . . Approximately one-fifth of all rapes, one-quarter of all physical assaults, and one-half of all stalkings were reported to the police."[1]

- Research by the US Department of Justice estimates that 22.1 percent of women (about one in five) have been a victim of intimate partner violence at some point in their life. The *method the abuser used* was reported as follows:

— 8.1 percent threw something that hurt
— 8.1 percent pushed, grabbed, or shoved
— 9.1 percent pulled hair
— 16 percent slapped or hit
— 5.5 percent kicked or bit
— 6.1 percent choked or tried to drown
— 5.0 percent hit with an object
— 8.5 percent beat up
— 3.5 percent threatened with a gun
— 2.8 percent threatened with a knife
— 0.7 percent used a gun
— 0.9 percent used a knife[2]

- Many abusers and victims of physical abuse *grew up in abusive homes.* The American Psychological Association reports that "each year an estimated 3.3 million children are exposed to violence against their mother or female caretaker by family members. A child's exposure to the father abusing the mother is the strongest risk factor for transmitting violent behavior from one generation to the next."[3]

- There are many *risk factors* associated with intimate partner violence.

— *Unmarried, cohabiting couples* have higher rates of intimate partner violence than do married couples.

— *Minorities* have higher rates of intimate partner violence than do whites.

— *Lower income women* have higher rates of intimate partner violence than do higher income women.

— *Less educated women* have higher rates of intimate partner violence than do more educated women.

— Couples with *income, educational, or occupational status disparities* have higher rates of intimate partner violence than do couples with no status disparity.

— *Experiencing and/or witnessing violence in one's family* of origin increases the chances of being a perpetrator or victim of intimate partner violence.

— Wife assault is more common in families where *power is concentrated in the hands of the husband or male partner* and the husband makes most of the decisions regarding family finances and strictly controls when and where his wife or female partner goes.

— *Women with a disability* are at greater risk of violence.[4]

- Many of the predictors of physical abuse are *present in the dating relationship*. Some of these predictors are

  — use of force or violence to solve problems

  — a male abuser's need to prove himself by acting tough

  — rigid ideas of what men and women should be like

  — the victim's fears of the abuser's anger

- In public, abusers tend to be charming and personable but *behave entirely differently in private*. In counseling sessions, abusers can seem quite reasonable and can try to influence you, portraying their wife as irrational or rebellious and wanting you to see their side.

Consequences of Abuse

- *Physical.* Women with a history of IPV report *higher rates of all health problems* than do women with no history of abuse. IPV victims report lasting negative health problems, such as chronic pain, gastrointestinal disorders, and irritable bowel syndrome, which can interfere with or limit daily functioning. The more severe the abuse, the greater its impact on a woman's physical and mental health. Other negative consequences include gynecological disorders, unwanted pregnancy, fibromyalgia, a compromised immune system, central nervous system disorders, premature labor and birth, and sexually transmitted diseases including HIV/AIDS. IPV victims have a higher prevalence of sexually transmitted diseases, hysterectomy, and heart or circulatory conditions.[5]

- *Psychological.* Often abused girls and women experience *adverse mental health conditions*, such as depression, anxiety, post-traumatic stress disorder, fear of intimacy, flashbacks, relational detachment, and low self-esteem. Women with a history of IPV experience increased levels of substance use and antisocial and suicidal behavior.[6]

- *Social. Children who witness IPV are at a great risk* of developing psychiatric disorders, developmental problems, school failure, violence against others, and low self-esteem. *Women in violent relationships* have been found to be restricted in the way they gain access to services, take part in public life, and receive emotional support from friends and relatives. [7]

Vulnerability to Victimization

- Women with any of the following as part of their past or present experience are *more vulnerable than other women* to IPV: history of physical abuse, prior injury from the same partner, having a verbally abusive partner, economic stress, partner history of alcohol or drug abuse, childhood abuse, being under the age of twenty-four, marital conflict, male dominance in the family, and poor family functioning.

ASSESSMENT INTERVIEW 3

If a couple comes into counseling together and you *suspect abuse, speak to each separately* to get an accurate understanding of the situation. To avoid putting the victim in danger, simply say that it is your practice to speak to each member of the couple individually.

Rule Outs

1. Do your fights ever get physical? (*This is an easier question to answer than one about abuse.*)
2. Do either of you use alcohol or drugs?
3. Do you feel safe with your spouse? (*If you have any questions about the presence of abuse, do not try to deal with marital issues when the couple is together until the issue of safety is thoroughly addressed.*)

General Questions

1. Has your husband or boyfriend ever hurt you physically or tried to physically intimidate you?
2. If yes, when was the last time it happened?
3. How often does this abuse happen?
4. Have you ever tried to get help?
5. What have you done to get help?
6. Has it worked?
7. Does your husband or boyfriend go through the cycle of tension, battering, and then remorse? (*See Definitions and Key Thoughts above.*)

8. Describe what usually happens. What has kept you from getting out and leaving the abuse?
9. Are you afraid for your children's safety [if you have children]?
10. Do you have a plan for safety if the abuse happens again?

4 WISE COUNSEL

The first goal is safety. Working out a plan of safety with the victim is essential. Sometimes what keeps a victim in the abusive situation is the lack of *resources to escape.* Be sure you investigate this need.

Many Christian women are taught that they should never leave their husband, even for reasons of physical safety, because to do so is not being submissive to him, and therefore, disobeying the commands of Scripture. Make it clear to the woman that *Scripture does not teach that a Christian woman should continually submit herself to an abusive man.* In situations of abuse, *separation for safety* is a must.

Help the woman set up an *action plan for times she feels threatened*, such as who to call, where to go, and what to do that will help her feel safe.

5 ACTION STEPS

1. Have a Plan to Stay Safe

- Work with a counselor or friend to develop an action plan in case there is another instance of potential abuse. Keeping yourself (and any children involved) safe is of utmost importance.
- Be sure that you have numbers to call—police, battered women's shelter, family shelter, trusted friend, relative, and counselor—in an easily accessible place.
- Have bags with essentials packed in an easily accessible location so you can leave quickly if needed.
- Photocopy important documents and plan ahead to have access to money and car keys.
- If you need to leave at some point when an abusive incident presents itself, do not take part in a discussion or argument with the abuser. Calmly exit and go to a predetermined location (with a trusted friend or family member).

2. Gain a Healthy Perspective

- Sometimes, in the midst of abuse, it's easy to believe the lie that the abuse is "deserved" or "punishment" for not being a "good enough" wife and/or mother. However, a husband's role of headship in a marriage never includes the right to control or abuse. And a wife's role never includes the right to control or abuse, nor does it include submitting to abuse.

3. Build a Support Network

- Ground yourself in the truth of who you are in Christ. Abuse does not have to define who you are. Be proactive in getting help and never feel that you are stuck.

- Join a support group in your church or community to connect with other women in similar situations. Seek out godly advice and input from leaders in your church or friends you trust.

- Pray. You don't have to go through this alone. In the midst of pain and heartache, Jesus aches to heal your wounds and carry you in His arms. Don't resist His love or try to push through on your own.

BIBLICAL INSIGHTS 6

[Moses] and Aaron gathered the assembly together in front of the rock and Moses said to them, "Listen, you rebels, must we bring you water out of this rock?" Then Moses raised his arm and struck the rock twice with his staff. Water gushed out, and the community and their livestock drank.

Numbers 20:10–11

Moses acted in anger. He did not obey God and was punished by not being allowed to lead his people into the Promised Land (Num. 20:12).

Anger can be the most damaging of all emotions, causing people to say or do things they regret. Out-of-control anger can ruin friendships and marriages and even cause nations to go to war.

Some people end up living forever with the consequences of choices made in a moment of heated anger. People who struggle with destructive anger must find help to discover alternative ways to manage it. This begins by admitting there is an out-of-control problem, seeking accountability and help, and turning it over to God.

[Abimelech] went to his father's home in Ophrah and on one stone murdered his seventy brothers, the sons of Jerub-Baal [Gideon]. But Jotham, the youngest son of Jerub-Baal, escaped by hiding.

Judges 9:5

The tragic story of Abimelech pictures extreme violence used for selfish reasons. This illegitimate son of Gideon and a concubine (Judg. 8:29–31) brought disaster on the rest of Gideon's family. Violence and murder became his way of dealing with all threats to his power (9:22–49). In the end, however, his violent ways resulted in his own destruction (vv. 50–56).

Violence doesn't resolve anything and ultimately leads to more violence and death. It comes from out-of-control emotions. If you are in a violent relationship, you have a right and a responsibility to protect yourself. While God promises to be with you and take care of you, this does not mean you have to let the abuse continue. Make the abuse known and seek help. You are only enabling the abuser by continuing to submit to physical abuse, and generally abuse worsens with time.

Husbands, love your wives and do not be harsh with them.

Colossians 3:19

And you, fathers, do not provoke your children to wrath, but bring them up in the training and admonition of the Lord.

Ephesians 6:4 NKJV

These verses describe healthy relationships within the family and within the body of Christ. Physical abuse and violence have no place here.

Husbands are commanded to love and not be harsh with their wives. Scripture never commands a woman to submit to a physically abusive husband. If you are in such a situation, do not continue to let yourself be abused. As God's daughter, you are precious to Him and deserve to be treated with respect and care. Get godly counsel and work to set physical and personal boundaries.

Although children are commanded to obey their parents, this does not give parents permission to be cruel or unreasonable in their treatment of their children. Parents who nag, belittle, deride, or beat their children destroy their self-esteem and discourage them. The purpose of parental discipline is to train children. Consistent discipline, administered with love, will help children grow into responsible adults.

7 PRAYER STARTER

Today Your child is worried and frightened, Lord. _____ needs Your help to know how best to deal with the difficult circumstances she is experiencing. Show her the best way for her to escape the violent situations she finds herself in and heal her wounds as only You can. Surround her with people who will support her, love her, and help her find healing. Give her courage to stand up to this individual and take the necessary steps to protect herself . . .

8 RECOMMENDED RESOURCES

Kroeger, Catherine Clark, and Nancy Nason-Clark. *No Place for Abuse: Biblical and Practical Resources to Counteract Domestic Violence*. InterVarsity, 2001.

Nason-Clark, Nancy, and Catherine Clark Kroeger. *Refuge from Abuse: Healing and Hope for Abused Christian Women*. InterVarsity, 2004.

Stewart, Donald. *Refuge: A Pathway Out of Domestic Violence and Abuse*. New Hope Publishers, 2004.

Vernick, Leslie. *The Emotionally Destructive Relationship: Seeing It, Stopping It, Surviving It*. Harvest House, 2007.

Pregnancy

PORTRAITS 1

- "We're having a baby!" Jasmine squealed when her husband, Chris, walked through the door. A million emotions swirled through Jasmine like a current of electricity—excitement about being a mother, love for Chris, pride that there was a little life growing inside of her, eager anticipation of the baby's birth, and a little bit of anxiety and fear. Two months later Chris couldn't take it. "I don't even feel like we're married anymore," he blurted out one day. "All you want to talk about is the baby. What happened to *us*?"

- Since she was a little girl, Paige had always dreamed of having a baby. But she didn't expect it to be in high school. Paige and her boyfriend, Tom, had been sexually active for a while but had always used protection, so Paige was shocked when she found out she was pregnant. Tom couldn't handle it. He ended the relationship right then and there. But as hard as it was, Paige was determined to give her baby a chance. Paige ran her hand over her swollen belly that was growing bigger by the day and smiled. *Another kick.*

- As Lauren sat in the doctor's office for her first prenatal appointment, she was excited and nervous. After her miscarriage two years ago, Lauren and Tim had been unsure whether they'd be able to have kids. But here she was, with a real, live baby inside of her. Leaving the office a few hours later, the doctor's words pounded through her head. *High-risk pregnancy*, he had said. "O God," she whispered through tears, "not again."

DEFINITIONS AND KEY THOUGHTS 2

- *Pregnancy is the period from conception to birth when a baby develops and grows in a woman's uterus.* In the United States there are an average of sixty million women each year who are of childbearing age—fifteen to forty-four years old.[1]

- Pregnancy can be determined through an *at-home urine test or a blood test given by a doctor.* All pregnancy tests work by detecting the presence of human chorionic gonadotropin (hCG), a hormone produced when a fertilized egg implants itself in a woman's uterine wall. While at-home tests are fairly accurate, if a woman suspects pregnancy, *she should see her doctor.*

- Pregnancy is a time of *joy and anticipation* for the mother-to-be but also a time of *unique challenges and stresses.* Especially if the pregnancy was unplanned, the news can strike fear in a woman's heart and cause her to *consider the option of abortion*. And statistics show that pregnancy *increases the possibility of violence* and abuse, often from the baby's father.

— 240,000 pregnant women are subject to domestic violence.

— 40 percent of assaults begin during the first pregnancy.

— Pregnant women have twice the risk of battery.[2]

- Each year, there are 468,988 babies born to *teenage mothers* in the United States. Many of these women have no idea how to care for themselves or their baby. In addition to needing access to medical care, most of these at-risk women *will need counseling in how to develop a healthy lifestyle to ensure the safety of their baby*.

- Many women are not aware of the *risks of certain behaviors* during pregnancy, or they don't think about the welfare of their unborn baby. A pregnant woman's use of the following substances has been proven to have *long-term effects on the health of the child*.

— 820,000 women smoke cigarettes while pregnant.

— 221,000 women use illicit drugs during pregnancy.

— 757,000 women drink alcohol while pregnant.[3]

- Each year there are approximately 6,000,000 pregnancies in the United States: 4,058,000 live births and 1,995,840 pregnancy losses. Among women who experience *pregnancy loss*:

— 600,000 women experience pregnancy loss through miscarriage.

— 1,200,000 women experience pregnancy loss through termination.

— 64,000 women experience pregnancy loss through ectopic pregnancy.

— 6,000 women experience pregnancy loss through molar pregnancies.

— 26,000 women experience pregnancy loss through stillbirth.[4]

- Every pregnancy has the possibility of *complications*, even among healthy women. Each year in the United States

— 875,000 women experience one or more pregnancy complications.

— 458,952 babies are born to mothers without adequate prenatal care.

— 467,201 babies are born prematurely.

— 307,030 babies are born with low birth weight.

— 154,051 children are born with birth defects.

— 27,864 infants die before their first birthday.[5]

- After nine months of pregnancy, the birth of a baby is a cause for *great joy and relief*, but many women also struggle with depression. Eleven percent of pregnant women are diagnosed with *postpartum depression*, otherwise known as the "baby blues."[6]

- While it's natural for a woman to feel overwhelmed for a while with the added stress of caring for and adjusting to a baby, *prolonged or deep depression should not be ignored*. The body's transition out of pregnancy involves significant changes in hormone levels, but if hormones continue to be unbalanced, causing depression, professional help may be necessary. Left untreated, *postpartum depression* can linger on for more than a year. Symptoms include:

  — loss of appetite
  — insomnia
  — intense irritability and anger
  — overwhelming fatigue
  — loss of interest in sex
  — lack of joy in life
  — feelings of shame, guilt, or inadequacy
  — severe mood swings
  — difficulty bonding with the baby
  — withdrawal from family and friends
  — thoughts of harming self or the baby[7]

ASSESSMENT INTERVIEW 3

1. When did you find out you were pregnant? How far along are you? Have you been to the doctor yet?
2. Was this pregnancy planned or unexpected?
3. How did you respond to the news? How did your boyfriend or husband respond to the news? Is he supportive of you?
4. Is this your first pregnancy? Have you had complications with a pregnancy in the past?
5. How are you feeling physically? What symptoms have been most prominent for you (for example, morning sickness, lack of energy, cravings)?
6. What precautions are you taking to ensure your baby's safety? Are you consuming alcohol, drugs, or excessive amounts of caffeine?
7. Are you in a situation where you feel you or your baby's physical safety is at risk? Have you experienced abuse, domestic violence, or battering in your home?
8. Pregnancy brings with it a whole new set of emotions and stresses. What feelings have been most prominent for you? How are you coping with these stresses?
9. How has your pregnancy changed the dynamics of your relationship with your boyfriend or husband? Has it had an impact on your friendships or your relationship with your parents?
10. Becoming a parent requires adjusting your schedule and lifestyle. What aspects do you think will be most difficult for you and your boyfriend or husband? Have you discussed this and begun to plan?

11. What are your greatest fears about having a baby?
12. Who is supporting you as you go through this journey?

4 WISE COUNSEL

Pregnancy is a time of *great joy*, but also a time for *important decisions*. A woman experiences *significant changes*—physical, hormonal, mental, and emotional—as her body adapts to pregnancy and she gets ready to be a mother. In a woman's first pregnancy, these changes can be scary and unsettling, and *many women feel self-conscious and insecure*.

Encourage the woman that *no question is stupid, no matter how strange or embarrassing it may feel to ask*. Discuss how she is feeling—not only physically but also emotionally. What are her stressors? What is she afraid of? What is frustrating her?

Work with the woman to strategize pros and cons for the *decisions she needs to make*, such as:

choosing a health-care provider

knowing the gender of the baby

deciding on the type of birth (natural or cesarean section)

creating a birthing plan

taking childbirth classes

employing a doula

deciding about cord blood banking

breastfeeding or using a bottle

deciding about circumcision

child care and career decisions after the baby is born

The journey of pregnancy is not a solo journey. It's essential that a pregnant woman gather a support network around her, including her doctor, her husband, her family, and her friends—especially women who have already experienced pregnancy and childbirth. *Assess the quality of the woman's relationships and her level of comfort with her pregnancy*. Suggest going to a support group for pregnant women and new moms.

5 ACTION STEPS

1. Take Care of Your Body and Get Prenatal Care

- With a baby growing inside of you, you can expect to feel different, but that doesn't mean you are destined to nine months of misery. Pregnancy is a time of change, adjustment, and challenges, but also a time of rejoicing.

- Right now, taking care of your baby means taking care of your body, and that includes eating a healthy and balanced diet (remember, weight gain is part of being pregnant), exercising regularly, getting proper rest, and avoiding toxic substances like alcohol, drugs, and excessive caffeine.

2. Connect with Other Women

- While prenatal appointments with your doctor will keep tabs on your physical health, you need to keep tabs on your emotional health as well. There's no substitute for spending time with other pregnant women—laughing, crying, talking, sharing stories and concerns, praying for each other, and enjoying this time of your life as a gift from God.

- Get involved in a pregnancy support group in your church or community. Seek out women who have "been there, done that," and ask them questions, rather than trying to figure it all out on your own.

- Consider employing a doula, a professional who is trained in childbirth and can offer emotional, physical, and informational support to you and your husband during your pregnancy journey. To find a doula, ask your physician, childbirth course instructor, or your friends who have children. You can also use the web to look up certified doulas in your area. Here are two sites to check:

  — CAPPAChildbirth and Postpartum Professional Association, www.cappa. net

  — DONADoulas of North America, www.dona.org

3. Talk, Plan Ahead, and Research

- Spend time with your husband or boyfriend to discuss responsibilities and expectations. That way, you know what to expect from him and he knows what to expect from you. This is crucial to maintain your intimacy. Begin planning how the two of you will stay focused and continue to cultivate your relationship throughout the pregnancy.

- Write out a birth plan with your doctor, your husband, and a trusted friend (if you wish), expressing your preferences for the birth of your baby. Consider who you want to be there, if you want a doula, what positions you hope to use, your preferences for pain relief, if you want an epidural, preferences for your baby's care, and so on. Make sure your doctor, husband, and any other important people have a copy of this document so there will be no doubt about your wishes.

- While you should not live in fear, it's important to know the risks of your pregnancy and the possibility of your baby arriving early. Talk to your doctor about your health risks, and research the symptoms of Rh factor incompatibility, gestational diabetes, preeclampsia, and other common health problems. Even if you don't appear to be at risk, it is wise to be prepared in case you develop health complications at some point during your pregnancy.

6 : BIBLICAL INSIGHTS

I praise you because I am fearfully and wonderfully made; your works are wonderful, I know that full well. My frame was not hidden from you when I was made in the secret place. When I was woven together in the depths of the earth, your eyes saw my unformed body.

Psalm 139:14–16

Life is a miracle, and no matter what the circumstances are surrounding your pregnancy, you can be joyful in the fact that the baby growing inside of you is being intimately woven together by God Almighty. Though you can't see your baby yet, God is intimately involved in the process of your baby's development and growth in "the secret place."

The reality of pregnancy is an opportunity for worship. Even in the midst of morning sickness, backaches, and possible health complications, God is sovereign over your life and your baby's life. Rather than living in fear of what may go wrong, choose to joyfully trust Him with your and your baby's health.

Like the psalmist, praise Him for the fearful and wonderful way your baby's unformed body is being put together by a loving God.

He tends his flock like a shepherd: He gathers the lambs in his arms and carries them close to his heart; he gently leads those that have young.

Isaiah 40:11

Pregnancy is not easy, and neither is raising little ones, but Jesus, the Good Shepherd, promises to gently lead you, nurturing, caring for, protecting, and providing for you as you do the same for your baby. So as you walk through the journey of pregnancy, know that you don't walk alone.

Invite Jesus into your marriage, your pregnancy, and your adjustment to being a parent. He loves you intimately and longs to be involved in every aspect of your life. Be honest with Him about your fears, anxieties, and frustrations and rejoice in His unconditional love and faithfulness that is new every day, even when they begin with morning sickness.

Do not be anxious about anything, but in everything, by prayer and petition, with thanksgiving, present your requests to God. And the peace of God, which transcends all understanding, will guard your hearts and your minds in Christ Jesus.

Philippians 4:6–7

During pregnancy, many women struggle with anxiety concerning their baby. *What if something's wrong with the baby? What if I have a miscarriage? What if . . .* The questions can go on and on, and left unchecked, the what-if game can steal the joy and wonder of bearing a child.

Rather than focusing on everything that could go wrong, choose to embrace this opportunity as a faith-building experience. While you are responsible to make wise choices, eat healthy, and take care of your body, God is the only one who can create and sustain life. So rather than falsely believing that you're in control, let God be God and rest in His peace. He promises to take care of you and to provide everything you need.

PRAYER STARTER : 7

Lord, we thank You for the gift of life, and the life that You are nurturing inside this woman. _____ is excited, Jesus, but also stressed, anxious, nervous, and a little worried, and so she brings these feelings to You today and gives them to You. Lord, You are sovereign over every single thing in this universe, including this little baby. Give this woman wisdom as she adjusts her lifestyle and makes important decisions. Surround her with Your love and grace. Bring people into her life who can support and encourage her . . .

RECOMMENDED RESOURCES : 8

Maclean, Heather, and Hollie Schultz. *The Baby Gizmo Buying Guide: What to Buy When You're Expecting*. Thomas Nelson, 2008.

McWhorter, Brette, and Bruce Rodgers. *The Everything Guide to Pregnancy Over 35*. Adams Media, 2007.

Murkoff, Heidi. *Eating Well When You're Expecting*. Workman, 2005.

Murkoff, Heidi, and Sharon Mazel. *What to Expect When You're Expecting*. Workman, 2005.

Polimino, Jennifer, and Carolyn Warren. *Praying through Your Pregnancy: An Inspirational Week-by-Week Guide for Moms-to-Be*. Gospel Light, 2009.

Puryear, Lucy. *Understanding Your Moods When You're Expecting: Emotions, Mental Health, and Happiness*. Houghton-Mifflin, 2008.

Stone, Joanne. *The Pregnancy Bible: Your Complete Guide to Pregnancy and Early Parenthood*. Firefly Books, 2009.

Prostitution

1 : PORTRAITS

- Candice had been prostituting herself for over a year and she thought she was doing fine. She was living in her pimp's lavish home and no longer had to avoid her father, who had sexually abused her since she was eleven years old. Life seemed to be going okay, until the night a "client" pulled a knife on her. Candice didn't know if she would make it out alive.

- Aubrey was from a middle-class, suburban neighborhood. Once Aubrey reached college, the bills and debt began to pile up. Then Aubrey met Roy, who promised to help her out with all her debt if she would work for him. Aubrey was desperate and agreed to turn to prostitution. Once Aubrey realized that being trapped in debt was simple compared to being trapped in prostitution, she didn't know where to turn.

- Sarah had so much responsibility weighing on her shoulders. Her family depended on her to bring in most of the money to support them because of their health issues. Sarah's minimum wage income just wasn't cutting it. One day she was hanging out with a friend and was introduced to some of her friend's friends. One of the guys pulled her aside after hearing her discuss her financial issues. He offered her a job that would make her quadruple the amount of money she was currently making. She just had to be willing to show off her body and perform a few sexual favors here and there. She agreed to it for the sake of her family and was to start the following night.

2 : DEFINITIONS AND KEY THOUGHTS

- *Prostitution*, known as the world's oldest profession, involves *selling one's body for sex and sexual favors*. It can also involve trading sex with someone for drugs or shelter or protection or any number of necessary services to maintain life.

- When someone under the age of 18 is prostituting, they are called a domestic minor trafficking victim. It is estimated that *1 million women and 1.2 million children* work as prostitutes, some as young as 10 years old. In the United States, 1 percent of women have worked as prostitutes at some point in their life.[1]

- The *legality of adult prostitution* varies in different parts of the world. It is legal and heavily regulated in Nevada, some states of Australia, and some European countries, but is punishable by death in numerous Middle Eastern countries.

- The *prostitution of minors is illegal in most countries*. Furthermore, many countries whose citizens most frequently engage in international child procurement, such as the United States, Australia, and European countries, enforce worldwide jurisdiction on their nationals traveling abroad.

- *In every city in America, prostitution rings are organized by pimps who "manage" the women*, sometimes including preteens living and working as sexual slaves. The pimps keep the bulk of the women's earnings in exchange for shelter and protection from other pimps and dangerous johns—*those who use prostitutes and other services. Many pimps are dangerous*, abusing drugs and beating their women into servile submission of the worst kind.

- According to one study, the number of full-time equivalent prostitutes in a typical area in the United States is *estimated at twenty-three per one hundred thousand, of which some 4 percent are under age eighteen.*[2]

- The length of the working careers of these prostitutes was estimated at a mean of 5 years. Another study revealed a mean number of *868 male sexual partners per prostitute per year* of active sex work and that the number of men who had prostitutes as sexual partners is seriously underreported.[3] One study found that 16 percent of 18- to 59-year-old men in a United States survey group had paid for sex.[4]

- *Street prostitutes* may be the *most common form of sex-for-sale* in the United States. Pimps stake out and defend key corners and streets in their communities. Then they parade the girls for a john passing in a car or they direct him to a certain hotel that offers rooms for an hour or all night to engage in sex.

- *Brothels* are *establishments specifically dedicated to prostitution* and may be confined to special red-light districts in big cities. Other names for a brothel include *bordello, whorehouse, cathouse,* or *knocking shop*. Prostitution also occurs in *some massage parlors.*

- *Escort prostitution* is considered a more high-class form of business and commonly takes place at the customer's hotel room (referred to as an *out-call*) or at the escort's place of residence or hotel room rented for the occasion by the escort (called *in-call*). This form of prostitution is delivered under the umbrella of *escort agencies*, which ostensibly supply attractive escorts for social occasions. While escort agencies claim to never provide sexual services, very few successful escorts are available exclusively for social companionship. Even where this type of prostitution is legal, the ambiguous term *escort service* is commonly used. In the United States, *escort agencies advertise frequently on the internet*, and advertisements can be readily found on any major search engine and on open forum sites.

- Research shows that prostitution *often involves abuse and assault*. In one study prostitutes reported that

  — 82 percent had been physically assaulted.
  — 83 percent had been threatened with a weapon.
  — 68 percent had been raped while working as a prostitute.
  — 84 percent experienced current or past homelessness.[5]

3 ASSESSMENT INTERVIEW

Prostitution should be approached primarily as if it were sexual violence and abuse, which it is. Being a victim carries stigma, shame, and fear, so some women are not likely to volunteer information about the situation. You can be sure that coercion and violence occur and that these acts can have negative consequences on reproductive and mental health. Through counseling, you can help identify women who are victims or potential victims and provide services, either directly or through referral. It is important that you listen carefully to the woman when discussing violence. You can establish trust and rapport and create an atmosphere of respect and privacy, elements that may be missing from the life of a woman who is a victim of sexual violence.

Questions for a woman who is involved in or was just recently rescued from a prostitution ring are:

1. How did you first become involved in prostitution?
2. When did this first occur? Tell me a little bit about your lifestyle and sexual activity now.
3. How has prostitution affected and changed you and your identity as a woman?
4. When you look back over it, what feelings are most prevalent?
5. Do you feel you are in immediate danger? Are you afraid to go home or be alone?
6. Do you use alcohol or drugs to help you cope with your experiences? How effective has that been?
7. How has prostitution affected your daily life, your friendships, your family, your boyfriend or husband?
8. How has prostitution affected your view of sexual relationships?
9. Tell me about your hopes and dreams. What's most important to you? Who do you want to be?
10. Have you ever felt hopeless or depressed before? Have you considered suicide?
11. What do you want to see change in your life? What are you willing to do to change and get help?
12. Who else in your life is aware of your involvement in prostitution? Do you have a family member or friend you can talk to about this?

4 WISE COUNSEL

Typically, prostitutes do not seek counseling for their problems because they are *suspicious of outsiders and authorities, fear rejection, and fear change.* Prostitutes may fear admitting they have been harmed. They may also fear their pimps, who monitor them 24/7 and will often accompany them to a doctor's office. They may have difficulty establishing enough control over their own lives to seek counseling and they may fear that health care and other services will not be available to them because they are prostitutes. Many prostitutes have a "*psychological paralysis*" that involves wanting help but rejecting it at the same time. *However, it has been found that if twenty-four-hour hotlines, counseling, advocacy, and shelter care are made available specifically to prostitutes, these services will be used.* Counseling has been found to help prostitutes recover from sexual trauma and improve self-esteem.[6]

Usually prostitutes fear *violent clients, pimps, and corrupt law-enforcement officers.* Those who engage in street prostitution are also sometimes the targets of serial killers, who consider them easy targets and who use the religious and social stigma associated with prostitutes as justification for their murder. *Being criminals in most jurisdictions, prostitutes are less likely than the law-abiding to be looked for by police if they disappear, making them favored targets of predators and serial killers.*

It's not unusual for Christians and some feminists to be on the same page regarding prostitution, believing that it is *degrading to all involved and inherently exploitative.* Commercial sex is seen as a *form of rape* enforced by poverty (and often by the pimps' violence). Those who believe that prostitution is degrading *reject the idea (for different reasons) that prostitution can be reformed and legalized,* challenging the *false assumptions* that women exist for men's sexual enjoyment, that all men "need" sex, or that the bodily integrity and sexual pleasure of women is irrelevant. These ideas, in fact, are what make prostitution an *inherently exploitative, sexist practice.*

One authority asserted that *venereal disease and suicide attempts* are the two greatest health risks for juvenile prostitutes. Fifteen percent of all *suicide* victims are prostitutes, and 75 percent of prostitutes have attempted suicide. In one study about half of the women reported having a *sexually transmitted disease (STD).* More than 90 percent of women in both street and off-street activities increased their *drug or alcohol usage* during prostitution. Furthermore, because many prostitutes have been sexually assaulted, *they suffer from the psychological effects of rape and child sexual abuse.* These include *rape trauma syndrome, low self-esteem, guilt, and self-destructiveness.*[7]

In working with those who have been victims of sexual violence or coercion, remember the following:

Be *sensitive and listen* carefully to the client's needs.

Treat any medical problems.

Ask about *safety.*

Ask about *substance abuse.*

Offer *a pregnancy test,* if available.

Provide *information about services* for STDs and HIV screening and treatment.

Offer *information about routine contraceptive use.*

Engage *professional intervention.*

Realize that prostitution is not just an act. It's an *identity.* Over time, a woman becomes known as a prostitute, and that is how she views herself. Even if she is no longer prostituting herself, it will take time to figure out who she is and reshape her identity. In this process, it's essential to *look to God's Word and seek out together what it truly means to be a woman* and a daughter of God.

5 ACTION STEPS

1. Be Patient and Rest in God

- Healing from sexual violence is a long, difficult process, and people will vary in the amount of time they need for healing. Don't put yourself on a time line or tell yourself you should be over this by now. You are courageous to seek help for healing, to talk about your experience, and to bring what was once in darkness into the light.

- For many women, prostitution is much more than a job—it truly becomes their identity. Even years later, it can sometimes be difficult not to think of themselves in that way. But our God is a redeemer of broken people, and there is nothing too hard for Him. Let Him begin to heal your heart and fill you with new life. Spend time reading Scripture, not as a spiritual exercise, but to discover and recount the promises of God and let them soak into your heart. Seek out a Christian support group, a safe place where you can be open and honest as you begin to work through the healing process.

- *If you are involved in a court matter with this case, focus on the data the court needs and when it is needed and question your client about her willingness and ability to further explore her experiences in the context of counseling.*

- *Prostitution carries with it extended issues for the woman seeking healing and restoration. If you are not qualified for the long-term process of work with victims of exploitation and sexual abuse, refer her to a trained counseling professional.*

2. Grieve Your Loss

- You have been violated. Free yourself to express emotive rage and tears when you are ready.

- *Some clients may have gone to the opposite, compensatory extreme and are numb, without affect at all as they face their losses. Do not push your client to be emotional if she isn't ready. Feel her pain and walk with her to grieve the loss she has experienced.*

3. Repent When Necessary

- If you entered into prostitution willingly, healing and transformation will happen only when you confess your sins to the Lord and repent of the wrongdoing. God is ready and waiting to forgive your sins and extend His grace to cover them. He wants to set you free from the lifestyle you have been living and use your testimony to bring glory to Himself.

4. Regain Control and Find Support

- Attending a group for survivors of sexual violence or rape can be a healing first step. Share your story with someone you trust. Consider restorative counseling as an aid in regaining control of your life.
- Realize how saddened God is by the abuse you have suffered. Jesus understands your pain completely, for He suffered unimaginably in His shameful trial and death on the cross.
- Being believed and being able to say what happened are important first steps in recovery. Your counselor will help you stand strong as you begin to realize that those who victimized you can no longer have any power over you.

5. Set Healthy Boundaries

- Here are some things you need to realize: You have a bright future. You're not a victim but a survivor. You may have lost a lot but you are not ruined for the future. Healing is possible.
- Survivors of sexual abuse need to learn how to practice self-care. One important step is to establish healthy boundaries. While boundaries may vary depending on your specific situation, some examples include avoiding certain parts of town, cutting off all contact with previous clients and pimps, seeking the financial help of your family or a local church, establishing accountability with a trusted individual about your daily schedule and activities, and attending counseling to begin to find healing. Be sure trusted people are aware of your personal boundaries so they can help you stand firm in them.

6. Consider Counseling and Psychotherapy

- You may need professional guidance to deal with the deep pain that sexual abuse and exploitation have caused. Seek out a counselor with expertise in counseling survivors of sexual abuse.
- *Be ready to refer the client to a counselor or therapist who has expertise in counseling victims of sexual violence.*

BIBLICAL INSIGHTS 6

When a woman who had lived a sinful life in that town learned that Jesus was eating at the Pharisee's house, she brought an alabaster jar of perfume, and as she stood behind him at his feet weeping, she began to wet his feet with her tears. Then she wiped them with her hair, kissed them and poured perfume on them. . . . Jesus said to her, "Your sins are forgiven." . . . "Your faith has saved you; go in peace."

Luke 7:37–38, 48, 50

Jesus welcomes the broken, discouraged, and hopeless. In this passage, He reached out to this immoral woman in love, forgave her sins, and spoke publicly of her faith. How ironic that a broken, hurting woman—not the "holy" Pharisee—was the one Jesus honored! He welcomed and praised the poured-out love of this prostitute, not the religious leader's dinner.

No matter what you have experienced, Jesus longs to forgive you, heal you, and help you build a new life. He looks past outward appearances and reads the deepest hurts and longings of your heart. He receives the one with a heart of brokenness and faith, one that is desperate to change—not a put-together, "holy" person who doesn't need His grace. So don't push away the only One who has the power to heal you. Invite Him into your pain. He will never judge or reject you, for He is love.

You intended to harm me, but God intended it for good to accomplish what is now being done, the saving of many lives.

Genesis 50:20

If anyone had good reason for revenge, it was Joseph. His brothers' jealousy provoked them to horrible abuse—selling him as a common slave to be taken away forever (Gen. 37:11–28). Before being raised to power in Egypt, Joseph had lost thirteen years of personal freedom. But he wisely understood that God had overruled his brothers' abuse, making their evil turn out for good. This response of strength and faith can come only from those who trust God to rule—and overrule evil—in their lives.

Sometimes people think they can hide portions of their lives from everyone. They try to hide angry tempers, deep jealousies, or sexual sin. Sexual violence hasn't escaped God's notice. The abuser may have thought he got away with it, but God knows—and God promises to judge appropriately.

Do not take revenge, my friends, but leave room for God's wrath, for it is written: "It is mine to avenge; I will repay," says the Lord. . . . Do not be overcome by evil, but overcome evil with good.

Romans 12:19, 21

God knows all that has occurred in our lives, including the pain, the betrayal, and brokenness. He was present in the darkness and continues to walk with us when we are coming out into the light. The offenses done to us were done to Him as well—including the shame of being disrobed at the cross.

He promises to repay—vengeance is His and His alone. Our job is to heal and to forgive. Do not let the evil overcome you; do not give the abuser that much power in your life. Overcome the evil by doing good to others and to yourself.

Have mercy on me, O God, according to your unfailing love; according to your great compassion blot out my transgressions. Wash away all my iniquity and cleanse me from my sin. For I know my transgressions, and my sin is always before me.

Psalm 51:1–2

No matter what shame or guilt you feel as a result of your prostitution, God's grace is greater. He longs to meet you in your pain and walk with you every step of the way toward healing. Don't think you can hide your past from God. He already knows every single thing about you, including every mistake and sin you've committed, and yet, He still pursues you with His unconditional love.

So do not be afraid and do not run from God. Instead, like David in this psalm, invite God into your brokenness and pain. Confess your particular sins to Him and cry out to Him for mercy. God's Word promises that "if we confess our sins, he is faithful and just and will forgive us our sins and purify us from all unrighteousness" (1 John 1:9). When you confess and repent of your sin, God promises to *forgive* and *cleanse* your heart.

PRAYER STARTER 7

Father in heaven, be the Father of lights and the Father of care and protection for _____. May she always look to You for the power to stay away from and never be sucked back into the evil system she was in. Walk with her in the journey of healing and redemption that You already can see and have prescribed for her. Bring into her life the people and organizations that will help heal her wounds and champion her as a person deserving respect and care . . .

RECOMMENDED RESOURCES 8

Alcorn, Nancy. *Violated: Mercy for Sexual Abuse.* Winepress, 2008.

Carmichael, Amy. *You Are My Hiding Place.* Bethany House, 1991.

Farley, Melissa, ed. *Prostitution, Trafficking, and Traumatic Stress.* Haworth, 2003. Not Christian but full of good information. She also has a website titled Prostitution Research and Education.

Grant, David, and Beth Grant. *Beyond the Soiled Curtain: Project Rescue's Fight for the Victims of the Sex-Slave Industry.* Onward Books, 2009.

Jewell, Dawn. *Escaping the Devil's Bedroom.* Monarch Books, 2008.

Langberg, Diane. *On the Threshold of Hope.* Tyndale, 1999.

Rock, Donna. *A Heart Set Free: My Story for His Glory.* Strang Communications, 2005.

Sands, Christa. *Learning to Trust Again: A Young Woman's Journey of Healing from Sexual Abuse.* Discovery House, 1999.

Schaumburg, Harry. *Undefiled: Redemption from Sexual Sin, Restoration for Broken Relationships.* Moody, 2009.

Tracy, Steven. *Mending the Soul: Understanding and Healing Abuse.* Zondervan, 2008.

DVD

Wildflowers. AACC Library: DVD training series; to order call 800-526-8673 or visit www.aacc.net.

Rape

1 PORTRAITS

- Jane and her husband were part of a church with a very rigid theological viewpoint that men were the indisputable head of the household and wives must be submissive in all things. When her doctor inquired about the bruising on her face and shoulders, she went numb and told him that it was her fault. If she could only learn to be more submissive, her husband would stop beating her and forcing her into rough sex. Their pastor had been counseling them both and strongly advised against Jane's leaving the home and marriage, even though this would provide for her safety and sanity. To her husband and her pastor, her leaving would be a selfish act of abandonment.

- Nancy was a freshman at the university and she really wanted to fit in. She was invited by a handsome young man to go to a fraternity party. After a few drinks, he led her into a back room where other couples were engaged in various stages of sexual acts. She protested, but in a drunken rage, he overpowered, violated, and raped her.

- Daniel and Bethany have been dating for almost two years. Bethany reports that about one year into their relationship, Daniel became very rigid in his desire for certain sexual practices that she was extremely uncomfortable performing. At first, she thought that it was just a phase of experimentation that he would get over, but he didn't. Daniel began to force Bethany to do these sexual acts. During a recent visit to her gynecologist, however, Bethany was told that she may never be able to have children due to injury she received after the most recent sexual encounter with Daniel.

2 DEFINITIONS AND KEY THOUGHTS

- Sexual violence is defined by the Centers for Disease Control and Prevention as any behavior that falls within one or more of the following categories:

1. use of physical force to compel a person to engage in a sexual act against his or her will, whether or not the act is completed;
2. attempted or completed sex act involving a person who is unable to understand the nature or condition of the act, to decline participation, or to communicate unwillingness to engage in the sexual act, e.g., because of

illness, disability, or the influence of alcohol or other drugs, or because of intimidation or pressure;

3. abusive sexual contact.[1]

- Rape is defined as sexual intercourse, or other forms of sexual penetration, without the consent of the victim. "Rape may be heterosexual (involving members of the opposite sex) or homosexual (involving members of the same sex). The legal definition of rape may also include forced oral sex, date rape, gang rape, and other sexual acts."[2]

- Historically, *marriage has been a defense against being charged by one's spouse with sexual violence.* However, in the past forty years, a growing number of states have criminalized sexual violence within marriage. Trends in the law clearly indicate that *such violence will no longer be tolerated in the United States.*

- The Centers for Disease Control report that sexual violence and rape are *significant problems in the United States.*

  — Among high school students surveyed nationwide, about *8 percent reported having been forced to have sex.* Females (11 percent) were more likely to report having been forced to have sex than males (4 percent).

  — An estimated *20–25 percent of college women* in the United States experience attempted or completed rape during their college career.

  — In the United States *one in six women and one in thirty-three men* reported experiencing an attempted or completed rape at some time in their lives.

  — These numbers underestimate what many experts consider to be a problem plagued by *secrecy and failure to report.* Many cases are not reported because victims are afraid to tell the police, friends, or family about the abuse. Often they are *threatened with further violence* or violence against their children, or they are simply afraid that telling will cause the *breakup of their family and they'd be left destitute* and without financial resources to raise their children.

  — Victims may think that *their stories of abuse will not be believed and that police cannot help them.* And intense feelings of *shame and embarrassment* can be too painful to expose.

  — Sexual violence may be linked to *risky behaviors* that affect physical health. For example, victims are more likely to smoke, abuse alcohol, use drugs, and engage in unsafe sexual activity.[3]

- The US Department of Justice reports:

  — *Every two minutes someone in the United States is sexually assaulted.*

  — Sexual assault is one of the most underreported crimes, with *60 percent being left unreported.* Males are the least likely to report a sexual assault, though they make up about 10 percent of all victims.

  — More often than not—73 percent of the time—*rape victims know their attacker.*[4]

3 ASSESSMENT INTERVIEW

1. Tell me about what happened when you were raped. What emotions or memories stick out to you the most?
2. Can you tell me who did this to you? (*If the person seems reticent, explain that you need to know to help her, others who might be abused, and the abuser himself. In addition, if your client is a minor and still in contact with the abuser, immediate reporting action needs to be taken.*)
3. Tell me about your family. How are things going at home?
4. Tell me about your past. Have you been abused or raped before? Is this the first time you've sought help as a victim of sexual violence or rape?
5. What problems are you currently having as a result of what happened? (*Listen to how the abuse affected her. No two people are alike in what happened to them or concerning the consequences of sexual violence or rape. Be aware that victims tend to minimize the impact of the abuse.*)
6. Tell me how you feel about what has happened to you. (*The client needs to have permission to feel her true emotions.*)
7. Do you feel responsible for the rape? (*Reassure her that she is not alone and that she is not responsible for the abuse.*)
8. What do you believe about yourself? (*Uncover unhealthy beliefs that have developed as a result of abuse. For example, what does she think about herself that she allowed the rape to happen or abuse to continue?*)
9. What do you believe about the person who raped you? (*Listen for rationalizations, such as "He couldn't help it; he was drunk." These defenses have helped the client cope but have also made her less capable of seeing herself as a true victim of abuse.*)
10. What would you like to have happen as a result of our meeting today?
11. What kinds of boundaries do you think need to be set up to protect you? What do you need if you are to heal from this?
12. Who else knows about this?
13. Do you have a personal support system in your life?
14. Where do you think God has been in all of this?

4 WISE COUNSEL

Shame, humiliation, fear, pain, and confusion are among the myriad feelings encircling a victim of sexual violence and rape. These victims have been violated and assaulted in the most demeaning way possible. *Personal boundaries were disregarded* as the victim lost control over her own body, leaving scars that run deep.

It is the responsibility of the counselor to establish safety and trust with the client before engaging in any kind of treatment strategy. The counselor-client relationship must be viewed as the primary initial intervention of utmost importance. Establishing rapport and creating safety take time, and the process cannot be forced.

Reasons a victim may seek the help of a counselor include:

fear for the safety of her life or the lives of her children

depression, anxiety, panic, or other mental health symptom that is presently preventing the client from daily functioning

referral by a pastor, mentor, doctor, family member, or trusted friend

requirement of a court due to a pending legal case against the perpetrator

A thorough assessment and an evaluation are needed to determine the *level of impairment and current dysfunction.* Areas to assess include personal history, current functioning or impairment, level of safety in current living arrangement, family history, abuse history, medical history, and suicidal or other self-harm ideation.

If danger is still present and the client's personal safety is an issue, you will need to *develop a safety plan* with her. This may include deciding on alternate living arrangements with a family member, trusted friend, or local safety shelter.

In her book *Trauma and Recovery,* Dr. Judith Herman wrote: "The core experiences of psychological trauma are disempowerment and disconnection from others. Recovery, therefore, is based upon the empowerment of the survivor and the creation of new connections. Recovery can take place only within the context of relationships; it cannot occur in isolation."[5]

Although Dr. Herman did not write her book from a Christian viewpoint, her insight is still valuable and can be aligned with Solomon's words in Ecclesiastes 4:9–10: "Two are better than one . . . : If one falls down, his friend can help him up. But pity the man who falls and has no one to help him up!"

We are *created for relationships.* Beginning with a counselor-client relationship that fosters empowerment and then reconnecting with others who are safe, victims of sexual violence and rape can discover God's healing power.

ACTION STEPS 5

1. Reconnect

- You will begin to find healing when you allow yourself to open up and talk about your feelings and what happened to you with another safe person, such as a counselor. When you were victimized, your ability to control and protect your own body was taken away. This is the gravest of violations for most people and can wreak emotional and relational havoc for years to come if not dealt with in the context of a safe environment. It is important to begin to find your voice again and become empowered to overcome the pain this abuse has caused in your life.

- *It is important for the counselor to move slowly and allow the client to explore her feelings at her own pace. She has suffered severe personal boundary violation and needs to feel that she is worthy of respect and honor again. Be a refuge of safety for her.*

- *Many victims will report feelings of guilt and/or shame, believing that they could have done something to prevent the abuse or that they deserved the abuse. Validate your client's feelings, yet reassure her that the abuse was not her fault. Challenge irrational thought patterns and discuss the importance of placing responsibility on the offender.*

2. Develop a Plan for Safety

- If you are still in danger, develop a plan with your counselor as to how you can establish physical and emotional safety for yourself and, if applicable, for your children. Write down the plan and exit strategy.
- Never attempt to escape without a clear plan and the assistance of a trusted person. In many cases when a victim has attempted to leave abruptly, she has been harassed, severely injured, or even killed by the perpetrator.

3. Reach Out

- Reach out for help by joining a support group, going to counseling on an ongoing basis, or reading about and researching sexual violence and rape. However you do it, reaching out will help you fight against fear and the desire for isolation. You do not have to go through this alone. We are broken through relationships, but we are also healed in safe, loving relationships.
- *Help your client come to an understanding of what it means to trust again. Provide education regarding safe versus unsafe people.*

4. Seek God's Healing and Wisdom

- At first, it may be very hard to turn to God for healing. You may be questioning where God has been in the midst of your pain. Find a way to work through this doubt and fear. Read verses in the Bible that remind you of your worth and significance in the eyes of God, such as Psalms 18:16–19; 34:7; 1 Peter 3:12. Ask God to help you deal with feelings of guilt, shame, and/or anger. Get involved in a local church and consider joining a small group so that you can surround yourself with a caring body of believers.

6 BIBLICAL INSIGHTS

If out in the country a man happens to meet a girl pledged to be married and rapes her, only the man who has done this shall die. Do nothing to the girl; she has committed no sin deserving death. This case is like that of someone who attacks and murders his neighbor, for the man found the girl out in the country, and though the betrothed girl screamed, there was no one to rescue her.

Deuteronomy 22:25–27

Rape is a serious offense in God's eyes because it twists and corrupts God's beautiful creation of sexual intimacy. Under the Old Testament law, rapists were sentenced to death.

It is biblical to report sexual violence and/or rape and for the offender to be duly punished by the law. Keeping quiet is *not* extending grace; it is failing to recognize one's immense value in the eyes of God.

Despite the victim's feelings of guilt and self-blame, rape and sexual violence are *never* her fault. God's Word states clearly that the girl "has committed no sin."

Therefore God gave them over in the sinful desires of their hearts to sexual impurity for the degrading of their bodies with one another. They exchanged the truth of God for a lie, and worshiped and served created things rather than the Creator—who is forever praised. Amen.

Because of this, God gave them over to shameful lust. . . .

Furthermore, since they did not think it worthwhile to retain the knowledge of God, he gave them over to a depraved mind, to do what ought not to be done.

Romans 1:24–26, 28

Do you not know that the wicked will not inherit the kingdom of God? Do not be deceived: Neither the sexually immoral nor idolaters nor adulterers nor male prostitutes nor homosexual offenders nor thieves nor the greedy nor drunkards nor slanderers nor swindlers will inherit the kingdom of God.

1 Corinthians 6:9–10

Rape is an evil corruption of the beautiful truth God intended to convey through human sexuality as a picture of Christ and His church. Rather than recognizing that the body is an offering to serve and please one's spouse, the abuser's goal is to control and terrorize the victim to satisfy his own desires. These behaviors degrade and ignore Christ's example—He laid down His life for His bride, the church.

God calls sexual immorality, including rape, "wicked," "shameful," and "depraved." God promises to bring just punishment on the offenders.

The LORD is close to the brokenhearted and saves those who are crushed in spirit.

Psalm 34:18

The Spirit of the Sovereign LORD is on me, because the LORD has anointed me to preach good news to the poor. He has sent me to bind up the brokenhearted, to proclaim freedom for the captives and release from darkness for the prisoners, to proclaim the year of the LORD's favor and the day of vengeance of our God, to comfort all who mourn, and provide for those who grieve in Zion—to bestow on them a crown of beauty instead of ashes, the oil of gladness instead of mourning, and a garment of praise instead of a spirit of despair. They will be called oaks of righteousness, a planting of the LORD for the display of his splendor.

Isaiah 61:1–3

God weeps over the pain and the damaging effects of sin in His children's lives, especially in the area of sexual violence. He created sexuality as a beautiful expression of marital intimacy between a man and a woman; but even more than that, it is a picture of His union with His bride, the church. Sexual violence mars this ideal of intimacy between God and man, grieving the heart of God.

Even in the face of unjust abuse, Jesus Christ can bring freedom from tormented memories, release from feelings of degradation, and comfort to the hurting victim.

Many victims of sexual violence view themselves as ugly, no good, and worthless, but God promises to bring beauty and gladness even out of unimaginable pain.

7 : PRAYER STARTER

Heavenly Father, we know Your heart breaks when people are hurt so deeply. Thank You for _____, who has come for help and healing. And thank You, Lord, for Your kindness and strength. Give wisdom and courage as she takes the next steps to be honest about the pain. It is so comforting to know You never abandon us and will help this dear person experience Your love and peace in the midst of this storm . . .

8 : RECOMMENDED RESOURCES

Fortune, Marie. *Sexual Violence: The Sin Revisited.* Pilgrims Press, 2005.

Holcomb, Lindsey and Justin. *Rid of My Disgrace: Hope and Healing for Victims of Sexual Assault.* Crossway Books, 2011.

Humbert, Cynthia. *Deceived by Shame, Desired by God.* NavPress, 2001.

Langberg, Diane. *On the Threshold of Hope.* Tyndale, 1999.

Meyer, Joyce. *The Love Revolution.* FaithWords, 2009.

Weaver, Andrew, Laura Flannelly, and John Preston. *Counseling Survivors of Traumatic Events.* Abingdon Press, 2004.

Wright, H. Norman. *The New Guide to Crisis and Trauma Counseling.* Gospel Light, 2003.

Relationships with Men

PORTRAITS 1

- Rachel did not understand why he was being so persistent. John, one of her classmates in her History 101 class at college, tried to talk to her every class they had together. Obviously he was interested in her and found her very attractive. Rachel could not bear to say more than a couple words to him, out of fear that he would pursue her even more. Her mom, who had gone through a nasty divorce, constantly told Rachel when she was growing up that men are evil. Though John seemed genuine and she knew he was a strong Christian, she just couldn't trust him.

- During her childhood, Sally never had a father figure in her life. Once she hit puberty and began realizing how much her body was changing, she became addicted to wearing outfits that got her the most attention from men. She loved flaunting her curves and shooting seductive glances at all the men she passed. Basically she loved the attention of guys.

- Kara did not think she could be any more in love with her boyfriend, Ryan. She absolutely adored him and could not see herself marrying anyone else. One night Ryan came over to her apartment looking very worried. Within minutes she realized he had come to break up with her, that he had found someone else. As he walked out her front door, leaving her crying uncontrollably on the floor, she swore she would never let another man into her heart or into her life.

DEFINITIONS AND KEY THOUGHTS 2

- *A relationship with someone of the opposite sex* involves a state of *connectedness* between people (especially an emotional connection).

- Relationships with men may consist of *family relationships, work relationships, or romantic relationships.* These three categories of relationship make up the majority of those a woman will have with a man.

- For many women, *goals and ambitions are chosen but remain fluid, depending on romantic relationships with men.* For these women, relationships with men are central to their conversations, friendships, and daily activities. The idea that women are focused on their relationships with men has been the subject of many pop culture movies, magazines, and television shows.

- When women have *suffered past abuse, victimization, or infidelity* at the hands of a man, they struggle with relationships with the opposite sex. *Alarming statistics* show that, compared to males, females are 10 times more likely to experience partner violence, around 572,032 women compared to 48,983 men.[1]

3 ASSESSMENT INTERVIEW

1. What specifically brings you here today?
2. Describe your relationship with your father.
3. Describe your relationship with God.
4. Growing up, how did you interact with your brothers or male friends?
5. Do you make friends with men easily?
6. Do you find it hard to be comfortable around men?
7. Have you had any experience in the past that made you skeptical of men?
8. Have you ever had your heart broken by a boyfriend, by more than one boyfriend? Is this something you're still hurting from?
9. Do you find yourself desiring the attention of men everywhere you go or do you find yourself trying to avoid the eye contact of men altogether? If you answered yes to either one of these questions, why do you think you feel this way?
10. What do you hope to gain from counseling?

4 WISE COUNSEL

Don't be surprised by what women may view as a normal relationship with a man. *Many women do not realize what is and is not a healthy relationship with the opposite sex.* When a girl is raised by her single mom, it is more likely that she will *desire attention* from many different males while growing up. On the other hand, many women *avoid having relationships* if they have had any sort of traumatic experience with men in the past.

A woman who *does not know how to relate to men in a healthy way* will find herself crippled in her job and social settings and may even be setting herself up for destructive romantic relationships. As hard as it may be, get to the core of *why she has a hard time* forming healthy relationships with the opposite sex.

This may require *pulling out painful information about her past*. For example, many women who have unhealthy views of men were raised in a home where their father had little or no positive impact on their life. Try to discover what makes her feel the way she does.

Talk with her about *how to behave around men* in a variety of different situations—work, home, school, social settings, and so on—so that she can form healthy relationships with them and be treated as a woman should be.

Help the woman gain *perspective*. She needs to understand that *not all men are like those in her past* who hurt her and broke her trust. Often healing comes *in the context of community*, as a woman sees and experiences relationships with godly men who genuinely care for her as a sister in Christ.

However, because not every man has the best intentions, it is vital that a woman *learn to be discerning* and stay away from men who want to use her. This means learning to *stand up for herself*, which for many women is a foreign idea.

Take time to evaluate the woman's view of guy-girl interactions. If she subconsciously slips into "doormat submission," work with her to restructure her behavior patterns and *develop a healthier normal*, according to *scriptural guidelines*. In the process, the woman will learn more about herself, who God is, and what is and is not appropriate in interacting with men.

ACTION STEPS : 5

1. Evaluate Your Relational Patterns

- Step back and take stock of your relationships with men. How is your relationship with your father, brothers, male friends, boyfriend, or husband? If you find yourself either being drawn to or afraid of interacting with men, it is important to address the root issues, though it may be emotionally painful. Unless you work through and get healing in these areas of your life, you will find yourself in a string of emotionally and physically unhealthy relationships.

2. Get to the Core Issue

- While it may feel unnatural and scary, because of unhealthy relational patterns, to relearn how to interact with men, realize that no woman is exempt from falling into harmful attachments with men. Get to the core of why you probably have a hard time forming healthy relationships with the opposite sex. This may require reliving your past, which may be quite painful. For example, many women who have unhealthy views of men were raised in a home where their father had little or no positive impact on their life.

3. Realize Your Worth

- Depending on your past, it may be easy to forget how much you are worth. If you have been belittled or abused in any way, you need to hear how much God loves you and to understand that men should treat you with the respect you deserve.
- To develop healthy relationships, you must learn how *not* to act around men and how *to* act around men. Ask your counselor to help you understand how men think and how they may view your actions. You may not realize it, but your innocent (or maybe intentional) actions and body language may communicate a lack of self-respect.
- *Encourage the woman to continue to view herself as a woman of integrity, whom men should respect and honor.*

6 BIBLICAL INSIGHTS

I also want women to dress modestly, with decency and propriety, not with braided hair or gold or pearls or expensive clothes, but with good deeds, appropriate for women who profess to worship God.

1 Timothy 2:9–10

God's desire for women is for them to act like women of God. He wants the best for His daughters, and in this passage He makes it clear how He wants women to portray themselves. The modesty and humility of a woman of God are not just outward characteristics, but ultimately heart attitudes. God looks past a woman's outward appearance and knows the thoughts, intentions, and motives of her heart. Self-care is important, but a woman's identity should not be grounded in her outward appearance. This passage reminds us that a joyful, loving, giving heart is precious and valuable.

A gracious woman attains honor.

Proverbs 11:16 NASB

A wife of noble character who can find? She is worth far more than rubies. Her husband has full confidence in her and lacks nothing of value.

Proverbs 31:10–11

As a woman's roots go down deep into Christ, she will carry herself with dignity and live graciously with both men and women in all arenas of her life. Her identity and behavior will be rooted in her position in Christ and His character rather than the norms of the culture in which she lives. Such a woman attains honor and respect for her strength, her compassion, her wisdom, and her kindness.

7 PRAYER STARTER

Lord, we come to You with a heart of humility. We ask You to help Your daughter, _____, understand just how special she is to You. Please help her realize the kind of attention she does and does not deserve from men. Mold her heart to Your will, so she will desire to develop healthy relationships with the men that are in her life . . .

8 RECOMMENDED RESOURCES

Antcliff, Amanda. *Women Rising: A Challenge to Stand Up and Step Out into a Life of Influence.* Creation House, 2010.

Cloud, Henry, and John Townsend. *Boundaries.* Zondervan, 1992.

DeMoss, Nancy Leigh, and Dannah Gresh. *Lies Young Women Believe: And the Truth That Sets Them Free.* Moody, 2008.

DiMarco, Hayley. *How Hot Is Too Hot?* Baker, 2006.

Ethridge, Shannon. *Every Woman's Battle: Discovering God's Plan for Sexual and Emotional Fulfillment.* Random House, 2003.

Relationship with Christ

1 PORTRAITS

- Tanya grew up in the typical Christian home. She attended youth group, Christ-centered summer camps, and even sang on the worship team for a number of years. After a women's conference, Tanya realized her relationship with Christ was stuck. She had built a great résumé, but the *relationship* was still at its beginning stages.

- Olivia knew what a relationship with Christ looked like, but having one seemed so out of reach. Olivia received Christ as her Savior at a young age, but growing up had been rough, and with no one to mentor her, Olivia had to go it alone. Now thirty-five years old and a mother of two, Olivia wants to experience a true relationship with Christ. *But how?* she wonders. *It all seems like drudgery to me.*

- Laura was a pastor's daughter. She grew up going to church every single time the doors were open. She knew how to do the Christian thing and portray herself as a good Christian girl. Once she was in college, she began to realize that she did not have much of a relationship with Christ. She had been doing all the right things to please her family and church and now needed to change if her relationship with her Lord was to be real.

2 DEFINITIONS AND KEY THOUGHTS

- Often *legalism* creates a gap between *knowing* who God is and *experiencing* a relationship with God. *Legalism* is a superficial and mechanical (going through the motions) way of displaying one's faith. Usually it entails rules, guidelines, and ideas of how one should look and act as a Christian.

- Numerous research studies by Gallup reveal a *growing dissatisfaction with the state of religion* in America. Only about half of Americans view religion as being very important, while nearly three-fourths of our nation see religion as *a waning influence* in American culture. In fact, three out of ten Americans view religion as *old-fashioned and out-of-date*, and that number appears to be growing.[1]

- Yet despite losing faith in the church, *the majority of Americans still believe in a higher Being.* A *Newsweek* poll found that 91 percent of American adults claim a belief in a god of some sort,[2] while *Time* magazine reported that 85 percent of Americans identify themselves as Christian.[3]

- A Gallup study reports that *73 percent of Americans "are convinced that God exists."* Only 3 percent of the American population identify themselves as atheists, being "convinced God does not exist." For the remaining 24 percent of Americans, the jury is still out.[4]

- Many women in today's world have been jaded by religion or hurt by the church, and now want something *real*, something fresh. Abstract theology, wooden benches, and dusty hymnbooks are out. But *the Holy Spirit is still at work in women's hearts*, drawing them into relationship with Him.

- *Spiritual growth* is not just about an emotional experience or praying a prayer. It is about being *rooted and grounded in the life-transforming truths of Scripture—*not just on a head level, but on a heart level. It is about knowing Jesus. There are three elements that factor into our spiritual growth: *experiences, disciplines, and relationships.*

- Experiencing God leads *to growth in an intimate relationship with Him.* Often God uses hardships, disappointments, and trials to draw us closer (see Rom. 5:3–5).

- A *relationship with Christ* is not based on works, rules, regulations, or appearances. A relationship with Christ is about *spending time getting to know Him,* just as women do with friends—making and spending time with one another. Through her *conversations with Christ in prayer and getting into His Word,* transformation will begin in the life of the woman who is wholeheartedly seeking Him.

- A *relationship with Christ* is also not about a checklist or a change list. Once the relationship with Christ begins to form through time in His Word and prayer, we begin to think differently about the old ways and the sins in our life, and we *begin to change because of our renewed mind and spirit*—not because of a checklist we have made. Change comes through Christ, and through change in Christ we can have *a relationship with Him that surpasses all others.*

- *Our own effort* is a key in growing our relationship with Christ. A relationship always requires two who are committed to it.

- Our *relationship with Christ* is also *somewhat dependent on our earthly relationships.* Those we surround ourselves with either model what it means to follow Christ or draw us away from following Him. As Scripture puts it, "Do not be misled: 'Bad company corrupts good character'" (1 Cor. 15:33). *It is important to have mentors.* Paul addresses older women in the church specifically to be mentors of younger women, showing them how to live out a life that is God-honoring (Titus 2:4–5).

- When asked about the *most important relationships* in their life, seven out of ten Americans choose their *earthly family over their heavenly Father.*[5] Also only one out of five, or 19 percent, of adults choose God or Jesus Christ as most important in their life. [6]

- A recent study conducted by Gallup revealed that Americans' *views of God* vary greatly, and not just denominationally. In a survey of 1,721 participants, researchers discovered that 31 percent of Americans view God as *judgmental*, 25 percent view God as *benevolent*, 23 percent view God as *distant*, and 16 percent view God as *critical.*[7]

243

3 ASSESSMENT INTERVIEW

1. How do you view Jesus Christ?
2. What are your experiences with Christ and His mercy, grace, and forgiveness?
3. Has there ever been a time when you accepted Christ as your Savior and Lord?
4. What was your home life like when you were growing up?
5. Were your parents and/or siblings Christians?
6. Has there ever been a person in your life who models a true relationship with Christ?
7. Do you often find yourself going through the motions of being a Christian?
8. Do you spend time alone (not in a group setting) with Christ in His Word and in prayer?
9. How would you describe a relationship with Christ?
10. What would it mean in your life to have such a relationship?
11. What are practical ways you can seek God with all of your heart?
12. When is the best time of day for you to pray, read His Word, and spend time with Him?

4 WISE COUNSEL

Many hear the church teaching that *being a Christian means being perfect, put together, and spiritually mature*, but this attitude misconstrues the true gospel—that Jesus Christ came to rescue sinners. The beauty and wonder of knowing God is this: "Because of his great love for us, God, who is rich in mercy, made us alive with Christ even when we were dead in transgressions—it is by grace you have been saved" (Eph. 2:4–5). We cannot save ourselves—it is entirely through the work of the Holy Spirit that we are given Christ's righteousness and are transformed, one day at a time, into Christ's likeness.

It is vital that a woman realize her relationship with Christ is a gift from God (we all deserve God's judgment!) and is not a moral self-improvement project. A do-it-yourself view of Christianity will lead to *legalism, a judgmental attitude, and, ultimately, giving up trying to "be good" in our own strength.* A woman must also realize that it is a team effort. She and God make up the relationship, not just God and His sovereignty alone.

Help the woman see that, just like any other relationship, getting to know God starts with *spending time with Him*—talking to Him in prayer, reading His Word, and worshiping Him for who He is. Encourage the woman to *set aside a time of day when she is fresh, awake, and alert to spend time with Jesus.* Though it may seem awkward at first, Scripture encourages us to talk to God like a trusted friend or a loving, gentle father.

While a relationship with Christ requires discipline and intentionality, more than anything, *God desires for us to be honest with Him.* Brainstorm with the woman to discover ways to build *God-oriented habits*—bringing God into every single aspect of life—eating, sleeping, work, school, shopping, hanging out with friends. The reality is that God is present *everywhere* and He longs for His children to learn to live in His grace.

ACTION STEPS 5

1. Delight in God

- As we are told in Psalm 1:2, those who seek to be righteous should delight in God and His Word. As you read God's Word and find pleasure and refuge in it, you will be filled with spiritual wisdom rather than worldly advice.
- Seek joy, happiness, and delight in Christ and His Word rather than in things of the earth; then you will be on the path to a healthy, vibrant relationship with Christ.

2. Meditate on God's Word Day and Night

- Take delight in God's Word and meditate on its life-changing truths. Meditating involves thinking on a verse, letting it resonate in your mind and heart, and asking God to show you how to apply it to your life. When you open, read, and shut the Bible, without thinking about what God may be saying to you in it, you have head knowledge but no real heart change.
- When you meditate on God's Word, focusing on what it says, the truths go with you throughout the day and night. God's Word is kept in the forefront of your mind and has influence on your heart. Meditation on God's Word allows it to become part of your life and heart. Ultimately it will change your attitudes and behavior.

3. Be Careful of the Company You Keep

- It is easy for women to get caught up in groups of other women who build their relationships on gossip and cliques. Building relationships with other women on the same path as you are—women who desire to know and please God and fight sin—will help you build a relationship with God.
- The company you keep should encourage you, challenge your faith, and honor God. It is also important to know that the company you keep want to be held accountable for their actions and behaviors. A true sister in Christ looks for accountability and correction when needed.

4. Spend Time with Jesus

- Building a relationship with Jesus means seeking God for yourself. Set aside time on a daily basis when you can talk to God, listen to His Spirit, confess sin, worship and thank Him, and read His Word.

- Group Bible studies and church services are great tools for spiritual growth, but there is no substitute for time alone with Christ, because at its core, your relationship with Him depends on the commitment you alone have to Him. Become intimate with Christ and share with Him every thought and need. Then praise Him with shouts of joy!

6 BIBLICAL INSIGHTS

Direct me in the path of your commands, for there I find delight. Turn my heart toward your statutes and not toward selfish gain. Turn my eyes away from worthless things; preserve my life according to your word.

Psalm 119:35–37

When we start out on the journey toward a personal relationship with Christ, we need direction and we must learn how to look to Christ for guidance. In Psalm 119 the writer's prayer to God is a model for those who need direction and a foundation for building their personal relationship with Christ. Getting rid of the old ways and learning new ways take God's help. The psalmist's cry to God here should be the cry of our heart.

Oh, the joys of those who do not follow the advice of the wicked, or stand around with sinners, or join in with mockers. But they delight in the law of the LORD, *meditating on it day and night.*

Psalm 1:1–2 NLT

Not only does our relationship with God require a commitment of our time to meditate and delight in His Word, but it also requires that we separate ourselves from the ungodly. We are still required to minister to the ungodly, but our relationships and our time should be spent in the counsel of the godly, not the ungodly. To build a relationship with God, we need godly relationships with others.

One thing I ask of the LORD, *this is what I seek: that I may dwell in the house of the* LORD *all the days of my life, to gaze upon the beauty of the* LORD *and to seek him in his temple.*

Psalm 27:4

Many things grab at the attention of women, but, ultimately, the most important thing in all of life is Jesus Christ. Though King David had the world at his fingertips, we see in this psalm that he realized, compared to the beauty of Christ and the delights of knowing Him intimately, nothing else matters. A relationship with Christ won't just happen. It requires turning aside from our own desires and our old way of life and being intentional about knowing Jesus. Just as in any other relationship, getting to know God personally requires time, commitment, and sacrifice, but, oh, is it worth it!

Now this is eternal life: that they may know you, the only true God, and Jesus Christ, whom you have sent.

John 17:3

Tragically, the gospel has been cheapened by many Christians today who view it as a free ticket out of hell, a voucher that Christ-followers get to cash in on judgment day. Such a perspective robs God of His glory and misses the heart of the gospel. To everyone who believes the promise of the gospel, salvation is far more than a free ticket. It is the miracle of redemption—no longer are we enemies of God. We are His children, His friends, His beloved. In this verse recorded in John, Jesus speaks of eternal life as not just a future promise, but, for the believer, a present reality. Eternal life comes from knowing God, and it begins now.

PRAYER STARTER : 7

Father, a relationship with You is the most fulfilling thing we can ever experience. Give _____ an unquenchable desire to have a personal relationship with You. Meet with her, Lord. Bring her fellowship and surround her with women who desire to know You and women who will show her what a relationship with You can be. Show her Your goodness and Your love . . .

RECOMMENDED RESOURCES : 8

Blackaby, Henry, Richard Blackaby, and Claude King. *Experiencing God: Knowing and Doing the Will of God.* B&H, 2008.

Brestin, Dee, and Kathy Troccoli. *Falling in Love with Jesus.* Thomas Nelson, 2001.

Clinton, Julie. *Living God's Dream: An Extraordinary Women Devotional.* Harvest House, 2008.

Curtis, Brent, and John Eldredge. *The Sacred Romance: Drawing Closer to the Heart of God.* Thomas Nelson, 1997.

Eldredge, John and Stasi. *Captivating: Unveiling the Mystery of a Woman's Soul.* Thomas Nelson, 2010.

Ethridge, Shannon. *Completely His.* WaterBrook, 2008.

Fuller, Cheri. *A Fresh Vision of Jesus.* Baker, 2004.

Meyer, Joyce. *Knowing God Intimately: Being as Close to Him as You Want to Be.* FaithWords, 2003.

Moore, Beth. *Believing God.* B&H, 2004.

Packer, J. I. *Knowing God.* InterVarsity, 1993.

Tozer, A. W. *The Pursuit of God.* Wingspread, 1993.

Roles of Women

1 PORTRAITS

- Charisa feels torn and frustrated. She always thought that finding the man of her dreams would make her life easier, but marrying Pete two years ago has brought with it a whole new set of challenges. Charisa works a high-stress job, and when she gets home in the evening, the *last* thing she wants to do is think about cooking dinner. *What am I supposed to do?* Charisa wonders. *Quit my job? Eat out every night?*

- Stuck between a rock and a hard place. That's reality for Jessica. Growing up, she was an independent, strong-headed little girl. Her dad wasn't around very much, and it was her mom who ran the home. As a young professional, Jess can hold her own in a conversation and is very comfortable speaking her mind. "It seems like I scare every guy off," Jess spurts out in frustration. "What am I supposed to do? I don't want to be single for the rest of my life but am I supposed to change who I am so guys will ask me out?"

- Ever since she was a little girl, Emily dreamed of a baby of her very own. When she gave birth to beautiful twin girls, Emily and her husband, Tim, couldn't be happier. But Emily never anticipated how much work it would be to care for kids. "I hardly have time to brush my own teeth, never mind spend time with Tim," Emily spills out through tears. "What happened to our marriage? What happened to *us*?"

2 DEFINITIONS AND KEY THOUGHTS

- *A woman's roles involve the responsibilities and expectations she carries in all areas of her life*—as an individual, a student, a professional, a volunteer, a wife, a mother, a grandmother, a neighbor, a friend . . . and the list goes on.

- Women's lives are very seasonal. *Each season—college, marriage, parenting, and so on—brings with it a unique set of joys and challenges.* While we can't do all things all the time, we can do them all (or almost all) when necessary, because the seasons of our life bring different responsibilities and freedoms, thus allowing for a rich, full life.

- Women in today's world wear many hats. *Trying to figure out how to combine the roles* of wife, mother, and professional can be a difficult challenge, leading to *stress, frustration, and conflict.* And being concerned about doing them *in a way that is pleasing to God* can add to the stress. *How do I know what I should do and what I should say no to? How can I organize my priorities so my husband knows I love him, my kids are taken care of, and I am making a difference in my profession? How should I interact with other men in my workplace?* Questions like these are important, and often there are many factors to consider.

- *The majority of women in the United States work outside the home.* Of the 122 million women age 16 years and over in the United States, 72 million (59.2 percent) are working or looking for work.[1]

- Research shows that, among women who are employed, *74 percent work at full-time jobs, while 26 percent work part-time.*[2]

- The most *common jobs* for women at present include:

  — secretaries and administrative assistants, 3,074,000

  — registered nurses, 2,612,000

  — elementary and middle school teachers, 2,343,000

  — cashiers, 2,273,000

  — nursing, psychiatric, and home health aides, 1,770,000

  — retail salespersons, 1,650,000

  — first-line supervisors or managers of retail sales workers, 1,459,000

  — waitresses, 1,434,000

  — maids and housekeeping cleaners, 1,282,000

  — customer service representatives, 1,263,000

  — child-care workers, 1,228,000[3]

- Though the professional world has been considered a "man's world," *some careers are actually dominated by women,* such as:

  — registered nurses (92 percent female)

  — meeting or convention planners (83.3 percent female)

  — elementary and middle school teachers (81.9 percent female)

  — tax examiners and revenue agents (73.8 percent female)

  — medical and health services managers (69.5 percent female)

  — social and community service managers (69.4 percent female)

  — psychologists (68.8 percent female)

  — business operations specialists (68.4 percent female)[4]

- No matter what her profession, biblically, *a woman's identity is found in Christ* and in her standing as a child of God, not in a marriage or in perfect kids or in a dream career. *Knowing who she is in Christ is vital to understanding and balancing differing roles in different seasons of life.*

- As of 2004 there had been a 15-percent increase in stay-at-home mothers over the preceding 10 years.[5] However, some women, especially single mothers or women whose husbands are in school, *have no choice but to maintain a full-time career as well as being a full-time mom.* And today's uncertain economy only adds to the stress of financial issues.

- Research shows that *12 percent of households in America are run by a single mom.* The average income for single moms is only 25,500 dollars per year, and it is estimated that *only 70 percent of single moms are employed.*[6]

- Many women *operate in multiple roles at the same time,* and the daily grind of marriage, family, and work can easily lead to burnout. It is *vital to set healthy boundaries* and avoid overcommitment. Though this may initially seem selfish, if a woman doesn't take care of herself, she can't take care of anyone else.

- In today's world, many women are raised with a drive for independence and performance, thinking they can do anything. To a certain extent, this is true, but *no woman can do everything.*

- Many women suffer from the *superwoman syndrome.* They feel the pressure to *pull themselves together and do it all,* and, as a result, live under unrealistic expectations. Sadly, society sets this "superwoman" standard for women, and additional pressure may come from a woman's husband, family, friends, and even herself. With good intentions, women *overcommit* themselves, making their lives miserable. Every day they fail to measure up to *an impossible standard of perfection,* leading them to feel *depressed, overwhelmed, and frustrated.*

- Though God intends for His children to work diligently and pursue excellence in whatever they do, He never intends for a woman to live under the pressure of trying to do it all. *A critical aspect of counseling consists in helping a woman establish healthy, realistic expectations for herself* and put in place *clear boundaries to protect her time and relationships.*

3 ASSESSMENT INTERVIEW

1. What brings you here today?
2. Describe your daily routine and the roles you are in.
3. What role is most difficult for you? What role is causing the most stress?
4. Are there any roles you see as conflicting? If so, how have you handled this?
5. What most frustrates you about your life right now? Where do you feel overwhelmed?
6. How often do you say no, and in which role? How did it feel? How did other people respond?
7. Have you set any boundaries about what you will and will not do?
8. How do you define success? What roles do you need to prioritize to be successful?
9. Take some time to make a list of your roles; then prioritize them. Which role is most important to you? Which role do you spend the most time on?
10. What season of life are you in right now? What are your primary commitments and goals for this season? Do you wish to change anything?

11. When was the last time you went out on a date with your husband or hung out with friends? When was the last time you did something just for *you*—just to relax and unwind?

12. What can you begin to say no to so you can focus on what you really value, the things that are most important to you?

13. How can you enlist help to fulfill your commitment to each role?

14. How would your life be different if you knew you had nothing to lose and nothing to prove?

WISE COUNSEL : 4

In today's independent culture, many women struggle with balancing their independent personality with the biblical commendation of a "gentle and quiet spirit" (1 Peter 3:4). Taken in context, however, this was not written with the intention of smothering women or taking away their rights. On the contrary, *in Christ, men and women can rejoice in their differences as unique and equal creations of God.*

How does a godly woman operate and interact in relationships with men? While every situation is different, biblically, every interaction should aim to *encourage and build up the other individual, should avoid even the appearance of sin, and should not belittle or demean a man's masculinity or a woman's femininity.* Flirtatiousness and coarse joking do not honor God, but neither does mindless submission.

Scripture commands a woman to submit to her husband, but this does not mean she must submit to every man. *Biblical submission to one's husband should be understood in its proper context.* It doesn't mean that the man is above his wife in some hierarchy. A husband is commanded to love his wife as Christ loves His bride, the church. This kind of *unselfish love is the exact opposite of domination,* control, or fear. It is servanthood, sacrifice, and putting the other's needs first.

God created women with *unique insight* that can carry great weight, and a woman of God should not feel it is necessary to stifle her personality or kill her desires to be godly. First and foremost, *a woman of God submits her heart, her personality, her words, her actions, and her relationships to God.* She is not her own—she is God's instrument to bring hope, encouragement, and healing to others.

Establishing *balance in a woman's roles* often begins with *gaining perspective.* Many women believe that crazy schedules, dysfunctional relationships, and lack of intimacy are realities of life, so they fail to take any steps to change. But God never intended for His daughters to run themselves into the ground, failing to enjoy life or interactions with others.

Help the woman to step back from the daily grind of life and evaluate her commitments. Ask her *why* she is doing the things she's doing and if she is content with her life now. Until a woman *sees the need to change her life,* she won't likely be willing to make changes.

Boundary setting is essential to maintaining a woman's sanity. Help the woman understand that if she is constantly stressed out, rushed, and torn between responsibilities, *something* needs to go. Gaining freedom from the "I have to do everything and help everyone" lie is *the first step to establishing boundaries.* God's Word instructs us to obey, to work hard, and to find enjoyment in our work. It doesn't say we must wear ourselves out trying to do everything.

Help the woman *evaluate the level at which she is trying to live as a superwoman.* Try to get to the root of this drive for performance. Is she trying to prove something? Is she weighed down by other people's expectations? What aspects of her life does she feel are out of control? Communicate to the woman that she does not have to keep living this way but that she must be proactive about *clarifying her roles and responsibilities.*

5 ACTION STEPS

1. Make Knowing God the Top Priority

- Getting to know God needs to be a lifelong journey. Knowing about God and knowing God are very different. You will need to give God times of undivided attention to create an intimate relationship with Him. Having moments of quiet and stillness with God will enable you to hear Him and be led by His Spirit.

2. Commit to Knowing and Living in Truth

- It is crucial to have your beliefs founded on biblical truths. This step requires digging through your belief system and grounding each and every belief in the truths of God's Word. Study Proverbs 31 for further insight into living as a woman of God.
- Many women have a hard time understanding and living God's truth due to past physical, sexual, or emotional abuse. Your counselor can help you identify the beliefs that are rooted in past offenses and then help you discover the biblical truth.

3. Seek Healthy Christian Relationships

- Ground your identity in God—not in what other people think about you. Often women find their self-worth in the affirmation and validation of others. This can lead to an addiction to approval, which is harmful and puts others above God!
- Rather than using relationships to gain approval or significance, make Christ the center of all your relationships—with family, friends, co-workers, husband or boyfriend, and all others. Remember, your life isn't about you anyway. Treat other people in a loving, encouraging way, and always keep the other person's best interest in mind. In your interactions with the opposite sex, be especially careful to act in a pure and righteous way.

4. Find a Godly Mentor

- It is important to find a mentor who models Christ-centered living and can encourage you both in your walk with God and your journey as a woman.

- Seek out a godly, older woman in your church or community and ask her if she will mentor you. Seek to develop a teachable, humble spirit and listen to her insights and counsel.

BIBLICAL INSIGHTS 6

Wives, in the same way be submissive to your husbands so that, if any of them do not believe the word, they may be won over without words by the behavior of their wives, when they see the purity and reverence of your lives. Your beauty should not come from outward adornment, such as braided hair and the wearing of gold jewelry and fine clothes. Instead, it should be that of your inner self, the unfading beauty of a gentle and quiet spirit, which is of great worth in God's sight. For this is the way the holy women of the past who put their hope in God used to make themselves beautiful. They were submissive to their own husbands, like Sarah, who obeyed Abraham and called him her master. You are her daughters if you do what is right and do not give way to fear.

1 Peter 3:1–6

These verses do not mean that women should not or cannot style their hair or wear jewelry and pretty clothes; rather, this passage teaches that women should not let their outward appearance and beauty be the only beauty they possess. Christian women need to focus more on their inward beauty and on developing a genuine, caring, and gentle spirit.

It is a good thing for Christian women to have flattering hairstyles, clothes, and jewelry, but outward beauty does not compare to a heart that truly loves, cares for, and invests in other people. Women with such a heart are truly beautiful, and their beauty does not fade with age. They get more beautiful as they become more like Jesus each day.

The older women likewise [should] be reverent in behavior, not slanderers, not given to much wine, teachers of good things—that they admonish the young women to love their husbands, to love their children, to be discreet, chaste, homemakers, good, obedient to their own husbands, that the word of God may not be blasphemed.

Titus 2:3–5 NKJV

Women have a very special role in the lives of one another. A woman of God is a tool God uses to teach other women, young women, how to live a life pleasing to the Lord. It takes humility to accept mentoring, but there is no better place to go for real-life answers about relationships, marriage, and weathering life's storms than to other godly women who have struggled with the same issues.

Do not rebuke an older man harshly, but exhort him as if he were your father. Treat younger men as brothers, older women as mothers, and younger women as sisters, with absolute purity.

1 Timothy 5:1–2

Many women in today's world wonder how to interact with men. The "modern woman" is independent, bold, and assertive, while the "Christian woman" is viewed as weak-willed, old-fashioned, and a submissive servant. Both of these extremes miss the mark of God's design for women. Thankfully, the principles of God's Word are timeless and help us sort out the puzzles in opposite-gender relationships.

This Scripture passage admonishes us to treat men with purity and respect, as brothers. As we interact with men on a daily basis, our prayer should be, "Lord, let me encourage and challenge him to be a better, more godly man. Let me build him up, not tear him down."

7 PRAYER STARTER

Father, You have a special design for women, whom You cherish. Father, help _____ understand her role as a woman, as a daughter of the King. Guide her, Father, and give her wisdom in knowing how to carry out her roles. Give her wisdom and strength to balance her responsibilities and to know how to relate to others—both men and women—in a real, genuine way . . .

8 RECOMMENDED RESOURCES

Brummett, Nancy, and Alice Scott-Ferguson. *Reconcilable Differences: Two Friends Debate God's Roles for Women.* David C. Cook, 2006.

Chancey, Jennie, and Stacy McDonald. *Passionate Housewives Desperate for God: Fresh Vision for the Hopeful Homemaker.* The Vision Forum, 2007.

Eldredge, John and Stasi. *Captivating: Unveiling the Mystery of a Woman's Soul.* Thomas Nelson, 2007.

Elliot, Elisabeth. *Let Me Be a Woman.* Living Books, 2009.

Hatmaker, Jen. *Makeover: Revitalizing the Many Roles You Fill.* NavPress, 2007.

LaCelle-Peterson, Kristina. *Liberating Tradition: Women's Identity and Vocation in Christian Perspective.* Baker, 2008.

Piper, John. *Recovering Biblical Manhood and Womanhood.* Crossway, 2006.

Sumner, Sarah. *Men and Women in the Church: Building Consensus on Christian Leadership.* InterVarsity, 2003.

Van Leeuwen, Mary. *Gender and Grace.* InterVarsity, 1990.

Weaver, Joanna. *Having a Mary Heart in a Martha World.* Random House, 2000.

Self-Worth and Approval

- Claire and her mother have never been very close. Claire's mother and father both worked full-time with many overtime hours, so as a child, Claire was often alone and neglected. She has always sought out approval and self-worth from the relationships she is in—whether it's with a co-worker, a friend from church, or a romantic interest. The feeling never lasts and Claire ends up alone and feeling worthless again. "I hate feeling worthless and no good, but I feel like I'm stuck," Claire says. "Approval is like my drug."

- For as long as Chelsea can remember, her need for approval has been her drive behind every accomplishment, every choice, and every friend she makes. Failures and disapproval hurtle her into depression and an even greater determination to gain approval. Rarely does Chelsea do something just because she would enjoy it. Everything she says, does, wears—everything—is all about getting the attention and affirmation of her family, friends, boss, and co-workers.

- Rebecca grew up constantly feeling pressured by her mom to look and act a certain way. Even after she had moved out of the house and away from home, she continued to wake up every morning and attempt to look the way her mom had always expected. If she did not have her makeup applied flawlessly, hair brushed just right, and clothes fitting perfectly, she immediately thought of her mother and felt insecure. She wanted her mom's approval more than anyone in the world, but it seemed like she could never be good enough.

DEFINITIONS AND KEY THOUGHTS 2

- *Self-esteem*, whether it's low, normal, or high, *and self-worth describe a woman's understanding of her value and identity.* A woman's self-esteem is a measuring stick for how she feels about herself.

- There are two major components to this measure of worth: *security and significance*. In other words, self-esteem and self-worth are based on *whether a woman feels loved and accepted.* For many women, physical appearance plays a role in the level of self-worth they feel.

- *Security* gives a woman certainty—a foundation on which to build relationships and carry out her daily life. A woman who is insecure feels very uncomfortable with herself. All she sees are her *weaknesses and failures.*

- *Significance* denotes having *a compelling meaning or purpose in life*. A woman seeking significance may struggle with feelings of *inadequacy and hopelessness* and even question the reason for her life.
- *Both self-esteem and self-worth* are developed during the childhood and teenage years. *Experiences, attachment styles, and family dynamics* play a huge role in an individual's self-esteem and self-worth.
- *Low self-esteem* can lead to risky sexual behaviors, suicidal ideations, and eating disorders. Research shows that half of all girls report having been on a diet at or before age nine while 80 percent of eighth-grade girls report being on a diet because they feel *insecure about their weight or body shape*.[1]
- Generally, *self-esteem peaks when a girl is between eight and ten years old*. Research reports that 72 percent of sixth-grade girls say they "have confidence in themselves," but only 55 percent of tenth graders say they have self-confidence.[2]
- Nearly every woman struggles *with insecurity about the way she looks*. Thin is in, as evidenced in television shows and movies, books and magazines, billboards and commercials. And if the way women spend money says anything, a lot of women believe they have to fit a certain cookie-cutter mold. *Women in America spend seven billion dollars on cosmetics every year*. But aside from the usual mascara, blush, and lipstick, a lot of women turn to surgery in attempts to be perfect. Each year, women in America pay for *expensive cosmetic surgeries*, such as:

  — breast augmentation (1.5 billion dollars per year)
  — lipoplasty (1.3 billion dollars)
  — eyelid surgery (684 million dollars)
  — tummy tucks (992 million dollars)
  — breast reduction (829 million dollars)[3]

- The following comment expresses *the pitfalls of an approval addiction*: "Seeking permanent security from imperfect people [or things] doesn't work. . . . Seeking permanent significance from our accomplishments doesn't have any lasting value, and we're left trying to accomplish more."[4]
- God created us to be *satisfied in Him*. Nothing else—even the biggest accomplishment we can imagine—can really fill the need we have to be affirmed, loved, and valued. Earthly approval is fleeting and short-lived, but a woman who knows Jesus desires to hear Him say, "Well done, good and faithful servant" more than anything else in the world. God's love for us, His children, is unconditional and never ending. His approval of us is based on the righteousness of Jesus Christ, not our own accomplishments. Thus we serve others as an overflow of His love in our hearts, not to try to earn God's love.

3 ASSESSMENT INTERVIEW

1. What makes you feel secure?
2. What makes you feel significant?

3. What are the standards you use to measure your self-worth?

4. When you are not accepted by a group or individual, how does this make you feel?

5. Are the opinions, standards, and approval of others very important to you? How much of your day would you say is controlled by trying to fulfill or earn them?

6. How much time do you spend on your outward appearance? How much time do you spend worrying about your outward appearance?

7. Describe your relationship with your mother.

8. Describe your relationship with your father.

9. Have you ever been in a romantic relationship that influenced your self-esteem?

10. Do you feel the need to excel constantly or to overachieve?

11. What do all these feelings accomplish for you? Have you achieved the desired feeling when you accomplish these things?

WISE COUNSEL 4

When dealing with women *suffering from low self-esteem or the need for approval*, it is important to note that low self-esteem begins with the *way in which women think*. To a certain extent, every woman struggles with low self-esteem, and if she has a history of unhealthy family or dating relationships, she may have very deep heart wounds. Low self-esteem stems from *comparison and perception of one's appearance and performance.*

The woman who thinks she isn't good enough, smart enough, talented enough, or sexy enough *fails to accept the woman God created her to be.* For her, life is all about trying—trying to measure up, trying to be like everyone else. Every action and decision, then, is motivated by a desperate pursuit of significance. *This kind of woman finds her identity in what she does, and she fails to realize that her true identity is in Jesus Christ.*

The process of developing a healthy self-worth is just that, *a process.* There is no magic prayer or quick fix. Lies built up over years and years of broken relationships take time to crumble, as *the truths of Scripture permeate a woman's heart.* God's Word tells us, "Do not conform any longer to the pattern of this world, but be transformed by the renewing of your mind" (Rom. 12:2). The more a woman focuses on Christ, she will increasingly be freed to live in the truth of who God created her to be.

ACTION STEPS 5

1. Retrain the Way You Think

- Self-worth and the need for approval begin in your thought patterns. It is critical to retrain your thoughts of what is true and what is not. Your counselor will help you do this.

- *The client needs to identify the thoughts and thought patterns that are contributing to harmful thinking. Once these are identified, you can help her retrain her thinking to be positive, eliminating the harmful, self-defeating thoughts.*
- Memorize Scripture passages that reinforce your significance and worth in Christ. Choose a modern translation, such as New International Version or New Living Translation, which are easier to memorize. Here are some valuable passages to know by heart:

  — I am God's workmanship (Eph. 2:10).

  — I am free from condemnation (Rom. 8:1–2).

  — I am Jesus's friend (John 15:15).

  — I have been redeemed and forgiven of every sin (Col. 1:13–14).

  — I have direct access to God (Heb. 4:14–16).

- It is important to note that just memorizing passages about self-worth will not facilitate the desired change, though it is important to memorize and apply Scripture in your everyday life. Appropriate Scripture passages can encourage and reassure you when you are slipping back into feelings of worthlessness. Ultimately, however, only a personal relationship with Christ can facilitate change in a woman's heart.
- The thoughts in our mind affect our heart. Changing what is in the mind will greatly impact your thinking about who you are and who God is. Ultimately, this will reshape your identity.

2. Partake in Self-Enriching Activities

- First, take a step back from media standards of self-worth. Put away the television shows, magazines, and movies that depict a false sense of a person's value.
- Second, get involved in church outreach, community projects, and service organizations that benefit others. This will create a more realistic view of reality that will help form a better idea of who you are and what your life is about.
- Use your natural gifts to invest yourself in church or community groups that seek to help others in need. For instance, you may want to help children from low-income families excel in their education, coach a kids' sports team, volunteer at a downtown youth center or homeless shelter. Make your life about more than yourself and your needs.

3. Set a Biblical Standard

- Set the standard for your self-worth by getting into God's Word and having a firm foundation in Him. Knowing where your self-worth comes from, and knowing the only approval needed is the approval of God, will radically change your self-image. When you know God intimately and are seeking His approval, a new significance and self-worth will develop that you have never experienced before.

BIBLICAL INSIGHTS : 6

So God created man in his own image, in the image of God he created him;
male and female he created them.

Genesis 1:27

We are made in the image of God—the crowning work of God's creation! Our self-worth will be like a roller coaster if we measure it by what others say or hold as a standard. Realizing that we are made in God's image and using *that* as our standard for self-worth and identity will never leave us feeling void or empty.

We are precious to God. We belong to Him. He knows each of us intimately and put us together the way He did for a reason.

I praise you because I am fearfully and wonderfully made; your works are
wonderful, I know that full well.

Psalm 139:14

This is not only a passage fit for praising the Father, but a passage worth *praying* to the Father. It is a passage to be held near and dear to our hearts. You are made *fearfully* and *wonderfully*! If we believe the truth of God's Word that He is our Savior, then the truth in His Word that says His works are wonderful and we were made wonderfully should encourage and sustain us. We should know it "*full well.*"

Are not two sparrows sold for a penny? Yet not one of them will fall to the
ground apart from the will of your Father. And even the very hairs of your head
are all numbered. So don't be afraid; you are worth more than many sparrows.

Matthew 10:29–31

If the Lord God Almighty takes notice and cares for sparrows, how much more care and notice does God give us, His creation that was made in His image? We are valuable and "worth more than many sparrows." God values us. This alone should instill in us great self-worth (not to be confused with pride) that relieves us from the need of approval from anyone other than the Lord God Himself.

But now, this is what the LORD says—he who created you, O Jacob, he who
formed you, O Israel: "Fear not, for I have redeemed you; I have summoned you
by name; you are mine."

Isaiah 43:1

Focus on the last three words of this passage: "you are mine." To be the Lord's is an honor and worth far more than the approval others can give us. Earthly standards of self-worth and approval are ever changing, but the standards of the Lord are concrete, never changing. And achieving God's standards does not take a lot of effort if we trust His Word and find our true worth in Him and in our relationship with Him.

7 PRAYER STARTER

Father, Your daughter is struggling with her feelings of self-worth and her need for approval—a trap the Evil One loves to hold us in. Free her from this stronghold. The value You place on each of us is above our comprehension. Help _____ find her worth and satisfy her need for approval in You and You alone! Give her the satisfaction only You can provide . . .

8 RECOMMENDED RESOURCES

Alexander, Myrna. *Behold Your God.* Zondervan, 1978.

Hathaway, Rick. *A Legacy of Faith: A Fresh Look at Blessing, Morality, Self-Worth, and Mentorship.* Tate Publishing, 2007.

Heald, Cynthia. *Becoming a Woman of Freedom.* NavPress, 2005.

McGee, Robert. *The Search for Significance: Seeing Your True Worth through God's Eyes.* Thomas Nelson, 2003.

Moore, Beth. *So Long Insecurity: You've Been a Bad Friend to Us.* Tyndale, 2010.

Reall, Scott. *Journey to a Life of Significance: Freedom from Low Self-Esteem.* Thomas Nelson, 2008.

Sex Addiction

PORTRAITS 1

- Cindy could hardly believe the predicament she was in. At her ten-year high school reunion, she had reunited with her old sweetheart. They were both in troubled marriages and were at the reunion without their spouses. One flaming night of sex resurfaced old feelings and recalled the wild times they had enjoyed together in high school. They met two other times that year for sex, and now her former boyfriend is leaving his wife and threatening to move to Cindy's town. She has to talk to someone about the panic she feels about his increasing compulsions and obsessive behavior. It's beginning to feel a lot like stalking.

- Rachel always viewed porn as a thing that only men got addicted to. Therefore, one night when she was feeling really lonely, she decided to search for porn websites to see what it was all about. She found herself very sexually aroused and desired to view it again the next night . . . and the next . . . and the next . . . until she felt as if she had no control over herself any longer.

- Maggie had a devastating, heartbreaking relationship in her past. Since then she has wanted nothing to do with the process of becoming emotionally attached to another guy for fear of getting hurt. So she began having purely sexual relationships with guys. Eventually she became numb to the possibility of turning into a slut. She didn't care anymore—she was becoming addicted to sex and the men who could give her the best sex she could find.

DEFINITIONS AND KEY THOUGHTS 2

- Midday soaps, love affair movies on Lifetime, late night shows on HBO, Showtime, or Cinemax. *It is clear—sex sells*. With a society so sexually obsessed and sex saturated, the opportunity for addiction abounds.

- An *addiction* is *a physical* (as to alcohol or most other drugs) *or psychological* (as to sex or gambling or shopping) *compulsion* to use a substance or activity *to cope with everyday life*. For example, without alcohol or access to a sexual partner or website, the addict *does not feel "normal" and cannot function well*.

- The *habitual misuse of sexual behavior* with the purpose of changing (ostensibly for improving) one's mood or psychological state of mind classifies as *an addiction to sex. Women use and abuse their sexual behaviors to forget their pains*

261

or anxieties. Substance abuse is often combined with addictive sexual behavior, commonly referred to as co- or poly-addiction.

- An addiction is a repetitive, compulsive behavior that is *difficult or seemingly impossible to control.* It leads to activity that is designed solely to *obtain the substance or access to the behavior and to cover up its use*—the housewife hiding her sex chat rooms on her computer, the drug addict shoplifting to support the habit, the gambler embezzling to pay off debts. Characterized by the *defense mechanisms of denial, minimization, and blame-shifting*, the addict attributes her problems to someone else or some difficult situation—the boss is too difficult, the job is too stressful, the spouse isn't affectionate enough, the kids are disobedient, or the friends are too persuasive. *The addict refuses to take responsibility for her behavior and to admit the seriousness of the problem.*

- *Sex addiction is the bio-psycho-social dependence* on the sexual behavior—such as internet porn, sadistic or masochistic behaviors, masturbation, or a relationship with a lover. Over time the body and the brain need the sexually arousing behavior in ever-increasing amounts to cope minimally and stave off the symptoms of withdrawal.

- While much of the focus on sexual addiction is directed toward men, research estimates that as many as one out of every six women struggle with some sort of sexual addiction.[1] In one specific study, 28 percent of females surveyed presented symptoms of a sexual addiction.[2]

- It is estimated that 17–20 percent of women struggle with a pornography addiction. In one study, "60 percent of the women who answered the survey admitted to having significant struggles with lust; 40 percent admitted to being involved in sexual sin in the past year; and 20 percent of the churchgoing female participants struggle with looking at pornography on an ongoing basis."[3]

Key Characteristics

The following are characteristics of addictions.

- Mood swings are common.
- Increasing use or pattern of behavior develops over time.
- Feelings of shame or worthlessness increase.
- There is a strong need to be liked or receive approval from others.
- Usually there are impulse-control problems—especially with food, sex, drugs, or money.
- The substance or behavior is used to raise a depressed mood or to reduce anxiety.
- Obsessing about the substance or behavior is common.
- Unmanageability of the addiction increases.
- Efforts to control the addiction fail.
- The addiction has caused negative consequences to self and others.

Causes of Addiction

- *Emotional.* Addicts are emotionally wounded; many have experienced severe trauma in childhood. One study of sex addicts found that 81 percent had been sexually abused, 74 percent had been physically abused, and 97 percent had been emotionally abused.[4]
- *Relational.* Addictive behaviors are positively related to troublesome early life relationships. For adults, addiction causes stress in interpersonal relationships—especially marriage and family life—and leads to many social difficulties.
- *Physical.* Addicts become physically dependent on their substances or behavior of abuse, experiencing withdrawal without them.
- *Cognitive and behavioral.* Often addicts have illogical or irrational thoughts that cause them to forget their own identity as children of God. Unrealistic expectations for themselves and others and reliance on quick and magical solutions are also common.
- *Spiritual.* At its core, addiction is rebellion against God. In addition, whether it is an addiction to drugs, alcohol, or sex, the substance or behavior becomes a false idol to the addict. Giving up this reliant idolatry is one of the most difficult and long-term struggles for the addict.

ASSESSMENT INTERVIEW 3

Remember that a key characteristic of addiction is denial. The behavior is never an issue for the addict. Breaking down this denial is part of your job in your assessment. When interviewing the addict, focus on asking concrete questions about circumstances, events, and symptoms. If questions are asked in a nonthreatening and nonjudgmental fashion, the counselee should respond fairly honestly. If speaking with a family member, reframe these questions and ask them about the addict.

Rule Outs

1. Has your use of sex and/or obsession with romance to cope with life increased or decreased over the years? Has there been a time when you were free of this use? Do you mix sexuality with drugs or other behaviors to keep enjoying the high it gives you? (*Tolerance, or the need for increasing amounts of the substance or behavior, is a key factor in distinguishing between a problem and a dependency. Also you want to assess strengths, including family strengths, and find reasons for reliance on sexual behavior by finding out about past periods of freedom from the addiction.*)
2. Have you ever experienced a time when you did not remember what you did while engaging in sexual escape? Have you ever experienced anxiety, panic attacks, shakes, or hallucinations after not engaging in sexual practices for a while?

3. Have you ever been treated for or received counseling for this problem or for anything else? (*This is asked to assess severity of the addiction and success or failure of prior treatment, and to assess whether a mental disorder or dual disorder is at the root of the problem.*)

4. Has anyone in your family ever been hurt by your sexual behaviors or said anything to you about your being obsessed with sex and/or romance? If so, why do you think the person said that?

5. Is your spouse threatening to leave you?

6. Are you in legal trouble as a result of your addiction? (*This is to assess the need for family help, crisis intervention, or legal referral.*)

General Questions

1. Have you ever been concerned about an addiction to sex and/or romance? If you saw that your best friend or spouse showed the same level of interest in sex and/or romance that you have, would you consider it a problem? What would you say to him or her?

2. How often do you engage in sexual behaviors, such as pornography or masturbation, or fantasize about romantic encounters?

3. Have you ever done anything while engaging in sexual behaviors that you later regretted?

4. Did anyone in your family of origin use sex or a substance in excess while you were growing up? Who was that? What did the person do? Did he or she ever break free of it? Do you remember how you felt when you saw the person in his or her addicted state?

5. Has your use of addictive sex and/or romance ever affected your job or your family? What happened?

6. Have you ever quit or tried to quit? How long did this last? What happened when you quit? How did you feel? How did others respond to you? What would it take for you to quit?

7. Do you want to quit for good? If "for good" is too impossible to contemplate, how long are you willing to commit to staying sexually pure? What will or should happen if you relapse?

8. How do you see your life improving without a sex and/or romance addiction? How will your relationships improve if you quit?

9. Do you believe that God can be a resource to turn to for strength in this struggle? How has He helped you experience freedom from sin in the past? Are you willing to do what it takes to break free now?

4 WISE COUNSEL

The effects of addiction include the following:

- *Unmanageability.* The dependency of addicts on their addiction is *out of their control.* They cannot manage it without help.

- *Neuro-chemical tolerance.* God designed our bodies to adapt to what is presented to them. Therefore, addicts experience tolerance—*their bodies need increasing amounts of a chemical or behavior* to procure the same effect.

- *Progression* (often to poly-addiction). Many addictions begin through simple experimenting—when a person tries out a drug, goes to a casino, takes a puff on a cigarette, views porn in a magazine. However, because more of a chemical or a behavior is needed to achieve an effect, *the addict will increase the strength or frequency of the substance or behavior use,* eventually combining and *mixing various addictive behaviors and/or substances.*

- *Feeding avoidance.* The addiction is used to *improve the addict's emotional or psychological state.* It is a way of avoiding such feelings as loneliness, anxiety, anger, sorrow, and depression.

- *Negative consequences.* Estrangement from God, the manifestation of habitual sin, poor health issues, chronic pain, and interpersonal problems are all *consequences common to addiction.*

Addicts need *hope and encouragement* to overcome their addiction and to know that *Christ is stronger than what pulls them down.* Have the client memorize and recite biblical passages of hope and strength in God so she can recall them in the difficult times of temptation.

In addition to the Biblical Insights section of this chapter, review Psalm 44:21, 51; 1 Corinthians 6:19–20; Ephesians 5:18; and Hebrews 10:22–25 so you can use them to encourage your client. Advise her to meditate on the truth of God's Word, which will fill her mind, leading to everlasting freedom and healing.

ACTION STEPS 5

1. Repent and Seek God's Forgiveness

- As you work through the counseling process, you will begin to see how the sinful nature can rage out of control if you are unable to recognize temptation. Sin is powerful, and Satan seeks to use it to destroy your life. Begin to take control; ask for God's forgiveness and strength to stand against temptation. He will answer and provide a way of escape to freedom in Christ!

- You may need to evaluate your relationships and assess the need to ask for the forgiveness of others in your life.

2. Be Accountable

- Make a commitment to God and the counseling process to remain consistent in attending sessions and living free of sexual sin and addiction. It would also be beneficial to write down your goals and commitment for both you and your counselor to keep as a reminder of your new vows.

- *Help your client commit to some form of accountability, at the most serious level she is willing. If she will sign a contract with you, she is serious about change.*

3. Pursue Regular Counseling

- Participate in ongoing individual counseling to begin to discover the underlying issues that perpetuate the addiction cycle in your life. Stay consistent in attendance and keep in mind that sessions may become harder before things get better. However, healing will begin to happen as you learn more positive ways of coping with life and stress.
- Consider attending group treatment or a local support group. In a group setting you will gain great insight and support from others who struggle with similar issues, helping you know that you are not alone in this battle for sexual purity.

6 BIBLICAL INSIGHTS

Now those who belong to Christ Jesus have crucified the flesh with its passions and desires. If we live by the Spirit, let us also walk by the Spirit.

Galatians 5:24–25 NASB

God offers hope—not judgment—to the addict, but repentance is required. God wants to free His daughters from anything that takes His rightful place in their lives. He wants to show them that He can meet all their needs. With God's help and their accountability to compassionate believers, addicts can be set free! But it takes time, energy, determination, and accountability.

Ephesians 4:19 says, "Having lost all sensitivity, they have given themselves over to sensuality so as to indulge in every kind of impurity, with a continual lust for more." Being led by the Holy Spirit, an addict can be victorious over the sin of sexual addiction. However, it takes serious discipline to stop engaging in the sexual acts that "desensitize" one from truly walking by the Spirit.

Put to death, therefore, whatever belongs to your earthly nature: sexual immorality, impurity, lust, evil desires and greed, which is idolatry. Because of these, the wrath of God is coming.

Colossians 3:5–6

These verses describe some of those sinful desires that believers should "put to death." Sexual sins, evil desires, and greed (a form of idolatry) should have no place in a believer's heart. It takes a conscious daily decision to say no to these sinful temptations and rely on the Holy Spirit's power to overcome them.

It is God's will that you should be sanctified: that you should avoid sexual immorality; that each of you should learn to control his own body in a way that is holy and honorable, not in passionate lust like the heathen, who do not know

God; and that in this matter no one should wrong his brother or take advantage of him. The Lord will punish men for all such sins, as we have already told you and warned you. For God did not call us to be impure, but to live a holy life.

1 Thessalonians 4:3–7

Christians represent Christ and we are called to be holy and pure. God desires His children to live lives that are holy because He is holy, and we are His ambassadors to a world that is being ruled by evil. Therefore, we have the responsibility to others to show them Christ so they too might believe in God and be rescued, redeemed, and restored to right relationship with Him.

PRAYER STARTER 7

Dear Lord, thank You that _____ has come here today to seek help for an addiction. Please help her to be open to considering that this might be a true addiction for which she needs to get help and find healing. Lead us by Your Holy Spirit to the resources that will be most helpful, and thank You for Your gift of forgiveness . . .

RECOMMENDED RESOURCES 8

Clinton, Tim. *Turn Your Life Around.* FaithWorks, 2006.

Ferree, Marnie. *No Stones: Women Redeemed from Sexual Addiction.* InterVarsity, 2010.

Hart, Archibald D. *Healing Life's Hidden Addictions: Overcoming the Closet Compulsions That Waste Your Time and Control Your Life.* Haworth Press, 1998.

Hawkins, David. *Breaking Everyday Addictions: Finding Freedom for the Things That Trip Us Up.* Harvest House, 2008.

Laaser, Mark. *Healing the Wounds of Sexual Addiction.* Zondervan, 2004.

Moore, Beth. *Breaking Free: Discover the Victory of Total Surrender.* B&H, 2007.

Schaumburg, Harry. *False Intimacy: Understanding the Struggle of Sexual Addiction.* NavPress, 1997.

Willingham, Russell. *Breaking Free: Understanding Sexual Addiction and the Healing Power of Jesus.* InterVarsity, 1999.

Sexual Desire and Expectations

1 PORTRAITS

- Samantha was never known to be "wild" but she really wanted her sex life with her husband to be more creative. Doing the same things every time bored her. When she tried new things or suggested trying them, her husband got upset. He said it was "crossing the line" and he would not have it.

- A few years ago Hannah and her husband had a wonderful sex life, even after their fourth child was born. But two years later, Hannah's husband's company downsized, and he lost his once well-paying job. He tried for several months to find a similar position but eventually gave up and began rigorous training for a new career. He hates his new job and his ego has taken quite a blow. He used to be energetic, creative, and full of life. Now he drifts through life—even his marriage—with little enthusiasm. He rarely initiates sex with Hannah, and when she initiates it, he seems just to be going through the motions. Hannah is sad and irritated and she feels as if her husband's love for her is fading—just like his enthusiasm. Now Hannah's husband feels like a failure more than ever.

- When Pam got pregnant, it took a toll on her and her husband's sex life. Her husband assured her it would get better after a few weeks but it didn't. Pam kept making excuses to avoid sex, even months after the birth of their child. She was either "too tired," "too sore," or "too busy" to be intimate. Recently Pam has noticed her husband's attention being drawn to other women.

2 DEFINITIONS AND KEY THOUGHTS

- *Sex is a gift from God.* He created us to be sexual beings and *He created the act of sex for married couples.* Sex is best seen as a continuing desire, an appetite that is fulfilled on an ongoing basis. Part of being human is to enjoy a rich, fulfilling sexual life, but it is often the case that *the desire for sexual contact is different for each spouse in a marriage.*

- Therefore sex, like most other issues, becomes a *matter of negotiation between the two partners* (with *negotiation* implying that each partner's desires and wishes regarding sex are given equal weight. It should not be presumed that, due to a couple's adherence to a theology of male headship, the man has any right to impose his sexual will on the woman—as many religious men presume).

- It may be necessary—especially to the man—to point out that *no one has ever died from not having sex! It is not essential to life like oxygen and water*. In spite of the notion that being cut off from sex is a crazy-maker or death sentence, it is neither. Sexual abstinence or learning alternative ways to be sexual is usually required at some point in any long marriage—due to pregnancy, illness, family emergencies, separations for business or work, attaining desired spiritual goals, or any number of situations that demand it.

- In 1 Corinthians Paul writes, "Do not deprive each other except by mutual consent and for a time, so that you may devote yourselves to prayer. Then come together again so that Satan will not tempt you because of your lack of self-control" (7:5). God intended for sexual intimacy to be a *vital part of a healthy marriage relationship*, but sensitivity to one's spouse is essential. Sexual intimacy was created to delight both husband *and* wife, not merely as a marital obligation.

- One barrier to mutual sexual satisfaction is that the frequency of having sex is dictated by contradictory desires and reasons—attributable to both the differences in men and women as well as their unique life experiences. Though it may be somewhat simplistic to assert, it is largely true that *men tend to want sex for physical pleasure and release, while women want sex more to reinforce the relationship and be assured again of their husband's desire and their primary place in his life*. These and other differences are important for both men and women to understand about each other.

- As couples begin to look at their sexual expectations and desires in the marriage, it's important to consider that barriers to sexual intimacy may be a *symptom of a much bigger and broader communication issue* between them. Sometimes couples can exist in the same house and live in their own worlds, seldom talking about anything more meaningful than their work and schedules. But some couples talk openly and honestly about everything in their lives—everything, that is, except sex—a subject too taboo for far too many couples.

- Research shows that "satisfaction in a relationship is one of the most *important predictors of sexual desire* . . . a woman's sexual desire is nearly inseparable from her relational environment."[1]

- *Building and rebuilding trust* are important to sexual communication. Many married people have been hurt because they feel misunderstood. After months or years these hurts may have festered into *deep resentments* that cloud every part of the relationship. *Trust can't be demanded; it must be earned over time by honesty, patience, integrity, and kindness.*

- Recent studies have confirmed *the link between trust and sexual desire*. Statistics show that "decreased sexual interest is related to self-reported negative emotions, including lower self-esteem, insecurity, and loss of femininity."[2]

- Additionally, *sexual desire may be altered by changes in a woman's body*. Even among women with healthy marriage relationships, nearly 50 percent of menopausal women have decreased sexual desire. One-fourth of those women experience distress as a result.[3]

- While sexual desire changes with time, *marital faithfulness has been shown to increase sexual satisfaction*. A definitive survey of sex in America reports that "of all sexually active people, married people with only one lifetime partner are most likely to report they are 'extremely' or 'very' satisfied with the amount of physical and emotional pleasure they experience in their sex lives."[4]

- *Connecting on an emotional level* takes time but it tears down barriers and builds strong bonds of trust, creating a relational environment in which sexual expectations can be safely discussed. As in all topics of communication, one of the most important steps forward is for *both parties to feel understood*, not just to understand the other person's point of view.

3 ASSESSMENT INTERVIEW

Some couples come together to talk with a counselor about their sexual desires and expectations, but frequently only one partner comes for help because the other is too embarrassed or too angry to join the discussion. If you sense that your client is reluctant to talk openly about sexual desires and expectations, consider going through a list of topics and asking her to pick the one (or several of them) about which she feels most frustrated. (A strength-based approach to intervention would be to have her list what's going right and to build on that.) You may want to have a written list of topics and ask the woman to check the ones that are most troubling to the relationship. The list might include:

frequency of sexual contact

quality of foreplay

preparation for sex

smells, sounds, and sensations during sex

places where you have sex

her frequency and quality of orgasm

premature ejaculation

creativity in positions and techniques

sex that's "over the line" (for example, it may seem too rough or too kinky)

the barriers of stress, worry about finances or kids, and busyness

shame or disgust over body image

distrust because of the partner's past sexual experiences

distrust because of irresponsible behavior

health issues that block sexual performance

breaking patterns of passivity

learning to talk openly about sexual desires

1. What would wonderful and satisfying sex between you and your husband be like?
2. What does your husband enjoy?
3. When was a time in your relationship when sex was at its best? Describe your relationship during that time. What made sex so good at that point?

4. Describe what attracted you to your husband and brought you together. What attracted him to you? Are these things still parts of your relationship?
5. What are some sexual experiences you enjoy (or want to enjoy) that you find to be creative and full of passion? You need to tell your spouse what these sexual experiences are.
6. What do you find easy to talk about? What topics are hard to discuss? What might be some reasons these are difficult?
7. To you, what is "over the line" sexually?
8. Has your husband told you his limits?
9. How would you describe your level of trust in your husband?
10. What would it mean for your husband to respect your sexual desires in your relationship?
11. What might be some genuine (if small) steps forward in setting healthy expectations for your sexual relationship?

WISE COUNSEL : 4

Help your client grasp the fact that men and women are *fundamentally different* in how they approach many aspects of life, including sex. Often *men need to be told what their wife wants*, sometimes even as they are having sex together. If women expect their husband to pick up on signals or read their mind, they'll probably be very disappointed. Men need to understand that *foreplay lasts all day long for women*, and they don't flip a switch in an instant as men can. Having men attend to and prepare their wives emotionally by extra kindness and respect during the day goes a long way to mutually satisfying sexual adventure that night.

Watch for the *big picture issue of trust* in a couple's relationship as the context for communication about their sexual life. If they can't trust each other, they'll feel used and even abused. Easily resolved misunderstandings and hurts can become resentments if they are not dealt with quickly, and then bitterness sets in, and the relationship suffers in every area.

Talking openly about their sexual life will enhance every other part of the couple's relationship. Effective communication lays a foundation for the expression of the couple's desires and expectations about their future, their children, their money, and everything else in their lives. *If a woman doesn't feel understood by her husband, she'll probably drift back into old habits and attitudes.*

ACTION STEPS : 5

1. Talk to Him

- Be honest with your husband about your experience and expectations in the area of sexual intimacy. Talk about what's working and what isn't. While this may seem awkward at first, and you might think that he should know, you will find that talking frankly about sexual intimacy will bring the two of you closer together and clear up miscommunication.

- Brainstorm new ideas. Address the frustrations, disappointments, and other concerns on your mind. Honesty and fond memories provide a strong foundation for a satisfying sex life.

2. Expect to Uncover Barriers

- As you communicate to your husband about your sex life, you will likely uncover barriers, distractions, and even brokenness. These feelings might include anger at his past indiscretions, guilt over your own past sexual sins, shame about body image, resentment about the focus being on children, or a host of other potential problems. If emotional barriers or past behaviors are affecting the level of sexual intimacy in your relationship, consider talking to a counselor to find emotional healing.

- Healing and greater intimacy won't happen overnight but they begin with the following:

  — being honest with yourself and your husband about the reality of your feelings and reasons for lack of connectedness (rather than discounting them as not a big deal)

  — repenting of any behaviors that are currently affecting the level of intimacy

  — forgiving your husband and yourself for past indiscretions, and working through associated guilt, shame, or resentment

  — learning to trust your husband on a deeper level

3. Show Him Respect

- As you communicate with your husband, be sensitive to his desires and expectations. Remember, sex is not just about you; it is about mutual pleasure. Discuss creative ways to express sexual desire—explore individual likes and dislikes of sexual relations. Even in an age of freedom for sexual expression, some people are very repressed sexually, so don't be surprised if your spouse does not want to do everything you may want to do. By the same token, do not feel pressured to try techniques that you are not comfortable with. Remember that sex is God's gift to be enjoyed to its fullest *by the two of you*.

- Never force sexual expectations. If you do, failure will likely be the result and trust will be shattered. Creativity may need to start small but it can grow as you both find new techniques you enjoy and as you feel increasingly safe with one another.

- *Train the woman to negotiate with and communicate desires and new expectations to her husband before urges take over.*

4. Spend Quality Time Together

- Identify the roadblocks and distractions in your life that erode the quality time you spend with your husband and provide excuses for your not spending time and energy on your sexual experience. For instance, if you find yourself continually drained by the stress and commitments of your life, you may need to reevaluate your priorities and let something go.
- Many couples try to compensate for dysfunction or distance in their relationship through sexual intimacy. However, intimacy in a relationship is not just built through sex. Discuss with your husband how you can spend quality time together—hang out, talk, play, engage in nonsexual touch, go on a date—have fun! Investing time in your relationship will deepen your love for each other and likely deepen your sexual intimacy as well.

5. Know God's Perspective

- Take time to research and read about God's perspective on sex and marital communication. Your counselor will suggest books that will be helpful and will show you how to take steps forward in clarifying your needs, communicating your expectations, and bringing passion and creativity back to your and your husband's sex life.

BIBLICAL INSIGHTS 6

Therefore, as God's chosen people, holy and dearly loved, clothe yourselves with compassion, kindness, humility, gentleness and patience. Bear with each other and forgive whatever grievances you may have against one another. Forgive as the Lord forgave you. And over all these virtues put on love, which binds them all together in perfect unity.

Colossians 3:12–14

Treating one another with love, respect, and kindness is a choice both partners can make. Negotiating desires and expectations begins with this commitment to honor and value one another instead of being selfish.

Forgiveness—of terrible past sins or minor present annoyances—is essential to a strong relationship and a great sex life.

How beautiful you are and how pleasing, O love, with your delights! Your stature is like that of the palm, and your breasts like clusters of fruit. I said, "I will climb the palm tree; I will take hold of its fruit." May your breasts be like the clusters of the vine, the fragrance of your breath like apples, and your mouth like the best wine.

Song of Songs 7:6–9

Song of Songs (or Song of Solomon), this beautiful and sensual book of the Bible, portrays the beauty of sex in marriage in poetic language. The metaphors of foreplay, desire, sensual touching, and intercourse show the pleasure, exhilaration, and creativity of a rich sexual life in the context of a committed relationship.

The beauty of loving, joyful, sensual sex deserves time and effort to maximize the pleasure. Poetry, music, flowers, scents, and special times and places can greatly enhance the couple's enjoyment.

7 : PRAYER STARTER

Father, thank You that _____ wants to experience Your gift of joyful sex in her relationship. She has come because she wants to grow in this area of her life and marriage. She is committed to You and to her husband. Help her, Lord, to take the steps to find even more fulfillment. Give her courage to talk openly about her desires and to listen intently to her husband and him to her. We trust You will be honored and that her relationship with her husband will grow stronger as they enjoy each other even more . . .

8 : RECOMMENDED RESOURCES

Chapman, Gary. *Making Love: The Chapman Guide to Making Sex an Act of Love.* Tyndale, 2008.

Dillow, Linda, and Lorraine Pintus. *Intimate Issues: 21 Questions Christian Women Ask about Sex.* Random House, 1999.

LaHaye, Tim, and Beverly LaHaye. *The Act of Marriage.* Zondervan, 1998.

_____. *The Act of Marriage after 40.* Zondervan, 2000.

Leman, Kevin. *Sheet Music: Uncovering the Secrets of Sexual Intimacy in Marriage.* Tyndale, 2003.

Penner, Clifford, and Joyce Penner. *The Gift of Sex: A Guide to Sexual Fulfillment.* Thomas Nelson, 2003.

Rosenau, Douglas E. *Celebration of Sex: A Guide to Enjoying God's Gift of Sexual Intimacy.* Thomas Nelson, 2002.

Wheat, Ed, and Gaye Wheat. *Intended for Pleasure: Sex Technique and Sexual Fulfillment in Christian Marriage.* 4th ed. Revell, 2010.

Sexual Harassment

PORTRAITS : 1

- Monica was angry, frustrated, and hurt. "It was pretty cut-and-dried," she explained. "My supervisor, in no uncertain terms, said that if I wanted to keep my job, I would have to put out. I refused and I was fired." Monica *was* a successful young professional but now she's without a job because she would not compromise her morals. *Where do I go from here?* she wonders.

- Brenda had been at the company for a few weeks, and during that time, she could tell that Alicia, her supervisor, had singled her out. A co-worker told her she thought Alicia was a lesbian, but Brenda didn't want to believe it. When Alicia found out that Brenda was thirty years old and single, she began sending Brenda emails that were a little too friendly in nature and borderline suggestive. Brenda was very uncomfortable when she received a voice mail from Alicia in which she made several comments about her physical attractiveness.

- As the branch secretary, Kathleen interacted with the office staff all the time but she especially enjoyed doing projects for Matt. Matt had a great personality and was always very appreciative of her effort. "You're my lifesaver, Kathleen," he often told her. Both of them worked long hours, and one night Matt asked Kathleen if she wanted to grab a late dinner after work. Kathleen didn't think anything of it, until he walked her to her car and tried to kiss her. Matt is married, with two kids, and Kathleen doesn't know what to do. She feels ashamed, violated, and angry.

DEFINITIONS AND KEY THOUGHTS : 2

- Sexual harassment is "*unwelcome verbal, visual, or physical conduct of a sexual nature that is severe or pervasive and affects working conditions or creates a hostile work environment.*"[1]

- Often, *sexually oriented conduct explicitly or implicitly affects an individual's employment, interferes with an individual's work performance, or creates an intimidating, hostile, or offensive work environment.*

- Sexual harassment is *a form of sexual discrimination* that violates Title VII of the Civil Rights Act of 1964.

- Sexual harassment *may include one or more of the following*:

> — *unwelcome sexual advances*
> — *requests for sexual favors*
> — *verbal conduct* of a sexual nature
> — *physical conduct* of a sexual nature

- Sexual harassment can occur *among a variety of people in a variety of circumstances*, including but not limited to the following:

  > — The target may be *male or female.*
  > — The harasser may be *male or female.*
  > — The target may be the *same sex or the opposite sex* of the harasser.
  > — The harasser may be *the target's supervisor, an agent of the employer, a supervisor in another area, a co-worker, or a nonemployee.*
  > — The target does not have to be the person harassed but could be *anyone affected by offensive conduct.*
  > — Sexual harassment may occur *without economic injury to or causing termination of employment* of the target.
  > — The harasser's conduct must be *unwelcome.*

- Sexual harassment is *common in the workplace, in social settings, and sometimes, even among "religious" people.* A few recent studies report that

  > — *62 percent of female college students* report having been sexually harassed at their university, while *51 percent of male college students* admit to sexually harassing someone in college.[2]
  > — In a telephone poll by Louis Harris and Associates of 782 US workers, 31 percent of female workers reported that they had been sexually harassed at work.[3]
  > — In a survey of 2,064 students in eighth through eleventh grades, 83 percent of girls and 79 percent of boys had been sexually harassed—38 percent by teachers or school employees and 36 percent by students. Among schoolteachers and employees, 42 percent had been harassed by each other.[4]

- In many cases, it is *helpful for the target to inform the harasser directly* that his or her conduct is unwelcome and request its immediate cessation. Or the target may use any complaint mechanism or grievance system available at the place of employment. Often sexual harassment will cease after an internal complaint is filed.

- According to one official at a US government department, the US Supreme Court has simplified matters concerning sexual harassment by describing two *basic types of unlawful sexual harassment* in the workplace.

  Type One: Quid pro quo. The first type of sexual harassment includes a *tangible employment action.* An example of this could be a supervisor who tells a subordinate that she must be sexually cooperative or she will be terminated, passed up for promotion, punished, and so on, and then takes punitive action when the employee does not cooperate. This is referred to as the quid pro quo type of sexual harassment because of its "this for that" nature.

Type Two: Hostile employment. Unlike the quid pro quo in which a supervisor gives an ultimatum, the hostile environment can result from the *unwelcome conduct of supervisors, co-workers, customers, or anyone else* with whom a harassed employee interacts. Behaviors that constitute hostile environment harassment include

— *threats* to impose a sexual quid pro quo
— discussion of sexual activities
— telling off-color jokes
— unnecessary or excessive touching
— comments on physical attributes of an employee
— displaying sexually suggestive pictures
— use of inappropriate nicknames, such as "Honey," "Doll," or "Babe"
— threatening or hostile physical conduct
— use of crude, crass, and offensive language

ASSESSMENT INTERVIEW 3

1. When did the sexual harassment begin?
2. What is the nature of the harassment? Is it interfering with your work?
3. Who else knows about this?
4. What did you do to try to end the harassment?
5. Did your attempts to stop the sexual harassment help? Why or why not?
6. Are you still being sexually harassed?
7. Do you feel that you are in physical danger?
8. Have you reported this to the authorities?
9. What is the next step in resolving the problem?
10. What can you do to protect future and current employees from sexual harassment from others?

WISE COUNSEL 4

All human beings are created in God's image and deserve respect. *Sexual harassment, exploitation, and abuse are destructive.* When a person is a victim of this type of injustice, her ability to develop and use her God-given gifts of creativity and wholeness are stifled.

Sexual harassment can occur in several ways. However, no matter how or when it occurs, it *erodes a woman's sense of comfort and safety.* When sexual harassment occurs at the hand of someone who is supposed to be an advocate (such as a pastor, counselor, teacher, or supervisor), it makes the experience even more confusing and painful for the target.

Women who complain about sexual harassment must be taken seriously. Perhaps there has been a misunderstanding, and both parties can grow from the process of resolution. But if harassment has occurred, *feelings of betrayal and pain* will be very real for the victim.

In many cases a victim will be *nervous or afraid to report sexual harassment.* She may be concerned about losing her job, especially if the sexual harasser is her supervisor or someone in a position of higher authority. *A victim may also fear being ridiculed, blamed, or called a liar.*

The following are general principles for counseling someone who has been sexually harassed:

1. The victim may have *very similar feelings and perceptions as a victim of rape.*
2. *The victim may feel insecure and ashamed* for not being able to prevent the harassment.
3. Almost certainly, the person accused will claim that he has been *grossly misunderstood* and may *blame the victim* for the problem.
4. The *response of the company* will determine if it is a safe place for the victim to go back to work.
5. Even if the company responds positively to the victim, charges take time to be addressed, and the accused will likely appeal negative findings, either to the company's human resources department or to the U.S. Equal Employment Opportunity Commission (EEOC). During this long process, *the victim will need reassurance and encouragement.*

It is important to *create a safe environment* for the client to feel respected, believed, and empowered to take control of her life.

Prevention

According to the *EEOC, prevention is the best tool* to eliminate sexual harassment in the workplace. *Prevention begins with employers and managers* communicating clearly to employees that *sexual harassment will not be tolerated.* They must create an open environment where sexual harassment, or even potential sexual harassment, can be reported without fear. This can be accomplished in part by establishing *complaint or grievance procedures* and also by taking *immediate and appropriate actions* if and when employee complaints occur.

Reporting Sexual Harassment

If a person believes or suspects she has been a target of sexual harassment, it is appropriate to *report the incident to the management* at the place of employment, or a *charge of sexual harassment can be filed* with the U.S. Equal Employment Opportunity Commission.

To file a charge with the EEOC:

- Charges may be filed in person, by mail, or by telephone. If there is no EEOC nearby to visit in person, call the EEOC toll-free at 800-699-4000 (or call 800-

669-6820 for the hearing impaired—TDD) for more information on filing a charge of sexual harassment.

- There are strict time limitations in which charges of sexual harassment or discrimination can be filed. To ensure the ability of the EEOC to act on the victim's behalf and to protect her right to file a private lawsuit (should one ultimately need to be filed), be sure to follow any guidelines provided by the EEOC when filing a charge.

ACTION STEPS : 5

1. Talk Honestly

- You may be asking, *Why me?* You may be experiencing many feelings, such as anger at the perpetrator, shame for not being able to stop it, worthlessness, and a sense of being used. It's important to talk to someone you trust—a family member, friend, or counselor—to sort through these feelings and receive validation. Talk honestly about what has happened to you.
- *Trust and safety are of vital importance. Validate and affirm your client's feelings. Help her realize the abuse was not her fault and encourage her to find appropriate ways to express her feelings outside of the counseling office, such as through journaling or writing out her story.*

2. Relinquish Self-Blame and Shame

- Develop an understanding of how this harassment happened and realize the abuse was not your fault. Work to relinquish blaming yourself and feelings of shame.
- What has happened to you is someone else's wrongdoing. You can regain control of your emotions and reassume ownership of your personal integrity.

3. Consider Joining a Support Group

- It always helps to talk with someone who has shared similar pain and receive guidance from the experience of others. In a group setting, individuals comment and discuss their own stories of sexual harassment and are able to provide support to each other—as well as advice on how to properly report and end the cycle of abuse.

4. Develop a Plan of Action

- Develop a plan of action with your counselor and take the necessary steps to ensure that the perpetrator is held responsible for his actions.

5. Pray

- Pray for God's strength to endure and the wisdom needed to properly report the abuse. Also trust that God will use this painful experience to bring good into your life and change and mature you to be more like Him.

6 BIBLICAL INSIGHTS

He heals the brokenhearted and binds up their wounds. He determines the number of the stars and calls them each by name. Great is our Lord and mighty in power; his understanding has no limit. The LORD sustains the humble but casts the wicked to the ground.

Psalm 147:3–6

Sexual harassment is a shattering experience that can jolt every aspect of a woman's safety and identity, but God promises to be close to the brokenhearted and offers to them His presence, peace, and wisdom. Victims can be assured that someday, somehow, God's justice will prevail.

Consider it pure joy, my brothers, whenever you face trials of many kinds, because you know that the testing of your faith develops perseverance. Perseverance must finish its work so that you may be mature and complete, not lacking anything.

James 1:2–4

God can use every experience in our lives—the good, the bad, and the confusing—to shape our character and draw us closer to Him, if we'll let Him. God will even use the traumatic experience of sexual harassment to produce more depth, wisdom, and hope than we've ever known before. Certainly, the abuse wasn't His perfect plan, but by His grace, He turns negatives into positives to bring glory to Himself.

If any of you lacks wisdom, he should ask God, who gives generously to all without finding fault, and it will be given to him. But when he asks, he must believe and not doubt, because he who doubts is like a wave of the sea, blown and tossed by the wind. That man should not think he will receive anything from the Lord; he is a double-minded man, unstable in all he does.

James 1:5–8

When harassment begins, the victim is often caught off guard and feels confused. Turning to God in prayer, the Scriptures, and a wise counselor, she can find genuine insight into the path God wants her to follow. The path may not be easy or straight. She may experience a lot of opposition from the perpetrator, and others may not understand why she brought the charge in the first place. But if she trusts God and follows His leading, she can stay strong and find healing.

PRAYER STARTER : 7

Lord, _____ comes to You today after a traumatic experience in her life. She has experienced sexual harassment in the workplace, Lord, and needs Your presence to help her know the correct course of action. She needs to experience Your healing touch and she needs to protect herself from further transgressions against her . . .

RECOMMENDED RESOURCES : 8

Balswick, Judith, and Jack Balswick. *Authentic Human Sexuality: An Integrated Christian Approach*. InterVarsity Academic, 2008.

Cloud, Henry, and John Townsend, *Boundaries*. Zondervan, 1992.

DeMoss, Nancy Leigh. *The Lies Women Believe and the Truth That Sets Them Free*. Moody, 2001.

Hawkins, Linda. *The Sexual Harassment Handbook*. Career Press, 2007.

VanVonderen, Jeffrey. *When God's People Let You Down*. Bethany House, 2005.

Wilson, Sandra. *Released from Shame: Moving beyond the Pain of the Past*. InterVarsity, 2002.

Wright, H. Norman. *The New Guide to Crisis and Trauma Counseling*. Gospel Light, 2003.

Wright, H. Norman, Matt Woodley, and Julie Woodley. *Surviving the Storms of Life: Finding Hope and Healing When Life Goes Wrong*. Revell, 2008.

Sexually Transmitted Diseases

1 PORTRAITS

- Mary hasn't been feeling well. She thought she had a virus, but it hasn't gone away in more than two months. She feels feverish, has a headache, feels pain when she urinates, and has vaginal discharge. She can't bring herself to think she might have contracted a sexually transmitted disease. A friend told her it might be genital herpes.

- Clara was devastated as she sat in her physician's office and heard that she is HIV positive. Her doctor's upbeat assertion that this is no longer a death sentence barely penetrated the cold horror that was overtaking her soul. As a nurse herself, she knew that effective treatment meant a cocktail of toxic drugs. Clara can't imagine how she was exposed to HIV because she wasn't sexually active. Her doctor suggested that perhaps she had contracted the virus from a patient in her care. Clara is angry and hurt. *How could God allow this?* she wonders. *I didn't do anything wrong. I was just doing my job!*

- Jeannie was horrified when her ob-gyn revealed she was carrying the AIDS virus. *I'm six months pregnant*, she thought and then went to the bathroom at her physician's office and vomited. She realized she must have contracted it from her husband, whom she suspected was sexually active with someone else while she was pregnant.

2 DEFINITIONS AND KEY THOUGHTS

- Sexually transmitted diseases (STDs, sometimes called sexually transmitted infections or STIs) have become *increasingly common in our society*. STDs are diseases and infections that are *transmitted, or passed, from person to person via sexual contact, most often, sexual intercourse.*[1] They require medical diagnosis and treatment, and the complications they bring to a person's life may necessitate emotional, relationship, and spiritual intervention by a counselor.

- *The United States has an epidemic of sexually transmitted diseases* (STDs). Every year, nineteen million STD infections occur with 50 percent of the cases being in fifteen-to-twenty-four year olds. It is estimated that as many as one in four teenage girls has an STD.[2]

- STDs can be caused by *bacteria* (for example, chlamydia, gonorrhea, syphilis), *viruses* (for example, HIV/AIDS, hepatitis, herpes, human papillomavirus—

HPV), or *parasites* (trichomoniasis). Chlamydia is the most common bacterial STD. HPV infection is the most common viral STD. People contract STDs during sexual activity, including vaginal sex, oral sex, and anal sex. A few infections—HPV and herpes—can even be spread by contact with infected skin. Others, such as HIV and hepatitis, can be spread through needle sharing. Many times you can pick up an STD from someone who does not even show symptoms.[3]

- The Medical Institute for Sexual Health reports that most people with STDs *will not immediately develop symptoms*; however, they *can still transmit the infection to sexual partners*.[4] The most common symptoms include an abnormal discharge from the penis or vagina, a burning sensation when urinating, and abdominal pain. Rashes, ulcers, and warts on the skin can also signal a sexually transmitted disease.

- *Most bacterial STDs can be treated with antibiotics*, and the symptoms of *other STDs (such as HIV/AIDS) can be treated but not cured*. A vaccine has recently been developed for eleven- and twelve-year-old girls to prevent HPV. The Centers for Disease Control recommendation allows for vaccination to begin at age nine. Vaccination is also recommended for females aged thirteen through twenty-six who have not been previously vaccinated, who have not completed the full series of shots, and who have not yet had sexual intercourse.[5]

- *Condom* use for vaginal sex *reduces the risk of infection* for

  — HIV by 85 percent
  — gonorrhea by about 50 percent
  — chlamydia by about 50 percent
  — herpes by about 50 percent
  — syphilis by about 50 percent
  — HPV by 50 percent or less[6]

- STDs can cause *serious and permanent health problems*. They can cause premature births, stillbirths, and spontaneous abortions. In women, complications from infection include pelvic inflammatory diseases (PID), tubal pregnancy, infertility, and cervical cancer. In pregnant women, STDs can lead to miscarriage, stillbirths, preterm delivery, and birth defects. In men, HPV infection can cause penile cancer. Some STDs, such as HIV, can be life threatening.

- Those infected with an STD are *two to five times more likely* than an uninfected individual to contract HIV when exposed to the virus via sexual contact.[7]

ASSESSMENT INTERVIEW 3

1. Where do you think you may have contracted a sexually transmitted disease?
2. What are your symptoms? How long have you experienced them?
3. Have you seen a doctor for diagnosis and treatment?
4. Are you being treated for the problem? Is it working?
5. How are you coping with the stress of this problem?

6. How is the problem affecting you emotionally? What feelings are most prominent?
7. How is it affecting your relationships? Who are you talking to about this?
8. Does your spouse know? Has he been tested and diagnosed?
9. How do you see a sexually transmitted disease changing your life?
10. What are your goals for counseling?

4 : WISE COUNSELING

STDs are *serious medical problems* and need to be addressed in counseling with a combination of *grace and gravity*.

Counselors need to refer clients who have or are suspected of having STDs to *a competent physician who can accurately diagnose and treat the infection*. The counselor's role is to *help the client process and resolve the emotional, relational, and spiritual implications* of the disease.

Become *a partner with the doctor*. When the client comes back to see you, support the doctor's assessment and treatment plan and offer encouragement about the benefits of addressing the problem. If it is appropriate and if you have a relationship with the doctor, ask for input about how you can further support the medical treatment plan. (Remember to obtain a letter of written consent from your client to speak to any third party.)

Many people experience shame because they contracted an STD from illicit sexual contact, but others innocently and unknowingly contracted the infection from a spouse who had been previously infected. *Treatment, then, must be tailored to the specifics of each person's case*, addressing the issues of grace, forgiveness, forgiving others, and restoring broken trust.

If the client is single, make *recommendations about abstinence*. If the client is married, she and her partner will benefit from being counseled together to resolve *difficult relational issues* brought on by the infection and its treatment.

5 : ACTION STEPS

1. Have a Medical Evaluation

- Make an appointment to see a doctor to be tested for STDs. Early diagnosis and intervention are the best methods of treatment. STDs are health problems that must be addressed as quickly as possible by a physician.
- Try to overcome the stigma of shame at the prospect of getting medical treatment. The benefits of early diagnosis and treatment cannot be stressed enough. Your counselor can help you find a doctor or clinician in your area.
- Return for counseling to learn how to deal with the complications of the STD.

2. Address Your Feelings

- Be open to discussing any feelings of guilt, shame, or anger that may be in your heart. Talk honestly and openly regarding perceptions you have about STDs. Stay consistent in attending counseling to fully address your emotions regarding this diagnosis.

- If you contracted the infection from illicit sexual behavior, you will need to repent of your sin and experience God's forgiveness. Remember that no sin is beyond God's grace.

- If you were unknowingly and innocently infected by your spouse, you will need help in being honest about the hurt and anger you feel, as well as in choosing to forgive him.

3. Take Responsibility

- If you have been diagnosed with an STD, take the proper steps to ensure that you will not infect your spouse.

- If you have concern that anyone other than your spouse may also be infected, be sure to act responsibly and notify that person. Even though this will be very difficult to do, it is the respectful thing to do.

- Remember that the process for healing, for both you and the one who infected you, will take time and courage.

BIBLICAL INSIGHTS 6

This is how God showed his love among us: He sent his one and only Son into the world that we might live through him. This is love: not that we loved God, but that he loved us and sent his Son as an atoning sacrifice for our sins.

1 John 4:9–10

No matter what we've done, God hasn't forgotten us and He hasn't stopped loving us. Whether a sexually transmitted disease is our fault or someone else's, God still has a gracious plan for our lives.

The measure of God's love is the sacrifice of Jesus to pay for our sins. His death on the cross communicates the wealth of His love and grace to us and makes it possible for every sin to be forgiven.

Not only so, but we also rejoice in our sufferings, because we know that suffering produces perseverance; perseverance, character; and character, hope. And hope does not disappoint us, because God has poured out his love into our hearts by the Holy Spirit, whom he has given us.

Romans 5:3–5

God wants to use everything in our lives—difficulties as well as blessings—to shape us and draw us closer to Him. Even when we are the victim of another's irresponsible behavior, we can trust God will somehow use it for good in our life. We may not see it soon, but we can trust God will eventually produce fruit in our life.

Get rid of bitterness, rage and anger, brawling and slander, along with every form of malice. Be kind and compassionate to one another, forgiving each other, just as in Christ God forgave you.

Ephesians 4:31–32

In a marriage, a sexually transmitted disease can cause tremendous heartache and anger. First, we need to remember that Christ paid for our sins. With God's grace we can then choose to forgive the one who has hurt us. We may not feel loving and warm toward the person, but forgiveness is a choice not to hold the past against him. And forgiveness sets us free.

7 PRAYER STARTER

Father, nothing is beyond Your sight, and nothing is beyond Your grace. _____ is hurting today because of a disease, and she needs Your care to overcome fear, doubts, hurt, and anger. Thank You, Lord, that You are near, that You are patient, and that You will help her take one step at a time toward hope and healing . . .

8 RECOMMENDED RESOURCES

Arterburn, Stephen. *The God of Second Chances: Experiencing His Grace for the Best of Your Life*. Thomas Nelson, 2010.

Grimes, Jill. *Seductive Delusions: How Everyday People Catch STDs*. Johns Hopkins University Press, 2008.

Marr, Lisa. *Sexually Transmitted Diseases: A Physician Tells You What You Need to Know*. Johns Hopkins University Press, 2007.

Nack, Adina. *Damaged Goods? Women Living with Incurable Sexually Transmitted Diseases*. Temple University Press, 2008.

Nelson, Anita, and Jo Ann Woodward. *Sexually Transmitted Diseases: A Practical Guide to Primary Care*. Humana Press, 2007.

Websites

The Centers for Disease Control and Prevention: www.cdc.gov/std.

The Medical Institute for Sexual Health: www.medinstitute.org.

WebMD: www.webmd.com/sexual-conditions.

Singleness

PORTRAITS 1

- Janelle is on the hunt. She uses online dating services and attends speed dating sessions, yet she rarely finds anyone who both interests her and is interested in her. Her heart has been broken over and over again, and she wonders if true love even exists. Most of her friends are seriously dating, engaged, or married. Janelle worries she will never find a man to spend her life with, and the thought of lifelong singleness has her desperate to find someone.
- Brittany was divorced within a year of a disastrous marriage. Now she can't seem to succeed in any relationship. Brittany struggles to figure out who she is as a single woman. When she was married, she found her identity solely in her husband and now she doesn't know how to function, how to relate to other couples, and how to move on.
- Rachel lives with her mother and rarely dates. She is painfully shy and feels that she will probably never marry. "I guess it's just my lot in life," Rachel concludes but she can't shake the desperate feeling of loneliness. Rachel doesn't like meeting new people. *But how*, she wonders, *am I ever supposed to find a man?*

DEFINITIONS AND KEY THOUGHTS 2

- Singleness means *being without a spouse*. People can be single because they *never married* or because they have *lost a spouse* through death or divorce.
- There are more than ninety million unmarried Americans over the age of eighteen, and 22.7 percent of them are women.[1] Overall, as of 2004, 49 percent of women in America were not married.[2]
- Some people remain *single by choice*, while others *have not met anyone* who attracts them and who is attracted to them.
- A major part of the *discontent* that surrounds the stereotype of singles is *fueled by the media*: movies, television shows, magazines, and books. The ever so popular image of *the single girl who is desperate to find love* yet seems to always end up alone and depressed overshadows *the single girl who is accomplishing her dreams and goals* and being perfectly content in the stage she is in.
- Since *Christian women have not been encouraged to be the initiators* in romantic relationships, singleness may feel like something that is beyond their control. Some call this idea "old school," while others adhere very much to the rules of

letting the male do the pursuing. Either way, it is a confusing, and often frustrating, place for singles to be.

- Those with *mental, emotional, or physical disabilities face particular challenges in finding a spouse.* Either they feel they cannot be themselves or they struggle with feeling unworthy of a spouse. Many times the issue of when to divulge the personal information becomes intimidating and leads to giving up on finding love.

- *Being single and being lonely are two different things.* Many single people would not characterize themselves as lonely or alone at all. Some singles enjoy the stage of singleness in their life. *Being single provides opportunity to explore one's self and one's interests, accomplish major goals and dreams, as well as establish lifelong friendships and memories.*

- It is very helpful *when churches make single people feel welcome.* Not every activity should be for families. Seek to use the gifts of the single people in your congregation.

3 ASSESSMENT INTERVIEW

Some churches provide a welcoming atmosphere for singles, while other churches are so family-oriented that singles feel out of place. If your church is one of the former, you may have singles to counsel. If they are seeking aid, they may be uncomfortable with their singleness.

1. In your opinion, what is the reason that you are single?
2. Is your singleness your choice?
3. What is your parents' attitude toward those who aren't married? (*Some parents make children without dates feel inadequate.*)
4. Are family members pressuring you to get married?
5. Have you ever been in a close relationship that might have led to marriage? What happened?
6. Describe your support system—friends and family members who are there for you. Does your support come primarily from other singles or from married people as well?
7. Do you have many opportunities to meet other singles? (*There is a wide range in singles' groups—from the dismal support group for the socially inept to the lively social group for well-adjusted singles.*)
8. What does it mean to be a well-adjusted single?
9. Do you think you fit into that category?
10. Do you have any leisure pursuits, such as sports, hobbies, or volunteer work?
11. What is your first thought when people tell you they want to set you up with a friend or acquaintance of theirs?
12. What, if anything, makes marriage preferable to singleness?
13. What advantages do you think married people have?
14. What, if anything, makes singleness preferable to marriage?
15. What advantages do you think single people have?

16. From the following terms, choose four that best describe what singleness means to you and then explain your choices:

> loneliness
> independence
> self-focus
> freedom
> poverty
> spontaneity
> burden
> outward focus
> isolation
> deprivation
> wealth

17. Does our culture view singleness (especially celibate singleness) as a positive or negative state?
18. How many television shows can you name that feature a mature single person who is celibate and happy?
19. Why are so many Christian singles made to feel incomplete?

WISE COUNSEL : 4

Encourage the woman to closely *examine her beliefs about singleness*. Investigate *the messages she received* from her family of origin. (Some parents communicated to their children that girls without dates must be unworthy and boys without girlfriends must be gay. These destructive messages can leave an adult bereft of feelings of self-worth and independence.)

Our culture pictures women who marry as victors who have won the conquest and prizes. So what does this tell a single woman? Help her understand the *unbiblical values exhibited by those who put down singles*. Paul made it clear that singleness is *a high calling* that allows single women to focus more intensely on God.

The single woman must *come to terms with being single*, knowing that she is *complete and whole* as an individual in her relationship with Christ.

Single mothers may be particularly needy, as parenting keeps them from pursuing many social engagements. They may also worry, rightly, about the effect of dating relationships on their children.

ACTION STEPS : 5

1. Accept Your Singleness with Joy

- Live life to its fullest as you seek God's purpose and direction. Accept your singleness as a high calling, giving you the ability, like Paul, to do things for Christ that you might not have the opportunity to do if you were married.

- Seek God in all you do. Never rush to get married.
- Realize that you are a complete and whole person in your relationship with God.

2. Remain Celibate

- You may be frustrated by your singleness because you are not sexually fulfilled.
- To be celibate is the ability to have complete control over your sexual desires. This doesn't necessarily mean you have the gift of celibacy, just that you have a biblical mandate to live a chaste life.
- Remaining chaste involves more than refraining from sexual activity; it also means bringing all sexual desires under submission to God. Your counselor will help you discover methods for coping with temptations and drives in positive ways.
- This is not easy, but if you wish to honor God with your life, you must allow God to be at the center, helping you handle your fears, desires, hopes, and dreams.

3. Get Involved in Community

- Pursue hobbies, sports, or volunteer work so you can meet new people.
- Find a church that has a strong singles program. Lacking that, find a church that provides opportunities for all church members to mix and have fun together. The activities will both encourage fellowship and sharing and help you get to know new people, including other singles.
- You need a community of friends whom you can trust and with whom you can share activities and interests.
- You need a balance of male and female friends.

4. Learn to Love the Quiet

- Learning to appreciate contemplation and solitude may help you feel more comfortable with being alone. You will realize that *alone* is not a synonym for *lonely*.
- Learn to listen to God in the undistracted quiet. Rest in God's love and know that He is sovereign over every aspect of your life, even your singleness. Enjoy being able to spend ample, undivided time with God.
- Take the times of quiet and the times of being alone (being alone, but not lonely) to really get to know yourself and who you are as a person. Grow, learn, and explore life and all that it has to offer. Though it may sound like a cliché, learning and growing will make you more grounded in who you are and prevent the problem of codependency and dependency in any future relationship.

BIBLICAL INSIGHTS : 6

And the Lord God said, "It is not good that man should be alone, I will make him a helper comparable to him."

Genesis 2:18 NKJV

God's provision of a "helper" for Adam was not a condescending comment on singleness but an approval of marriage. God was concerned for Adam's loneliness, for He created people to have relationships—with Him and with others.

Though issues may differ, each one faces the potential problems of aloneness, such as isolation, insecurity, and feelings of rejection. Being unattached can foster destructive responses or it can encourage the development of a deeper relationship with God. There's nothing wrong with being single—just don't go it alone!

Then Miriam the prophetess, the sister of Aaron, took the timbrel in her hand; and all the women went out after her with timbrels and with dances.

Exodus 15:20 NKJV

Miriam, most likely a single woman, played a significant role in the spiritual life of Israel, and she is the first woman to be called a prophetess. Singleness never denotes inferiority. God has special work for all of His people, whether they are single or not.

Now there was one, Anna, a prophetess, the daughter of Phanuel, of the tribe of Asher. She was of a great age, and had lived with a husband seven years from her virginity; and this woman was a widow of about eighty-four years, who did not depart from the temple, but served God with fastings and prayers night and day.

Luke 2:36–37 NKJV

Anna was very young when her husband died and then she was a widow for eighty-four years. Anna remained single, choosing to give her life to serving God through fasting and prayer.

People are single for a number of reasons and they respond to singleness in different ways. Some single people, like Anna, seek to serve God without concern about marriage; others long deeply for a spouse.

It is important to remember that the key to a fulfilled single life is contentment in God. He has places of service for all people—married or single.

But I say to the unmarried and to the widows: It is good for them if they remain even as I am.

1 Corinthians 7:8 NKJV

Some have understood this passage to mean that all single people should remain that way. But Paul's words must be understood with his analysis of his cultural context and his mission.

As a single man, Paul understood the need for people to be able to do whatever it took to share the gospel with unbelievers. He knew that persecution could come at any time. His words reveal his total commitment to his call.

He encouraged single people not to apologize for their singleness. They should not seek to be married as if that were all that mattered. God has an important calling for single women, since they can "serve the Lord without distraction" (1 Cor. 7:35 NKJV).

A married woman has many responsibilities. A single person can be freer to work for the gospel. Neither state is better than the other, but different circumstances create different opportunities.

Singleness can be used for God's glory. Whether a woman has never been married or has become single by way of divorce or bereavement, she is not set aside by God. He has great things for her to accomplish for His kingdom.

Single women must get their own priorities straight—seeking God and His will above all. Single women are never alone; God is always with them.

7 PRAYER STARTER

Dear Lord, _____ is feeling uncomfortable with being single. Please reveal to her Your special purpose for her life as a single woman. Encourage her; bring friends and family around her who can help her achieve a new appreciation for her singleness. Give her the wisdom to see her opportunities for service and enable her to serve You with joy . . .

8 RECOMMENDED RESOURCES

Ethridge, Shannon. *Every Woman's Battle: Discovering God's Plan for Sexual and Emotional Fulfillment*. Random House, 2003.

Hammond, Michelle McKinney. *Sassy, Single, and Satisfied: Secrets to Loving the Life You're Living*. Harvest House, 2003.

Kendall, Jackie, and Debby Jones. *Lady in Waiting: Becoming God's Best while Waiting for Mr. Right*. Destiny Image, 2005.

Leutwiler, Carolyn. *Singleness Redefined: Living Life to the Fullest*. P&R Publishing, 2008.

Ludy, Eric, and Leslie Ludy. *Meet Mr. Smith: Revolutionize the Way You Think about Sex, Purity, and Romance*. Thomas Nelson, 2007.

Martin, Cheryl. *First Class Single*. Salem Communications, 2003.

Rinehart, Paula. *Better Than My Dreams: Finding What You Long For Where You Might Not Think to Look*. Thomas Nelson, 2007.

Single Parenting

PORTRAITS : 1

- Jamie married a soldier, so she wasn't surprised when, even before the birth of her child, her husband was on a tour thousands of miles away. Even though she's married, she's dealing with the daunting task of single motherhood for months at a time.
- After the car accident in which her husband died, Andrea's title changed from proud mother and wife to frightened single mom. Now Andrea faces the task of raising two very young, confused, and hurting kids, while she is dealing with the loss of her husband.
- Darlene thought she and Ted were in it for the long haul. After two kids and finally buying their own home, she knew she was settling into her life. However, when the going got tough, Ted got going. He left her without even saying good-bye or attempting to do anything to fix their marriage. Now Darlene has joined the single mothers club.

DEFINITIONS AND KEY THOUGHTS : 2

- Single parenting for women involves *taking responsibility for parenting one's children* without the benefit of (and sometimes with the direct sabotage of) the husband and/or father—*usually as a result of divorce, abandonment, or death* but sometimes due to military or other service.
- There are *few things more difficult than being a single parent*. A common problem faced by single parents is *the overwhelming amount of work to be done*. The demands of life and living come at the single parent 24-7. Earning a living, fixing meals, caring for kids, helping with homework, cleaning house, paying bills, repairing the car, handling insurance, doing the banking and the income tax, grocery shopping, and everything else can require twelve hours a day or more.
- Often single mothers have *unmet social and emotional needs*. Their time is spent on being a full-time mother and trying to fill the role of father as well. There is little to no time for their own social and emotional needs to be met.
- The *deterioration of fatherhood* in America is considered our most serious social ill. Nearly 40 percent of children fall asleep in homes where their father is not present.[1]

- The National Commission on Children found that nearly *half of all children* in disrupted families have not seen their father at all in the past year.[2]
- *Fatherlessness* is associated with crime, suicide, teenage pregnancy, drug and alcohol abuse, and incarceration.[3]
- Research shows youth from single-parent homes have *more physical and mental health problems* than children living with married parents, and are two to three times more likely to develop emotional and behavioral problems.[4]
- Almost 75 percent of children living in fatherless homes will *experience poverty, and are ten times more likely*—as compared to children living with two parents—*to experience extreme poverty.*[5]

3 ASSESSMENT INTERVIEW

Asking the following questions will help you get a better idea of how the single mother is coping with the task of raising a child (or children) alone.

1. How long have you been a single parent?
2. Describe a typical day or week for you.
3. What kind of support system do you have? Are your parents around? Do they help out with raising your child?
4. How do you provide emotional support to your child? Does your child have the healthy support of adult males?
5. Is the child's father involved with the child at any time? When he is around, is it disruptive or helpful to your child?
6. How are you taking care of yourself as a single mother? When was the last time you went out with friends to have fun? Who cares for the child when you are out? How difficult is it to care for your own needs right now?
7. What are ways you can begin to alleviate some of the burden?

4 WISE COUNSEL

The key to successful single parenting is recruitment and commitment of other *"substitute parents"* who can become part of the family—grandparents, aunts and uncles, friends, neighbors, Big Brother and Big Sister mentors, anyone trustworthy who will commit to assisting your child to grow up as healthy as possible. A healthy church with youth mentors and pastors is another source of support for single parents.

Practically speaking, a single parent may have to *cut back financially* on services such as cell phone, cable television, internet, and other expenses for a period of time. Setting up a reasonable and doable *financial plan* and budget will help cut excessive spending and ensure the single parent is able to pay for basic necessities.

If the single parent is considering a dating relationship, advise her to wait *at least* one year following a divorce. And when the single parent decides to begin dating, it is important to be aware that *the child may feel abandoned for the dating partner.* It is advisable to monitor the amount of exposure the child has to the dating partner—

minimal to not at all in the beginning stages of the relationship and increasing as the single parent becomes more comfortable and trusting of the dating partner.

The single parent must not neglect the time and attention the child needs, while giving time and attention to the dating relationship. *The single parent's child is the most important relationship that she has.*

It is particularly challenging for a single mother to parent a son by herself. Single mothers should try to find *quality and trustworthy males* who will be involved in the child's life. A grandfather, an uncle, youth pastor or leader, scout leaders, and coaches are some men who may be able to fill this role.

Discipline is important for the well-being and self-esteem of children. Many single parents have the tendency to make their son or daughter a friend. Instead, *children need the discipline of a loving parent.*

Help the single mother think of *practical ways of showing love to her son or daughter.* She could hide notes in the child's book bag, have dinner with her child often, go on short day trips over the weekend, visit the zoo, go to a park. During special activities such as these, she may want to invite other single-parent families to join them. Not only can the cost of the trip be split between the families, going together provides a friend for the single parent as well as friends for her child. *Single mothers should make an effort to laugh with their child, play outside with him or her, help with homework, show up for sporting events and extracurricular activities, and encourage their child often.*

Also single mothers need to *find a church* that will provide them meaningful *encouragement and helpful support*—never judgment or criticism for being a single parent.

ACTION STEPS 5

The following guidelines are called the "super Ts" and are the foundation of any good parenting, whether the parent is single or not. They are a basic guide for all parents on how to build a relationship and bring up a happy and healthy child. (It should be apparent that for many of these tasks, the single parent will need the help of other adults. No one person can accomplish all these alone.)

1. Time

- Kids spell love t-i-m-e. There is no substitute for every hour, minute, and second of quality time mothers (and fathers) spend with their children. Kids need heavy doses of you every day, if possible.
- There are many ways to spend time with your child. A few examples are helping with homework, making dinner together, watching a favorite television show together, going for ice cream, taking the child to a movie, or just sitting together and talking.
- The time spent with your child will leave a lasting impression on him or her throughout life. Quality time is one of the most common ways to show and receive love.

2. Touch

- A hug and kiss, holding hands, brushing hair, high fives, even cuddling on the couch—most child experts agree kids need at least eleven touches a day.
- Christian child psychiatrist Grace Ketterman believes children need at least one hundred loving touches a day!
- Children seek affection from their parents, which they interpret as approval and acceptance.

3. Talk

- Find the interests you and your child share, and talk! Ask your child about his or her day. Remember, communication is more nonverbal than verbal, so be careful of all the different ways you "speak" to your child.
- Having regular conversation with your child will form a bond that will, later in life, keep the door open for more serious conversations about life and other issues that may arise.
- When talking to your child, try to make it a conversation and listen. Try not to lecture or find fault with what your child says. If you begin to criticize or lecture, your child may close up and shut you out.

4. Truth

- Deuteronomy 6:6–7 says, "These commandments that I give you today are to be upon your hearts. Impress them on your children. Talk about them when you sit at home and when you walk along the road, when you lie down and when you get up." Parents' morals fill the minds and hearts of their children. Therefore, ground your children in the truth of God's Word so that when they become teenagers, there is no question as to what they should believe or how they should behave.
- The best way to instill biblical principles in your child is to live them out yourself. Not only will your child trust the words you say to him or her but the child will see the Word of God alive and active in you.
- Remember that your child will go through periods of life when he or she will question God's goodness. Be there as a reminder of His truth and that the Word of God will never change.

5. Tenderness

- Tenderness is loving unconditionally and having a soft hand of discipline—even when children irritate, argue, or disappoint. It is the same message Jesus shouts to us—in any condition of sin or grace, we are worth everything to Him!
- Also learn the way your child gives and receives love and overdose him or her with that love! According to Christian child psychologist Fran Stott, "Every child needs at least one person who's crazy about him."

6. Teaching

- Whether they realize it or not, parents are always teaching something to their child. Children learn what they live—what is modeled to them. Your child learned something from you today, guaranteed.
- Don't miss a moment to teach your child important life lessons. And if one parent is absent, assure the child that he or she deserves two parents—even though one might not be around.

7. Tenacity

- Today kids need structure and stability more than ever, for their lives are more erratic, confusing, and rapidly changing than for any generation in history! Be a reference point, an anchor, for your child, holding firmly against powerful countercurrents.
- The hardest part of parenting is staying consistent. With all the other pressures on your plate, it can be easy to slack off in any of the above-mentioned areas. Your investment now is what your child has to "bank" on as he or she grows into a compassionate, competent adult. The truth is children grow up way too soon. Never quit being the parent your child needs.

8. Tomorrow

- The most beautiful part of God's love for us is what Scripture calls the "blessed hope"—an eternity with Him in heaven. Fill your child's heart with hope. Believe in your child. Dream with him or her. Look expectantly to the future. Be big on praise, forgiveness, and grace and be small on criticism.
- There is no better inheritance—no amount of money or privilege or worldly power—that can compare to a legacy of hope in a godly future.

BIBLICAL INSIGHTS 6

But the mercy of the LORD is from everlasting to everlasting on those who fear Him, and His righteousness to children's children, to such as keep His covenant, and to those who remember His commandments to do them.

Psalm 103:17–18 NKJV

One of the great promises of the Bible is that the mercy of the Lord continues from one generation to the next, even to our children's children. This does not mean that the children of believers will automatically believe in God, but that God's mercy and goodness are available to each generation that follows the good example set by the previous generation.

For I have told [Eli] that I will judge his house forever for the iniquity which he knows, because his sons made themselves vile, and he did not restrain them.

1 Samuel 3:13 NKJV

Eli did not discipline his sons, even though they were priests under his supervision. These men were treating the sacrifices of the people with contempt (2:12–17) and were committing sexual sin with women of the tabernacle.

Certainly Eli, as a parent and high priest, had the authority to deal with his sons but he chose to do nothing. Eventually God stepped in.

God gives parents authority over their children, expecting parents to use their authority wisely to guide their children away from sin.

Let the word of Christ dwell in you richly as you teach and admonish one another with all wisdom, and as you sing psalms, hymns, and spiritual songs with gratitude in your hearts to God.

Colossians 3:16

Parents are the child's best and most influential teacher. The schools, churches, and organizations of today are slowly creeping into the position of "parent" in many ways. Here in Colossians 3:16, we are instructed to let God's Word teach and admonish others through us as we worship in our hearts. For parents, this is so important in raising children—especially for single parents.

God the Father can be a single mother's best companion in single parenting. Letting the worship in her heart teach and admonish her children is a major part of providing healthy emotional and spiritual parenting.

7 PRAYER STARTER

Lord, I don't think there is a job in the world more difficult than being a single parent. For this task _____ needs an extra blessing from You to help her walk the road that lies ahead. May she feel Your presence and leading in her life . . .

8 RECOMMENDED RESOURCES

Chisholm, Dana. *Single Moms Raising Sons: Preparing Boys to Be Men When There's No Men Around.* Beacon Hill Press, 2007.

Frisbe, David and Lisa. *Raising Great Kids on Your Own: A Guide and Companion for Every Single Parent.* Harvest House, 2007.

Howe, Michele. *Going It Alone: Meeting the Challenges of Being a Single Mom.* Hendrickson, 1999.

Leman, Kevin. *Single Parenting That Works: Six Keys to Raising Happy, Healthy Children in a Single Parent Home.* Tyndale, 2006.

Meyer, Nancy. *Spiritually Single Moms: Raising Godly Kids When Dad Doesn't Believe.* NavPress, 2007.

Richmond, Gary. *Successful Single Parenting.* Harvest House, 1998.

Whitehurst, Teresa. *God Loves Single Moms: Practical Help for Finding Confidence, Strength, and Hope.* Revell, 2010.

Strength in Conflict and Stress

1 PORTRAITS

- Miranda sat on the side of the hospital bed and put on her shoes. Yesterday she had been sure she was having a heart attack. Her chest had been tight and she had struggled to breathe. But today, after many tests, her doctor told her that her heart is fine. Nothing was *physically* wrong. "I think you're under a lot of stress," her doctor told her. The doctor recommended that she see a counselor.

- Carey is trying to focus on school and be a good student, but for the past few months, things with her roommates have become tense and heated. The pressing issues with her roommates are consuming her usual study time and even her thoughts during class. The pressure she feels to make everything better, while at the same time focusing on all the work she has for school, is overwhelming her. Carey feels as if she could burst into tears at any moment.

- Kailey has been through a lot lately. Her husband lost his job, and the bill collectors are beginning to call. In addition, her mom has been sick, her kids have been having a difficult time in school, and the water heater just broke. Kailey feels as though she is going nuts and does not think she can handle one more crisis.

2 DEFINITIONS AND KEY THOUGHTS

- *Stress* is the common term for *general adaption syndrome* (GAS), or the *fight or flight syndrome*. It is the body's natural response to threatening situations, which prepares us to fight or to flee—it arouses us and gives us the energy we need to resolve or remove ourselves from the stressor. Stress is a normal part of life and can be *both negative and positive*, alerting us to a problem needing attention.

- Stress is usually *negative* when a woman experiences it constantly, without relief or relaxation between challenges. Women are more likely to experience *physical symptoms of stress*, whereas men often use the "fight or flight" method of coping.[1]

- *Chronic stress* may be a function of the *constant negative appraisals* a woman makes about life, seeing things as more threatening than they really are.

- *Seventy percent* of women who are married and have children less than eighteen years of age work outside the home—this juggling act of being mother, wife, and career woman is a major leading cause of stress in women.[2] Sometimes stress comes from a *difficult life situation*, but stress can also result from *negative perceptions about life situations*, such as worries about failure and perfectionist tendencies. It is critically important to help clients understand the *difference between stressful events and perceived stress*—your counseling approach will be different, depending on which kind of stress exists. Some personalities, referred to as Type A, *cause stress* in themselves and in others. Some people may have extremely driven or perfectionist personalities or live or work with someone who does, thereby feeling the stress of the other person's drivenness.

- For women, premenstrual, postpartum, and menopausal changes are major factors leading to stress and depression.[3] Stress without relief can lead to *physical symptoms*, such as headaches, an upset stomach, elevated blood pressure, chest pain, and difficulty sleeping. Stress can also *affect a woman's relationships* adversely as well as her *body, mind, and spirit*. We must pay attention to each area to reduce the effects of stress on overall well-being.

- If we do not learn to control stress, *it will eventually control us*. We need not be overwhelmed by stress. Philippians 4:7 says, "The peace of God, which transcends all understanding, will guard your hearts and your minds in Christ Jesus."

ASSESSMENT INTERVIEW 3

1. What would you say are the stressors in your life right now? Is something or someone in your life causing you stress (for example, a stressful spouse or boss)? Or are you causing your own stress by being a perfectionist or trying to control situations over which you have no control?

2. What percentage of your total stress is being caused by each of these stressors? How long has each of these stressors been present?

3. Tell me about each stressor. (*Get as many details as you can so you can begin to assess how the woman views these stressors.*)

4. How realistic is the possibility of the things you're worried about actually happening? (*For example, if the woman is experiencing persistent fears of job loss, is this fear based on current reality?*)

5. To whom do you talk about the stress in your life? Are these conversations helpful to you? (*The impact of stress is greater if the individual feels that he or she is alone in handling it.*)

6. Are you using other things to help you handle the stress (such as sports, drugs [OTC or prescription], alcohol, sexual activity, excessive television or computer use)? What has helped?

7. When do you experience the least stress in your life? Is there any time when you do not experience stress?

8. Do you believe you are in control of changing these stressors? Is change possible? Is there anything you can think of that would reduce your stress level?

9. Are you overloading yourself with commitments? When could you say no so that you would be able to enjoy life again?

10. If there is no way to limit your commitments, what are some healthy ways you can think of to handle the stress you're currently under?

4 WISE COUNSEL

If the woman is experiencing *physical effects* of the stress and hasn't seen a physician, encourage her to *schedule a physical*.

Determine if there are *immediate situational stressors* that need attention, such as resolving a problem in the workplace or finding help to deal with a difficult child. *Often stress is just a symptom of a deeper issue, such as conflict, dysfunction, or burnout.*

Assess ways to *provide a break from the stress*. Suggest

exercise (with a doctor's review and permission)

frequent breaks throughout the day to *pray and meditate* on Scripture

sharing burdens with a trusted friend

taking a *vacation* (even a day or two off can help)

Because stress affects the mind, body, and spirit, it *poses a triple threat*. The woman needs to protect all three aspects of her life. Advise her to do the following:

To protect your mind: remind yourself of the truth, confess God's power over stressful events, refuse to make mountains out of molehills, refuse to see only bad things, set priorities, and gain perspective.

To protect your body: increase your exercise regimen, get enough sleep, eat well, and breathe deeply.

To protect your spirit: meditate on God and His Word, thank God for the good things in your life, learn to trust God more by confessing your lack of trust in stressful times, and pray without ceasing—use stressful thoughts as cues to switch into a prayer mode.

5 ACTION STEPS

1. Consider What God Is Doing

- Gain perspective on what is causing the stress. Is it relationships, work responsibilities, marital conflict, misbehaving children? As you think about the various areas of your life that are stressful, you break apart the "I'm so stressed" mind-set into manageable pieces. Then you can begin to address each part. Sometimes, stress is a result of overcommitment or codependency, but, to a certain extent, stress is part of life.

- One of the best antidotes to stress is seeing God's purpose in the difficulties and developing faith to believe that God is always working for your good and His glory, even in the midst of stress.

- God can use stress to reveal the sin in your heart and develop the fruits of the Spirit in you. Knowing that God uses every situation—even the petty, irritating situations of life—to teach you to become more like Jesus can help you feel less stressed by things you cannot control.

2. Get Alone with God

- In today's fast-paced world, it's so easy to get caught up in the rat race of going, doing, and accomplishing. Planned times of quiet and solitude can be difficult to fit in but are essential to balance the busyness of life.

- God says, "Be still, and know that I am God" (Ps. 46:10). Cultivating a heart of prayer—both talking and listening to God—helps you see God's perspective and to experience more fully His presence throughout the day (Ps. 16:8–11).

- Many times prayer does not change the situation as much as it changes you and your orientation to stressful people and situations. As you purposely quiet your heart each day, the Holy Spirit has a chance to change the way you see your stressful situation.

3. Share Your Burden with Others

- If you're feeling stressed and overwhelmed, *talk to someone about it*. You don't have to figure it out on your own and you don't have to do it all. Get advice from people you respect.

- You can share your burden literally or figuratively. In other words, you can ask others to help with some of your responsibilities and you can talk about your stressors, which can bring relief and prayer support.

- Perhaps some of the stress is because you're doing too much. It may be time to reevaluate, cut back, say no, or slow down. Even Moses had to delegate when he got overwhelmed (Exod. 18:13–23). Maybe you can do the same.

4. Guard Your Heart

- Stress has a way of orienting us toward the things that are wrong in our lives. It pushes us to forget the good and godly things, and we begin to believe that only bad things are going on. Guard your heart and mind against such stress-induced negativity and pessimism. Take time each day to check your thinking and take every thought captive to the obedience of Christ (2 Cor. 10:5), focusing on God and allowing Him to change your perspective.

- Your heart is the fountain from which your emotions, feelings, and thoughts spring. Guarding your heart allows you to have God honoring emotions, feelings, and thoughts that also carry you on the path to freedom.

5. Live Intentionally

- Stop focusing on minor things. At the end of life, many will realize that they spent most of their time on what mattered least, and the least time on what mattered most. Become more intentional about the way you spend your time and energy. Learn to say no to things that are just not that important.

- Frequently our lives become filled with stress because we refuse to accept our limits or we are completely boxed in and paralyzed by them. Decide what is really important, choose your priorities, and live for them.
- Allow for some levity in your life. Take time for laughter, joking, and amusement.

6 : BIBLICAL INSIGHTS

You will keep him in perfect peace, whose mind is stayed on You, because he trusts in You.

Isaiah 26:3 NKJV

Jesus reminded His followers "in this world you will have trouble" (John 16:33). The prophet Isaiah wrote that God gives peace in spite of conflict and turmoil.

Peace is so basic to God's nature that it is part of His name. God the Father is the "God of peace" (Phil. 4:9; Heb. 13:20). God the Son is the Prince of Peace (Isa. 9:6).

The Holy Spirit produces peace in our lives (Gal. 5:22). To have "perfect peace," wrote Isaiah, we must focus our minds on God and trust in Him.

Let not your heart be troubled; you believe in God, believe also in Me.

John 14:1 NKJV

The disciples were bewildered and discouraged. Jesus had said He was going away, that He would die, that one of His disciples was a traitor, and that Peter would deny Him.

"Let not your heart be troubled," Jesus told them. Believers can rest their troubled hearts, knowing that Jesus is in control regardless of the circumstances.

Persecuted, but not forsaken; struck down, but not destroyed.

2 Corinthians 4:9 NKJV

For us, each day is filled with different levels of stress. Regardless of occupation, age, social status, or lifestyle, we experience stress.

We bring some stressors on ourselves, because of poor planning, saying yes too often, or being disorganized. We need to learn from these experiences so we don't allow ourselves to become overwhelmed again.

Stress also arises from factors outside our control—the weather, a broken computer, an unexpected difficulty or sorrow. At these times, we can control only our reactions to the stress. Our reactions reveal our character and our trust in God.

Be anxious for nothing, but in everything by prayer and supplication, with thanksgiving, let your requests be made known to God; and the peace of God, which surpasses all understanding, will guard your hearts and minds through Christ Jesus.

Philippians 4:6–7 NKJV

Stress and its companion, worry, do their best to immobilize believers. People are anxious about the future; they are anxious about events that haven't happened but *could* happen.

So what can believers do about their stresses? When we give our stress to God, He replaces it with His peace that "surpasses all understanding."

When we feel stress rising, we should turn to God in prayer. He will give us the peace He promised.

My brethren, count it all joy when you fall into various trials, knowing that the testing of your faith produces patience.

James 1:2–3 NKJV

Everyone faces trials in one form or another. We cannot control what we will encounter but we can control the level of stress that situations cause us if we focus on the joy God gives rather than on the stressor.

Joy is not a natural reaction to difficulty but one that the Holy Spirit can provide. For this to happen, we must choose an attitude that looks expectantly to the lessons God will teach and the wisdom He will provide. There's no better prescription for dealing with stress.

PRAYER STARTER : 7

Thank You, Lord, that _____ has come today for help in relieving her burden of stress. You never intended for Your children to live overwhelmed and unhealthy lives by carrying undue amounts of stress all by ourselves. Help _____ to face and handle what she can, and give her wisdom to turn over to You, Lord, all the difficult people and situations that are beyond her control . . .

RECOMMENDED RESOURCES : 8

Colbert, Don. *Deadly Emotions.* Thomas Nelson, 2006.

Ensley, Eddie. *Prayer That Relieves Stress and Worry.* Contemplative Press, 2007.

Hager, W. David, and Linda Carruth Hager. *Stress and the Woman's Body.* Revell, 1998.

Pegues, Deborah Smith. *30 Days to Taming Your Stress.* Harvest House, 2007.

Powlison, David. *Stress: Peace Amid Pressure.* P&R Publishing, 2004.

Swenson, Richard A. *Margin: Restoring Emotional, Physical, Financial, and Time Reserves to Overloaded Lives.* NavPress, 2004.

———. *The Overload Syndrome: Learning to Live within Your Limits.* NavPress, 1999.

Final Thoughts

Helping Women in Crisis

Diane Langberg

As counselors, we have had the privilege of caring for countless hurting women over the years. They have come with histories of sadistic, chronic sexual abuse. They have come bruised and swollen because of the battering of people who were supposed to love them. They have come because spouses have left them. They have buried children and spouses. Some have lived with chronic illness—their own or another's. They have struck me dumb with the depths of their suffering. They have told stories of evil and pain that have been incomprehensible to me. They have highlighted in living color my own inadequacies and failures, and they've challenged me, frustrated me, frightened me, loved me, hated me, and enriched my life beyond words.

I assume that because you are reading this, you care about and desire to minister to people who are suffering or in crisis. A crisis is literally "a separating," something in life that is so significant that it becomes a marker—you think of life before and life after a crisis. A rape, the first time someone hits you, learning you have cancer, the loss of a child, the death of a spouse, financial ruin, and infidelity are all separating moments. Each is a turning point, a crucial time in a person's life. It is also a frightening time. The road map with which you are familiar no longer points the way. What was known is gone, what felt safe now feels unsafe, and what seemed predictable is totally uncertain. A crisis is essentially what we might call an alarm moment in a life.

Oswald Chambers talks about having "staying power in the alarm moments of others' lives." Think about those times when you have accidentally set off an alarm and you have a little flavor of what people are experiencing when they are in crisis. There is a lot of emotional noise in their lives; there is chaos. They cannot think what to do. They are afraid. They feel that they are in danger, something is wrong. They want someone to help. They want the noise to stop, the fear to subside. They want to feel safe and to be able to think.

If people seek you out during their alarm moments, one of the things they will bring you is their noise. They will walk into your life and bring anger, violence, sobbing, ranting, terror, panic, fear, and anxiety. You may even become the focus of their anger, accusations, or fear. How hard it is to have staying power at such times!

They will also bring you their silence. Pain brings silence, for often suffering is so great that there are no words. Trauma silences; death silences. The psalmist says, "I am shut up, and I cannot come forth" (Ps. 88:8 KJV). They will bring tears, sometimes wrenching sobs. We tend to respond by simply handing out tissues, which can be a subtle hint that the crying should be over by now. We prefer human beings with clean faces. We feel awkward with loud sobbing. We are uneasy in the face of unadulterated terror or pain. How are we to have staying power in alarm moments such as these?

When an alarm goes off, we want to turn it off. The noise bothers us; it disrupts our world. When an alarm goes off, it makes us want to flee—a normal response. Alarms mean things are not okay, and we want our world to be okay. Anytime a person in crisis walks into your world, you are facing an alarm moment. It is a separating time for that person. It is actually a separating time for you as well. The fact is that anytime someone brings you her crisis, the person is actually creating one for you as well. Will you enter in, and if so, how should you conduct yourself so that your presence is a help and support, not a contributor to the noise and chaos?

It is crucial that we understand something of what we encounter if we are to minister to women in crisis. There are characteristics that we need to grapple with if we are to really understand what it is we need to do. I fear we may think that helping people in crisis is simply about telling them good and true things; then they will listen and get better. But it is rarely as simple as that.

AMBIGUITY, CHANGE, AND REPETITION

One of the things you will encounter as you move in to help is ambiguity. Interactions between humans on a good day are often fuzzy and confusing. And while a life alarm is going off, interactions are frequently unclear. You think you understand an issue and then it shows up in someone's life and what you know does not seem to fit. Or someone brings you a problem, and then you realize it is not the real problem at all. People want to feel better. They want answers. You may quickly feel that you have no idea what to do or you may realize that what you thought was the right response ends up producing a more complicated mess.

Those in crisis want change—or do they? They do, oh how they do—but we forget that change makes human beings nervous. Change requires massive effort, and they are exhausted. Change is not something that usually occurs simply because someone told you the right answer. Not only that, when a person does decide to do the work of changing, she may make other people frightened and angry. They push back; that creates more crises! It feels as though things are going in the wrong direction!

Change is not just in the wings for the person who is suffering; it is there for you as well. Somebody in crisis walks into your life with a story yet untold. This person and her story *will* impact you. Suffering people will take you places you have never been and maybe do not want to go. You cannot let yourself down into another's life without being impacted. You cannot be present to abuse, violence, trafficking, deceit, brokenness, terminal illness, and darkness without being affected. You will find yourself thrown by the things humans do to one another. You will struggle with disbelief. You will want to say it could not be true.

Repetition is necessary for someone in crisis. You say something and then you say it again. You live it out in the flesh for her and she still questions its truth. You cannot confront the debilitating effects of chronic childhood abuse, domestic violence, oppression, or addiction without being repetitious. You speak truth and watch it devoured by a sea of lies. Over and over you rework the ground of trust, only to have someone say, "But can I trust you here too?" And so you must restate, rework, relive what you thought was so clear.

LEARNING TO WAIT

You will have to learn how to wait. You will wait for a thought to bubble to the surface of a confused mind. You will wait for truth to penetrate a dark mind. You will wait while an addict fails *again*, and old ground has to be covered again. You will wait while the Spirit of God works internally in a life with yet no outward sign of growth. You will wait because God's timetable is not yours, and He is teaching you about waiting as much as He is teaching the person you are caring for. He is teaching you how to think and love *while* the alarm is still going off.

You must never forget that you are dealing with a combination of suffering and sin when you work with people in crisis. Suffering silences people and scars lives. Silence and scars are not proof of sin in a life—you have only to look at the life of Christ to know that. You do not push a woman to tell you how the alarm got set off while it is still screaming in her ears. At that moment she cannot think clearly.

ENCOUNTERING SIN

Sometimes we set off our own alarm moments; sometimes another has done so. Often, but not always, it is a combination. Many women suffer because of another's sin, not their own. David suffered because of what Saul did. His suffering was undeserved. Remember that when you sit across from suffering. Do not add to the burden of the suffering one by assuming the need to go on a sin hunt.

Sometimes we suffer because we live in a fallen world and no one's sin is involved. A person who lives with chronic illness is faced with never-ending grief and loss, pain and body chemicals that may result in unremitting depression, not due to sinful actions on anyone's part.

You will, of course, also encounter deep and habituated sin. Not necessarily in the person you are caring for but perhaps in others in the person's life. It is critical that we not be naive about the impact of such sin on a person's life. A woman who grew up with chronic sexual abuse has been shaped and trained by evil. A person who has endured someone else's control, rage, battering, or constant verbal abuse has been profoundly impacted in her thinking, emotions, spiritual life, and relationships. A person who has had a drug, sex, or gambling addiction has practiced self-deception for a long time and will be so wrapped up in it that truth will penetrate slowly and in very small doses. People who have been beaten down by sin for years, their own or another's, cannot stand up straight all of a sudden. People who have lived with habituated sin, their own or another's, are altered, or shaped, by that sin. Their spiritual hearing and seeing have been crippled.

We are careful about our children's diets because we know that the food they consume can affect everything, both now and in the future. We are careful about what they read or see for the same reasons. We become good at those things we habituate and we know that what is done frequently has profound consequences. If you practice silence and a blank mind to deal with battering over a period of twenty years, then you will not be able to think or articulate clearly just because someone has stepped in to help.

MINISTERING LIKE JESUS

So if simply speaking the truth is not sufficient on its own when responding to those in crisis, how can we respond so that they are helped and ultimately transformed? We can, of course, learn from our Lord. He stepped into the alarm moments of our lives. He entered the chaos and noise. He encountered the suffering and the sin of this world and had staying power. He has called us to be like Him. Let us consider something of what that was like for Him so that we might follow Him into the lives of those He brings to us.

Leave Glory

The first thing one must do to enter into the alarm moments of others' lives is leave glory. The leaving must occur before the entering can happen. Jesus left His world, its beauty, its comfort, its safety, and its peace. He left what was rightfully His and entered what was foreign to Him. He left perfect love for hatred, order for chaos, beauty for ugliness, and light for darkness. He left behind functioning as the self He is in heaven so that He might function as a self like us. He put on the cloak of humanity.

You must leave glory if you are to help those in crisis. You must leave that which is familiar, ordered, predictable, and comfortable for you. You must enter into foreign territory that you do not know, encountering what is unfamiliar. You will be forever changed by the sufferings and sin of others.

Become Little

Second, in leaving glory, Jesus became little. He is the Creator and Sustainer of the universe. He is eternal, immortal, and infinite. He became unlike Himself. He reduced Himself in size, power, impact, words, and potential to help. He became little for our sakes. He became like us so we could receive Him. His becoming like us is a kind of listening unlike any the world has ever seen. He allowed Himself, as it were, to be "taught" by us about what it is like to be human.

When you enter a life in crisis, you must become little. You will not help if you swoop in, tell people what to do, and take over. You need to leave glory and enter in, in small doses, so you can truly listen and understand and be touched by their infirmities.

If you have never been chronically sexually abused, you do not know what that kind of life is like. If you have been, you know only your experience, not theirs. Enter in, listen, live with, observe, and learn. Be little; it is about them, not you. You will put yourself into the mix by eye dropper amounts, just the way the Lord of the universe has done with you. If He poured everything in His mind into yours, yours would blow up. You could not hold it, organize it, understand it, or use it.

Enter the Darkness

Third, in leaving glory, Jesus entered darkness. He dwelt in the unfamiliar, and it had an impact on Him. He, who is the beginning and the end, could not see tomorrow. He who is the light of the world was eclipsed. He who is the Word became silent. He who is perfection was scarred. His life was touched by many things that were utterly foreign to Him, things that were an assault on Him.

Typically, when we enter into another's suffering, we try to drag the person into our world. We want her to think what we think, choose what we would choose, understand what we see, and live more in the way we do. These are not necessarily bad goals, but you can get people to reach them only if you enter into their darkness. You must go in and get them so that you can bring them out. You cannot call people out of suffering. You must go in to them and sit with them and listen and understand and then little by little you can begin to walk with them toward a new and different place. You cannot help if you do not enter the darkness.

Bring Christ's Character with You

Fourth, Jesus was not lost in the darkness. He brought the character of the Father with Him when He became little and entered our darkness. He brought truth and love manifest in the flesh when He came and sat with us. When He came into the darkness and sat down, He was bearing the character of the Father, full of grace and truth. He lived out that character while He walked with us and ate with us and talked with us. Who He was when He was with us explained the Father to us. Light began to dawn for us because it was lived out in the flesh in front of us.

So often we think we need techniques, programs, plans—and these can all be very helpful. However, suffering and sinful humanity needs the character of God the Father manifest in the flesh before them. People do not need just knowledge about the character of God but the actual demonstration of it in the flesh, in you—His truth, His love, His mercy, and His grace. As we sit with them and live with them, they are greeted with evidence of Him through us. Someone who has been abused has been saturated with evil, lies, manipulation, humiliation, and rage. Oh, how they need to sit with the loving and truthful character of the Father in you! They need more than hearing about it. They need to experience it (love, mercy, grace) in you, in the flesh.

Don't Abandon Them

Fifth, our Lord did not abandon us. He left glory and entered into our darkness and did not run, even when facing the cross. He felt like running. He was overwhelmed by what He faced but He did not abandon humanity. He did not leave us alone in our mess, our alarm moments. He does not leave us now. Had He abandoned us, we would not have ever found our way out. We could not see; we could not think; we could not walk upright. He stays and waits and calls us to come to Him, to come with Him.

You will want to run away but you cannot. Your client will make one phone call too many, one mistake too many, one bad choice too many. You will get weary and it will feel heavy. You will want a life free of crises and alarms. But the love of the Father does not abandon His own. Many times I see how we in the body of Christ start off well with a crisis but do not have staying power. We find it difficult to maintain connection with crises, especially chronic ones, and so we abandon those who have no choice about the presence of suffering in their lives. They are left to endure it alone. Our Friend, who entered in, never abandons us.

Maintain Spiritual Strength

Sixth, our Lord left glory and entered the darkness but He did not catch the disease from which we suffer. It is very easy when working with alarm moments to get caught up in the crisis and lose perspective. He did not. He did not sin, even when He suffered with our sufferings. He did not allow the chaos, darkness, evil, and noise to destroy Him. He entered into the darkness but stayed light. He entered into frailty but did not get sick.

How can we work with women in crisis and not catch the soul diseases they bring with them? How can we have staying power in the alarm moments of others' lives? How do we maintain spiritual strength so we do not become twisted and crippled by an ongoing exposure to evil?

Staying power means having the ability to endure, holding out against discouragement, sustaining our involvement without impairment, bearing with patience the ups and downs of the relationship. If we are to help those in crisis, then clearly we need a place to stand. We will abandon them or end up impaired without that place. We will become cynical, bitter, or despairing.

Handley Moule, Bishop of Durham, said the following (slightly adapted): "If you would deal aright with the people in crisis, earnest Christian of the church, live at the Center. Dwell deep. From the person turn back evermore to Jesus Christ, that from Jesus Christ you may the better go back to the person, bringing the peace and power of the Lord Himself with you." In other words, it is only as we come to Him and drink deeply that we can endure in the carrying of living water to dry and thirsty places.

THREE ESSENTIALS TO REMEMBER

I would have you remember three things if you are to minister to suffering people in the body of Christ. *First, you are doing God's work with Him*. Do not make the mistake of thinking of this as *your* work. Yes, you are the one bringing down the character of God into flesh and blood, but it is not your work. It is a piece of the work of God in this world and He has given you the privilege of sharing in it. It is His work, the people are His people, and you are not your own. You are not the Redeemer, merely His servant. If you remember that it is His work, you will continually run to Him about the piece of that work He has for you to do. If it is His work, the results are in His hands, and you will not need to demand certain outcomes by a certain time, thereby pressuring hurting women to get better so that you feel successful.

It is not only His work to do *with* Him, but *it is His work done for Him.* You are not working for the suffering; you are not working for anyone else looking for their approval or certain status in the church. You are Christ's worker, working for Him. If you do the work as if it is for the suffering, then you will be governed by them. Their needs will be your ruler, and you will end up in their noise and chaos. They are central, they are considered, and they must be understood, but the work is done *in* their life and *for* your God. He says this, not that; these limits, not those; this response, not that one. The needs of others are not the call nor are they your governance. The call is from God, the governance is God's alone, and from *that* place you enter into the suffering of another.

Third, you can only *do this work by God and through Him.* You cannot do the work of God in suffering lives, nor will you please God with your work, unless He works redemptively in and through you. The work of the Redeemer in this world is a difficult work. He was a Man of Sorrows and acquainted with grief. I prefer to be familiar with comfort. He was despised and rejected. I prefer to be honored and accepted. He took up our sickness, frailties, and disabilities. I prefer health, strength, and wholeness. He was pierced and crushed and oppressed. I prefer no injuries, no smashing, and no injustice.

I do not like alarm-moment work and I cannot do it. God has taught me through the lives of many suffering people that I cannot do His work. Yet He has called me to this work. The resolution of this dilemma has come as I have learned to bow to the work of redemption in me. I have had to allow God to alter me, fit me, for His work. If I would bend down to bear the burdens of my sisters, then I must first be made a fit burden-bearer. To be a fit burden-bearer is to be like Jesus and wherever I am not like Him, I am not fit, for I will misrepresent Him to those who suffer.

I can attest to the fact that working with suffering people, bending down to bear their burdens, will expose you to yourself. You can tell yourself you are very patient but unless that patience is tested, you will not know the truth of your belief. As I said early on, crises are separating, not just for the one in crisis but also for the one coming to her aid. You will have a time of "this is what I thought I was" and then a time of "this is who I turned out to be." God is always working both sides. He has not just called you to care for the person in crisis. He is also creating a crisis in you so that He might show you areas of yourself where you are in desperate need of His work. It is only as we bow to the work of His Spirit, exposing and calling us to repentance, that we will truly be able to go out to the circumferences and carry His grace to those in need. The call of God to care for those who suffer is ultimately a call to be made to look like Jesus Christ in this world.

THREE ESSENTIALS FOR DOING THIS WORK

One last set of things in closing. There are three essentials for doing this work. *First, you must know about people.* Read, please read. Read about trauma, sexual abuse, domestic abuse, grief, chronic illness, depression, addictions, cancer, or whatever God is bringing across your path. If you do not read and understand, you will make wrong judgments. You will expect change prematurely and you will give wrong answers. Study avidly. Listen acutely. You cannot appropriately care for people you do not understand.

Second, know God. Know His Word. Be an avid student of that Word. If we are going to serve as His representatives to others, we need to know Him well. We need to be so permeated by His Word that we learn to think His thoughts. And we must remember that to know His Word, according to Him, means it is woven into our lives and we are obedient to Him. Where we do not live in accord with His Word, we do not truly know Him.

Third, do not do this work without utter dependence on the Spirit of God. Where else will you find wisdom? How will you know when to speak and when to be silent? How will you discern the lies from the truth? How else will you love when you are weary or be patient when you are depleted? How can you know the mind of God apart from the Spirit of God? How can we possibly expect to demonstrate the character of God in the flesh apart from the indwelling power of His Spirit? How can we think that the life-giving power of Christ crucified will be released into other lives unless we have allowed the cross to do its work in our own lives? To work with crises is to work with lies, darkness, and evil. You cannot fight the litter that hell leaves in a life unless you walk dependent on the Spirit of God.

Such a work will change you; it will challenge you; it will force you to your knees, hungry for more of Christ. Frankly, whether a particular person you counsel ever changes or makes good choices or truly comes to grasp the grace of God in her life, *you* will be changed into His likeness by walking His way and learning of Him.

Notes

Introduction

1. Doug Clark, "Jesus and Women," *Enrichment Journal* (November 15, 2009), http://enrichmentjournal .ag.org/200102/024_jesus_and_women.cfm.

Abortion

1. The Alan Guttmacher Institute (1996–2008), http:// www.abortionno.org/Resources/fastfacts.html.

2. "Abortion Surveillance—United States" (2006), http://www.cdc.gov/reproductivehealth/Data_Stats/ index.htm#Abortion.

3. Ibid.

4. The Alan Guttmacher Institute (1996–2008), http:// www.abortionno.org/Resources/fastfacts.html.

5. Ibid.

6. Ibid.

7. Yvonne Florczak-Seeman, *A Time to Speak: A Healing Journal for Post-Abortive Women*, http://lfa.axiom -server.com.

Aging

1. Department of Health and Human Services, Administration on Aging, "Aging Statistics" (May 11, 2010), http://www.aoa.gov/aoaroot/aging_statistics/index.aspx.

2. Centers for Disease Control and Prevention, "Leading Causes of Death in Females, United States, 2006," http://www.cdc.gov/women/lcod/index.htm.

3. Centers for Disease Control and Prevention, "Strength Training among Adults over 65 Years—United States, 2001," http://www.cdc.gov/mmwr/preview/ mmwrhtml/mm5302a1.htm.

4. Centers for Disease Control and Prevention, http:// www.cdc.gov/women/natstat/aging.htm.

5. All statistics taken from the United States Census Bureau (2001), reported in "Diseases and Conditions That Affect Older Women," http://www.womancando .org/womancando/olderwomenconditions2.htm.

Anger

1. Jane Brody, "Women and Anger: To Vent or Not to Vent Isn't the Question," *New York Times*, http://www .nytimes.com/1993/12/01/science/women-and-anger- to-vent-or-not-to-vent-isn-t-the-question.html?page wanted=1.

2. Mental Health Organization, "Mental Health Organization Boiling Point Report 2008," http://www.mental health.org.uk/campaigns/anger-and-mental-health /boiling-point-report/.

Birth Control

1. Centers for Disease Control and Prevention, "Unintended Pregnancy Prevention: Contraception," http:// www.cdc.gov/reproductivehealth/unintendedpregnancy/ contraception.htm; Centers for Disease Control and Prevention, "FastStats: Contraceptive Use," http://www.cdc .gov/nchs/fastats/contraceptive.htm.

2. All statistics taken from Planned Parenthood, "Diaphragms, Caps, and Shields," http://www.ppsev .org/services/diaphragm.html.

3. Robert Hatcher, "Managing Contraception Questions and Answers," Emory University School of Medicine (January 21, 2009), http://www.managingcontraception .com/qa/questions.php?questionid=1146.

4. The Nemours Foundation, "About Birth Control: The Birth Control Shot," http://kidshealth.org/parent/ growth/sexual_health/bc_shot.html.

5. University of Cincinnati, "Implantable Birth Control New Option for Women," *Science Daily* (2006), http:// www.sciencedaily.com/releases/2006/11/061110090542 .htm.

6. "Emergency Contraception's Mode of Action Clarified," *Population Briefs* (May 2005).

7. Royal College of Obstetricians and Gynaecologists, "Vasectomy," *Male and Female Sterilisation: Evidence-based Clinical Guideline 4* (2004): 38, http://www.rcog .org.uk/files/rcog-corp/uploaded-files/NEBSterilisation Full060607.pdf; Harvard Medical School, "Vasectomy and Vasovasostomy (Reversal Surgery)," *Well Connected* (2001), http://www.vasectomy-information.com/pages/ wellconn2001.pdf.

8. H. B. Peterson et al., "The Risk of Ectopic Pregnancy after Tubal Sterilization," *New England Journal of Medicine* 336 (1997): 762–67.

9. The Alan Guttmacher Institute (1996–2008), http:// www.abortionno.org/Resources/fastfacts.html.

Cancer

1. National Cancer Institute, "Definition of Cancer," http://www.cancer.gov/dictionary/?CdrID=45333.

2. Centers for Disease Control and Prevention, "FastStats: Women's Health" (2006), http://www.cdc.gov/nchs/fastats/womens_health.htm.

3. Centers for Disease Control and Prevention, "Cancer and Women," http://www.cdc.gov/features/womenandcancer.

4. National Cancer Institute, "Cancer Statistics," http://www.cancer.gov/cancertopics/types/womenscancers.

5. L. Ries et al., "SEER Cancer Statistics Review, 1975–2005," http://seer.cancer.gov/csr/1975_2005/.

Child Sexual Abuse

1. National Center on Child Abuse and Neglect, http://www.findcounseling.com/journal/child-abuse/sexual-abuse.html.

2. D. Kilpatrick, B. Saunders, and D. Smith, "Youth Victimization: Prevalence and Implications," *National Institute of Justice Report* (U.S. Department of Justice, 2003).

3. Centers for Disease Control and Prevention, "ACE Study: Prevalence of Adverse Childhood Experiences," http://www.cdc.gov/nccdphp/ace/prevalence.htm.

4. Darkness to Light, "Statistics Surrounding Child Sexual Abuse," http://www.darkness2light.org/knowabout/statistics_2.asp.

5. B. V. Molnar, S. L. Buka, and R. C. Kessler, "Child Sexual Abuse and Subsequent Psychopathology: Results from the National Comorbidity Study," *American Journal of Public Health* 9 (2001): 753–60.

6. Darkness to Light, "Statistics Surrounding Child Sexual Abuse," http://www.darkness2light.org/knowabout/statistics_2.asp.

Chronic Pain

1. American Chronic Pain Association, "What Is Chronic Pain?" http://www.theacpa.org/faqlisting.aspx.

2. Chronic Pain Outreach, "Who Does Chronic Pain Affect?" http://www.chronicpain.org/.

3. American Academy of Pain Medicine, "AAPM Facts and Figures on Pain," http://www.painmed.org/patient/facts.html.

4. Centers for Disease Control and Prevention, "Chronic Disease and Health Promotion," http://www.cdc.gov/chronicdisease/overview/index.htm.

5. Siang-Yang Tan and George Ohlschlager, "Pain: Problem, Puzzle, Parable" in *The Bible for Hope: Caring for People God's Way*, ed. Dr. Tim Clinton (Nashville: Thomas Nelson, 2001).

Codependency and Relationship Addiction

1. C. Hughes-Hammer, D. S. Martsolf, and R. A. Zeller, "Depression and Codependency in Women," *Archives of Psychiatric Nursing* 12, no. 6 (1998): 326–34, http://www.ncbi.nlm.nih.gov/pubmed/9868824.

2. Melody Beattie, *Codependent No More* (Center City, MN: Hazelden, 1992), 36.

3. A. J. Mahari, "Enmeshment, Codependency, and Collusion," *Soul Self Help* (2007), http://www.soulselfhelp.on.ca/coenmesh.html.

4. Mental Health America, "Factsheet: Codependency," http://www.nmha.org/go/codependency.

Depression

1. "Definition of Depression," http://wordnetweb.princeton.edu/perl/webwn?s=depression.

2. Archibald D. Hart and Catherine Hart Weber, *A Woman's Guide to Overcoming Depression* (Grand Rapids: Revell, 2007).

3. "Statistics of Depression," http://depressiontreatmenthelp.org/depression-statistics.php.

4. National Alliance on Mental Illness, "Women Depressed at Twice the Rate of Men" (April 29, 2008), http://www.upi.com/Health_News/2008/04/29/Women-depressed-at-twice-the-rate-of-men/UPI-67861209491371/.

5. "Statistics of Depression," http://depressiontreatmenthelp.org/depression-statistics.php.

6. National Institutes of Mental Health, http://www.nimh.nih.gov/health/topics/depression/index.shtml.

7. "Statistics of Depression," http://depressiontreatmenthelp.org/depression-statistics.php.

8. American Psychiatric Association, *Diagnostic and Statistical Manual of Mental Disorders: DSM-IV-TR* (2000), 356.

Diet and Nutrition

1. "Definition of Nutrition," http://wordnetweb.princeton.edu/perl/webwn?s=nutrition.

2. National Eating Disorders Association, "Statistics: Eating Disorders and Their Precursors" (2005), http://www.sc.edu/healthycarolina/pdf/facstaffstu/eatingdisorders/EatingDisorderStatistics.pdf.

3. Centers for Disease Control and Prevention, "Nutrition Resources for Health Professionals: Data and Statistics," http://www.cdc.gov/nutrition/professionals/data/index.html.

4. U.S. Department of Health and Human Services, "Fruit and Vegetable Consumption Data and Statistics," http://apps.nccd.cdc.gov/5ADaySurveillance/.

5. Centers for Disease Control and Prevention, "FastStats: Women's Health," http://www.cdc.gov/nchs/fastats/womens_health.htm.

6. National Eating Disorders Association, "Statistics: Eating Disorders and Their Precursors" (2005), http://www.sc.edu/healthycarolina/pdf/facstaffstu/eatingdisorders/EatingDisorderStatistics.pdf.

7. Ibid.

8. Ibid.

Divorce

1. "Divorce Law and Legal Definition," *US Legal*, http://definitions.uslegal.com/d/divorce/.

2. Ibid.

3. Ibid.

4. The Barna Group, "New Marriage and Divorce Statistics Released" (March 31, 2008), http://www.barna.org/barna-update/article/15-familykids/42-new-marriage-and-divorce-statistics-released.

5. Gary Picariello, "A New Study Reveals the Effects of Divorce on Health," *Associated Content* (September 28, 2006), http://www.associatedcontent.com/article/64864/a_new_study_reveals_the_effects_of_pg2.html?cat=5.

6. Ibid.

7. National Center for Health Statistics, "New Report Sheds Light on Trends and Patterns in Marriage, Divorce, and Cohabitation" (July 24, 2002), http://www.cdc.gov/nchs/pressroom/02news/div_mar_cohab.htm.

Drug and Alcohol Addiction

1. National Drug and Alcohol Abuse Hotline, "Alcohol Statistics" (2002), http://www.drug-rehabs.org/alcohol-statistics.php.

2. Ibid.

3. US No Drugs, "Drug Addiction Statistics" (2009), http://www.usnodrugs.com/drug-addiction-statistics.htm.

4. National Institute of Drug Abuse, "Women and Drug Abuse," http://archives.drugabuse.gov/womendrugs/Women-DrugAbuse.html.

5. M. Smith, J. Saisan, and J. Segal, "Alcoholism and Alcohol Abuse," *Help Guide*, www.helpguide.org/mental/alcohol_abuse_alcoholism_signs_effects_treatment.htm.

Eating Disorders

1. National Eating Disorders Association, "Statistics: Eating Disorders and Their Precursors" (2005), http://www.nationaleatingdisorders.org/uploads/file/Statistics%20%20Updated%20Feb%2010,%202008%20B.pdf.

2. The Alliance for Eating Disorders Awareness, "Eating Disorders Statistics," http://www.eatingdisorderinfo.org/Resources/EatingDisordersStatistics.aspx.

3. National Eating Disorders Association, "Statistics: Eating Disorders and Their Precursors" (2005), http://www.nationaleatingdisorders.org/uploads/file/Statistics%20%20Updated%20Feb%2010,%202008%20B.pdf.

4. The Alliance for Eating Disorders Awareness, "Eating Disorders Statistics," http://www.eatingdisorderinfo.org/Resources/EatingDisordersStatistics.aspx.

5. National Eating Disorders Association, "Statistics: Eating Disorders and Their Precursors" (2005), http://www.nationaleatingdisorders.org/uploads/file/Statistics%20%20Updated%20Feb%2010,%202008%20B.pdf.

6. The Alliance for Eating Disorders Awareness, "Eating Disorders Statistics," http://www.eatingdisorderinfo.org/Resources/EatingDisordersStatistics.aspx.

7. Media Awareness Network, "Beauty and Body Image in the Media," http://www.media-awareness.ca/english/issues/stereotyping/women_and_girls/women_beauty.cfm.

8. South Carolina Department of Mental Health, "Eating Disorder Statistics," http://www.state.sc.us/dmh/anorexia/statistics.htm.

9. National Eating Disorders Association, "Statistics: Eating Disorders and Their Precursors" (2005), http://www.nationaleatingdisorders.org/uploads/file/Statistics%20%20Updated%20Feb%2010,%202008%20B.pdf.

10. "Anorexia Nervosa," *Merriam Webster Dictionary*, http://www.merriam-webster.com/dictionary/anorexia+nervosa.

11. The Alliance for Eating Disorders Awareness, "Eating Disorders Statistics," http://www.allianceforeatingdisorders.com/.

12. National Eating Disorders Association, "Statistics: Eating Disorders and Their Precursors" (2005), http://www.sc.edu/healthycarolina/pdf/facstaffstu/eatingdisorders/EatingDisorderStatistics.pdf.

Emotional Abuse

1. "Emotional Abuse Facts," *Woman Abuse Prevention*, http://www.womanabuseprevention.com/html/emotional_abuse_facts.html.

2. "Emotional Abuse Statistics," *Child Abuse Effects*, http://www.child-abuse-effects.com/emotional-abuse-statistics.html.

3. Bonnie Fisher et al., "The Sexual Victimization of College Women" (U.S. Department of Justice, 2000), http://www.ncjrs.gov/pdffiles1/nij/182369.pdf.

4. A. J. Z. Henderson, K. Bartholomew, and D. G. Dutton, "He Loves Me, He Loves Me Not: Attachment and Separation Resolution of Abused Women," *Journal of Family Violence* 12, no. 2 (1997): 186.

Fear and Anxiety

1. "Top 6 Women's Fears," *FemLive: Women's Lifestyle* (June 2, 2009), http://www.femlive.com/archives/new/857.

2. "Anxiety," http://wordnetweb.princeton.edu/perl/webwn?s=anxiety.

3. National Institute of Mental Health, "The Numbers Count: Mental Disorders in America" (2010), http://www.nimh.nih.gov/health/publications/the-numbers-count-mental-disorders-in-america/index.shtml; Centers for Disease Control and Prevention, "Anxiety and Depression," http://www.cdc.gov/features/dsBRFSSDepressionAnxiety/.

4. Anxiety Disorders Association of America, "Facts and Statistics," http://www.adaa.org/about-adaa/press-room/facts-statistics.

5. "Phobia," http://wordnetweb.princeton.edu/perl/webwn?s=phobia.

6. "Specific Phobia Statistics," http://www.phobias-help.com/phobia_statistics.html.

7. Ibid.

8. "Panic Attack," *MedTV*, http://anxiety.emedtv.com/panic-attacks/panic-attack.html.

Forgiveness

1. "Power of Forgiveness—Forgive Others," *Harvard Health Publications* (2005), http://www.health.harvard.edu/press_releases/power_of_forgiveness.

2. Ibid.; "Research into the Strength of Forgiveness," *A Campaign for Forgiveness Research*, http://www.forgiving.org/campaign/harness.asp.

3. Ibid.

4. "Power of Forgiveness—Forgive Others," *Harvard Health Publications* (2005), http://www.health.harvard.edu/press_releases/power_of_forgiveness.

5. Dr. Frederick Luskin, "Forgiveness Research," Statistics from Stanford University research (June 10, 2009), http://www.forgivenessasanactofpower.com/members/faaaop/blog/VIEW/00000001/00000001/Forgiveness-Research.html#00000001.

6. "Research Examines Physical Dimensions of Forgiveness," Hope College Press Releases (1998), http://www.hope.edu/pr/pressreleases/content/view/full/671.

7. Everett Worthington Jr., *Forgiving and Reconciling: Bridges to Wholeness and Hope* (Westmont, IL: Inter Varsity, 2003), 73.

Gossip

1. "Gossip," *Merriam Webster*, http://www.merriam-webster.com/dictionary/gossip.

2. Dianna Booher, "The Power of Gossip," in *The Bible for Hope: Caring for People God's Way*, ed. Dr. Tim Clinton (Nashville: Thomas Nelson, 2001), 838–39.

3. "Slander," *Merriam Webster*, http://www.merriam-webster.com/dictionary/slander.

4. Kate Fox, "Evolution, Alienation, and Gossip: The Role of Mobile Communications in the 21st Century," Social Issues Research Centre (June 1, 2010), http://www.sirc.org/publik/gossip.shtml.

5. Indiana University Newsroom, "Gossip in the Workplace: A Weapon or Gift" (October 28, 2009), http://newsinfo.iu.edu/news/page/normal/12357.html.

Grief and Loss

1. "Annual Grieving Statistics," *Grief Recovery*, http://www.mygriefrecovery.com/Site/Welcome.html.

2. "Overcoming Loss: Grief Counseling," *Theravive*, http://www.theravive.com/services/grief-and-loss.htm.

3. Ibid.

4. This information is summarized from groundbreaking research on grief, as summarized in Elisabeth Kübler-Ross, *On Death and Dying* (New York: Scribner, 1997).

Infertility

1. National Institutes of Health, "Infertility," http://www.nlm.nih.gov/medlineplus/infertility.html.

2. Centers for Disease Control and Prevention, "Fertility, Family Planning, and Reproductive Health of U.S. Women: Data from the 2002 National Survey of Family Growth," tables 67, 69, 97, http://www.cdc.gov/nchs/data/series/sr_23/sr23_025.pdf. http://www.cdc.gov/nchs/data/series/sr_23/sr23_025.pdf.

3. Ibid.

4. Ibid.

5. Centers for Disease Control and Prevention, "Annual ART Success Rates Report: 2003," http://www.cdc.gov/art/artreports.htm.

Lesbianism and Same-Sex Attraction

1. Centers for Disease Control, "Prevalence of Bisexuality and Lesbianism in the U.S.," findings from the CDC Sex Study for Lesbians and Bisexual Women, http://lesbianlife.about.com/od/lesbiansex/a/SameSexBehavior.htm.

2. Ibid.

3. Ibid.

4. Richard Redding, "It's Really about Sex: Same-Sex Marriage, Lesbigay Parenting, and the Psychology of Disgust," *Duke Journal of Gender Law and Policy* (January 2008), 127–93.

Masturbation

1. The Kinsey Institute, "Masturbation" (2002), http://www.iub.edu/~kinsey/resources/FAQ.html.

2. Ibid.

3. Tim and Beverly LaHaye and Mike Yorkey, *The Act of Marriage after 40* (Grand Rapids: Zondervan, 2000), 189.

Menopause

1. Jacobs Institute of Women's Health, "Guidelines for Counseling Women on the Management of Menopause," North American Menopause Society (2000), http://www.jiwh.org/Resources/Guidelines%20for%20Menopause.pdf.

2. Ibid.

Miscarriage

1. American Pregnancy Association, "Miscarriage," http://www.americanpregnancy.org/pregnancycomplications/miscarriage.html.

Obesity

1. Centers for Disease Control and Prevention, "Overweight and Obesity," http://www.cdc.gov/obesity/causes/index.html.

2. Ibid.

3. "Food Statistics: McDonalds Restaurants by Country," *NationMaster* (2007), http://www.nationmaster.com/graph/foo_mcd_res-food-mcdonalds-restaurants.

4. Centers for Disease Control and Prevention, "FastStats: Women's Health" (2008), http://www.cdc.gov/nchs/fastats/womens_health.htm.

5. American Heart Association, "Physical Inactivity, Overweight and Obesity" (2006), http://www.americanheart.org/presenter.jhtml?identifier=742.

6. Ibid.

Physical Abuse

1. U.S. Department of Justice, "Extent, Nature, and Consequences of Intimate Partner Violence" (July 2000), iv–v.

2. Ibid., 10–11.

3. American Psychological Association, "Violence and the Family: Report of the APA Presidential Task Force on Violence and the Family" (1996), http://www .apa.org.

4. U.S. Department of Justice, "Extent, Nature, and Consequences of Intimate Partner Violence" (July 2000), 33.

5. Centers for Disease Control and Prevention, "Intimate Partner Violence: Consequences," http://www. cdc.gov/violenceprevention/intimatepartnerviolence/ consequences.html.

6. Ibid.

7. Ibid.

Pregnancy

1. American Pregnancy Association, "Statistics: Pregnancy," http://www.americanpregnancy.org/main/ statistics.html.

2. Ibid.

3. Ibid.

4. Ibid.

5. Ibid.

6. Ibid.

7. Mayo Clinic, "Postpartum Depression" (June 3, 2010), http://www.mayoclinic.com/health/postpartum -depression/DS00546/DSECTION=symptoms.

Prostitution

1. Hawaii AIDS Education and Training Center, "Prostitution," John A. Burns School of Medicine, http:// www.hawaii.edu/hivandaids/Prostitution%20Statistics %20IL.pdf.

2. J. J. Potterat et al., "Estimating the Prevalence and Career Longevity of Prostitute Women," *Journal of Sex Research* 27 (1990): 233–43.

3. D. D. Brewer et al., "Prostitution and the Sex Discrepancy in Reported Number of Sexual Partners," *Proceedings of the National Academy of Science U.S.A.* 97.22 (October 2000): 12385–88.

4. R. T. Michael et al., *Sex in America* (Boston: Little Brown, 1994).

5. Melissa Farley and Howard Barkan, "Prostitution, Violence against Women, and Post-traumatic Stress Disorder," *Women & Health* 27, no. 3 (1998): 37–49.

6. M. H. Silbert, *Victims of Sexual Aggression: Treatment of Prostitute Victims of Sexual Assault* (New York: Van Nostrand Reinhold, 1984).

7. All statistics in this paragraph from Hawaii AIDS Education and Training Center, "Prostitution," John A. Burns School of Medicine, http://www.hawaii.edu/hivan daids/Prostitution%20Statistics%20IL.pdf.

Rape

1. Centers for Disease Control and Prevention, "Intimate Partner Violence: Definitions," http://www.cdc .gov/ncipc/factsheets/ipvoverview.htm.

2. "Definition of Rape," *MedicineNet*, http://www. medterms.com/script/main/art.asp?articlekey=12412.

3. Centers for Disease Control and Prevention, "Sexual Violence" (Spring 2008), http://www.cdc.gov/ ViolencePrevention/pdf/sv-datasheet-a.pdf.

4. Rape, Abuse and Incest National Network, "Statistics," http://www.rainn.org/statistics.

5. Judith Herman, *Trauma and Recovery* (New York: Basic Books, 1997), 133.

Relationships with Men

1. Abuse, Rape, Domestic Violence, Aid and Resource Collection (AARDVARC), "Domestic Violence Statistics," http://www.aardvarc.org/dv/statistics.shtml.

Relationship with Christ

1. Gallup, "Religion" (2009), http://www.gallup.com/ poll/1690/religion.aspx?.

2. "The God Debate," *Newsweek* (April 9, 2007), http:// www.newsweek.com/id/35784.

3. Nathan Black, "Poll: 9 of 10 Americans Believe in God; Nearly Half Rejects Evolution," *Christian Post* (2007), http://www.christianpost.com/Society/Polls_reports /2007/04/poll-9-of-10-americans-believe-in-god-nearly- half-rejects-evolution-02/index.html.

4. Gallup, "Who Believes in God and Who Doesn't?" (2006), www.gallup.com.

5. Jennifer Riley, "Study: God Relationship Not Most Important to Americans," *Christian Post* (March 17, 2008), http://www.christianpost.com/article/20080317/study- god-relationship-not-most-important-to-americans /index.html.

6. Ibid.

7. "Your Views of God Say a Lot about You, Study Shows," *Jet*, http://www.google.com/hostednews/ap/article /ALeqM5jn4ZlxW24L322-0sC7NftpnM_YZQD97H 3V0O0http://www.google.com/hostednews/ap/article /ALeqM5jn4ZlxW24L322-0sC7NftpnM_YZQD97 H3V0O0.

Roles of Women

1. Department of Labor, "Statistics on Women Workers" (2009), http://www.dol.gov/wb/stats/main.htm.

2. Ibid.

3. Ibid.

4. Ibid.

5. Lesley Stahl, "Staying at Home," CBS News (October 10, 2004), http://www.cbsnews.com/stories/ 2004/10/08/60minutes/main648240.shtml.

6. Renee Spraggins, *We the People: Women and Men in the United States,* Census 2000 Special Report, CENSR-20 (Washington, DC: U.S. Census Bureau, 2005), 8, http:// www.census.gov/prod/2005pubs/censr-20.pdf.

Self-Worth and Approval

1. "Media and Girls," Media Awareness Network, http://www.media-awareness.ca/english/issues/stereo typing/women_and_girls/women_girls.cfm.
2. Ibid.
3. "Beauty at Any Cost," YWCA, www.ywca.org/site/pp.asp?c=djISI6PIKpG&b=4427615.
4. Darla Walker, "Women and Self-Esteem," *Women Today*, http://powertochange.com/discover/life/women esteem/.

Sex Addiction

1. Survey conducted by *Today's Christian Woman* (Fall 2003), http://www.transitioning.org/2010/03/23/sex-addiction-in-women-is-a-reality-sexualaddiction recovery-com/.
2. Safe Families, "Statistics on Pornography, Child Sexual Abuse, and Online Perpetrators," http://www.safefamilies.org/sfStats.php.
3. Blazing Grace, "Statistics and Information on Pornography in the USA," http://www.blazinggrace.org/cms/bg/pornstats.
4. Mark Laaser, cited in William Cutrer and Sandra Glahn, *Sexual Intimacy in Marriage* (Grand Rapids: Kregel, 2007), 219.

Sexual Desire and Expectations

1. J. D. DeLamater and M. Sill, "Sexual Desire in Later Life" (Society for the Scientific Study of Sexuality, 2005), http://www.thefreelibrary.com/Sexual+desire+in+later+life-a0133315406.
2. U. Hartmann et al., "Low Sexual Desire in Midlife and Older Women: Personality Factors, Psychosocial Development, Present Sexuality," *Menopause* 11 (2004): 726–40.
3. RTI International, "Half of Menopausal Women Have Low Sexual Desire, Study Finds," (2008), http://www.rti.org/news.cfm?nav=386&objectid=121923A8-868A-4672-91D27CA0C1A79D7A.
4. Robert T. Michael et. al., *Sex in America: A Definitive Survey* (Boston: Little, Brown, 1994), 1, 131.

Sexual Harassment

1. "Know Your Rights: Equal Employment at Work," Equal Rights Advocates, http://www.equalrights.org/publications/kyr/shwork.asp.
2. Study conducted by the American Association of University Women, "Statistics: Sexual Harassment," http://www.umich.edu/~sapac/info/stats-sh.html.
3. Sexual Harassment Support, http://www.sexual harassmentsupport.org/SHworkplace.html.

4. Sexual Harassment Support (2002), http://www.sexualharassmentsupport.org.ED.html.

Sexually Transmitted Diseases

1. Centers for Disease Control and Prevention, "Sexually Transmitted Diseases," http://www.google.com/search?client=safari&rls=en&q=centers+for+disease+control+stds&ie=UTF-8&oe=UTF-8.
2. Ibid.
3. Ibid.
4. The Medical Institute for Sexual Health, "STD Fact Sheets," http://www.medinstitute.org/public/251.cfm.
5. Centers for Disease Control and Prevention, "Sexually Transmitted Diseases," http://www.google.com/search?client=safari&rls=en&q=centers+for+disease+control+stds&ie=UTF-8&oe=UTF-8.
6. Ibid.
7. Ibid.

Singleness

1. U.S. Census Bureau, "America's Families and Living Arrangements" (2007), http://www.census.gov/prod/2004pubs/p20-553.pdf.
2. "Professional Women: Vital Statistics" (2006), http://www.pay-equity.org/PDFs/ProfWomen.pdf.

Single Parenting

1. David Blankenhorn, *Fatherless America: Confronting Our Most Urgent Social Problem* (New York: Harper Perennial, 1996), 1.
2. National Commission on Children Statistics, as referenced in National Center for Fathering, "Trends in Fathering," http://www.fathers.com/content/index.php?option=com_content&ask=view&id=412.
3. Ibid.
4. Paul R. Amato, Laura S. Loomis, and Alan Booth, "Parental Divorce, Marital Conflict, and Offspring Well-Being during Early Adulthood," *Social Forces* 73, no. 3 (1995): 895–915.
5. U.S. Census Bureau, "Income," http://www.census.gov/hhes/www/income/income.html.

Strength in Conflict and Stress

1. Department of Health and Human Services, "Stress and Your Health," Womenshealth.gov, http://www.womens health.gov/faq/stress-your-health.cfm#d.
2. Cleveland Clinic, "Stress and Women," http://my.clevelandclinic.org/healthy_living/Stress_Management/hic_Stress_and_Women.aspx.
3. Ibid.